Hadoop 2.x Administration Cookbook

Administer and maintain large Apache Hadoop clusters

Gurmukh Singh

Packt

BIRMINGHAM - MUMBAI

Hadoop 2.x Administration Cookbook

First published: May 2017

Production reference: 1220517

Published by Packt Publishing Ltd.
Livery Place
35 Livery Street
Birmingham B3 2PB, UK.

ISBN 978-1-78712-673-2

`www.packtpub.com`

Credits

Author
Gurmukh Singh

Reviewers
Rajiv Tiwari
Wissem EL Khlifi

Commissioning Editor
Amey Varangaonkar

Acquisition Editor
Varsha Shetty

Content Development Editor
Deepti Thore

Technical Editor
Nilesh Sawakhande

Copy Editors
Laxmi Subramanian
Safis Editing

Project Coordinator
Shweta H Birwatkar

Proofreader
Safis Editing

Indexer
Francy Puthiry

Graphics
Tania Dutta

Production Coordinator
Nilesh Mohite

Cover Work
Nilesh Mohite

About the Author

Gurmukh Singh is a seasoned technology professional with 14+ years of industry experience in infrastructure design, distributed systems, performance optimization, and networks. He has worked in big data domain for the last 5 years and provides consultancy and training on various technologies.

He has worked with companies such as HP, JP Morgan, and Yahoo.

He has authored Monitoring Hadoop by Packt Publishing (`https://www.packtpub.com/big-data-and-business-intelligence/monitoring-hadoop`).

I would like to thank my wife, Navdeep Kaur, and my lovely daughter, Amanat Dhillon, who have always supported me throughout the journey of this book.

About the Reviewers

Rajiv Tiwari is a freelance big data and cloud architect with over 17 years of experience across big data, analytics, and cloud computing for banks and other financial organizations. He is an electronics engineering graduate from IIT Varanasi, and has been working in England for the past 13 years, mostly in the financial city of London. Rajiv can be contacted on Twitter at `@bigdataoncloud`.

He is the author of the book *Hadoop for Finance*, an exclusive book for using Hadoop in banking and financial services.

I would like to thank my wife, Seema, and my son, Rivaan, for allowing me to spend their quota of time on reviewing this book.

Wissem El Khlifi is the first Oracle ACE in Spain and an Oracle Certified Professional DBA with over 12 years of IT experience.

He earned the Computer Science Engineer degree from FST Tunisia, Master in Computer Science from the UPC Barcelona, and Master in Big Data Science from the UPC Barcelona.

His area of interest include Cloud Architecture, Big Data Architecture, and Big Data Management and Analysis.

His career has included the roles of: Java analyst / programmer, Oracle Senior DBA, and big data scientist. He currently works as Senior Big Data and Cloud Architect for Schneider Electric / APC.

He writes numerous articles on his website `http://www.oracle-class.com` and is avaialble on twitter at `@orawiss`.

Customer Feedback

Thanks for purchasing this Packt book. At Packt, quality is at the heart of our editorial process. To help us improve, please leave us an honest review on this book's Amazon page at `https://www.amazon.com/dp/1787126730`.

If you'd like to join our team of regular reviewers, you can e-mail us at `customerreviews@packtpub.com`. We award our regular reviewers with free eBooks and videos in exchange for their valuable feedback. Help us be relentless in improving our products!

Table of Contents

Preface

Hadoop is a distributed system with a large ecosystem, which is growing at an exponential rate, and hence it becomes important to get a grip on things and do a deep dive into the functioning of a Hadoop cluster in production. Whether you are new to Hadoop or a seasoned Hadoop specialist, this recipe book contains recipes to deep dive into Hadoop cluster configuration and optimization.

What this book covers

Chapter 1, Hadoop Architecture and Deployment, covers Hadoop's architecture, its components, various installation modes and important daemons, and the services that make Hadoop a robust system. This chapter covers single-node and multinode clusters.

Chapter 2, Maintaining Hadoop Cluster – HDFS, wraps the storage layer HDFS, block size, replication, cluster health, Quota configuration, rack awareness, and communication channel between nodes.

Chapter 3, Maintaining Hadoop Cluster – YARN and MapReduce, talks about the processing layer in Hadoop and the resource management framework YARN. This chapter covers how to configure YARN components, submit jobs, configure job history server, and YARN fundamentals.

Chapter 4, High Availability, covers high availability for a Namenode and Resourcemanager, ZooKeeper configuration, HDFS storage-based policies, HDFS snapshots, and rolling upgrades.

Chapter 5, Schedulers, talks about YARN schedulers such as fair and capacity scheduler, with detailed recipes on configuring Queues, Queue ACLs, configuration of users and groups, and other Queue administration commands.

Chapter 6, Backup and Recovery, covers Hadoop metastore, backup and restore procedures on a Namenode, configuration of a secondary Namenode, and various ways of recovering lost Namenodes. This chapter also talks about configuring HDFS and YARN logs for troubleshooting.

Chapter 7, Data Ingestion and Workflow, talks about Hive configuration and its various modes of operation. This chapter also covers setting up Hive with the credential store and highly available access using ZooKeeper. The recipes in this chapter give details about the process of loading data into Hive, partitioning, bucketing concepts, and configuration with an external metastore. It also covers Oozie installation and Flume configuration for log ingestion.

Chapter 8, Performance Tuning, covers the performance tuning aspects of HDFS, YARN containers, the operating system, and network parameters, as well as optimizing the cluster for production by comparing benchmarks for various configurations.

Chapter 9, Hbase and RDBMS, talks about HBase cluster configuration, best practices, HBase tuning, backup, and restore. It also covers migration of data from MySQL to HBase and the procedure to upgrade HBase to the latest release.

Chapter 10, Cluster Planning, covers Hadoop cluster planning and the best practices for designing clusters are, in terms of disk storage, network, servers, and placement policy. This chapter also covers costing and the impact of SLA driver workloads on cluster planning.

Chapter 11, Troubleshooting, Diagnostics, and Best Practices, talks about the troubleshooting steps for a Namenode and Datanode, and diagnoses communication errors. It also covers details on logs and how to parse them for errors to extract important key points on issues faced.

Chapter 12, Security, covers Hadoop security in terms of data encryption, in-transit encryption, ssl configuration, and, more importantly, configuring Kerberos for the Hadoop cluster. This chapter also covers auditing and a recipe on securing ZooKeeper.

What you need for this book

To go through the recipes in this book, users need any Linux distribution, which could be Ubuntu, Centos, or any other flavor, as long as it supports running JVM. We use Centos in our recipe, as it is the most commonly used operating system for Hadoop clusters.

Hadoop runs on both virtualized and physical servers, so it is recommended to have at least 8 GB for the base system, on which about three virtual hosts can be set up. Users do not need to set up all the recipes covered in this book all at once; they can run only those daemons that are necessary for that particular recipe. This way, they can keep the resource requirements to the bare minimum. It is good to have at least four hosts to practice all the recipes in this book. These hosts could be virtual or physical.

In terms of software, users need JDK 1.7 minimum, and any SSH client, such as PuTTY in Windows or Terminal, to connect to the Hadoop nodes.

Who this book is for

If you are a system administrator with a basic understanding of Hadoop and you want to get into Hadoop administration, this book is for you. It's also ideal if you are a Hadoop administrator who wants a quick reference guide to all the Hadoop administration-related tasks and solutions to commonly occurring problems.

Sections

In this book, you will find several headings that appear frequently (Getting ready, How to do it, How it works, There's more, and See also).

To give clear instructions on how to complete a recipe, we use these sections as follows:

Getting ready

This section tells you what to expect in the recipe, and describes how to set up any software or any preliminary settings required for the recipe.

How to do it...

This section contains the steps required to follow the recipe.

How it works...

This section usually consists of a detailed explanation of what happened in the previous section.

There's more...

This section consists of additional information about the recipe in order to make the reader more knowledgeable about the recipe.

See also

This section provides helpful links to other useful information for the recipe.

Conventions

In this book, you will find a number of text styles that distinguish between different kinds of information. Here are some examples of these styles and an explanation of their meaning.

Code words in text, database table names, folder names, filenames, file extensions, pathnames, dummy URLs, user input, and Twitter handles are shown as follows: "You will see a tarball under the `hadoop-2.7.3-src/hadoop-dist/target/` folder."

A block of code is set as follows:

```
<property>
    <name>dfs.hosts.exclude</name>
    <value>/home/hadoop/excludes</value>
    <final>true</final>
</property>
```

Any command-line input or output is written as follows:

```
$ stop-yarn.sh
```

> Warnings or important notes appear in a box like this.

> Tips and tricks appear like this.

Reader feedback

Feedback from our readers is always welcome. Let us know what you think about this book—what you liked or disliked. Reader feedback is important for us as it helps us develop titles that you will really get the most out of.

To send us general feedback, simply e-mail `feedback@packtpub.com`, and mention the book's title in the subject of your message.

If there is a topic that you have expertise in and you are interested in either writing or contributing to a book, see our author guide at `www.packtpub.com/authors`.

Customer support

Now that you are the proud owner of a Packt book, we have a number of things to help you to get the most from your purchase.

Downloading the example code

You can download the example code files for this book from your account at http://www.packtpub.com. If you purchased this book elsewhere, you can visit http://www.packtpub.com/support and register to have the files e-mailed directly to you.

You can download the code files by following these steps:

1. Log in or register to our website using your e-mail address and password.
2. Hover the mouse pointer on the **SUPPORT** tab at the top.
3. Click on **Code Downloads & Errata**.
4. Enter the name of the book in the **Search** box.
5. Select the book for which you're looking to download the code files.
6. Choose from the drop-down menu where you purchased this book from.
7. Click on **Code Download**.

Once the file is downloaded, please make sure that you unzip or extract the folder using the latest version of:

- WinRAR / 7-Zip for Windows
- Zipeg / iZip / UnRarX for Mac
- 7-Zip / PeaZip for Linux

The code bundle for the book is also hosted on GitHub at https://github.com/PacktPublishing/Hadoop-2.x-Administration-Cookbook. We also have other code bundles from our rich catalog of books and videos available at https://github.com/PacktPublishing/. Check them out!

Downloading the color images of this book

We also provide you with a PDF file that has color images of the screenshots/diagrams used in this book. The color images will help you better understand the changes in the output. You can download this file from http://www.packtpub.com/sites/default/files/downloads/Hadoop2.xAdministrationCookbook_ColorImages.pdf.

Errata

Although we have taken every care to ensure the accuracy of our content, mistakes do happen. If you find a mistake in one of our books—maybe a mistake in the text or the code—we would be grateful if you could report this to us. By doing so, you can save other readers from frustration and help us improve subsequent versions of this book. If you find any errata, please report them by visiting `http://www.packtpub.com/submit-errata`, selecting your book, clicking on the **Errata Submission Form** link, and entering the details of your errata. Once your errata are verified, your submission will be accepted and the errata will be uploaded to our website or added to any list of existing errata under the Errata section of that title.

To view the previously submitted errata, go to `https://www.packtpub.com/books/content/support` and enter the name of the book in the search field. The required information will appear under the **Errata** section.

Piracy

Piracy of copyrighted material on the Internet is an ongoing problem across all media. At Packt, we take the protection of our copyright and licenses very seriously. If you come across any illegal copies of our works in any form on the Internet, please provide us with the location address or website name immediately so that we can pursue a remedy.

Please contact us at `copyright@packtpub.com` with a link to the suspected pirated material.

We appreciate your help in protecting our authors and our ability to bring you valuable content.

Questions

If you have a problem with any aspect of this book, you can contact us at `questions@packtpub.com`, and we will do our best to address the problem.

1
Hadoop Architecture and Deployment

In this chapter, we will cover the following recipes:

- Overview of Hadoop Architecture
- Building and compiling Hadoop
- Installation methods
- Setting up host resolution
- Installing a single-node cluster - HDFS components
- Installing a single-node cluster - YARN components
- Installing a multi-node cluster
- Configuring Hadoop Gateway node
- Decommissioning nodes
- Adding nodes to the cluster

Introduction

As Hadoop is a distributed system with many components, and has a reputation of getting quite complex, it is important to understand the basic Architecture before we start with the deployments.

In this chapter, we will take a look at the Architecture and the recipes to deploy a Hadoop cluster in various modes. This chapter will also cover recipes on commissioning and decommissioning nodes in a cluster.

The recipes in this chapter will primarily focus on deploying a cluster based on an Apache Hadoop distribution, as it is the best way to learn and explore Hadoop.

> While the recipes in this chapter will give you an overview of a typical configuration, we encourage you to adapt this design according to your needs. The deployment directory structure varies according to IT policies within an organization. All our deployments will be based on the Linux operating system, as it is the most commonly used platform for Hadoop in production. You can use any flavor of Linux; the recipes are very generic in nature and should work on all Linux flavors, with the appropriate changes in path and installation methods, such as `yum` or `apt-get`.

Overview of Hadoop Architecture

Hadoop is a framework and not a tool. It is a combination of various components, such as a filesystem, processing engine, data ingestion tools, databases, workflow execution tools, and so on. Hadoop is based on client-server Architecture with a master node for each storage layer and processing layer.

Namenode is the master for **Hadoop distributed file system** (**HDFS**) storage and ResourceManager is the master for **YARN** (**Yet Another Resource Negotiator**). The Namenode stores the file metadata and the actual blocks/data reside on the slave nodes called Datanodes. All the jobs are submitted to the ResourceManager and it then assigns tasks to its slaves, called NodeManagers. In a highly available cluster, we can have more than one Namenode and ResourceManager.

Both masters are each a single point of failure, which makes them very critical components of the cluster and so care must be taken to make them highly available.

Although there are many concepts to learn, such as application masters, containers, schedulers, and so on, as this is a recipe book, we will keep the theory to a minimum.

Building and compiling Hadoop

The pre-build Hadoop binary available at `www.apache.org`, is a 32-bit version and is not suitable for the 64-bit hardware as it will not be able to utilize the entire addressable memory. Although, for lab purposes, we can use the 32-bit version, it will keep on giving warnings about the "not being built for the native library", which can be safely ignored.

In production, we will always be running Hadoop on hardware which is a 64-bit version and can support larger amounts of memory. To properly utilize memory higher than 4 GB on any node, we need the 64-bit complied version of Hadoop.

Getting ready

To step through the recipes in this chapter, or indeed the entire book, you will need at least one preinstalled Linux instance. You can use any distribution of Linux, such as Ubuntu, CentOS, or any other Linux flavor that the reader is comfortable with. The recipes are very generic and are expected to work with all distributions, although, as stated before, one may need to use distro-specific commands. For example, for package installation in CentOS we use `yum` package installer, or in Debian-based systems we use `apt-get`, and so on. The user is expected to know basic Linux commands and should know how to set up package repositories such as the `yum` repository. The user should also know how the DNS resolution is configured. No other prerequisites are required.

How to do it...

1. `ssh` to the Linux instance using any of the ssh clients. If you are on Windows, you need PuTTY. If you are using a Mac or Linux, there is a default terminal available to use `ssh`. The following command connects to the host with an IP of `10.0.0.4`. Change it to whatever the IP is in your case:

   ```
   $ ssh root@10.0.0.4
   ```

2. Change to the user root or any other privileged user:

   ```
   $ sudo su -
   ```

3. Install the dependencies to build Hadoop:

   ```
   # yum install gcc gcc-c++ openssl-devel make cmake jdk-
   1.7u45(minimum)
   ```

4. Download and install Maven:

   ```
   wget mirrors.gigenet.com/apache/maven/maven-3/3.3.9/binaries/
   apache-maven-3.3.9-bin.tar.gz
   ```

5. Untar Maven:

   ```
   # tar -zxf apache-maven-3.3.9-bin.tar.gz -C /opt/
   ```

6. Set up the Maven environment:

   ```
   # cat /etc/profile.d/maven.sh
   export JAVA_HOME=/usr/java/latest
   export M3_HOME=/opt/apache-maven-3.3.9
   export PATH=$JAVA_HOME/bin:/opt/apache-maven-3.3.9/bin:$PATH
   ```

7. Download and set up `protobuf`:

```
# wget https://github.com/google/protobuf/releases/download/
v2.5.0/protobuf-2.5.0.tar.gz
# tar -xzf protobuf-2.5.0.tar.gz -C /root
# cd /opt/protobuf-2.5.0/
# ./configure
# make;make install
```

8. Download the latest Hadoop stable source code. At the time of writing, the latest Hadoop version is 2.7.3:

```
# wget apache.uberglobalmirror.com/hadoop/common/stable2/hadoop-
2.7.3-src.tar.gz
# tar -xzf hadoop-2.7.3-src.tar.gz -C /opt/
# cd /opt/hadoop-2.7.2-src
# mvn package -Pdist,native -DskipTests -Dtar
```

9. You will see a tarball in the folder `hadoop-2.7.3-src/hadoop-dist/target/`.

How it works...

The tarball package created will be used for the installation of Hadoop throughout the book. It is not mandatory to build a Hadoop from source, but by default the binary packages provided by Apache Hadoop are 32-bit versions. For production, it is important to use a 64-bit version so as to fully utilize the memory beyond 4 GB and to gain other performance benefits.

Installation methods

Hadoop can be installed in multiple ways, either by using repository methods such as `Yum/apt-get` or by extracting the tarball packages. The project Bigtop `http://bigtop.apache.org/` provides Hadoop packages for infrastructure, and can be used by creating a local repository of the packages.

All the steps are to be performed as the **root** user. It is expected that the user knows how to set up a `yum` repository and Linux basics.

Getting ready

You are going to need a Linux machine. You can either use the one which has been used in the previous task or set up a new node, which will act as repository server and host all the packages we need.

How to do it...

1. Connect to a Linux machine that has at least 5 GB disk space to store the packages.
2. If you are on CentOS or a similar distribution, make sure you have the package `yum-utils` installed. This package will provide the command `reposync`.
3. Create a file `bigtop.repo` under `/etc/yum.repos.d/`. Note that the file name can be anything—only the extension must be `.repo`.
4. See the following screenshot for the contents of the file:

```
[hadoop@rt1 ~]$ cat /etc/yum.repos.d/bigtop.repo
[bigtop]
name=Bigtop
enabled=1
gpgcheck=1
type=NONE
baseurl=http://bigtop-repos.s3.amazonaws.com/releases/1.1.0/centos/6/x86_64
gpgkey=https://dist.apache.org/repos/dist/release/bigtop/KEYS
```

5. Execute the command `reposync -r bigtop`. It will create a directory named `bigtop` under the present working directory with all the packages downloaded to it.
6. All the required Hadoop packages can be installed by configuring the repository we downloaded as a repository server.

How it works...

From step 2 to step 6, the user will be able to configure and use the Hadoop package repository. Setting up a `Yum` repository is not required, but it makes things easier if we have to do installations on hundreds of nodes. In larger setups, management systems such as Puppet or Chef will be used for deployment configuration to push configuration and packages to nodes.

In this chapter, we will be using the tarball package that was built in the first section to perform installations. This is the best way of learning about directory structure and the configurations needed.

Setting up host resolution

Before we start with the installations, it is important to make sure that the host resolution is configured and working properly.

Getting ready

Choose any appropriate hostnames the user wants for his or her Linux machines. For example, the hostnames could be `master1.cluster.com` or `rt1.cyrus.com` or `host1.example.com`. The important thing is that the hostnames must resolve.

This resolution can be done using a DNS server or by configuring the `/etc/hosts` file on each node we use for our cluster setup.

The following steps will show you how to set up the resolution in the `/etc/hosts` file.

How to do it...

1. Connect to the Linux machine and change the hostname to `master1.cyrus.com` in the file as follows:

```
[root@master1 ~]# cat /etc/sysconfig/network
NETWORKING=yes
HOSTNAME=master1.cyrus.com
```

2. Edit the `/etc/hosts` file as follows:

```
[root@master1 ~]# cat /etc/hosts
127.0.0.1    localhost localhost.localdomain
10.0.0.104   master1.cyrus.com
```

3. Make sure the resolution returns an IP address:

```
# getent hosts master1.cyrus.com
```

4. The other preferred method is to set up the DNS resolution so that we do not have to populate the `hosts` file on each node. In the example resolution shown here, the user can see that the DNS server is configured to answer the domain `cyrus.com`:

```
# nslookup master1.cyrus.com
Server:             10.0.0.2
Address:      10.0.0.2#53

Non-authoritative answer:
Name:  master1.cyrus.com
Address: 10.0.0.104
```

How it works...

Each Linux host has a resolver library that helps it resolve any hostname that is asked for. It contacts the DNS server, and if it is not found there, it contacts the `hosts` file. Users who are not Linux administrators can simply use the `hosts` files as a workaround to set up a Hadoop cluster. There are many resources available online that could help you to set up a DNS quickly if needed.

Once the resolution is in place, we will start with the installation of Hadoop on a single-node and then progress to multiple nodes.

Installing a single-node cluster - HDFS components

Usually the term cluster means a group of machines, but in this recipe, we will be installing various Hadoop daemons on a single node. The single machine will act as both the master and slave for the storage and processing layer.

Getting ready

You will need some information before stepping through this recipe.

Although Hadoop can be configured to run as root user, it is a good practice to run it as a non-privileged user. In this recipe, we are using the node name `nn1.cluster1.com`, preinstalled with CentOS 6.5.

> Create a system user named `hadoop` and set a password for that user.

Install JDK, which will be used by Hadoop services. The minimum recommended version of JDK is 1.7, but Open JDK can also be used.

How to do it...

1. Log into the machine/host as root user and install jdk:

```
# yum install jdk -y
or it can also be installed using the command as below
# rpm -ivh jdk-1.7u45.rpm
```

2. Once Java is installed, make sure Java is in `PATH` for execution. This can be done by setting `JAVA_HOME` and exporting it as an environment variable. The following screenshot shows the content of the directory where Java gets installed:

   # export JAVA_HOME=/usr/java/latest

```
[root@nn1 ~]# ls -l /usr/java/
total 4
lrwxrwxrwx 1 root root   16 Mar 11  2016 default -> /usr/java/latest
drwxr-xr-x 8 root root 4096 Mar 11  2016 jdk1.8.0_11
lrwxrwxrwx 1 root root   21 Mar 11  2016 latest -> /usr/java/jdk1.8.0_11
```

3. Now we need to copy the tarball `hadoop-2.7.3.tar.gz`–which was built in the Build Hadoop section earlier in this chapter—to the home directory of the user root. For this, the user needs to login to the node where Hadoop was built and execute the following command:

   # scp -r hadoop-2.7.3.tar.gz root@nn1.cluster1.com:~/

4. Create a directory named`/opt/cluster` to be used for Hadoop:

   # mkdir -p /opt/cluster

5. Then untar the `hadoop-2.7.3.tar.gz` to the preceding created directory:

   # tar -xzvf hadoop-2.7.3.tar.gz -C /opt/Cluster/

6. Create a user named `hadoop`, if you haven't already, and set the password as `hadoop`:

   # useradd hadoop

   # echo hadoop | passwd --stdin hadoop

7. As step 6 was done by the root user, the directory and file under `/opt/cluster` will be owned by the root user. Change the ownership to the Hadoop user:

   # chown -R hadoop:hadoop /opt/cluster/

8. If the user lists the directory structure under `/opt/cluster`, he will see it as follows:

```
[root@nn1 ~]# ls -l /opt/cluster/
total 0
drwxr-xr-x 10 hadoop hadoop 150 Oct 16 23:33 hadoop-2.7.3
```

9. The directory structure under `/opt/cluster/hadoop-2.7.3` will look like the one shown in the following screenshot:

```
[root@nn1 ~]# ls -l /opt/cluster/hadoop-2.7.3/
total 116
drwxr-xr-x 2 hadoop hadoop  4096 Oct 16 13:55 bin
drwxr-xr-x 3 hadoop hadoop    19 Oct 16 13:55 etc
drwxr-xr-x 2 hadoop hadoop   101 Oct 16 13:55 include
drwxr-xr-x 3 hadoop hadoop    19 Oct 16 13:55 lib
drwxr-xr-x 2 hadoop hadoop  4096 Oct 16 13:55 libexec
-rw-r--r-- 1 hadoop hadoop 84854 Oct 16 13:55 LICENSE.txt
drwxrwxr-x 2 hadoop hadoop   138 Oct 16 23:35 logs
-rw-r--r-- 1 hadoop hadoop 14978 Oct 16 13:55 NOTICE.txt
-rw-r--r-- 1 hadoop hadoop  1366 Oct 16 13:55 README.txt
drwxr-xr-x 2 hadoop hadoop  4096 Oct 16 13:55 sbin
drwxr-xr-x 4 hadoop hadoop    29 Oct 16 13:55 share
```

10. The listing shows `etc`, `bin`, `sbin`, and other directories.
11. The `etc/hadoop` directory is the one that contains the configuration files for configuring various Hadoop daemons. Some of the key files are `core-site.xml`, `hdfs-site.xml`, `hadoop-env.xml`, and `mapred-site.xml` among others, which will be explained in the later sections:

```
drwxr-xr-x 2 hadoop hadoop 4096 Oct 16 23:32 hadoop
[root@nn1 ~]# ls -l /opt/cluster/hadoop-2.7.3/etc/hadoop/
total 152
-rw-r--r-- 1 hadoop hadoop  4436 Oct 16 13:55 capacity-scheduler.xml
-rw-r--r-- 1 hadoop hadoop  1335 Oct 16 13:55 configuration.xsl
-rw-r--r-- 1 hadoop hadoop   318 Oct 16 13:55 container-executor.cfg
-rw-r--r-- 1 hadoop hadoop   348 Oct 16 23:31 core-site.xml
-rw-r--r-- 1 hadoop hadoop  3589 Oct 16 13:55 hadoop-env.cmd
-rw-r--r-- 1 hadoop hadoop  4224 Oct 16 13:55 hadoop-env.sh
-rw-r--r-- 1 hadoop hadoop  2598 Oct 16 13:55 hadoop-metrics2.properties
-rw-r--r-- 1 hadoop hadoop  2490 Oct 16 13:55 hadoop-metrics.properties
-rw-r--r-- 1 hadoop hadoop  9683 Oct 16 13:55 hadoop-policy.xml
-rw-r--r-- 1 hadoop hadoop   590 Oct 16 23:32 hdfs-site.xml
```

12. The directories `bin` and `sbin` contain executable binaries, which are used to start and stop Hadoop daemons and perform other operations such as filesystem listing, copying, deleting, and so on:

```
[root@nn1 ~]# ls -l /opt/cluster/hadoop-2.7.3/bin/
total 376
-rwxr-xr-x 1 hadoop hadoop 131122 Oct 16 13:55 container-executor
-rwxr-xr-x 1 hadoop hadoop   6488 Oct 16 13:55 hadoop
-rwxr-xr-x 1 hadoop hadoop   8514 Oct 16 13:55 hadoop.cmd
-rwxr-xr-x 1 hadoop hadoop  12223 Oct 16 13:55 hdfs
-rwxr-xr-x 1 hadoop hadoop   7238 Oct 16 13:55 hdfs.cmd
-rwxr-xr-x 1 hadoop hadoop   5953 Oct 16 13:55 mapred
-rwxr-xr-x 1 hadoop hadoop   6094 Oct 16 13:55 mapred.cmd
-rwxr-xr-x 1 hadoop hadoop   1776 Oct 16 13:55 rcc
-rwxr-xr-x 1 hadoop hadoop 157730 Oct 16 13:55 test-container-executor
-rwxr-xr-x 1 hadoop hadoop  13352 Oct 16 13:55 yarn
-rwxr-xr-x 1 hadoop hadoop  11054 Oct 16 13:55 yarn.cmd
```

```
[root@nn1 ~]# ls -l /opt/cluster/hadoop-2.7.3/sbin/
total 120
-rwxr-xr-x 1 hadoop hadoop 2752 Oct 16 13:55 distribute-exclude.sh
-rwxr-xr-x 1 hadoop hadoop 6452 Oct 16 13:55 hadoop-daemon.sh
-rwxr-xr-x 1 hadoop hadoop 1360 Oct 16 13:55 hadoop-daemons.sh
-rwxr-xr-x 1 hadoop hadoop 1597 Oct 16 13:55 hdfs-config.cmd
-rwxr-xr-x 1 hadoop hadoop 1427 Oct 16 13:55 hdfs-config.sh
-rwxr-xr-x 1 hadoop hadoop 2291 Oct 16 13:55 httpfs.sh
-rwxr-xr-x 1 hadoop hadoop 3128 Oct 16 13:55 kms.sh
```

13. To execute a command `/opt/cluster/hadoop-2.7.3/bin/hadoop, a` complete path to the command needs to be specified. This could be cumbersome, and can be avoided by setting the environment variable `HADOOP_HOME`.
14. Similarly, there are other variables that need to be set that point to the binaries and the configuration file locations:

```
[root@nn1 ~]# cat /etc/profile.d/hadoopenv.sh
export JAVA_HOME=/usr/java/latest
export HADOOP_HOME=/opt/cluster/hadoop

export HADOOP_MAPRED_HOME=$HADOOP_HOME
export HADOOP_COMMON_HOME=$HADOOP_HOME
export HADOOP_HDFS_HOME=$HADOOP_HOME
export YARN_HOME=$HADOOP_HOME
export HADOOP_CONF_DIR=$HADOOP_HOME/etc/hadoop
export YARN_CONF_DIR=$HADOOP_HOME/etc/hadoop

export HADOOP_HOME_WARN_SUPPRESS=True
PATH=$JAVA_HOME/bin:$HADOOP_HOME/bin:$HADOOP_HOME/sbin:$PATH
export PATH
```

15. The environment file is set up system-wide so that any user can use the commands. Once the `hadoopenv.sh` file is in place, execute the command to export the variables defined in it:

```
[root@nn1 ~]# . /etc/profile.d/hadoopenv.sh
```

16. Change to the `Hadoop` user using the command `su - hadoop`:

```
[root@nn1 ~]# su - hadoop
Last login: Sat Oct 22 13:34:57 IST 2016 on pts/0
[hadoop@nn1 ~]$ id
uid=1003(hadoop) gid=1003(hadoop) groups=1003(hadoop)
```

17. Change to the `/opt/cluster` directory and create a symlink:

```
[hadoop@nn1 cluster]$ pwd
/opt/cluster
[hadoop@nn1 cluster]$ ls -l
total 0
drwxr-xr-x 10 hadoop hadoop 150 Oct 16 23:33 hadoop-2.7.3
[hadoop@nn1 cluster]$ ln -s hadoop-2.7.3 hadoop
[hadoop@nn1 cluster]$ ls -l
total 0
lrwxrwxrwx  1 hadoop hadoop  12 Oct 22 14:08 hadoop -> hadoop-2.7.3
drwxr-xr-x 10 hadoop hadoop 150 Oct 16 23:33 hadoop-2.7.3
```

18. To verify that the preceding changes are in place, the user can execute either the `which Hadoop` or `which java` commands, or the user can execute the command `hadoop` directly without specifying the complete path.
19. In addition to setting the environment as discussed, the user has to add the `JAVA_HOME` variable in the `hadoop-env.sh` file.
20. The next thing is to set up the Namenode address, which specifies the `host:port` address on which it will listen. This is done using the file `core-site.xml`:

```
[hadoop@nn1 cluster]$ cat hadoop/etc/hadoop/core-site.xml
<?xml version="1.0"?>
<?xml-stylesheet type="text/xsl" href="configuration.xsl"?>

<!-- Put site-specific property overrides in this file. -->

<configuration>

<property>
<name>fs.defaultFS</name>
<value>hdfs://nn1.cluster1.com:9000</value>
</property>

</configuration>
```

21. The important thing to keep in mind is the property `fs.defaultFS`.
22. The next thing that the user needs to configure is the location where Namenode will store its metadata. This can be any location, but it is recommended that you always have a dedicated disk for it. This is configured in the file `hdfs-site.xml`:

```
[hadoop@nn1 cluster]$ cat hadoop/etc/hadoop/hdfs-site.xml
<?xml version="1.0"?>
<?xml-stylesheet type="text/xsl" href="configuration.xsl"?>

<!-- Put site-specific property overrides in this file. -->

<configuration>

<property>
<name>dfs.name.dir</name>
<value>/data/namenode</value>
</property>
```

23. The next step is to format the Namenode. This will create an HDFS file system:

    ```
    $ hdfs namenode -format
    ```

24. Similarly, we have to add the rule for the `Datanode` directory under `hdfs-site.xml`. Nothing needs to be done to the `core-site.xml` file:

```
[hadoop@nn1 hadoop]$ cat hdfs-site.xml
<?xml version="1.0"?>
<?xml-stylesheet type="text/xsl" href="configuration.xsl"?>

<!-- Put site-specific property overrides in this file. -->

<configuration>

<property>
<name>dfs.name.dir</name>
<value>/data/namenode</value>
</property>

<property>
<name>dfs.datanode.data.dir</name>
<value>/data/datanode</value>
</property>

</configuration>
```

25. Then the services need to be started for Namenode and Datanode:

    ```
    $ hadoop-daemon.sh start namenode
    $ hadoop-daemon.sh start datanode
    ```

26. The command `jps` can be used to check for running daemons:

```
[hadoop@nn1 cluster]$ jps
2161 DataNode
2107 NameNode
2254 Jps
```

How it works...

The master Namenode stores metadata and the slave node Datanode stores the blocks. When the Namenode is formatted, it creates a data structure that contains `fsimage`, `edits`, and `VERSION`. These are very important for the functioning of the cluster.

The parameters `dfs.data.dir` and `dfs.datanode.data.dir` are used for the same purpose, but are used across different versions. The older parameters are deprecated in favor of the newer ones, but they will still work. The parameter `dfs.name.dir` has been deprecated in favor of `dfs.namenode.name.dir` in Hadoop 2.x. The intention of showing both versions of the parameter is to bring to the user's notice that parameters are evolving and ever changing, and care must be taken by referring to the release notes for each Hadoop version.

There's more...

Setting up ResourceManager and NodeManager

In the preceding recipe, we set up the storage layer—that is, the HDFS for storing data—but what about the processing layer?. The data on HDFS needs to be processed to make a meaningful decision using MapReduce, Tez, Spark, or any other tool. To run the MapReduce, Spark or other processing framework we need to have ResourceManager, NodeManager.

Installing a single-node cluster - YARN components

In the previous recipe, we discussed how to set up Namenode and Datanode for HDFS. In this recipe, we will be covering how to set up YARN on the same node.

After completing this recipe, there will be four daemons running on the `nn1.cluster1.com` node, namely `namenode`, `datanode`, `resourcemanager`, and `nodemanager` daemons.

Getting ready

For this recipe, you will again use the same node on which we have already configured the HDFS layer.

All operations will be done by the `hadoop` user.

How to do it...

1. Log in to the node `nn1.cluster1.com` and change to the `hadoop` user.
2. Change to the `/opt/cluster/hadoop/etc/hadoop` directory and configure the files `mapred-site.xml` and `yarn-site.xml`:

```
[hadoop@nn1 hadoop]$ cat mapred-site.xml
<?xml version="1.0"?>
<?xml-stylesheet type="text/xsl" href="configuration.xsl"?>

<!-- Put site-specific property overrides in this file. -->

<configuration>

<property>
<name>mapreduce.framework.name</name>
<value>yarn</value>
</property>

</configuration>
```

3. The file `yarn-site.xml` specifies the shuffle class, scheduler, and resource management components of the ResourceManager. You only need to specify `yarn.resourcemanager.address`; the rest are automatically picked up by the ResourceManager. You can see from the following screenshot that you can separate them into their independent components:

```
[hadoop@nn1 hadoop]$ cat yarn-site.xml
<?xml version="1.0"?>
<configuration>

<property>
<name>yarn.nodemanager.aux-services</name>
<value>mapreduce_shuffle</value>
</property>

<property>
<name>yarn.nodemanager.aux-services.mapreduce.shuffle.class</name>
<value>org.apache.hadoop.mapred.ShuffleHandler</value>
</property>

<property>
<name>yarn.resourcemanager.resource-tracker.address</name>
<value>nn1.cluster1.com:9001</value>
</property>

<property>
<name>yarn.resourcemanager.scheduler.address</name>
<value>nn1.cluster1.com:9002</value>
</property>

<property>
<name>yarn.resourcemanager.address</name>
<value>nn1.cluster1.com:9003</value>
</property>


</configuration>
```

4. Once the configurations are in place, the `resourcemanager` and `nodemanager` daemons need to be started:

```
[hadoop@nn1 hadoop]$ yarn-daemon.sh start resourcemanager
starting resourcemanager, logging to /opt/cluster/hadoop-2
t
[hadoop@nn1 hadoop]$ yarn-daemon.sh start nodemanager
starting nodemanager, logging to /opt/cluster/hadoop-2.7.3
[hadoop@nn1 hadoop]$ jps
2673 Jps
2582 NodeManager
2344 ResourceManager
2107 NameNode
```

5. The environment variables that were defined by `/etc/profile.d/hadoopenv.sh` included `YARN_HOME` and `YARN_CONF_DIR`, which let the framework know about the location of the YARN configurations.

How it works...

The `nn1.cluster1.com` node is configured to run HDFS and YARN components. Any file that is copied to the HDFS will be split into blocks and stored on Datanode. The metadata of the file will be on the Namenode.

Any operation performed on a text file, such as word count, can be done by running a simple MapReduce program, which will be submitted to the single node cluster using the ResourceManager daemon and executed by the NodeManager. There are a lot of steps and details as to what goes on under the hood, which will be covered in the coming chapters.

> The single-node cluster is also called pseudo-distributed cluster.

There's more...

A quick check can be done on the functionality of HDFS. You can create a simple text file and upload it to HDFS to see whether it is successful or not:

```
$ hadoop fs -put test.txt /
```

This will copy the file `test.txt` to the HDFS. The file can be read directly from HDFS:

```
$ hadoop fs -ls /
$ hadoop fs -cat /test.txt
```

See also

- The *Installing multi-node cluster* recipe

Installing a multi-node cluster

In the previous recipes, we looked at how to configure a single-node Hadoop cluster, also referred to as pseudo-distributed cluster. In this recipe, we will set up a fully distributed cluster with each daemon running on separate nodes.

There will be one node for Namenode, one for ResourceManager, and four nodes will be used for Datanode and NodeManager. In production, the number of Datanodes could be in the thousands, but here we are just restricted to four nodes. The Datanode and NodeManager coexist on the same nodes for the purposes of data locality and locality of reference.

Getting ready

Make sure that the six nodes the user chooses have JDK installed, with name resolution working. This could be done by making entries in the `/etc/hosts` file or using DNS.

In this recipe, we are using the following nodes:

- **Namenode**: `nn1.cluster1.com`
- **ResourceManager**: `jt1.cluster1.com`
- **Datanodes and NodeManager**: `dn[1-4].cluster1.com`

How to do it...

1. Make sure all the nodes have the `hadoop` user.
2. Create the directory structure `/opt/cluster` on all the nodes.
3. Make sure the ownership is correct for `/opt/cluster`.
4. Copy the `/opt/cluster/hadoop-2.7.3` directory from the `nn1.cluster.com` to all the nodes in the cluster:

   ```
   $ for i in 192.168.1.{72..75};do scp -r hadoop-2.7.3 $i:/opt/
   cluster/ $i;done
   ```

5. The preceding IPs belong to the nodes in the cluster. The user needs to modify them accordingly. Also, to prevent it from prompting for password for each node, it is good to set up pass phraseless access between each node.
6. Change to the directory `/opt/cluster` and create a symbolic link on each node:

   ```
   $ ln -s hadoop-2.7.3 hadoop
   ```

7. Make sure that the environment variables have been set up on all nodes:

   ```
   $ . /etc/profile.d/hadoopenv.sh
   ```

8. On Namenode, only the parameters specific to it are needed.
9. The file `core-site.xml` remains the same across all nodes in the cluster.

10. On Namenode, the file `hdfs-site.xml` changes as follows:

```
<property>
<name>dfs.name.dir</name>
<value>/data/namenode</value>
</property>
```

11. On Datanode, the file `hdfs-site.xml` changes as follows:

```
<property>
<name>dfs.datanode.data.dir</name>
<value>/data/datanode</value>
</property>
```

12. On Datanodes, the file `yarn-site.xml` changes as follows:

```
[hadoop@nn1 hadoop]$ cat yarn-site.xml
<?xml version="1.0"?>
<configuration>

<property>
<name>yarn.nodemanager.aux-services</name>
<value>mapreduce_shuffle</value>
</property>

<property>
<name>yarn.nodemanager.aux-services.mapreduce.shuffle.class</name>
<value>org.apache.hadoop.mapred.ShuffleHandler</value>
</property>

<property>
<name>yarn.resourcemanager.resource-tracker.address</name>
<value>jt1.cluster1.com:9001</value>
</property>

<property>
<name>yarn.resourcemanager.scheduler.address</name>
<value>jt1.cluster1.com:9002</value>
</property>

<property>
<name>yarn.resourcemanager.address</name>
<value>jt1.cluster1.com:9003</value>
</property>


</configuration>
```

13. On the node jt1, which is ResourceManager, the file `yarn-site.xml` is as follows:

```
[hadoop@nn1 hadoop]$ cat yarn-site.xml
<?xml version="1.0"?>
<configuration>

<property>
<name>yarn.nodemanager.aux-services</name>
<value>mapreduce_shuffle</value>
</property>

<property>
<name>yarn.nodemanager.aux-services.mapreduce.shuffle.class</name>
<value>org.apache.hadoop.mapred.ShuffleHandler</value>
</property>

<property>
<name>yarn.resourcemanager.resource-tracker.address</name>
<value>jt1.cluster1.com:9001</value>
</property>

<property>
<name>yarn.resourcemanager.scheduler.address</name>
<value>jt1.cluster1.com:9002</value>
</property>

<property>
<name>yarn.resourcemanager.address</name>
<value>jt1.cluster1.com:9003</value>
</property>


</configuration>
```

14. To start Namenode on `nn1.cluster1.com`, enter the following:

    $ hadoop-daemon.sh start namenode

15. To start Datanode and NodeManager on `dn[1-4]`, enter the following:

    $ hadoop-daemon.sh start datanode

    $ yarn-daemon.sh start nodemanager

16. To start ResourceManager on `jt1.cluster.com`, enter the following:

    $ yarn-daemon.sh start resourcemanager

17. On each node, execute the command `jps` to see the daemons running on them. Make sure you have the correct services running on each node.
18. Create a text file `test.txt` and copy it to HDFS using `hadoop fs -put test.txt /`. This confirms that HDFS is working fine.

19. To verify that YARN has been set up correctly, run the simple "Pi" estimation program:

```
$ yarn jar /opt/cluster/hadoop/share/hadoop/mapreduce/hadoop-
example.jar Pi 3 3
```

How it works...

Steps 1 through 7 copy the already extracted and configured Hadoop files to other nodes in the cluster. From step 8 onwards, each node is configured according to the role it plays in the cluster.

The user should see four Datanodes reporting to the cluster, and should also be able to access the UI of the Namenode on port `50070` and on port `8088` for ResourceManager.

To see the number of nodes talking to Namenode, enter the following:

```
$ hdfs dfsadmin -report
  Configured Capacity: 9124708352 (21.50 GB)
  Present Capacity: 5923942400 (20.52 GB)
  DFS Remaining: 5923938304 (20.52 GB)
  DFS Used: 4096 (4 KB)
  DFS Used%: 0.00%
Live datanodes (4):
```

The same information can also be retrieved using the Namenode Web UI as shown in the following screenshot:

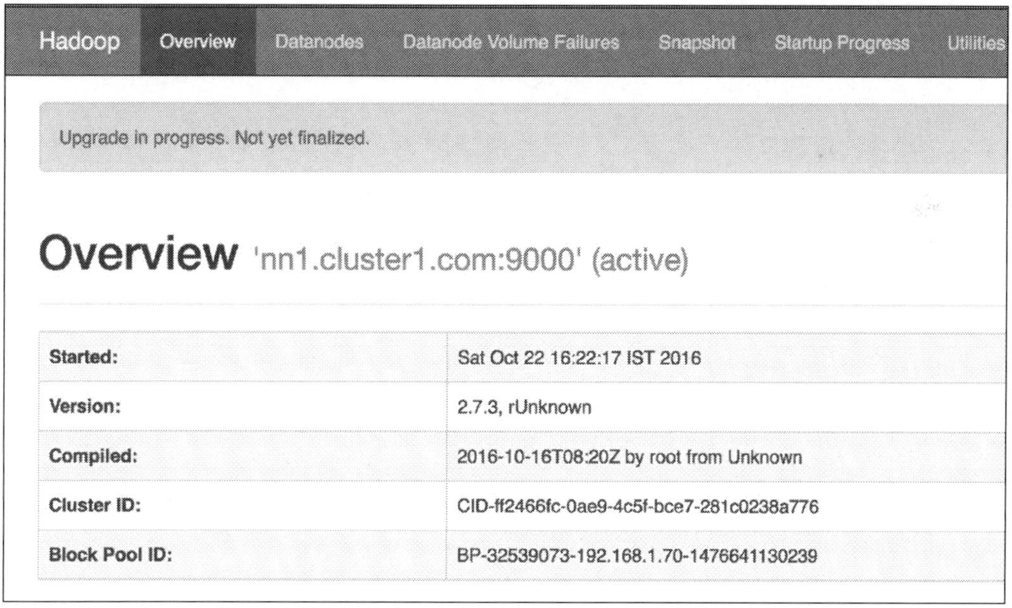

> The user can configure any customer port for any service, but there should be a good reason to change the defaults.

Configuring the Hadoop Gateway node

Hadoop Gateway or edge node is a node that connects to the Hadoop cluster, but does not run any of the daemons. The purpose of an edge node is to provide an access point to the cluster and prevent users from a direct connection to critical components such as Namenode or Datanode.

Another important reason for its use is the data distribution across the cluster. If a user connects to a Datanode and performs the data copy operation `hadoop fs -put file /`, then one copy of the file will always go to the Datanode from which the copy command was executed. This will result in an imbalance of data across the node. If we upload a file from a node that is not a Datanode, then data will be distributed evenly for all copies of data.

In this recipe, we will configure an edge node for a Hadoop cluster.

Getting ready

For the edge node, the user needs a separate Linux machine with Java installed and the user `hadoop` in place.

How to do it...

1. `ssh` to the new node that is to be configured as Gateway node. For example, the node name could be `client1.cluster1.com`.
2. Set up the environment variable as discussed before. This can be done by setting the `/etc/profile.d/hadoopenv.sh` file.
3. Copy the already configured directory `hadoop-2.7.3` from Namenode to this node (`client1.cluster1.com`). This avoids doing all the configuration for files such as `core-site.xml` and `yarn-site.xml`.
4. The edge node just needs to know about the two master nodes of Namenode and ResourceManager. It does not need any other configuration for the time being. It does not store any data locally, unlike Namenode and Datanode.
5. It only needs to write temporary files and logs. In later chapters, we will see other parameters for MapReduce and performance tuning that go on this node.
6. Create a symbolic link `ln -s hadoop-2.7.3 hadoop` so that the commands and Hadoop configuration files are visible.

7. There will be no daemon started on this node. Execute a command from the edge node to make sure the user can connect to `hadoop fs -ls /`.
8. To verify that the edge node has been set up correctly, run the simple "Pi" estimation program from the edge node:

```
$ yarn jar /opt/cluster/hadoop/share/hadoop/mapreduce/hadoop-
example.jar Pi 3 3
```

How it works...

The edge node or the Gateway node connects to Namenode for all HDFS-related operation and connects to ResourceManager for submitted jobs to the cluster.

In production, there will be more than one edge node connecting to the cluster for high availability. This is can be done by using a load balancer or DNS round-robin. No user should run any local jobs on the edge nodes or use it for doing non Hadoop-related tasks.

See also

Edge node can be used to configure many additional components, such as PIG, Hive, Sqoop, rather than installing them on the main cluster nodes like Namenode, Datanode. This way it is easy to segregate the complexity and restrict access to just edge node.

- The *Configuring Hive* recipe

Decommissioning nodes

There will always be failures in clusters, such as hardware issues or a need to upgrade nodes. This should be done in a graceful manner, without any data loss.

When the Datanode daemon is stopped on a Datanode, it takes approximately ten minutes for the Namenode to remove that node. This has to do with the heartbeat retry interval. At any time, we can abruptly remove the Datanode, but it can result in data loss.

It is recommended that you opt for the graceful removal of the node from the cluster, as this ensures that all the data on that node is drained.

Getting ready

For the following steps, we assume that the cluster that is up and running with Datanodes is in a healthy state and the one with the Datanode `dn1.cluster1.com` needs maintenance and must be removed from the cluster. We will login to the Namenode and make changes there.

How to do it...

1. ssh to Namenode and edit the file `hdfs-site.xml` by adding the following property to it:

```
<property>
<name>dfs.hosts.exclude</name>
<value>/home/hadoop/excludes</value>
<final>true</final>
</property>
```

2. Make sure the file `excludes` is readable by the user `hadoop`.
3. Restart the Namenode daemon for the property to take effect:

```
$ hadoop-daemons.sh stop namenode
$ hadoop-daemons.sh start namenode
```

4. A restart of Namenode is required only when any property is changed in the file. Once the property is in place, Namenode can read the changes to the contents of the file `excludes` by simply refreshing nodes.
5. Add the `dn1.cluster1.com` node to the file `excludes`:

```
$ cat excludes
dn1.cluster1.com
```

6. After adding the node to the file, we just need to reload the file by doing the following:

```
$ hadoop dfsadmin -refreshNodes
```

7. After sometime, the node will be decommissioned. The time will vary according to the data the particular Datanode had. We can see the decommissioned nodes using the following:

```
$ hdfs dfsadmin -report
```

8. The preceding command will list the nodes in the cluster, and against the `dn1.cluster1.com` node we can see that its status will either be decommissioning or decommissioned.

How it works...

Let's have a look at what we did throughout this recipe.

In steps 1 through 6, we added the new property to the `hdfs-site.xml` file and then restarted Namenode to make it aware of the changes. Once the property is in place, the Namenode is aware of the `excludes` file, and it can be asked to re-read by simply refreshing the node list, as done in step 6.

With these steps, the data on the Datanode `dn1.cluster1.com` will be moved to other nodes in the cluster, and once the data has been drained, the Datanode daemon on the node will be shutdown. During the process, the node will change the status from normal to decommissioning and then to decommissioned.

Care must be taken while decommissioning nodes in the cluster. The user should not decommission multiple nodes at a time as this will generate lot of network traffic and cause congestion and data loss.

See also

- The *Add nodes to the cluster* recipe

Adding nodes to the cluster

Over a period of time, our cluster will grow in data and there will be a need to increase the capacity of the cluster by adding more nodes.

We can add Datanodes to the cluster in the same way that we first configured the Datanode started the Datanode daemon on it. But the important thing to keep in mind is that all nodes can be part of the cluster. It should not be that anyone can just start a Datanode daemon on his laptop and join the cluster, as it will be disastrous. By default, there is nothing preventing any node being a Datanode, as the user has just to untar the Hadoop package and point the file "core-site.xml" to the Namenode and start the Datanode daemon.

Getting ready

For the following steps, we assume that the cluster that is up and running with Datanodes is in a healthy state and we need to add a new Datanode in the cluster. We will login to the Namenode and make changes there.

How to do it...

1. ssh to Namenode and edit the file `hdfs-site.xml` to add the following property to it:

```
<property>
<name>dfs.hosts</name>
<value>/home/hadoop/includes</value>
<final>true</final>
</property>
```

2. Make sure the file `includes` is readable by the user `hadoop`.

3. Restart the Namenode daemon for the property to take effect:

   ```
   $ hadoop-daemons.sh stop namenode
   $ hadoop-daemons.sh start namenode
   ```

4. A restart of Namenode is required only when any property is changed in the file. Once the property is in place, Namenode can read the changes to the contents of the `includes` file by simply refreshing the nodes.
5. Add the `dn1.cluster1.com` node to the file `excludes`:

   ```
   $ cat includes
   dn1.cluster1.com
   ```

6. The file `includes` or `excludes` can contain a list of multiple nodes, one node per line.
7. After adding the node to the file, we just need to reload the file by entering the following:

   ```
   $ hadoop dfsadmin -refreshNodes
   ```

8. After some time, the node will be available in the cluster and can be seen:

   ```
   $ hdfs dfsadmin -report
   ```

How it works...

The file `/home/hadoop/includes` will contain a list of all the Datanodes that are allowed to join a cluster. If the file `includes` is blank, then all Datanodes are allowed to join the cluster. If there is both an `include` and `exclude` file, the list of nodes must be mutually exclusive in both the files. So, to decommission the node `dn1.cluster.com` from the cluster, it must be removed from the `includes` file and added to the `excludes` file.

There's more...

In addition to controlling the nodes as we described, there will be firewall rules in place and separate VLANs for Hadoop clusters to keep the traffic and data isolated.

2

Maintaining Hadoop Cluster HDFS

In this chapter, we will cover the following recipes:

- Configuring HDFS block size
- Setting up Namenode metadata location
- Loading data into HDFS
- Configuring HDFS replication
- HDFS balancer
- Quota configuration
- HDFS health and FSCK
- Configuring rack awareness
- Recycle or trash bin configuration
- Distcp usage
- Controlling block report storm
- Configuring Datanode heartbeat

Introduction

In this chapter, we will take a look at the storage layer, which is HDFS, and how it can be configured for storing data. It is important to ensure the good health of this distributed filesystem, and make sure that the data it contains is available, even in the case of failures. In this chapter, we will take a look at the replication, quota setup, and balanced distribution of data across nodes, as well as covering recipes on rack awareness and heartbeat for communication with the master.

The recipes in this chapter assume that you already have a running cluster and have completed the steps given in *Chapter 1, Hadoop Architecture and Deployment*.

> While the recipes in this chapter will give you an overview of a typical configuration, we encourage you to adapt this proposal according to your needs. The block size plays an important role in the performance and the amount of data that is worked on by a mapper. It is good practice to set up passphrase less access between nodes, so that the user does not need to enter a password while doing operations across nodes.

Overview of HDFS

Hadoop distributed file system (**HDFS**)is inspired from the **Google File system** (**GFS**). The fundamental idea is to split the files into smaller chunks called blocks and distribute them across nodes in the cluster. HDFS is not the only filesystem used in Hadoop, but there are other filesystems as well such as MapR-FS, ISILON, and so on.

HDFS is a pseudo filesystem that is created on top of other filesystems, such as ext3, ext4, and so on. An important thing to keep in mind is that to store data in Hadoop, we cannot directly write to native filesystems such as ext3, ext4, or xfs. In this chapter, we will cover recipes to configure properties of HDFS.

Configuring HDFS block size

Getting ready

To step through the recipes in this chapter, make sure you have completed the recipes in *Chapter 1, Hadoop Architecture and Deployment* or at least understand the basic Hadoop cluster setup.

How to do it...

1. `ssh` to the master node, which is Namenode, and navigate to the directory where Hadoop is installed. In the previous chapter, Hadoop was installed at `/opt/cluster/hadoop`:

   ```
   $ ssh root@10.0.0.4
   ```

2. Change to the `Hadoop` user, or any other user that is running Hadoop, by using the following:

   ```
   $ sudo su - hadoop
   ```

3. Edit the `hdfs-site.xml` file and modify the parameter to reflect the changes, as shown in the following screenshot:

   ```
   <property>
   <name>dfs.blocksize</name>
   <value>67108864</value>
   </property>
   ```

4. `dfs.blocksize` is the parameter that decides on the value of the HDFS block size. The unit is bytes and the default value is 64 MB in Hadoop 1 and 128 MB in Hadoop 2. The block size can be configured according to the need.
5. Once the changes are made to `hdfs-site.xml`, copy the file across all nodes in the cluster.
6. Then restart the Namenode and `datanode` daemons on all nodes.
7. The block size can be configured per file by specifying it during the copy process, as shown in the following screenshot:

```
[hadoop@nn1 ~]$ hadoop fs -Ddfs.blocksize=67108864 -put file1 /
```

How it works...

The best practice is to keep the configurations the same across all nodes in the cluster, but it is not mandatory. For example, the block size of Namenode can be different from that of the edge node. In that case, the parameters on the source node will be effective. It means that the parameter on the node from which the copying is done will be in effect.

Setting up Namenode metadata location

The most critical component of Hadoop is Namenode, and it is important to safeguard the information it stores. It stores metadata, which is a combination of namespace and inode structure.

All the steps are to be performed as the `hadoop` user. It is expected that the user has gone through *Chapter 1, Hadoop Architecture and Deployment* and understands the uses and function of Namenode.

Getting ready

You are going to need a preinstalled Hadoop as discussed in *Chapter 1, Hadoop Architecture and Deployment*. In the following recipes, we will configure the parameters for a copy of Hadoop that is already installed.

How to do it...

1. `ssh` to the Namenode, which in this case is `nn1.cluster1.com`.
2. Navigate to the `/opt/cluster/hadoop/etc/hadoop` directory. This is the directory where we installed Hadoop in the first chapter. If the user has installed it at a different location, then navigate to this directory.
3. Configure the `dfs.namenode.name.dir` parameter, which defines the location where Namenode will persist its metadata.
4. See the following screenshot for the contents of the file:

```
<property>
<name>dfs.namenode.name.dir</name>
<value>/data/namenode</value>
</property>
```

5. It is good practice to have the `/data/namenode` mount point on a different disk drive, rather than from a disk on which the OS is installed.
6. In production, there will always be more than one directory to store the metadata, as shown in the following screenshot:

```
<property>
<name>dfs.namenode.name.dir</name>
<value>/data/namenode,/data/namenode1</value>
</property>
```

7. Once the changes are made, save the file and restart the `namenode` daemon.
8. We need to format the Namenode so that all the directories listed are in sync and initialized.
9. If the user already had a running cluster, then copy the contents across the directories and do not format the Namenode, as it will result in the loss of data.

How it works...

With steps 3 to 5, the user will be able to configure the Namenode metadata store location. Usually, in production, one of the common separated lists of directories is a cross mount from the NFS server. This is done to make sure that, if the Namenode server goes down, we can still access the data by quickly mounting it on another machine.

Please start the Datanode daemons on all nodes configured to run as Datanodes. If the Datanodes were initially connected to another Namenode, then the Datanode directories specified using `dfs.datanode.data.dir` must be cleaned.

Loading data in HDFS

It is important to make sure that the cluster is working fine and the user can perform file operations on the cluster.

Getting ready

Log in to any of the nodes in the cluster. It's best to use the edge node, as stated in *Chapter 1, Hadoop Architecture and Deployment*, and switch to user `hadoop`.

Create a simple text file named `file1.txt` using any of your favorite text editors, and write some content in it.

How to do it...

1. Connect to the `client1.cluster1.com` edge node and switch to the `hadoop` user.
2. Copy the `file1.txt` file to HDFS, as shown in the following screenshot:

```
[hadoop@nn1 ~]$ hadoop fs -put file1.txt /
[hadoop@nn1 ~]$ hadoop fs -ls /file1.txt
-rw-r--r--   2 hadoop supergroup         24 2016-11-09 22:38 /file1.txt
```

3. The user can check for the status of a file, as shown in the following screenshot:

```
[hadoop@nn1 ~]$ hadoop fs -test -f /file1.txt
[hadoop@nn1 ~]$ echo $?
0
```

4. The user can make sure that the file exists and its type is correct, as shown in the following screenshot. The user can execute the commands to see the sub options:

   `$ hadoop fs (and hit enter to see the options)`

How it works...

Steps 2 and 3 create a simple text file on the local filesystem and then copy it to HDFS to make sure that the storage layer of Hadoop is working correctly. If there are errors in copying files, make sure the daemons are up and running. This can be done by using the `jps` command.

Configuring HDFS replication

For redundancy, it is important to have multiple copies of data. In HDFS, this is achieved by placing copies of blocks on different nodes. By default, the replication factor is 3, which means that for each block written to HDFS, there will be three copies in total on the nodes in the cluster.

It is important to make sure that the cluster is working fine and the user can perform file operations on the cluster.

Getting ready

Log in to any of the nodes in the cluster. It is best to use the edge node, as stated in Chapter 1, and switch to the user `hadoop`.

Create a simple text file named `file1.txt` using any of your favorite text editors, and write some content in it.

How to do it...

1. `ssh` to the Namenode, which in this case is `nn1.cluster1.com`, and switch to user `hadoop`.
2. Navigate to the `/opt/cluster/hadoop/etc/hadoop` directory. This is the directory where we installed Hadoop in *Chapter 1, Hadoop Architecture and Deployment*. If the user has installed it at a different location, then navigate to this directory.
3. Configure to the `dfs.replication` parameter in the directory `hdfs-site.xml` file.
4. See the following screenshot for this configuration:

```
<property>
<name>dfs.replication</name>
<value>2</value>
</property>
```

5. Once the changes are made, save the file and make changes across all nodes in the cluster.
6. Restart the Namenode and Datanode daemons across the cluster. The easiest way of doing this is using the `stop-dfs.sh` and `start-dfs.sh` commands.
7. See the following screenshot, which shows the way to restart the daemons:

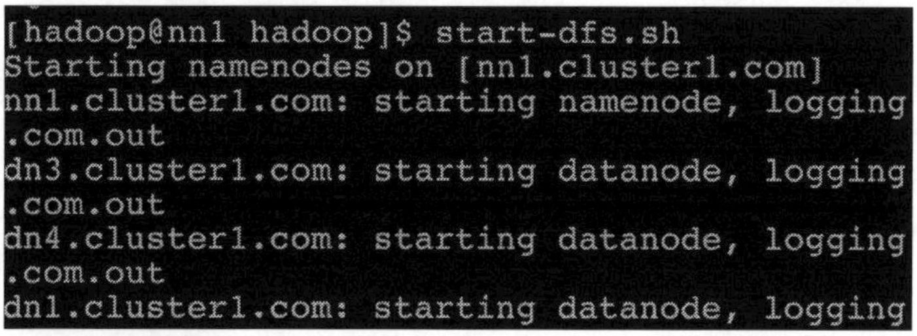

[hadoop@nn1 hadoop]$ start-dfs.sh
Starting namenodes on [nn1.cluster1.com]
nn1.cluster1.com: starting namenode, logging
.com.out
dn3.cluster1.com: starting datanode, logging
.com.out
dn4.cluster1.com: starting datanode, logging
.com.out
dn1.cluster1.com: starting datanode, logging

How it works...

The `dfs.replication` parameter is usually the same across the cluster, but it can be configured to be different across all nodes in the cluster. The source node from which the copy operation is done will define the replication factor for a file. For example, if an edge node has replication set to 2, then the blocks will be replicated twice, irrespective of the value on Namenode.

See also

- The *Configuring HDFS block size* recipe

HDFS balancer

In a long-running cluster, there might be unequal distribution of data across Datanodes. This could be due to failures of nodes or the addition of nodes to the cluster.

To make sure that the data is equally distributed across Datanodes, it is important to use Hadoop balancer to redistribute the blocks.

Getting ready

For this recipe, you will again use the same node on which we have already configured Namenode.

All operations will be done by user `hadoop`.

How to do it...

1. Log in the nn1.cluster1.com node and change to user `hadoop`.
2. Execute the balancer command as shown in the following screenshot:

```
[hadoop@master1 ~]$ hdfs balancer
16/11/17 23:48:40 INFO balancer.Balancer: namenodes  = [hdfs://master1.cyrus.com:9000]
16/11/17 23:48:40 INFO balancer.Balancer: parameters = Balancer.Parameters[BalancingPolicy.Node,
 of nodes to be excluded = 0, number of nodes to be included = 0]
Time Stamp               Iteration#  Bytes Already Moved  Bytes Left To Move  Bytes Being Moved
16/11/17 23:48:41 INFO net.NetworkTopology: Adding a new node: /default-rack/10.0.0.37:50010
16/11/17 23:48:41 INFO net.NetworkTopology: Adding a new node: /default-rack/10.0.0.75:50010
16/11/17 23:48:41 INFO net.NetworkTopology: Adding a new node: /default-rack/10.0.0.39:50010
16/11/17 23:48:41 INFO net.NetworkTopology: Adding a new node: /default-rack/10.0.0.40:50010
16/11/17 23:48:41 INFO net.NetworkTopology: Adding a new node: /default-rack/10.0.0.74:50010
16/11/17 23:48:41 INFO net.NetworkTopology: Adding a new node: /default-rack/10.0.0.38:50010
16/11/17 23:48:41 INFO balancer.Balancer: 0 over-utilized: []
16/11/17 23:48:41 INFO balancer.Balancer: 0 underutilized: []
The cluster is balanced. Exiting...
Nov 17, 2016 11:48:41 PM          0                  0 B                 0 B               -1 B
Nov 17, 2016 11:48:41 PM Balancing took 1.103 seconds
```

3. By default, the balancer threshold is set to 10%, but we can change it, as shown in the following screenshot:

```
[hadoop@master1 ~]$ hdfs balancer -threshold 40
16/11/18 01:14:53 INFO balancer.Balancer: Using a threshold of 40.0
16/11/18 01:14:53 INFO balancer.Balancer: namenodes  = [hdfs://master1.cyrus.com:9000]
16/11/18 01:14:53 INFO balancer.Balancer: parameters = Balancer.Parameters[BalancingPolicy.Node,
 of nodes to be excluded = 0, number of nodes to be included = 0]
Time Stamp               Iteration#  Bytes Already Moved  Bytes Left To Move  Bytes Being Moved
16/11/18 01:14:54 INFO net.NetworkTopology: Adding a new node: /default-rack/10.0.0.74:50010
16/11/18 01:14:54 INFO net.NetworkTopology: Adding a new node: /default-rack/10.0.0.40:50010
16/11/18 01:14:54 INFO net.NetworkTopology: Adding a new node: /default-rack/10.0.0.38:50010
16/11/18 01:14:54 INFO net.NetworkTopology: Adding a new node: /default-rack/10.0.0.39:50010
16/11/18 01:14:54 INFO net.NetworkTopology: Adding a new node: /default-rack/10.0.0.75:50010
16/11/18 01:14:54 INFO net.NetworkTopology: Adding a new node: /default-rack/10.0.0.37:50010
16/11/18 01:14:54 INFO balancer.Balancer: 0 over-utilized: []
16/11/18 01:14:54 INFO balancer.Balancer: 0 underutilized: []
The cluster is balanced. Exiting...
```

How it works...

The balancer threshold defines the percentage of cluster disk space utilized, compared to the nodes in the cluster. For example, let's say we have 10 Datanodes in the cluster, with each having 100 GB of disk storage totaling to about 1 TB.

So, when we say the threshold is 5%, it means that if any Datanode's disk in the cluster is utilized for more than 50 GB (5% of total cluster capacity), the balancer will try to balance the node by moving the blocks to other nodes. It is not always possible to balance the cluster, especially when the cluster is running near maximum disk utilization.

> Always run the balancer in off-peak hours and with `hdfs dfsadmin -setBalancerBandwidth`.

Quota configuration

In a multitenancy cluster, it is important to control the utilization both in terms of HDFS space, memory, and CPU utilization. In this recipe, we will be looking at how we can restrict a user or a project from using more than the allotted HDFS space.

Getting ready

Make sure that there is a running cluster, and that the user is already well versed in the recipes that we have looked at so far.

How to do it...

1. Connect to Namenode and change the user to `hadoop`.
2. Create a directory named `projects` on HDFS, as shown in the following screenshot:

```
$ hadoop fs -mkdir /projects
$ hadoop fs -ls /projects
```

3. By default, there is no quota configured on any directory.
4. To see what options can be set on the `projects` directory, use the following command:

```
$ hadoop fs -count -q /projects
```

5. The two leftmost fields show the namespace and disk space quota, which currently is not set, as shown in the following screenshot:

```
[hadoop@master1 ~]$ hadoop fs -count -q /projects
        none             inf            none             inf
```

6. To set the namespace quota, which will define how many inodes can be allocated for this `projects` directory, enter the following code. Inodes is the same as what we have in Linux. It is a data structure that defines a filesystem object:

```
$ hdfs dfsadmin -setQuota 100 /projects
```

7. To set the disk space quota, which will define how many blocks can be allocated for this `projects` directory, enter the following code:

```
$ hdfs dfsadmin -setSpaceQuota 4G /projects
```

8. With the preceding commands, we have set a namespace quota of 100 and a disk space quota of 4 GB, as shown in the following screenshot:

```
[hadoop@master1 ~]$ hdfs dfsadmin -setQuota 100 /projects
[hadoop@master1 ~]$ hadoop fs -count -q /projects
        100              99             none             inf
[hadoop@master1 ~]$ hdfs dfsadmin -setSpaceQuota 4G /projects
[hadoop@master1 ~]$ hadoop fs -count -q /projects
        100              99       4294967296      4294967296
```

9. To remove the quota on a directory, the user can use the commands as shown in the following screenshot:

```
[hadoop@master1 ~]$ hdfs dfsadmin -clrSpaceQuota  /projects
[hadoop@master1 ~]$ hadoop fs -count -q /projects
        100              99             none             inf
[hadoop@master1 ~]$ hdfs dfsadmin -clrQuota  /projects
[hadoop@master1 ~]$ hadoop fs -count -q /projects
       none             inf             none             inf
```

How it works...

In steps 1 through 9, we configured the quota to restrict any one directory from using the entire cluster space. The namespace controls how many files can be created in that path and the space quota tells us what the total size will be.

So now it is up to the user whether they want to create just a single file of 4 GB or 10 smaller files. This way, we are forcing the user not to create small files, as, if they do, they will run out of namespace quota.

The following commands show the total space available in the cluster, but the first command takes into account the replication factor:

```
$ hadoop fs -count -q /
9223372036854775807 9223372036854774414
$ hdfs dfsadmin -report | head
Configured Capacity: 378046439424 (352.08 GB)
Present Capacity: 357588590592 (333.03 GB)
DFS Remaining: 355012579328 (330.63 GB)
DFS Used: 2576011264 (2.40 GB)
```

> The user quota can be configured by restricting users to particular directories by using the Linux kind of permissions. It is easier to group users together and assign group permissions to directories.

HDFS health and FSCK

The health of the filesystem is very important for data retrieval and optimal performance. In a distributed system, it becomes more critical to maintain the good health of the HDFS filesystem so as to ensure block replication and near-parallel streaming of data blocks.

In this recipe, we will see how to check the health of the filesystem and do repairs, if any are needed.

Getting ready

Make sure you have a running cluster that has already been up for a few days with data. We can run the commands on a new cluster as well, but for the sake of this lab, it will give you more insights if it is run on a cluster with a large dataset.

How to do it...

1. ssh to the `master1.cyrus.com` Namenode and change the user to `hadoop`.
2. To check the HDFS root filesystem, execute the `hdfs fsck /` command, as shown in the following screenshot:

[hadoop@master1 ~]$ hdfs fsck /
Connecting to namenode via http://master1.cyrus.com:50070/
FSCK started by hadoop (auth:SIMPLE) from /10.0.0.104 for

3. We can also check the status of just one file instead of the entire filesystem, as shown in the following screenshot:

```
[hadoop@master1 ~]$ hdfs fsck /input/new.txt
Connecting to namenode via http://master1.cyrus.com:50070/fsck
FSCK started by hadoop (auth:SIMPLE) from /10.0.0.104 for path
.Status: HEALTHY
 Total size:    3707474 B
 Total dirs:    0
 Total files:   1
 Total symlinks:                0
 Total blocks (validated):      1 (avg. block size 3707474 B)
 Minimally replicated blocks:   1 (100.0 %)
 Over-replicated blocks:        0 (0.0 %)
 Under-replicated blocks:       0 (0.0 %)
 Mis-replicated blocks:         0 (0.0 %)
 Default replication factor:    3
 Average block replication:     2.0
 Corrupt blocks:                0
 Missing replicas:              0 (0.0 %)
 Number of data-nodes:          6
 Number of racks:               1
FSCK ended at Fri Nov 18 21:45:57 UTC 2016 in 0 milliseconds


The filesystem under path '/input/new.txt' is HEALTHY
```

4. The output of the `fsck` command will show the blocks for a file, the replication status, whether blocks are corrupted, and many more details, as shown in the following screenshot:

```
............Status: CORRUPT
 Total size:    850199694 B
 Total dirs:    179
 Total files:   1213
 Total symlinks:                0
 Total blocks (validated):      1209 (avg. block size 703225 B)
  ********************************
  UNDER MIN REPL'D BLOCKS:      2 (0.16542597 %)
  dfs.namenode.replication.min: 1
  CORRUPT FILES:        2
  MISSING BLOCKS:       2
  MISSING SIZE:         2471 B
  CORRUPT BLOCKS:       2
  ********************************
 Minimally replicated blocks:   1207 (99.83457 %)
 Over-replicated blocks:        0 (0.0 %)
 Under-replicated blocks:       0 (0.0 %)
 Mis-replicated blocks:         0 (0.0 %)
 Default replication factor:    3
 Average block replication:     2.8908188
 Corrupt blocks:                2
 Missing replicas:              0 (0.0 %)
 Number of data-nodes:          6
 Number of racks:               1
FSCK ended at Fri Nov 18 21:38:11 UTC 2016 in 148 milliseconds


The filesystem under path '/' is CORRUPT
```

5. We can also look at how the blocks of a file are laid across the cluster using the commands as shown in the following screenshot:

```
[hadoop@master1 ~]$ hdfs fsck /input/new.txt -files -blocks -racks -locations
Connecting to namenode via http://master1.cyrus.com:50070/fsck?ugi=hadoop&files=
h=%2Finput%2Fnew.txt
FSCK started by hadoop (auth:SIMPLE) from /10.0.0.104 for path /input/new.txt at
/input/new.txt 3707474 bytes, 1 block(s):  OK
0. BP-1100651502-10.0.0.104-1463464153571:blk_1073749762_8939 len=3707474 repl=2
default-rack/10.0.0.75:50010]
```

6. In the cluster named `cyrus`, you can see that there are some corrupt blocks. We can simulate this by manually deleting a block of a file on the lower filesystem. Each of the HDFS blocks, is a file at the lower filesystem such as EXT4.

```
.........................................................................
/user/hadoop/examples/apps/streaming/job.properties: CORRUPT blockpool BP-1100651502-
k blk_1073749593

/user/hadoop/examples/apps/streaming/job.properties: MISSING 1 blocks of total size 1
/user/hadoop/examples/input-data/text/data.txt: CORRUPT blockpool BP-1100651502-10.0.
_1073749610

/user/hadoop/examples/input-data/text/data.txt: MISSING 1 blocks of total size 1409 B
```

7. The corrupt blocks can be fixed by deleting them, and for an under replicated block we can use the `hdfs dfs -setrep 2 /input/new.txt` command, so that a particular file is set to the desired number of replications. If we need to set many files to a specified number of replications, just loop through the list and do a `setrep` on them.

How it works...

The `hdfs fsck /`command is similar to the Linux `fsck` command. In Hadoop, it does not repair the filesystem automatically and needs a manual intervention. To see what options there are for this command, please use the `hdfs fsck -help` help command.

See also

- The *Configuring rack awareness* recipe

Configuring rack awareness

There will always be failures in clusters, such as hardware issues with servers, racks, switches, power supplies, and so on.

To make sure that there is no single point of failure across the entire Hadoop infrastructure, and to ensure that the contention of resources is in a distributed manner, rack awareness plays an important role. Rack awareness is a concept in which Namenode is made aware of the layout of servers in a cluster, thus making intelligent decisions on block placement.

Getting ready

For the following steps, we assume that the cluster that is up and running with Datanodes is in a healthy state. We will log in to the Namenode and make changes there.

How to do it...

1. ssh to Namenode and edit the `hdfs-site.xml` file to add the following property to it:

```
<property>
<name>topology.script.file.name</name>
<value>/opt/cluster/topology.sh</value>
</property>
```

2. Make sure that the `topology.sh` file is readable by the user `hadoop`.
3. Create two files, `topology.sh` and `topology.data`, and add the contents as shown in the following screenshot:

```
[hadoop@master1 cluster]$ cat topology.sh
while [ $# -gt 0 ] ; do
  nodeArg=$1
  exec< /opt/cluster/topology.data
  result=""
  while read line ; do
    ar=( $line )
    if [ "${ar[0]}" = "$nodeArg" ] ; then
      result="${ar[1]}"
    fi
  done
  shift
  if [ -z "$result" ] ; then
    echo -n "/default"
  else
    echo -n "$result "
  fi
done
[hadoop@master1 cluster]$ cat topology.data
10.0.0.37       /rack1
10.0.0.38       /rack1
10.0.0.39       /rack2
10.0.0.40       /rack2
10.0.0.74       /rack3
10.0.0.75       /rack3
```

4. Restart the `namenode` daemon for the property to take effect:

   $ hadoop-daemons.sh stop namenode

   $ hadoop-daemons.sh start namenode

5. Once the changes are made, the user will start seeing the rack field in the output of the `hdfs dfsadmin -dfsreport` command, as shown in the following screenshot:

Name: 10.0.0.74:50010 (dn5.cyrus.com)
Hostname: dn5.cyrus.com
Rack: /rack3

6. We can have multiple levels in the topology by specifying `topology.data`:

   $ cat topology.data

   10.0.0.37 /sw1/rack1

   10.0.0.38 /sw1/rack2

   10.0.0.39 /sw2/rack3

7. `sw1` and `sw2` are rack switches, so the failure of `sw1` will cause the outage of `rack1` and `rack2`. Namenode will make sure that all the copies of a block are not placed across `rack1` and `rack2`:

   $ hadoop dfsadmin -refreshNodes

How it works...

Let's have a look at what we did throughout this recipe.

In steps 1 through 3 we added the new property to the `hdfs-site.xml` file and then restarted Namenode to make it aware of the changes. Once the property is in place, the Namenode becomes aware of the `topology.sh` file and it will execute it to find the layout of the Datanodes in the cluster.

When the Datanodes register with Namenode, the Namenode verifies their IP or hostname and places it in a rack map accordingly. This is dynamic in nature and is never persisted to disk.

In Hadoop 2, there are multiple classes, such as `simpleDNS` and table-based, that can be used to perform a resolution of hosts in the rack awareness algorithm. The user can use any scripting language or Java to configure this. We do not need to do anything if we are using a script as shown in the preceding method, but for Java invocations and other tabular formats, we need to modify the `topology.node.switch.mapping.impl`.

To troubleshoot this, there are some common things to look at, such as the file permissions and the path to the file. We will be able to see this if we check the Namenode logs.

See also

- The *Adding nodes to the Cluster* recipe in *Chapter 1, Hadoop Architecture and Deployment*
- *Chapter 6, Backup and Recovery*, on cluster planning

Recycle or trash bin configuration

There will also be cases where we need to restore an accidently deleted file or directory. This may be due to a user error or some archiving policy that cleans data periodically.

For such situations, we can configure the recycle bin so that the deleted files can be restored for a specified amount of time. In this recipe, we will see that this can be configured.

Getting ready

This recipe shows the steps needed to edit the configuration file and add new parameters to the file to enable trash in the Hadoop cluster.

How to do it...

1. ssh to Namenode and edit the `core-site.xml` file to add the following property to it:

   ```
   <property>
   <name>fs.trash.interval</name>
   <value>10080</value>
   </property>
   ```

2. The `fs.trash.interval` parameter defines the time in minutes after which the checkpoint will be deleted.
3. Restart the `namenode` daemon for the property to take effect:

   ```
   $ hadoop-daemons.sh stop namenode
   $ hadoop-daemons.sh start namenode
   ```

4. Once trash is enabled, delete any unimportant files, as shown in the following screenshot. You will see a different message--rather than saying `deleted`, it says `moved to trash`:

```
[hadoop@master1 cluster]$ hadoop fs -rm /input/new.txt
16/11/19 00:00:00 INFO fs.TrashPolicyDefault: Namenode trash configuration
tier interval = 45 minutes.
Moved: 'hdfs://master1.cyrus.com:9000/input/new.txt' to trash at: hdfs://m
/Current
```

5. The deleted file can be restored by using the following command:

```
$ hadoop fs -cp /user/hadoop/.Trash/Current/input/new.txt /input/
```

How it works...

Any deleted data is moved to the `.Trash` directory under the home of the user who executed the command. Every time the check pointer runs, it creates a new checkpoint out of current and removes any checkpoints created more than `fs.trash.interval` minutes ago.

There's more...

In addition to the preceding method, there is a `fs.trash.checkpoint.interval` parameter that defines the number of minutes between checkpoints.

Distcp usage

In Hadoop, we deal with large data, so performing a simple copy operation might not be the optimal thing to do. Imagine copying a 1 TB file from one cluster to another, or within the same cluster to a different path, and after 50% of the copy operation it times out. In this situation, the copy has to be started from the beginning.

Getting ready

This recipe shows the steps needed to copy files within and across the cluster. Ensure that the user has a running cluster with YARN configured to run MapReduce, as discussed in *Chapter 1, Hadoop Architecture and Deployment*.

For this recipe, there is no configuration needed to run `Distcp`; just make sure HDFS and YARN is up and running.

How to do it...

1. ssh to Namenode or the edge node and execute the following command to copy the `projects` directory to the `new` directory:

```
$ hadoop distcp /projects /new
```

2. The preceding command will submit a MapReduce job to the cluster, and once the job finishes we can see the data copied at the destination.

3. We can perform an incremental copy as well by using the following command:

```
[hadoop@master1 ~]$ hadoop distcp -update /projects /new
16/11/19 23:06:01 INFO tools.DistCp: Input Options: Dist
ng=false, ignoreFailures=false, maxMaps=20, sslConfigura
ting=null, sourcePaths=[/projects], targetPath=/new, tar
16/11/19 23:06:01 INFO client.RMProxy: Connecting to Res
```

4. The copy can be performed across clusters as a backup, or simply to move data from one cluster to another:

```
$ hadoop distcp hdfs://master1.cyrus.com:9000/projects hdfs://nn1.cluster1.com:9000/projects
```

How it works...

Distcp is similar to `sync`, but it works in a distributed manner. Rather than just using one node, it uses multiple nodes in the cluster to copy parts of the data. It uses MapReduce to perform this operation, so any failures are taken care of automatically by the framework.

Control block report storm

When Datanodes come up in large clusters with more than 200 nodes, Namenode will be overwhelmed by the block reports and this can cause Namenode to become unresponsive.

Getting ready

This recipe makes more sense for large clusters, not in terms of the number of nodes, but the number of blocks in the cluster.

How to do it...

1. ssh to Namenode and edit the `hdfs-site.xml` file to add the following property to it:

```
<property>
<name>dfs.blockreport.initialDelay</name>
<value>20</value>
</property>
```

2. Copy `hdfs-site.xml` across all nodes in the cluster.
3. Restart HDFS daemons across the nodes for the property to take effect:

```
$ stop-dfs.sh
$ start-dfs.sh
```

How it works...

The `dfs.blockreport.initialDelay` parameter specifies the time in seconds. This is the upper limit of the allotted time, and it is chosen randomly by all Datanodes. What it means is that a few Datanodes can take the value of 1, others may be 2, and a few others 10, but the maximum values are capped at 20 seconds.

Now, instead of the block report being sent immediately when the Datanodes come up, it will be delayed by the specified number of seconds. This will reduce the block advertisement storm on Namenode.

Configuring Datanode heartbeat

The Datanodes periodically update the Namenode about its presence or any changes in the blocks. The default Datanode heartbeat time is three seconds. But this does not mean that if a Datanode does not send a heartbeat for, say, 10 seconds, that the node will be marked dead.

In this recipe, we will look at how a heartbeat is configured and the parameters that play a role in its function.

Getting ready

You have a running cluster, and the user is familiar with Datanode communication with Namenode.

How to do it...

1. ssh to Namenode and edit the `hdfs-site.xml` file to add the following property to it:

   ```
   <property>
   <name>dfs.heartbeat.interval</name>
   <value>3</value>
   </property>

   <property>
   <name>dfs.namenode.heartbeat.recheck-interval</name>
   <value>300000</value>
   </property>
   ```

2. Copy `hdfs-site.xml` across all nodes in the cluster.
3. Restart HDFS daemons across nodes for the property to take effect:

   ```
   $ stop-dfs.sh
   $ start-dfs.sh
   ```

How it works...

These parameters are default parameters, which control how often the Datanodes send updates and when a Datanode will expire or be marked dead. Remember that `dfs.heartbeat.interval` is in seconds and the `dfs.heartbeat.interval` parameter is in milliseconds.

So, when a Datanode is dead, for any reason, it will take 10 minutes and 30 seconds for Namenode to mark it as dead. This is not true whenever a graceful removal of a node is performed, as discussed in *Chapter 1, Hadoop Architecture and Deployment*. There are a lot of factors that govern when a Namenode marks a Datanode as dead and how quickly it does this. But, if the user simply shuts down a Datanode and executes `hdfs dfsadmin -report`, the node will still be seen there. The formula that defines when a Datanode is marked as stale is as follows:

```
Datanode Removal time = (2 x dfs.namenode.heartbeat.recheck-interval )
+ (10 X dfs.heartbeat.interval
```

3

Maintaining Hadoop Cluster – YARN and MapReduce

In this chapter, we will cover the following recipes:

- Running a simple MapReduce program
- Hadoop streaming
- Configuring YARN history server
- Job history web interface and metrics
- Configuring ResourceManager components
- YARN containers resource allocations
- ResourceManager Web UI and JMX metrics
- Preserving ResourceManager states

Introduction

In the previous chapters, we learned about the storage layer HDFS, how to configure it, and what are its different components. We mainly talked about Namenode, Datanode, and its concepts.

In this chapter, we will take a look at the processing layer which is MapReduce and the resource management framework YARN. Prior to Hadoop 2.x, MapReduce was the only processing layer for Hadoop, but the introduction of YARN as a framework, provided a pluggable processing layer, which could be MapReduce, Spark, and so on.

While the recipes in this chapter will give you an overview of a typical configuration, we encourage you to adapt this proposal according to your needs. The deployment directory structure varies according to IT policies within an organization.

Running a simple MapReduce program

In this recipe, we will look at how to make sense of the data stored on HDFS and extract useful information out of the files like the number of occurrences of a string, a pattern, or estimations, and various benchmarks. For this purpose, we can use MapReduce, which is a computation framework that helps us answer many questions we might have about the data.

With Hadoop, we can process huge amount of data. However, to get an understanding of its working, we'll start with a simple program such as *pi* estimation or a word count example.

ResourceManager is the master for **Yet another Resource Negotiator** (**YARN**). The Namenode stores the file metadata and the actual blocks/data reside on the slave nodes called Datanodes. All the jobs are submitted to the ResourceManager and it then assigns tasks to its slaves, called NodeManagers.

When a job is submitted to **ResourceManager** (**RM**), it will check for the job queue it is submitted to and whether the user has permissions to do so or not. Then it will ask **Application Master launcher** (**AM Launcher**) to launch an **Application Master** (**AM**) container on a node. Going forward, AM is the one responsible for running Map and Reduce containers with the help of inputs from RM.

AM takes care of failures and relaunches the containers if needed. Although there are many concepts, such as resource grant, AppManager, and retry logic, this being a recipe book we will keep the theory to the minimal. The following diagram shows the relationship between AM, RM, and NodeManager.

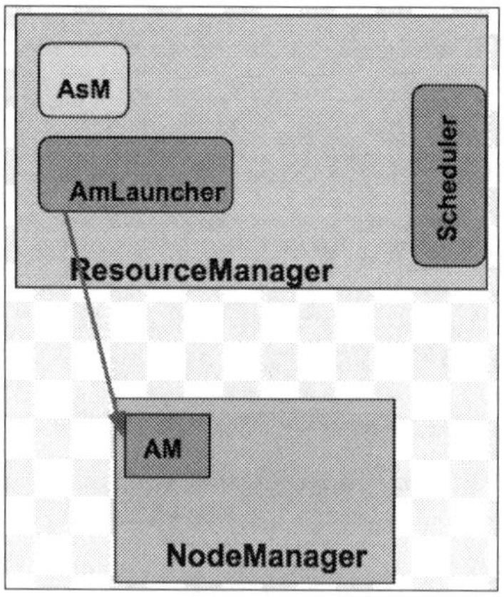

Getting ready

To step through the recipes in this chapter, make sure you have a running cluster with HDFS and YARN setup correctly as discussed in the previous chapters. This can be a single node cluster or a multinode cluster, as long as the cluster is configured correctly.

How to do it...

1. Connect to an edge node in the cluster as this is the preferred way, but you can connect to any node in the cluster. If you are connecting to a Datanode, please go through *Chapter 2, Maintain Hadoop Cluster HDFS* to understand the disadvantages of doing so.
2. Switch to user `hadoop`.
3. Navigate to the directory were Hadoop is installed. Hadoop is bundled with many examples to run and test the cluster and get the user started.
4. Under `/opt/cluster/hadoop/share/hadoop/mapreduce/`, there are lot of example JARs.
5. To see all programs a JAR can run, execute the JAR without any arguments:

    ```
    yarn jar /opt/cluster/hadoop/share/hadoop/mapreduce/hadoop-
    mapreduce-examples-2.7.2.jar
    ```

6. To run a pi estimation job, execute `mapreduce-examples-2.7.2.jar`, with arguments as shown in the following screenshot:

[hadoop@master1 ~]$ yarn jar /opt/cluster/hadoop/share/hadoop/mapreduce/hadoop-mapreduce-examples-2.7.2.jar pi 10
10
Number of Maps = 10
Samples per Map = 10
Wrote input for Map #0
Wrote input for Map #1
Wrote input for Map #2

Similarly, there are many other examples that can be run using the example JAR. To run a wordcount example, create a simple test file and copy it to HDFS and execute the program as follows:

```
yarn jar /opt/cluster/hadoop/share/hadoop/mapreduce/hadoop-
mapreduce-examples-2.7.2.jar wordcount /input_file /out_directory
```

1. The JAR `hadoop-mapreduce-examples-2.7.2.jar`, is a bundled JAR, which has various classes to call such as `wordcount`, `pi` and many more. Each class we call takes some input and writes some output. We can write our own classes/jars and use just a section of the above bundled JAR.

Hadoop streaming

In this recipe, we will look at how we can execute jobs on an Hadoop cluster using scripts written in Bash or Python. It is not mandatory to use only Java for programming MapReduce code; any language can be used by evoking the Hadoop streaming utility. Do not confuse this with real-time streaming, which is different from what we will be discussing here.

Getting ready

To step through the recipes in this chapter, make sure you have a running cluster with HDFS and YARN setup correctly as discussed in the previous chapters. This can be a single node cluster or a multinode cluster, as long as the cluster is configured correctly.

It is not necessary to know Java to run MapReduce programs on Hadoop. Users can carry forward their existing scripting knowledge and use Bash or Python to run the job on Hadoop.

How to do it...

1. Connect to an edge node in the cluster and switch to user `hadoop`.
2. The streaming JAR is also under the location as Hadoop `/opt/cluster/hadoop/share/hadoop/tools/lib/hadoop-streaming-2.7.2.jar`.
3. The map script of the wordcount example using Python is shown in the following screenshot:

```
[hadoop@master1 ~]$ cat mapper.py
#!/usr/bin/env python

import sys

# input comes from STDIN (standard input)
for line in sys.stdin:
    # remove leading and trailing whitespace
    line = line.strip()
    # split the line into words
    words = line.split()
    # increase counters
    for word in words:
        # write the results to STDOUT (standard output);
        # what we output here will be the input for the
        # Reduce step, i.e. the input for reducer.py
        #
        # tab-delimited; the trivial word count is 1
print '%s\t%s' % (word, 1)
```

4. The reduce script is as shown next:

```
#!/usr/bin/env python

from operator import itemgetter
import sys

current_word = None
current_count = 0
word = None

# input comes from STDIN
for line in sys.stdin:
    # remove leading and trailing whitespace
    line = line.strip()

    # parse the input we got from mapper.py
    word, count = line.split('\t', 1)

   # convert count (currently a string) to int
    try:
        count = int(count)
    except ValueError:
        # count was not a number, so silently
        # ignore/discard this line
        continue

    # this IF-switch only works because Hadoop sorts map output
    # by key (here: word) before it is passed to the reducer
    if current_word == word:
        current_count += count
    else:
        if current_word:
            # write result to STDOUT
            print '%s\t%s' % (current_word, current_count)
        current_count = count
        current_word = word

# do not forget to output the last word if needed!
if current_word == word:
print '%s\t%s' % (current_word, current_count)
```

5. The user can execute the script as shown in the following screenshot:

```
[hadoop@master1 ~]$ hadoop jar hadoop/tools/lib/hadoop-streaming-2.7.2.jar -file
 /home/hadoop/mapper.py -mapper /home/hadoop/mapper.py -file /home/hadoop/reduce
r.py  -reducer /home/hadoop/reducer.py -input /input -output /output
```

How it works...

In this recipe, `mapper.py` and `reducer.py` are simple Python scripts, which can be executed directly on the command line, without the need for Hadoop as shown next:

```
$ cat file | ./mapper.py | ./reducer.py
```

Here, `file` is a simple text file. Make sure you understand the indentation in Python to troubleshoot this script.

If the users are finding it difficult to write scripts or configurations, all these are available at GitHub: `https://github.com/netxillon/hadoop/tree/master/map_scripts`

Configuring YARN history server

Whenever a MapReduce job runs, it launches containers on multiple nodes and the logs for that container are only written on that particular node. If the user needs details of the job, he needs to go to all the nodes to fetch the logs, which could be very tedious in large clusters.

A better approach will be to aggregate the logs at a common location once the job finishes and then it can be accessed using a web server or other means. To address this, History Server was introduced in Hadoop, to aggregate logs and provide a Web UI, for users to see logs for all the containers of a job at one place.

Getting ready

You need to have a running cluster with YARN set up and should have completed the previous recipe to make sure the cluster is working fine in terms of HDFS and YARN.

The following steps will guide you through the process of setting up Job history server.

How to do it...

1. Connect to the ResourceManager node, which is the YARN master and switch to user `hadoop`.
2. Navigate to the directory `/opt/cluster/hadoop/etc/hadoop`.
3. Edit the `yarn-site.xml` file to add the following configurations, as shown in the upcoming steps and screenshots.

4. Firstly, enable `yarn.log` aggregation using the following parameter:

```
<property>
    <name>yarn.log-aggregation-enable</name>
    <value>true</value>
</property>
```

5. Add `jobhistory` server address. The following is the RPC configuration parameter:

```
<property>
    <name>mapreduce.jobhistory.address</name>
    <value>master1.cyrus.com:10020</value>
</property>
```

6. Add the `jobhistory` web server address:

```
<property>
    <name>mapreduce.jobhistory.webapp.address</name>
    <value>master1.cyrus.com:19888</value>
</property>
```

7. Configure a location to store logs on HDFS:

```
<property>
    <description>Where to aggregate logs to.</description>
    <name>yarn.nodemanager.remote-app-log-dir</name>
    <value>/tmp/logs</value>
</property>
```

8. Copy the `yarn-site.xml` file to all nodes in the cluster.
9. Start history server on the master using the following command:

```
$ mr-jobhistory-daemon.sh start historyserver
```

10. Restart YARN daemons for changes to take effect, as shown next:

```
$ stop-yarn.sh
$ start-yarn.sh
```

How it works...

Let's take a look at what we did throughout this recipe. In steps 1 through 7, we enabled YARN log aggregation, which is disabled by default. Then, we configured the RPC and web server ports and also the location where logs will be stored.

Whenever a container is cleaned, a log collection thread wakes up and does an upload of the logs to the configured location. The log location is similar to a web hosting directory, where the history server can publish its contents and is accessible through Web UI. There is a retention period, for how long the logs must be stored by the `yarn.log-aggregation.retain-seconds` parameter.

There's more...

In the upcoming releases, a new server for maintaining the history logs is used, which is called `Timeline server` and its job history server might be deprecated in the future.

Job history web interface and metrics

In the previous recipe, we enabled history server, and now we will use the Web UI to the explore YARN metrics and job history.

Getting ready

Make sure you have completed the previous recipe and have a History Server running as daemon, as shown here in the list of processes:

```
[hadoop@master1 hadoop]$ jps
5155 ApplicationHistoryServer
3462 SecondaryNameNode
5288 JobHistoryServer
6331 Jps
3228 NameNode
4781 ResourceManager
```

How to do it...

1. Using web browser, connect to the JobHistoryServer Web UI port, which in this case is port `19888` and host IP `master1.cyrus.com`.
2. Once connected to the Web UI, the user can see **JobHistory** and other details as shown here:

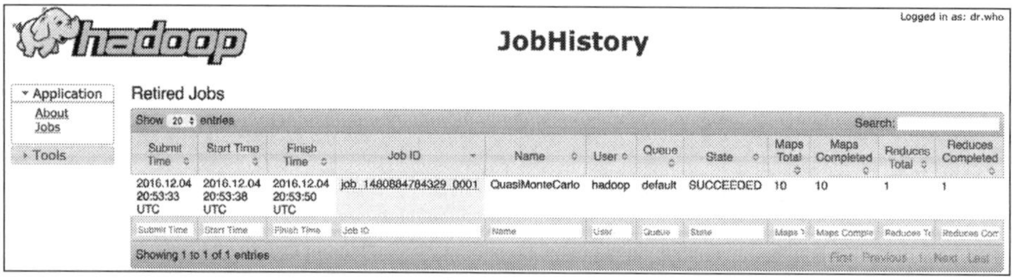

3. Under the **Tools** section on the left-most side, the user can see links to view YARN parameters currently in effect, using the link `configuration` as shown here:

```
▼<configuration>
  ▼<property>
     <name>dfs.journalnode.rpc-address</name>
     <value>0.0.0.0:8485</value>
     <source>hdfs-default.xml</source>
   </property>
  ▼<property>
     <name>yarn.ipc.rpc.class</name>
     <value>org.apache.hadoop.yarn.ipc.HadoopYarnProtoRPC</value>
     <source>yarn-default.xml</source>
   </property>
  ▼<property>
     <name>mapreduce.job.maxtaskfailures.per.tracker</name>
     <value>3</value>
     <source>mapred-default.xml</source>
   </property>
```

4. Another section is metrics, which gives information about JvmMetrics, stats, and so on. The output format is JSON:

```
{
  "beans": [
    {
      "name": "Hadoop:service=JobHistoryServer,name=UgiMetrics",
      "modelerType": "UgiMetrics",
      "tag.Context": "ugi",
      "tag.Hostname": "master1.cyrus.com",
      "LoginSuccessNumOps": 0,
      "LoginSuccessAvgTime": 0.0,
      "LoginFailureNumOps": 0,
      "LoginFailureAvgTime": 0.0,
      "GetGroupsNumOps": 0,
      "GetGroupsAvgTime": 0.0
    },
```

5. The preceding output can also be viewed from the command line, as shown in the following screenshot:

```
[hadoop@master1 hadoop]$ curl http://master1.cyrus.com:19888/jmx?qry=
Hadoop:service=JobHistoryServer,name=JvmMetrics
{
  "beans" : [ {
    "name" : "Hadoop:service=JobHistoryServer,name=JvmMetrics",
    "modelerType" : "JvmMetrics",
    "tag.Context" : "jvm",
    "tag.ProcessName" : "JobHistoryServer",
    "tag.SessionId" : null,
    "tag.Hostname" : "master1.cyrus.com",
    "MemNonHeapUsedM" : 50.889282,
    "MemNonHeapCommittedM" : 52.4375,
    "MemNonHeapMaxM" : -9.536743E-7,
    "MemHeapUsedM" : 97.7354,
    "MemHeapCommittedM" : 315.5,
    "MemHeapMaxM" : 889.0,
    "MemMaxM" : 889.0,
    "GcCount" : 8,
    "GcTimeMillis" : 136,
```

How it works...

In Hadoop, each daemon has a built-in web server, which is a jetty server. Each server exposes metrics, which can be captured or explored using the JMX API calls. The JMX interface is very important for writing plugins for health checks or for triggering some events on a condition, as it can be queried simply using a CURL call.

Configuring ResourceManager components

In YARN, ResourceManager is modular in nature, primarily limited to scheduling and not bothered about application state management, which is delegated to Application Masters. Although there are many components of RM, the core ones are: **ApplicationsManager** (**AsM**), Application Master Launcher, scheduler, and ResourceManager. AsM keeps track of which AM got assigned for which job and requests the launch of AM using AM Launcher. These are all part of the ResourceManager and are depicted in the following diagram. These components can be segregated for better control and management of resources:

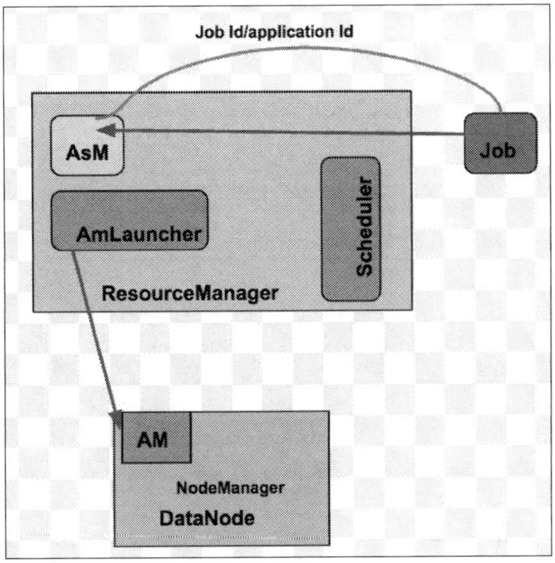

In this recipe, we will see how different components can be separated out, although not necessary, and controlled independently.

Getting ready

Before starting with this recipe, it is good to read about the components of ResourceManager and what each component does. There are lot of good resources available online for this. Also, make sure that there is a running cluster and the recipes so far have been completed or at least understood:

> This is not a comprehensive list of components and configurations that can be done. Users are highly recommended to read Apache documentation on this, for more details.

How to do it...

1. Connect to the `master1.cyrus.com` master node and switch to user `hadoop`.
2. Navigate to the directory `/opt/cluster/hadoop/etc/hadoop`.

3. Edit the configuration file `yarn-site.xml`, to explicitly specify the scheduler, `resource-tracker` and `resourcemanager`, as shown in the following screenshot:

```
<property>
<name>yarn.resourcemanager.resource-tracker.address</name>
<value>master1.cyrus.com:9001</value>
</property>

<property>
<name>yarn.resourcemanager.scheduler.address</name>
<value>master1.cyrus.com:9002</value>
</property>

<property>
<name>yarn.resourcemanager.address</name>
<value>master1.cyrus.com:9003</value>
</property>
```

4. The expiry for the liveliness of AM is defined by the following parameter:

   `yarn.am.liveness-monitor.expiry-interval-ms`

5. The number of attempts to launch AM for a single application is different from the number of retries for container launch:

   `yarn.resourcemanager.am.max-attempts`

6. There can be multiple schedulers, which can be used, such as capacity or fair scheduler. The scheduler to run for YARN is defined using the following parameter:

   `yarn.resourcemanager.scheduler.class`

7. Once the changes are done, save the file and copy it across to all the nodes in the cluster.
8. Restart the YARN daemons for the changes to take effect, as shown next:

```
$ stop-yarn.sh
$ start-yarn.sh
```

How it works...

Steps 1 through 6, explain how to make changes to the configuration file, which allows the separation of the ResourceManager components and also tunes the basic application liveliness and the schedulers to use.

> It is best practice to change one parameter at a time and see what difference it makes to the cluster or the ports listening, and so on.

If the user does not specify any parameter, the default values are used for it. Each of the configuration files have a default file. For example, `yarn-defaults.xml` has all the possible parameters defined and the user only overrides them by specifying them in the `yarn-site.xml` file.

There's more...

This is a very general introduction to the Yarn components. We will be covering the details in the performance tuning section.

See also

- The *YARN containers resource allocations* recipe

YARN containers and resource allocations

In YARN, there are many configuration parameters, which control the memory available to AM, containers, or the total memory that can be allocated for MapReduce or JVM heap size to be used and the number of CPU cores to be used for a job. This is covered in more detail in *Chapter 8, Performance Tuning*, but a rough idea is to have one core for each container and each Mapper container should have a memory of about 1 GB and the Reducer should have a memory twice the size of the Mapper. In addition to this, each node must have about 20% spare for the operating system and Hadoop daemons.

Getting ready

For this recipe, you will again need a running cluster and should have completed the previous recipes to make sure the cluster is working fine in terms of HDFS and YARN.

How to do it...

1. Connect to the `master1.cyrus.com` master node and switch to user `hadoop`.
2. Navigate to the directory `/opt/cluster/hadoop/etc/hadoop`.
3. Edit the configuration file `yarn-site.xml`, to make the necessary changes as shown in the following steps.

4. The maximum memory that can be used by Yarn in total on a node to launch containers is specified by the `yarn.nodemanager.resource.memory.mb` parameter. This can be configured as shown in the following screenshot:

```
<property>
<name>yarn.nodemanager.resource.memory.mb</name>
<value>11264</value>
</property>
```

5. The memory to be used by the AM container is defined by the parameter as shown in the following screenshot:

```
<property>
<name>yarn.app.mapreduce.am.resource.mb</name>
<value>1536</value>
</property>
```

6. The smallest memory that can be asked for by a container. All allocations are multiple of this value and it is defined as shown in the following screenshot:

```
<property>
<name>yarn.scheduler.minimum-allocation-mb</name>
<value>64</value>
</property>
```

7. The largest container that can be created on any node defined by `yarn.scheduler.maximum-allocation-mb`, which cannot be greater than the total memory available on that node for yarn `yarn.nodemanager.resource.memory.mb`.

```
<property>
<name>yarn.scheduler.maximum-allocation-mb</name>
<value>11264</value>
</property>
```

8. The number of CPU cores that can be used for scheduling is defined by the parameters as shown in the following screenshot:

```
<property>
<name>yarn.scheduler.minimum-allocation-vcores</name>
<value>1</value>
</property>

<property>
<name>yarn.scheduler.maximum-allocation-vcores</name>
<value>32</value>
</property>
```

9. The virtual memory and physical memory ratio can be controlled by enabling the parameters as follows:

```
<property>
<name>yarn.nodemanager.vmem-pmem-ratio</name>
<value>3.0</value>
</property>

<property>
<name>yarn.nodemanager.pmem-check-enabled</name>
<value>true</value>
</property>

<property>
<name>yarn.nodemanager.vmem-check-enabled</name>
<value>true</value>
</property>
```

How it works...

Steps 1 through 9 show how to configure resources for running YARN and make sure things work reasonably well.

There are lots of details, which will be covered in performance tuning, but with this bare minimum, users can get a fair understanding of resource allocation and what things to take care of. After making changes, make sure to restart the YARN daemons for changes to take effect.

There's more...

In addition to the YARN parameters, there are other MapReduce parameters, which are used for controlling resources for mappers and reducers, and which are configured in the `mapred-site.xml` file:

```
<property>
<name>mapreduce.map.memory.mb</name>
<value>1536</value>
</property>

<property>
<name>mapreduce.reduce.memory.mb</name>
<value>2048</value>
</property>

<property>
<name>mapreduce.map.java.opts</name>
```

```
<value>-Xmx1152m</value>
</property>

<property>
<name>mapreduce.reduce.java.opts</name>
<value>-Xmx1280m</value>
</property>

<property>
<name>mapreduce.job.counters.max</name>
<value>200</value>
</property>
```

The preceding parameters define the memory and heap space for Map and Reduce respectively. The heap size must obviously be less than the memory allocated to Map and Reduce.

See also

- *Chapter 8, Performance Tuning*

ResourceManager Web UI and JMX metrics

In the previous recipe, we presented how to configure parameters for YARN and MapReduce. As stated initially, each daemon runs a Jetty web server, which can be accessed using a web browser.

Users must take note of the fact that their RPC ports are different from HTTP ports and must not be confused with the options we used in the previous recipe. There are default web ports such as Namenode `50070`, ResourceManager `8088`, Datanode `50075`. All these can be configured to custom ports, if needed.

Getting ready

Make sure that the user has a running cluster with YARN and HDFS configured. The user must be able to run MapReduce jobs on it.

How to do it...

1. Point your web browser to `http://master1.cyrus.com/8088`, to access the ResourceManager Web UI:

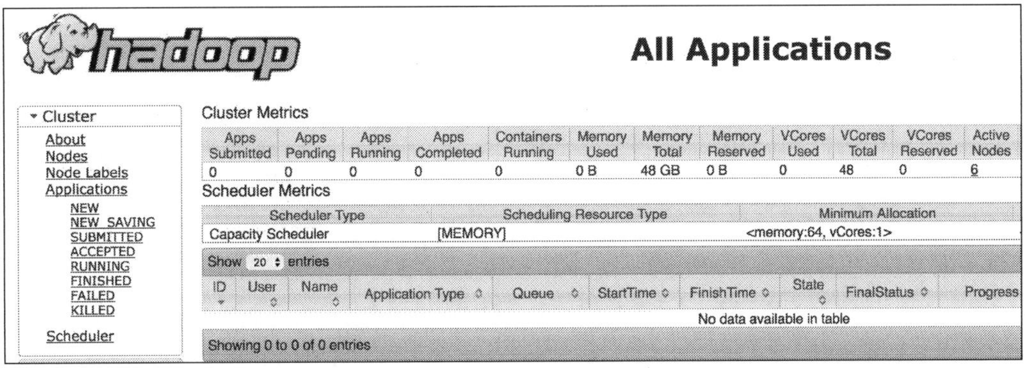

2. The Web UI gives information on running the application and the resources it uses, as shown in the following screenshot:

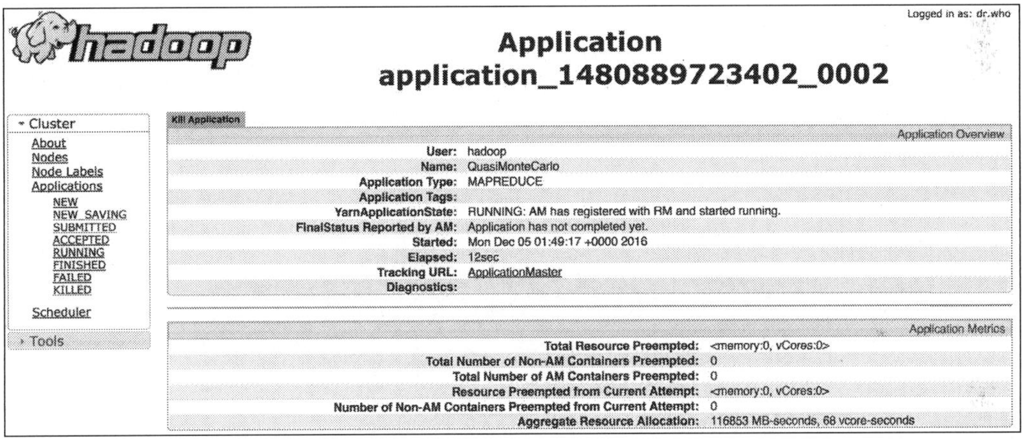

3. The web interface also shows the scheduler used, which is by default capacity scheduler:

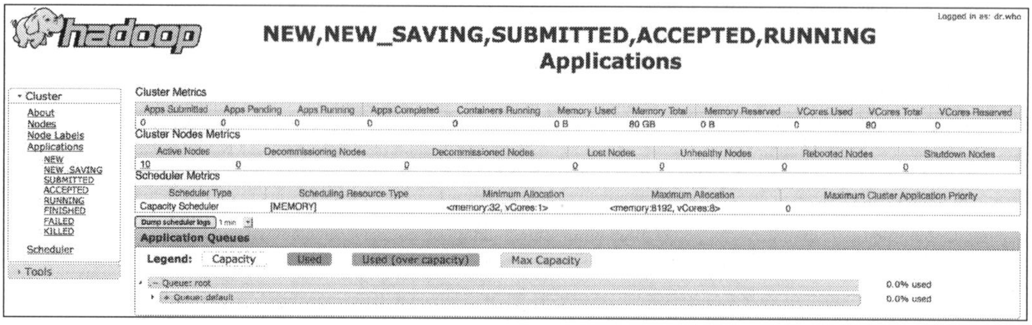

4. The ResourceManager metrics, in terms of what applications are running and what the cluster state is, can be fetched using the URL `http://master1.cyrus.com:8088/jmx?qry=Hadoop:*`.

5. The same can be accessed using the curl API and can be used to write monitoring plugins or to send alerts, as shown in the following screenshot:

```
[hadoop@master1 ~]$ curl http://master1.cyrus.com:8088/ws/v1/cluster
{"clusterInfo":{"id":1480889723402,"startedOn":1480889723402,"state":"STARTED","haState":"ACTIVE","rmStateSt
oreName":"org.apache.hadoop.yarn.server.resourcemanager.recovery.NullRMStateStore","resourceManagerVersion":
"2.7.2","resourceManagerBuildVersion":"2.7.2 from Unknown by root source checksum c63f7cc71b8f63249e35126f0f
7492d","resourceManagerVersionBuiltOn":"2016-05-16T04:01Z","hadoopVersion":"2.7.2","hadoopBuildVersion":"2.7
.2 from Unknown by root source checksum d0fda26633fa762bff87ec759ebe689c","hadoopVersionBuiltOn":"2016-05-16
T03:56Z","haZooKeeperConnectionState":"ResourceManager HA is not enabled."}}[hadoop@master1 ~]$
```

6. The metrics can be collected using REST API calls to `curl http://master1.cyrus.com:8088/ws/v1/cluster/metrics`, as shown in the following screenshot:

```
[hadoop@master1 ~]$ curl http://master1.c
{"clusterMetrics":{"appsSubmitted":2,"app
illed":0,"reservedMB":0,"availableMB":491
:48,"allocatedVirtualCores":0,"containers
```

7. Now, we will track how many applications are currently running and what is the total utilization in the cluster:

```
[hadoop@master1 ~]$ curl http://master1.cyrus.com:8088/ws/v1/cluster/scheduler
{"scheduler":{"schedulerInfo":{"type":"capacityScheduler","capacity":100.0,"used
100.0,"queueName":"root","queues":{"queue":[{"type":"capacitySchedulerLeafQueueI
apacity":0.0,"maxCapacity":100.0,"absoluteCapacity":100.0,"absoluteMaxCapacity":
:0.0,"numApplications":0,"queueName":"default","state":"RUNNING","resourcesUsed"
dReservationQueues":false,"nodeLabels":["*"],"numActiveApplications":0,"numPend
ilers":0,"maxApplications":10000,"maxApplicationsPerUser":10000,"userLimit":100,
r":1.0,"AMResourceLimit":{"memory":4928,"vCores":1},"usedAMResource":{"memory":0
```

8. To see what applications ran in the cluster and what their stats are, we can query the resources REST API, as shown in the following screenshot:

```
[hadoop@master1 ~]$ curl http://master1.cyrus.com:8088/ws/v1/cluster/apps
{"apps":{"app":[{"id":"application_1480889723402_0002","user":"hadoop","name":"QuasiMonteCarlo","queue":"def
ault","state":"FINISHED","finalStatus":"SUCCEEDED","progress":100.0,"trackingUI":"History","trackingUrl":"ht
tp://master1.cyrus.com:8088/proxy/application_1480889723402_0002/","diagnostics":"","clusterId":148088972340
2,"applicationType":"MAPREDUCE","applicationTags":"","startedTime":1480902557125,"finishedTime":148090257078
6,"elapsedTime":13661,"amContainerLogs":"http://dn6.cyrus.com:8042/node/containerlogs/container_148088972340
2_0002_01_000001/hadoop","amHostHttpAddress":"dn6.cyrus.com:8042","allocatedMB":-1,"allocatedVCores":-1,"run
ningContainers":-1,"memorySeconds":130085,"vcoreSeconds":78,"preemptedResourceMB":0,"preemptedResourceVCores
":0,"numNonAMContainerPreempted":0,"numAMContainerPreempted":0},{"id":"application_1480889723402_0001","user
":"hadoop","name":"QuasiMonteCarlo","queue":"default","state":"FINISHED","finalStatus":"SUCCEEDED","progress
":100.0,"trackingUI":"History","trackingUrl":"http://master1.cyrus.com:8088/proxy/application_1480889723402_
0001/","diagnostics":"","clusterId":1480889723402,"applicationType":"MAPREDUCE","applicationTags":"","starte
dTime":1480902526464,"finishedTime":1480902542342,"elapsedTime":15878,"amContainerLogs":"http://dn4.cyrus.co
m:8042/node/containerlogs/container_1480889723402_0001_01_000001/hadoop","amHostHttpAddress":"dn4.cyrus.com:
8042","allocatedMB":-1,"allocatedVCores":-1,"runningContainers":-1,"memorySeconds":150294,"vcoreSeconds":90,
"preemptedResourceMB":0,"preemptedResourceVCores":0,"numNonAMContainerPreempted":0,"numAMContainerPreempted"
```

How it works...

All the metrics are presented as JMX and can easily be retrieved using REST API calls, which can be parsed for useful information, such as monitoring and alerting, and can be fed to other metric collections used for useful analytics and performance analytics.

Preserving ResourceManager states

It is important to preserve the state of ResourceManager during the restart of RM, so as to keep the application running with minimal interruptions. The concept is that the RM preserves the application state in a store and reloads it on restart. **ApplicationMasters** (**AM**) and NodeManagers continuously poll RM for status and re-register with it when available, thus resuming the containers from saved state.

Getting ready

For this recipe, you will again need a running cluster and have completed the previous recipes to make sure the cluster is working fine in terms of HDFS and YARN.

How to do it...

1. Connect to the `master1.cyrus.com` master node and switch to user `hadoop`.
2. Navigate to the directory `/opt/cluster/hadoop/etc/hadoop`.
3. Edit the `yarn-site.xml` configuration file to make the necessary changes as shown in the following steps.

4. Enable RM recovery by making changes as shown in the following screenshot:

```
<property>
    <name>yarn.resourcemanager.recovery.enabled</name>
    <value>true</value>
</property>
```

5. Specify the `state-store` to be used for this, as shown in the following screenshot:

```
<property>
    <name>yarn.resourcemanager.store.class</name>
    <value>org.apache.hadoop.yarn.server.resourcemanager.recovery.FileSystemRMStateStore</value>
</property>
```

6. The store location is on HDFS, and by default is pointed to `<hadoop.tmp.dir>/yarn/system/rmstore`. This is shown in the following screenshot:

```
<property>
    <name>yarn.resourcemanager.fs.state-store.uri</name>
    <value>hdfs://localhost:9000/rmstore</value>
</property>
```

How it works...

The state-store stores the state of the queue, the RM state and AM communicate the states and registers when the RM is restarted. This enables the job to be restarted without failures.

Make sure you restart the daemons after making the necessary changes to the configuration files.

There's more...

There is lot more to RM states such as submitted, accepted, running, and killed, and it is important to understand the state diagram of YARN workflow to see what happens from end-to-end.

4
High Availability

In this chapter, we will cover the following recipes:

- Namenode HA using shared storage
- ZooKeeper configuration
- Namenode HA using Journal node
- Resourcemanager HA using ZooKeeper
- Rolling upgrade in HA
- Configuring shared cache manager
- Configuring HDFS cache
- HDFS snapshots
- Configuring storage-based policies
- Configuring HA for Edge nodes

Introduction

In this chapter, we will configure high availability for Namenode and Resourcemanager, as both of them are single points of failure. We will also walk through the various options of configuring high availability, cache configuration, storage policies, and snapshots for backup.

> In this chapter, HA is from the Hadoop perspective only and there is no HA at Linux level. The Hadoop cluster is not the same as the Linux cluster. If users are finding it difficult to write scripts or configurations, all these are available at my GitHub: `https://github.com/netxillon/hadoop`.

Namenode HA using shared storage

In Hadoop, we do not recommend NAS or SAN as storage for Datanodes, as it defeats the purpose of localized data. However, for critical components such as Namenode, there will be a storage mount point to store Namenode metadata. This is specified as a comma-separated list under the `dfs.namenode.name.dir` parameter.

For Namenode **High Availability** (**HA**), we need a shared location to store metadata, which can be accessed from both Namenodes. Only primary or active Namenodes can write to the shared location, but both Namenodes can read from it.

The active Namenode is the writer and the standby node is the reader node only. Namenode can failover from one node to another, but only one node can be Active at any given time. Another important thing to keep in mind is that the Datanodes talk to both the Namenodes so that after failure between Namenodes, there is no time taken to update the block report.

The shared storage can be any NFS server or a simple filer that can export the filesystem as NFS.

> Filer is a specialized hardware that provides optimized NFS share.

Getting ready

Before going through the recipes in this chapter, make sure you have two nodes that can be used as primary and secondary Namenodes. The installation is on Linux, and it may be useful to go through previous recipes to understand the set up. Make sure Hadoop is untarred and Java is installed on all the participating nodes in the cluster.

Configure the NFS server; it can be any node in the cluster. In production, this will be a separate server or a reliable filler. On that node, make sure that `nfs` and `rpcbind` services are up and running, as shown in the following screenshot:

[ec2-user@master1 ~]$ sudo /etc/init.d/nfs start
Initializing kernel nfsd: [OK]
Starting NFS services: [OK]
Starting NFS quotas: [OK]
Starting NFS mountd: [OK]
Starting NFS daemon: [OK]
Starting RPC idmapd: [OK]
[ec2-user@master1 ~]$ sudo /etc/init.d/rpc
rpcbind rpcgssd rpcidmapd rpcsvcgssd
[ec2-user@master1 ~]$ sudo /etc/init.d/rpcbind status
rpcbind (pid 2402) is running...

It is assumed that the user has basic Linux knowledge and knows how the NFS server works. Export a directory from the NFS server, as shown in the following screenshot, and make sure it is visible. Make sure the directory is owned by the user `hadoop`:

```
[ec2-user@master1 ~]$ sudo /etc/init.d/nfs start
Initializing kernel nfsd:                                  [  OK  ]
Starting NFS services:                                     [  OK  ]
Starting NFS quotas:                                       [  OK  ]
Starting NFS mountd:                                       [  OK  ]
Starting NFS daemon:                                       [  OK  ]
Starting RPC idmapd:                                       [  OK  ]
[ec2-user@master1 ~]$ sudo /etc/init.d/rpc
rpcbind    rpcgssd    rpcidmapd    rpcsvcgssd
[ec2-user@master1 ~]$ sudo /etc/init.d/rpcbind status
rpcbind (pid  2402) is running...
```

How to do it...

1. Connect to a master node in the cluster. The user can start with any master node, either `master1` or `master2`. Both of these will be used as Namenodes.
2. As the user `root`, create a directory named `/shared`.
3. Mount the `nfs` share on the first Namenode, as shown in the following screenshot:

```
[ec2-user@master1 ~]$ sudo mkdir -p /shared
[ec2-user@master1 ~]$ sudo mount -t nfs master1.cyrus.com:/nfs /shared
```

4. Correct the permissions on the `/shared` directory and make sure it is owned by the user `hadoop`. Refer to the following screenshot for details:

```
[ec2-user@master1 ~]$ ls -ld /shared/
drwxr-xr-x 2 hadoop hadoop 4096 Dec  5 09:31 /shared/
```

5. Switch to the user `hadoop`.
6. Navigate to the directory where Hadoop is installed:

   `/opt/cluster/hadoop/etc/hadoop.`
7. Edit `core-site.xml` to add the name service string, instead of any specific Namenode address, as shown in the following screenshot:

```
<property>
  <name>fs.defaultFS</name>
  <value>hdfs://mycluster</value>
</property>
```

8. Edit `hdfs-site.xml` to add `nameservice`, metadata location, and cluster members, as follows:

```
<property>
    <name>dfs.nameservices</name>
    <value>mycluster</value>
</property>

<property>
    <name>dfs.namenode.name.dir</name>
    <value>file:/data/namenode</value>
</property>

<property>
    <name>dfs.ha.namenodes.mycluster</name>
    <value>master1,master2</value>
</property>
```

9. The important thing to note here is that `master1` and `master2` are not the names of the Namenodes. They can be anything; they are just aliases for longer names. Users can call them anything they want regardless of hostname.
10. Add the `rpc` and web server settings to the `hdfs-site.xml` file as shown here:

```
<property>
    <name>dfs.namenode.rpc-address.mycluster.master1</name>
    <value>master1.cyrus.com:9000</value>
</property>


<property>
    <name>dfs.namenode.rpc-address.mycluster.master2</name>
    <value>master2.cyrus.com:9000</value>
</property>

<property>
    <name>dfs.namenode.http-address.mycluster.master1</name>
    <value>master1.cyrus.com:50070</value>
</property>

<property>
    <name>dfs.namenode.http-address.mycluster.master2</name>
    <value>master2.cyrus.com:50070</value>
</property>
```

11. Next we will configure the failover proxy provider using the configuration in the following code:

```
<property>
    <name>dfs.client.failover.proxy.provider.mycluster</name>
    <value>org.apache.hadoop.hdfs.server.namenode.ha.ConfiguredFai
loverProxyProvider</value>
</property>
```

12. Configure the shared store location to store the edit files:

```
<property>
    <name>dfs.namenode.shared.edits.dir</name>
    <value>file:///shared</value>
</property>
```

Similarly, all these changes need to be made to the other master Namenode, which in this case is `master2.cyrus.com`. The best way is to copy the files across to the other node, rather than performing manual changes.

The next step is to configure the Datanodes so that they are aware that there are two Namenodes in the cluster:

13. Copy `core-site.xml` from Namenode and copy it to all Datanodes in the cluster.
14. On any Datanode, edit `hdfs-site.xml` and include the `nameservice`, `rpc` configuration, and proxy failover settings as shown in the following code:

```
<property>
    <name>dfs.nameservices</name>
    <value>mycluster</value>
</property>

<property>
    <name>dfs.ha.namenodes.mycluster</name>
    <value>master1,master22</value>
</property>

<property>
    <name>dfs.namenode.rpc-address.mycluster.master1</name>
    <value>master1.cyrus.com:9000</value>
</property>

<property>
    <name>dfs.namenode.rpc-address.mycluster.master2</name>
    <value>master2.cyrus.com:9000</value>
</property>

<property>
    <name>dfs.client.failover.proxy.provider.mycluster</name>
```

```
    <value>org.apache.hadoop.hdfs.server.namenode.ha.ConfiguredFai
loverProxyProvider</value>
</property>
```

15. Once the changes are made, save the configuration files and copy them across Datanodes. Make sure the Datanodes were not part of the old cluster, as you might need to clean Datanodes if you re-format the Namenodes.
16. Starting with any Namenode of your choice, format it to initialize the HDFS filesystem. Make sure that you format only one of the two Namenodes.

    ```
    $ hdfs namenode -format
    ```

17. Once the formatting is done, make sure both the directories `/shared` and `/data/namenode` are formatted.
18. Log in to the other Namenode `master1.cyrus.com` and either copy the metadata from `master1.cyrus.com` to its local `dfs.namenode.name.dir` directory or execute the `hdfs namenode -bootstrapStandby` command from the other Namenode.
19. Once the other Namenode has pulled the metadata, start the Namenode daemon on both the Namenodes.
20. When the Namenodes are started, both will be in standby mode. The user has to explicitly switch the Namenode to Active mode, as shown in the following screenshot:

    ```
    $ hdfs haadmin -getServiceState master1
      master1 is Standby
    $ hdfs haadmin -transitionToActive master1
    ```

21. Start the Datanode daemons on all the nodes and test by writing some data to HDFS.

How it works...

In this recipe, the two Namenodes are configured, with both starting in standby mode and then transitioning to Active mode by explicitly executing a command.

As the **Namespace identifier** (**namespaceID**) is a random number created during the formatting of Namenode, it must be the same for both Namenodes. Only one Namenode is formatted, and the other is just bootstrapped from it. The Datanodes, with the help of the failover proxy provider, know which is the active master.

This approach is a manual failover and the Namenodes need to be switched either using a script to detect failure or by using the Hadoop administrator.

See also

- The *Namenode HA using Journal node* recipe

ZooKeeper configuration

In a distributed system, it is important to keep things coordinated and in sync with each other. In a cluster, if we have more than one master, so there should be a mechanism to control who should be the leader or decision maker and can make changes or writes to metadata, and who are just readers or have read-only access.

To do this, we need a co-ordination service that can do all of this, for which we will use the ZooKeeper service.

Getting ready

Before going through the recipe in this section, we need at least one node to install ZooKeeper. This could be a dedicated node or it can be co-located with other nodes in the cluster. In production, ZooKeeper is configured to run on minimum three nodes, which makes it highly available and there must always be odd number of nodes in the ZooKeeper quorum.

Mostly, ZooKeeper nodes are co-located with master nodes in the cluster. Never run them on slave nodes as they will be replaced often due to Datanode failures. In this recipe, we will use two Namenodes and one Resourcemanager node to configure the ZooKeeper quorum. If the reader does not have these many nodes, three instances of ZooKeeper can be run on a single node, by just changing the ports.

How to do it...

1. Download the latest stable release of the ZooKeeper package from `http://zookeeper.apache.org/releases.html`.
2. Connect to the `master1.cyrus.com` master node and the cluster and switch to the user `hadoop`.
3. Untar the tarball `tar -xzvf zookeeper-3.4.9.tar.gz -C /opt/cluster`.
4. Change to the directory `/opt/cluster/` and create a sym-link as follows:

   ```
   $ ln -s zookeeper-3.4.9 zoo
   ```

5. Next, set up an environment variable in `.bash_profile` as follows:

   ```
   export ZOOKEEPER_HOME=/opt/cluster/zoo
   ```

6. Make sure the environment variable is exported and available:

   ```
   $ echo $ZOOKEEPER_HOME
   /opt/cluster/zoo
   ```

7. Change to the directory `/opt/cluster/zoo/conf`.

8. Edit the `zoo.cfg` file and add the lines, as shown in the following code:

   ```
   dataDir=/data/zookeeper
   ```

9. Make sure to create the preceding directory with the correct permissions for the user `hadoop` to write to it.
10. Create a file named `myid` on each node under the `dataDir` directory, with the corresponding IDs, as shown in the following screenshot:

```
[hadoop@master1 zoo]$ id
uid=501(hadoop) gid=501(hadoop) groups=501(hadoop)
[hadoop@master1 zoo]$ pwd
/opt/cluster/zoo
[hadoop@master1 zoo]$ bin/zkServer.sh start
ZooKeeper JMX enabled by default
Using config: /opt/cluster/zoo/bin/../conf/zoo.cfg
Starting zookeeper ... STARTED
```

11. Add the list of servers to the file:

    ```
    server.1=master1.cyrus.com:2888:3888
    server.2=master2.cyrus.com:2888:3888
    server.3=rm1.cyrus.com:2888:3888
    ```

12. Copy the `ZooKeeper` directory to the other two nodes in the cluster and start the service on each node as shown in the following screenshot:

```
[hadoop@master1 zoo]$ ls -l /data/zookeeper/
total 12
-rw-rw-r-- 1 hadoop hadoop    2 Aug 23 02:12 myid
drwxrwxr-x 2 hadoop hadoop 4096 Aug 29 07:53 version-2
-rw-rw-r-- 1 hadoop hadoop    4 Jan  3 22:48 zookeeper_server.pid
[hadoop@master1 zoo]$ ls -l /data/zookeeper/myid
-rw-rw-r-- 1 hadoop hadoop 2 Aug 23 02:12 /data/zookeeper/myid
[hadoop@master1 zoo]$ cat /data/zookeeper/myid
1
```

13. Verify that the ZooKeeper service is up and running, as shown in the following screenshot:

```
[hadoop@master1 zoo]$ bin/zkServer.sh status
ZooKeeper JMX enabled by default
Using config: /opt/cluster/zoo/bin/../conf/zoo.cfg
Mode: follower
```

How it works...

In this recipe, we configured ZooKeeper services to run on three nodes in the cluster and to set up a quorum between them. This will be used to maintain the state of the Namenodes in the cluster and detect failures. ZooKeeper is a coordination service, with one leader and other nodes as followers. There is an election process to elect the master and then a quorum is formed.

Namenode HA using Journal node

In this recipe, we look to configure Namenode high availability using Journal nodes, ZooKeeper, and **ZooKeeper failover controller** (**ZKFC**). This is an automatic failover, rather than the manual one discussed previously.

Getting ready

Before going through the recipes in this chapter, make sure you have two nodes that can be used as Namenodes. The following steps will guide you through the process of setting up Namenode HA using the Journal node.

The role of the Journal node is to keep the Namenodes in sync and prevent split brain. Journal nodes are distributed systems for storing edits.

How to do it...

1. Connect to the master node in the cluster. The user can start with any master node, either `master1` or `master2`. Both of these will be used Namenodes.
2. Switch to the user `hadoop`.
3. Navigate to the directory where Hadoop is installed:

   `/opt/cluster/hadoop/etc/hadoop`

4. Edit `core-site.xml` to add the name service string instead of any specific Namenode address, as shown in the following screenshot:

```
<property>
  <name>fs.defaultFS</name>
  <value>hdfs://mycluster</value>
</property>
```

5. In `core-site.xml`, add the following ZooKeeper settings:

```
<property>
     <name>ha.zookeeper.quorum</name>
     <value>master1.cyrus.com:2181, master2.cyrus.com:2181, rm1.
cyrus.com:2181</value>
</property>
```

6. Edit `hdfs-site.xml` to add `nameservice`, metadata location, and cluster members, as shown in the following code:

```
<property>
     <name>dfs.nameservices</name>
     <value>mycluster</value>
```

```
</property>

<property>
    <name>dfs.namenode.name.dir</name>
    <value>file:/data/namenode</value>
</property>

<property>
    <name>dfs.ha.namenodes.mycluster</name>
    <value>master1,master2</value>
</property>
```

7. The important thing to note here is that `master1` and `master2` are not the names of the Namenodes. They can be anything; here, they are just aliases for longer names. Users can call them anything they want regardless of hostname.
8. Add the `rpc` and web server settings to the `hdfs-site.xml` file as shown in the following code:

```
<property>
    <name>dfs.namenode.rpc-address.mycluster.master1</name>
    <value>master1.cyrus.com:9000</value>
</property>


<property>
    <name>dfs.namenode.rpc-address.mycluster.master2</name>
    <value>master2.cyrus.com:9000</value>
</property>

<property>
    <name>dfs.namenode.http-address.mycluster.master1</name>
    <value>master1.cyrus.com:50070</value>
</property>

<property>
    <name>dfs.namenode.http-address.mycluster.master2</name>
    <value>master2.cyrus.com:50070</value>
</property>
```

9. Next we will configure the failover proxy provider using the following configuration:

```
<property>
    <name>dfs.client.failover.proxy.provider.mycluster</name>
    <value>org.apache.hadoop.hdfs.server.namenode.ha.ConfiguredFai
loverProxyProvider</value>
</property>
```

10. Configure the Journal node settings and enable automatic failover:

```
<property>
    <name>dfs.ha.automatic-failover.enabled</name>
    <value>true</value>
</property>

<property>
    <name>dfs.journalnode.edits.dir</name>
    <value>/data/mycluster</value>
</property>

<property>
<name>dfs.namenode.shared.edits.dir</name>
<value>qjournal://master1.cyrus.com:8485;master2.cyrus.
com:8485;rm1.cluster1.com:8485/mycluster</value>
</property>
```

Similarly, all these changes need to be made to the other master Namenode, which in this case is `master2.cyrus.com`. The best way is to copy the files across to the other node, rather than performing manual changes.

The next step is to configure the Datanodes so that they are aware there are two Namenodes in the cluster.

11. Copy the `core-site.xml` from Namenode and copy to all Datanodes in the cluster.
12. On any Datanode, edit the `hdfs-site.xml` file and include the `nameservice`, `rpc` configuration, and proxy failover settings, as shown here:

```
<property>
    <name>dfs.nameservices</name>
    <value>mycluster</value>
</property>

<property>
    <name>dfs.ha.namenodes.mycluster</name>
    <value>master1,master22</value>
</property>

<property>
    <name>dfs.namenode.rpc-address.mycluster.master1</name>
    <value>master1.cyrus.com:9000</value>
</property>

<property>
    <name>dfs.namenode.rpc-address.mycluster.master2</name>
    <value>master2.cyrus.com:9000</value>
```

```
</property>

<property>
    <name>dfs.client.failover.proxy.provider.mycluster</name>
    <value>org.apache.hadoop.hdfs.server.namenode.ha.ConfiguredFai
loverProxyProvider</value>
</property>
```

13. Once the changes are made, save the configuration files and copy them across Datanodes. Make sure the Datanodes were not part of the old cluster, as you might need to clean the Datanodes if you re-format the Namenodes.
14. Make sure the ZooKeeper services are up from the previous recipe.
15. Start the journal node on all the master nodes (`master1`, `master2`, and `rm1`):

    ```
    $ hadoop-daemon.sh start journalnode
    ```

16. Starting with any Namenode of your choice, format it to initialize the HDFS filesystem. But, make sure that you format only one of the two Namenodes:

    ```
    $ hdfs namenode -format
    ```

17. Format the ZooKeeper failover controller:

    ```
    $ hdfs zkfc -formatZK
    ```

18. Start the Namenode on the node where formatting was completed:

    ```
    $ hadoop-daemon.sh start namenode
    ```

19. Start ZKFC:

    ```
    $ hadoop-daemon.sh start zkfc
    ```

20. Log in to the other Namenode `master2.cyrus.com` and either copy the metadata from `master1.cyrus.com` to its local `dfs.namenode.name.dir` directory or execute the `hdfs namenode -bootstrapStandby` command from the other Namenode.
21. Once the other Namenode has pulled the metadata, start the Namenode daemon on the second Namenode, which will be the standby node.
22. Start ZKFC on the standby node.
23. Start the Datanode daemons on all nodes and test them by writing some data to HDFS.
24. Fail one Namenode at a time and test the automatic failover of Namenodes.

How it works...

Make sure the order in which the services are started is the same as mentioned earlier, else the services will fail to start up. The ZKFC will make sure only one Namenode should be active at a time. In production, it is recommended to configure the fencing method, even when using **Quorum Journal Manager** (**QJM**).

> If users are finding it difficult to write configurations, all these are available at my GitHub `https://github.com/netxillon/hadoop/tree/master/HA_QJM`.

Resourcemanager HA using ZooKeeper

In this recipe, we will be covering **Resourcemanager** (**RM**) high availability. In a Hadoop cluster, if the RM goes offline for any reason, all the jobs on the cluster will fail. In production, there will be critical jobs that might be running for a long time and it does not make sense to start them again due to the failure of RM. HA for Resourcemanager was introduced in Hadoop 2.4 and it supports both manual and automatic failover.

Similar to Namenode HA discussed in the earlier recipes, Resourcemanager HA also has only one active node at any given point of time. The failover is either initiated by an admin command or by using ZooKeeper for automatic failover.

Resourcemanager HA can be configured by either using `FileSystemRMStore` or using ZooKeeper store. In this recipe, we will configure automatic failover using `ZKRMStateStore`.

Getting ready

Before starting with this recipe, it is mandatory to complete the earlier recipe on ZooKeeper configuration and to make sure it is accessible from both masters. For this recipe, we will be using the same nodes which were used for Namenode HA—`master1.cyrus.com` and `master2.cyrus.com`. The preconfigured ZooKeeper nodes will be `master1.cyrus.com`, `master2.cyrus.com`, and `rm1.cyrus.com`. Refer to the *Operating Hive with ZooKeeper* recipe in *Chapter 7*, *Data Ingestion and Workflow* on ZooKeeper Configuration for details on how to configure ZooKeeper quorum.

Refer to the recipe on Namenode HA to make sure both the nodes have Hadoop configured with the appropriate environment variables and prerequisites such as JDK. In this recipe, we will use the same set of nodes for both Namenode and Resourcemanager, but actually in production there could be two nodes for both Namenode and Resourcemanager high availability.

How to do it...

1. Connect to the master node in the cluster. The user can start with any master node, either `master1` or `master2`. Both of these will be used as Resourcemanager.
2. Switch to the user `hadoop`.
3. Navigate to the directory were Hadoop is installed:

   /opt/cluster/hadoop/etc/Hadoop

4. Edit the `yarn-site.xml` file and add the following lines to enable Resourcemanager HA and assign a cluster ID:

```
<property>
    <name>yarn.resourcemanager.ha.enabled</name>
    <value>true</value>
</property>

<property>
    <name>yarn.resourcemanager.cluster-id</name>
    <value>cyrus</value>
</property>
```

5. Edit the `yarn-site.xml` file to specify the participating nodes in the cluster:

```
<property>
    <name>yarn.resourcemanager.ha.rm-ids</name>
    <value>rm1,rm2</value>
</property>

<property>
    <name>yarn.resourcemanager.hostname.rm1</name>
    <value>master1.cyrus.com</value>
</property>

<property>
    <name>yarn.resourcemanager.hostname.rm2</name>
    <value>master2.cyrus.com</value>
</property>
```

6. Edit the `yarn-site.xml` file to configure Resourcemanger Web UI:

```
<property>
    <name>yarn.resourcemanager.webapp.address.rm1</name>
    <value>master1.cyrus.com:8088</value>
</property>

<property>
```

```
        <name>yarn.resourcemanager.webapp.address.rm2</name>
        <value>master2.cyrus.com:8088</value>
    </property>
```

7. Edit the `yarn-site.xml` file to add ZooKeeper configuration:

```
<property>
    <name>yarn.resourcemanager.zk-address</name>
    <value>master1.cyrus.com:2181,master2.cyrus.com:2181,rm1.
cyrus.com:2181</value>
</property>
```

8. Copy the `yarn-site.xml` file to all the nodes in the cluster and restart the Resourcemanager and Nodemanager daemons:

```
$ yarn-daemon.sh start resourcemanager
```

9. Verify that one of the Resourcemanager nodes is `active` and the other is in `standby` state, as shown in the following screenshot:

```
[hadoop@master1 ~]$ yarn rmadmin -getServiceState rm1
active
[hadoop@master1 ~]$ yarn rmadmin -getServiceState rm2
standby
```

10. Verify by doing a switch to the other Resourcemanger and submitting a simple test job. The command to switch is shown in the following screenshot:

```
[hadoop@master1 ~]$ yarn rmadmin -transitionToActive  rm2
Automatic failover is enabled for org.apache.hadoop.yarn.client.RMHAServiceTarget@1e67a849
Refusing to manually manage HA state, since it may cause
a split-brain scenario or other incorrect state.
If you are very sure you know what you are doing, please
specify the --forcemanual flag.
```

11. Note that if automatic failover is enabled, you cannot use the manual transition command. Though you can override this using the `-forcemanual` flag, it will warn us about the split-brain scenario it can go into and discourages doing that. The first thing is to make the `active` node as `standby` and then `standby` to `active` using the commands shown in the following screenshot:

```
[hadoop@master1 ~]$ yarn rmadmin -transitionToStandby  rm1 --forcemanual
You have specified the --forcemanual flag. This flag is dangerous, as it can induce a split-brain scenar
io that WILL CORRUPT your HDFS namespace, possibly irrecoverably.

It is recommended not to use this flag, but instead to shut down the cluster and disable automatic failo
ver if you prefer to manually manage your HA state.

You may abort safely by answering 'n' or hitting ^C now.

Are you sure you want to continue? (Y or N) Y
17/05/10 10:02:58 WARN ha.HAAdmin: Proceeding with manual HA state management even though
automatic failover is enabled for org.apache.hadoop.yarn.client.RMHAServiceTarget@1e67a849
```

12. When the Resourcemanager is restarted or failover happens, the job state will be lost. The Application Master attempt will be retried, forcing the completed containers to run again. To avoid this, RM has a feature of state store and support restart. This can be done using the following configuration:

```
<property>
    <name>yarn.resourcemanager.recovery.enabled</name>
    <value>true</value>
</property>

<property>
    <name>yarn.resourcemanager.work-preserving-recovery.
scheduling-wait-ms</name>
    <value>master2.cyrus.com:8088</value>
    <description>Set the amount of time RM waits before allocating
new containers on RM work-preserving recovery.
    </description>
</property>
```

13. The RM configuration can be made more granular using the specific ports for scheduler and tracker instead of just using the Resourcemanager address `yarn.resourcemanager.hostname.rm1` as shown in the following configuration:

```
<property>
    <name>yarn.resourcemanager.resource-tracker.address.rm1</name>
    <value>master1.cyrus.com:9001</value>
</property>

<property>
    <name>yarn.resourcemanager.scheduler.address.rm1</name>
    <value>master1.cyrus.com:9002</value>
</property>

<property>
    <name>yarn.resourcemanager.address.rm1</name>
    <value>master1.cyrus.com:9003</value>
</property>
```

How it works...

In this recipe, we configured high availability for RM using automatic failover. This can also be done using the manual method or by having the RM state store on HDFS filesystem, instead of with ZooKeeper. Whenever RM failover happens, it is transparent to the end user, but in logs we can see that a new AM attempt was made and with recovery enabled the same container states were picked up.

Rolling upgrade with HA

In the previous few recipes, we enabled high availability using different methods. In this section, we will look at how we can upgrade from one version of Hadoop to another.

The support for rolling upgrades became quite stable in Hadoop 2.4.1 and the clusters can be upgraded without a downtime. HA must be in place if there is a requirement for no downtime in the cluster. In HA, there are Namenodes, Datanodes, ZooKeeper, and Journal nodes. ZooKeeper and Journal nodes are generally stable and do not need an upgrade.

Getting ready

To complete this recipe, the user must have a running cluster with HA set up, as discussed previously. Download the latest stable Hadoop release and untar the package and update the sym-links to point to the newer versions. Refer to the Hadoop installation recipe for details on how the initial setup has been done. Secondly, make sure that the recipes before this have been completed or at least understood.

How to do it...

1. Connect to the Namenodes and prepare them for upgrade. Make sure the command is executed on both the Namenodes. This process creates fsimage for rollback, in case something goes wrong:

   ```
   $ hdfs dfsadmin -rollingUpgrade prepare
   ```

2. Check the status of the prepare command to make sure it is complete:

   ```
   $ hdfs dfsadmin -rollingUpgrade query
   ```

3. Now connect to the standby Namenode (`master2`) and perform the upgrade:

   ```
   $ hadoop-daemon.sh stop namenode
   $ hdfs dfsadmin -rollingUpgrade started
   ```

4. Connect to the Namenode (`master1`) and transition `master2` to be active and Namenode `master1` to be standby master:

   ```
   $ hdfs haadmin -transitionToActive master2
   ```

5. Now, on standby Namenode (`master1`), perform the upgrade:

   ```
   $ hadoop-daemon.sh stop namenode
   $ hdfs dfsadmin -rollingUpgrade started
   ```

6. Upgrade Datanodes in a group of nodes per rack. Make sure Datanodes are shut down before restarting them:

```
$ hdfs dfsadmin -shutdownDatanode <DATANODE_HOST:IPC_PORT> upgrade
$ hdfs dfsadmin -getDatanodeInfo <DATANODE_HOST:IPC_PORT>
```

7. Change the sym-links to point to the latest Hadoop version and restart Datanodes.
8. Once the user is satisfied with the state of the cluster, the upgrade can be finalized. Remember, we cannot rollback after finalization:

```
$ hdfs dfsadmin -rollingUpgrade finalize
```

How it works...

The rolling upgrade is done by upgrading the standby master and then switching it to the Active node and doing the same for the other master in the cluster. During upgrade, things might go wrong and there might be a need to go back to the previous version or state of the cluster.

The cluster can be downgraded or rolled back to the previous version, unless it has not been finalized. In downgrade, the preupgrade software version as well as the state of user data is maintained, but in rollback only the software version is retained. The rollback or downgrade cannot be done without a downtime.

Configure shared cache manager

In YARN, whenever a job is submitted, it sets up a distributed cache for jars and configuration files per job. What this means is that the jars will be cached during the execution life cycle of a job. However, often the jars or the code does not change across different users of the cluster.

To solve the problem of loading jars for every job, which consume network bandwidth, a proposal is in place to implement a shared cache across the cluster for all users to use it.

Getting ready

You will need a running cluster with HDFS and YARN set up properly so that the user can run test jobs such as pi or wordcount examples on it.

> This feature is not yet production ready and is scheduled to be a standard feature in Hadoop 2.9.0, but users can still play with it and test it. Users will not see many improvements for small jobs with very few jars or common code.

How to do it...

1. Connect to the `master1.cyrus.com` master node and switch to user `hadoop`.
2. Create a directory on HDFS called `sharedcache`:

   ```
   $ hadoop fs -mkdir /sharedcache
   ```

3. Start the shared cache daemon on the master Namenode:

   ```
   $ yarn sharedcachemanager
   ```

4. Once the daemon is up and running, the user will see a process for it, as shown in the following screenshot:

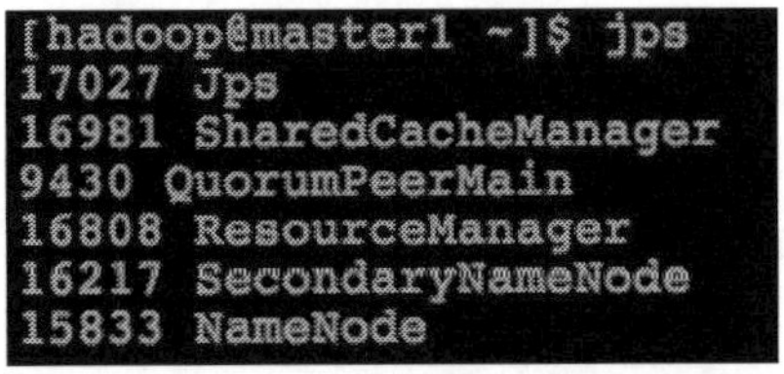
[hadoop@master1 ~]$ jps
17027 Jps
16981 SharedCacheManager
9430 QuorumPeerMain
16808 ResourceManager
16217 SecondaryNameNode
15833 NameNode

There's more...

This is a general introduction caching. Take a look at caching at the HDFS layer.

See also

- The *Configure HDFS cache* recipe

Configure HDFS cache

In Hadoop, centralized cache management is an explicit mechanism for caching the most frequently used files. Users can configure the path to be cached by HDFS, which prevents them from being evicted from memory. Namenode is responsible for coordinating all the Datanode caches in the cluster and periodically receives a cache report.

Getting ready

For this recipe, you will again need a running cluster with at least the HDFS daemons running in the cluster.

How to do it...

1. Connect to the `master1.cyrus.com` master node and switch to user `hadoop`.
2. The first step is to define a cache pool, which is a collection of cache directives. Refer to the following command and screenshot:

   $ hdfs cacheadmin -addPool sales

```
[hadoop@master1 ~]$ hdfs cacheadmin -addPool sales
Successfully added cache pool sales.
[hadoop@master1 ~]$ hdfs cacheadmin -listPools -stats
Found 1 result.
NAME   OWNER  GROUP  MODE            LIMIT  MAXTTL  BYTES_NEEDED  BYTES_CACHED
sales  hadoop hadoop rwxr-xr-x   unlimited   never             0             0
```

3. Then, we need to define a cache directive, which can be a path to a directory or a file:

   $ hdfs cacheadmin -addDirective -path /projects -pool sales -replication 2

```
[hadoop@master1 ~]$ hdfs cacheadmin -addDirective -path /projects -pool sales -replication 2
Added cache directive 1
[hadoop@master1 ~]$ hdfs cacheadmin -listDirectives
Found 1 entry
 ID POOL    REPL EXPIRY  PATH
  1 sales      2 never   /projects
```

4. Load a test file to the cached directory and see how the parameters change as shown in the following screenshot:

```
[hadoop@master1 ~]$ hadoop fs -put test /projects
[hadoop@master1 ~]$ hdfs cacheadmin -listPools -stats
Found 1 result.
NAME   OWNER  GROUP  MODE            LIMIT  MAXTTL  BYTES_NEEDED  BYTES_CACHED  BYTES_OVERLIMIT  FILES_NEEDED
sales  hadoop hadoop rwxr-xr-x   unlimited   never            84             0                0             1
```

5. We can display statistics on a directive or a cache pool as shown in the following screenshot:

```
[hadoop@master1 ~]$ hdfs cacheadmin -listDirectives -stats
Found 1 entry
 ID POOL    REPL EXPIRY  PATH          BYTES_NEEDED  BYTES_CACHED  F
  1 sales      2 never   /projects               84             0
[hadoop@master1 ~]$ hdfs cacheadmin -listPools -stats
Found 1 result.
NAME   OWNER  GROUP  MODE            LIMIT  MAXTTL  BYTES_NEEDED
sales  hadoop hadoop rwxr-xr-x   unlimited   never            84
```

6. The cache pools or directive can be removed or modified for TTLs and replication:

```
$ hdfs cacheadmin -removeDirective <id>
$ hdfs cacheadmin -removeDirective <path>
$ hdfs cacheadmin -removePool <name>
$ hdfs cacheadmin -modifyDirective -id 1 -path /projects
-replication 1 -ttl 3600s
```

How it works...

The steps 1 through 6, show how to configure the HDFS cache and reduce the latency to access files stored on HDFS. Cluster, by caching frequently used files in off-heap memory on the Datanodes and constantly updating the Namenode with the respective cache stores can be useful.

An important thing to keep in mind is that the directory path is nonrecursive and only the files at the first level will be cached. A directive needs to be set for each subdirectory if needed.

See also

- The *YARN shared cache manager* recipe

HDFS snapshots

In spite of having high availability and replication factor as three, there are chances of data loss due to accidental deletions or corruptions. What if the user wants to restore the HDFS state to a previous point in time? Can that be done?

To address these issues, HDFS supports snapshots, which is a kind of backup in a point of time. However, snapshots do not occupy any extra space, as these are simply pointers to the original data blocks.

In this recipe, we will see how the snapshots can be enabled and configured.

Getting ready

Make sure that the user has a running cluster with HDFS configured. The user must be able to execute HDFS commands and copy some data to the cluster.

How to do it...

1. Connect to the `master1.cyrus.com` Namenode and switch to the user `hadoop`.
2. The first step is to enable a snapshot on a directory, as shown in the following command:

   ```
   $ hdfs dfsadmin -allowSnapshot /projects
   ```

3. The preceding command makes a directory snapshot able and `.snapshot` directory will be created under it. Although it cannot be listed, it still exists inside every directory that is enabled to snapshots, as shown in the following screenshot:

```
[hadoop@master1 ~]$ hdfs dfsadmin -allowSnapshot /projects
Allowing snaphot on /projects succeeded
[hadoop@master1 ~]$ hdfs dfs -ls /projects
Found 1 items
-rw-r--r--   1 hadoop supergroup         42 2017-01-05 02:10 /projects/test
[hadoop@master1 ~]$ hdfs dfs -ls /projects/.snapshot
[hadoop@master1 ~]$
```

4. The next step is to create a snapshot with the following command.

   ```
   $ hdfs dfs -createSnapshot /projects jan52016
   ```

5. List the contents of the snapshot, as shown in the following screenshot:

```
[hadoop@master1 ~]$ hdfs dfs -ls /projects/.snapshot
Found 1 items
drwxr-xr-x   - hadoop supergroup          0 2017-01-05 03:39 /projects/.snapshot/jan52016
```

6. A snapshot-enabled directory cannot be deleted, as shown in the following screenshot:

```
$ hdfs dfs -rm -r /projects/
INFO fs.TrashPolicyDefault: Namenode trash configuration: Deletion interval = 10080 minutes, Emptier interval = 45 minutes.
 to trash: hdfs://master1.cyrus.com:9000/projects: The directory /projects cannot be deleted since /projects is snapshottable
```

7. There can be multiple snapshots for a directory and they can also be deleted with the following command:

   ```
   $ hdfs dfs -deleteSnapshot /projects 5jan2016
   ```

8. Snapshots can also be disabled, as shown in the following command:

   ```
   $ hdfs dfs -disallowSnapshot /projects
   ```

How it works...

Although there are a lot of details that make snapshots work, the basic logic behind snapshots is creating an extra reference to the data blocks. The reference metadata is simply a data structure and it does not make any additional copies of the data, keeping the disk usage same for a snapshot-enabled path.

Apache Hadoop distribution does not support automatic or scheduled snapshots. The user has to write scripts to do this in production.

Configuring storage based policies

Over a period of time, the Hadoop clusters grow in size and the hardware will change. More powerful nodes, with faster CPU, disks, and RAM, will be added and there will be an uneven performance of nodes across the cluster.

This can be controlled at the node level using YARN labels, which we will see at a later stage in the book. We can also configure storage-based policies according to the disk drives we have such as SSDs, SATA, and PATA.

Getting ready

For this recipe, you will again need a running cluster with at least HDFS configured and Datanodes in the cluster with different types of hard drives. Some nodes have slow disk drives and others have fast disk drives.

The segregation can also be based on the cost factor, as SSDs are expensive and must be on nodes, which are SLA stringent. The classification can be done into cold storage for the archiving of data and the hot storage of live data in the cluster. Users can store performance-critical data in SSD or memory, where high-density nodes with less compute power can be used for cold storage.

How to do it...

1. Connect to the `master1.cyrus.com` master node and switch to the user `hadoop`.
2. The first thing is to list the storage policies available using the following command:

   ```
   $ hdfs storagepolicies -listPolicies
   ```

3. Navigate to the directory `/opt/cluster/hadoop/etc/hadoop`.

4. Edit the `hdfs-site.xml` file and add the following configuration:

```
<property>
    <name>dfs.storage.policy.enabled</name>
    <value>true</value>
</property>
```

5. Now add the storage types on each Datanode, as shown in the following screenshot. Modify `hdfs-site.xml` according to the disk types on each datanode:

```
<property>
<name>dfs.datanode.data.dir</name>
<value>[DISK]file:///grid/dn/disk0,
       [SSD]file:///grid/dn/ssd0,
       [ARCHIVE]file:///grid/dn/archive0,
       [RAM_DISK]file:///grid/dn/ram0</value>
<description>A datanode storage location /grid/dn/disk0 on DISK</description>
<description>A datanode storage location /grid/dn/ssd0 on SSD</description>
<description>A datanode storage location /grid/dn/archive0 on ARCHIVE</description>
<description>A datanode storage location /grid/dn/ram0 on RAM_DISK</description>
</property>
```

6. Copy the `hdfs-site.xml` file across all the nodes and if the nodes are heterogeneous, make sure to make the Datanode-specific changes.
7. Apply the policy for a path using the following command:

```
$ hdfs storagepolicies -setStoragePolicy -path <path> -policy
<policy>
```

How it works...

There are different storage polices such as HOT, COLD, WARM, All_SSD, One_SSD, and there is a policy table that maps them to a numeric value. You can read though the Apache storage policies documentation for details on this.

The policies we applied earlier can be unregistered and modified. Make sure that the correct policies are configured according to the storage type per node, else the user might see strange performance benchmarks. It should not be that a node has slow disk and we apply a HOT policy to it.

Configuring HA for Edge nodes

Edge node is the access point for the cluster and it is always good to have multiple nodes to load balance and also to maintain high availability in case one node goes down.

This can be done in multiple ways, by either using a dedicated hardware load balancer in front of Edge nodes or by setting a DNS round robin with a health check.

Getting ready

Make sure that the user has a running cluster with at least two Edge nodes with Hadoop installed. Refer to *Chapter 1, Hadoop Architecture and Deployment*, for Edge node and DNS configurations. It is presumed that the users are aware about the working of DNS and is from Linux Administration background.

How to do it...

1. Connect to the `client1.cyrus.com` Edge node.
2. Check the DNS resolution of the node using the following command:

   ```
   $ nslookup client1.cyrus.com
   ```
3. The preceding command will return an IP address, something like `10.0.0.11`.
4. Check the resolution on the other Edge node `client2.cyrus.com` as well. It will also return an IP address such as `10.0.0.12`.
5. Now, in the DNS server, create host records as shown in the following command:

   ```
   Client          IN      A 10.0.0.11
   Client          IN      A 10.0.0.12
   ```
6. Save the zone file and reload the zone files. The following command is for Centos:

   ```
   # service named reload
   ```
7. Now test the DNS resolution for the `client.cyrus.com` record; it will return two IP addresses: `10.0.0.11` and `10.0.0.12`.
8. Set the caching TTL for these records to be very low so that they are not cached.
9. Also, on the two nodes `client1` and `client2`, make sure the ssh host fingerprints are the same, else we will get ssh key failures.

How it works...

Instead of connecting to a particular node, we are connecting to a floating round robin host record. Also, make sure that the two Edge nodes or whatever number of nodes are acting as Edge nodes, have the same ssh fingerprint, which is defined by the `/etc/ssh/ssh_host_rsa_key` file. The `ssh-keygen -l -f /etc/ssh/ssh_host_rsa_key` command can be used to see the fingerprints on each Edge node.

5
Schedulers

In this chapter, we will cover the following recipes:

- Configuring users and groups
- Fair Scheduler configuration
- Fair Scheduler pools
- Configuring job queues
- Job queue ACLs
- Configuring Capacity Scheduler
- Queuing mappings in Capacity Scheduler
- YARN and Mapred commands
- YARN label-based scheduling
- YARN SLS

Introduction

In this chapter, we will configure YARN schedulers and job queues so that multiple users can use the cluster at the same time and make a legitimate use of the resources provided to them. There are two approaches: either setup a separate cluster for different business units or share the clusters.

The first approach is fine if there are a few clusters, but managing a large number of clusters is challenging. A better approach is to build multitenancy clusters, which can support different users with varied use cases.

> If users are finding it difficult to write scripts or configurations, all these are available at my GitHub at `https://github.com/netxillon/hadoop`.

Configuring users and groups

In our previous recipes, we installed or configured Hadoop clusters as user `hadoop`. But, in production, it is good to run jobs as different users and also the Hadoop daemons can be separated to run with different user IDs, so as to have better control and security.

The security aspects will be covered in the security chapter, but it is important to understand the user segregation and grouping users per project or business units.

In this recipe, we will see how to create users and groups for job submission. These recipes do not talk about the HDFS user permissions or file ACLs, but only about the permission to submit jobs and what percentage of cluster capacity each user or department can use within an organization.

Getting ready

Before tackling the recipes in this chapter, make sure you have gone through the previous recipes or have at least gone through the steps to install the Hadoop cluster. In addition to this, the user must know the basics of Linux User Management and also understand the users and groups concepts in Linux.

In production, all users come from a central user management system such as NIS or LDAP, but in this recipe, our talk is limited to manual user creation on each host in the cluster.

How to do it...

1. Connect to any node in the cluster; user can start with any master node, `master1`, and then these steps are repeated on all the nodes in the cluster.
2. As a user root, create the required users as follows. The assumption is that the group `hadoop` already exists, as the cluster is pre-existing:

```
# useradd -G hadoop user1
# useradd -G hadoop user2
```

3. Create directories for the user and update permissions on HDFS as user `hadoop`:

    $ hadoop fs -mkdir /user/user1/

    $ hadoop fs -mkdir /user/user2/

    $ hadoop fs -chown -R user1:hadoop /user/user1/

    $ hadoop fs -chown -R user2:hadoop /user/user2/

4. Make sure you are able to write files to HDFS as that user, as shown in the following screenshot:

```
[user1@master1 ~]$ id
uid=503(user1) gid=503(user1) groups=503(user1),501(hadoop)
[user1@master1 ~]$ hadoop fs -put test.txt /user/user1/
[user1@master1 ~]$ hadoop fs -ls /user/user1/
Found 1 items
-rw-r--r--   1 user1 hadoop         20 2017-02-02 10:36 /user/user1/test.txt
```

5. Create a group named `prod` and `dev` and add few users to it, as shown in the following screenshot:

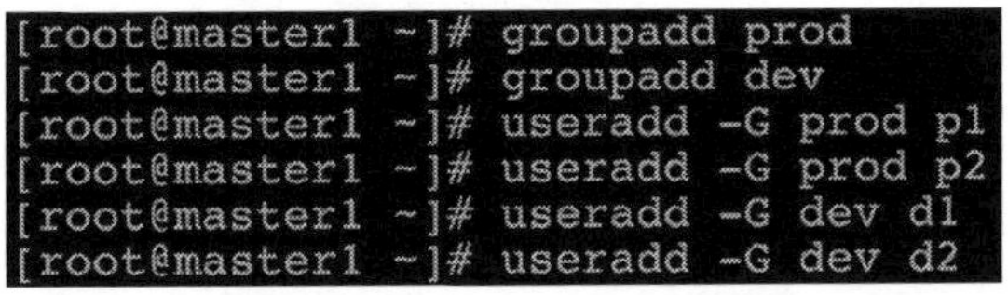

```
[root@master1 ~]# groupadd prod
[root@master1 ~]# groupadd dev
[root@master1 ~]# useradd -G prod p1
[root@master1 ~]# useradd -G prod p2
[root@master1 ~]# useradd -G dev d1
[root@master1 ~]# useradd -G dev d2
```

6. Create the same users on all the nodes in the cluster.

In the preceding recipe, we created users and groups to get readers familiar with the concepts, which will be used in the next recipes to create job queues. As stated initially, it could be cumbersome to create users manually on all nodes. A better approach is to use LDAP or configuration management systems such as Puppet or Chef.

How it works...

In the preceding recipe, different users can access Hadoop cluster to store data and process data. The groups used previously are just examples that readers can customize according to their needs. Usually, each daemon will run as a separate user and will be part of a common group so that it can write or read data. The preceding recipe is not addressing the security issues; it is just to facilitate different users to access data and submit jobs.

See also

- The *Fair Scheduler and Capacity Scheduler – Queue Management* recipe

Fair Scheduler configuration

Getting ready

To go through the recipe in this section, we need Hadoop Cluster setup and running. By default, Apache Hadoop 1.x distribution uses FIFO scheduler and Hadoop 2.x uses Capacity Scheduler. In a cluster with multiple jobs, it is not good to use FIFO scheduler, as it will starve the jobs for resources and only the very first job in the queue is executed; all other jobs have to wait.

To address the preceding issue, there are two commonly used Schedulers: Fair Scheduler, and Capacity Scheduler, to allocate the cluster resources in a fair manner. In this recipe, we will see how to configure Fair Scheduler. Simply put, Fair Scheduler shares resources fairly among running jobs based on queues and weights assigned.

How to do it...

1. Connect to the `master1.cyrus.com` master node in the cluster and switch as user `hadoop`.
2. Edit the `yarn-site.xml` as follows:

```
<property>
    <name>yarn.resourcemanager.scheduler.class</name>
    <value>org.apache.hadoop.yarn.server.resourcemanager.
scheduler.fair.FairScheduler</value>
</property>
```

3. Add the Fair Scheduler allocation file location to `yarn-site.xml` as follows:

```
<property>
    <name>yarn.scheduler.fair.allocation.file</name>
    <value>/opt/cluster/hadoop/etc/Hadoop/fair-scheduler.xml</
value>
</property>
```

4. Make sure the files are owned by the correct user `hadoop`.

5. Edit the allocation file `fair-scheduler.xml` as shown in the following screenshot:

```
[hadoop@master1 ~]$ cat /opt/cluster/hadoop/etc/hadoop/fair-scheduler.xml
<allocations>
  <queue name="prod_queue">
    <minResources>10000 mb,0vcores</minResources>
    <maxResources>90000 mb,0vcores</maxResources>
    <maxRunningApps>50</maxRunningApps>
    <maxAMShare>0.3</maxAMShare>
    <weight>2.0</weight>
    <schedulingPolicy>fair</schedulingPolicy>
  </queue>

  <queueMaxAMShareDefault>0.5</queueMaxAMShareDefault>

  <queue name="dev_queue">
  <minResources>5000 mb,0vcores</minResources>
  <maxResources>10000 mb,0vcores</maxResources>
  <maxRunningApps>30</maxRunningApps>
  <maxAMShare>0.1</maxAMShare>
  <weight>2.0</weight>
  <schedulingPolicy>fair</schedulingPolicy>
  </queue>
</allocations>
```

6. Copy the `yarn-site.xml` and `fair-scheduler.xml` files to all nodes in the cluster.
7. Restart the Resource manager and Node manager daemons as follows:

   $ stop-yarn.sh

   $ start-yarn.sh

8. Connect to the ResourceManager port `8088` and verify the changes as shown in the following screenshot:

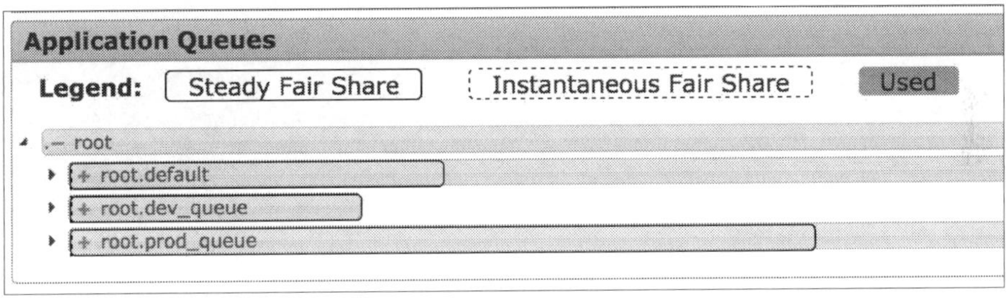

9. Submit any job as user `hadoop` and observe the ResourceManager page. You should see a queue as shown in the following screenshot:

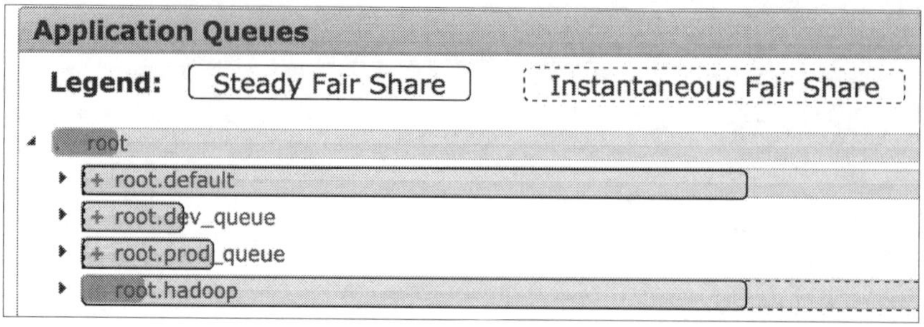

10. Submit a job as user `d1` and see the ResourceManager page, as shown in the following screenshot:

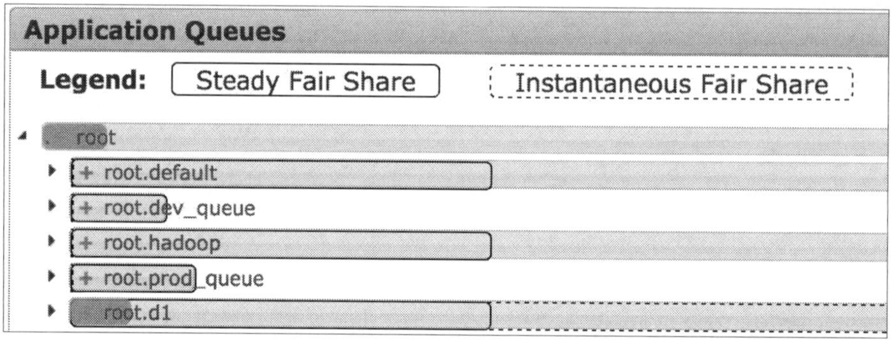

11. Make sure to change the Hadoop `tmp` directory ownership and create the home directory for user `d1`, as shown in the following screenshot:

```
[d1@master1 ~]$ hadoop fs -ls -d /user/d1
drwxr-xr-x   - d1 d1          0 2017-02-03 02:06 /user/d1
[d1@master1 ~]$ hadoop fs -ls -d /tmp
drwxrwxrwt   - hadoop supergroup          0 2017-02-03 01:59 /tmp
```

How it works...

In the preceding recipe, we configured Fair Scheduler for YARN, and users can submit jobs. The preceding configuration is not yet production ready, but this is to give the readers a glimpse of the Scheduler behavior. When a user named `hadoop` submits a job, it goes to the queue `root.hadoop` and, similarly, for user `d1` it goes to `root.d1`. This behavior is due to the queue placement policy, in which create queue is set to true by default. So, this means it will automatically create a queue for the user for the submitted job.

In the upcoming sections, we will look at how job submission can be done to particular queues, and control which users can submit to it and look into the queue placement policy details.

Fair Scheduler pools

In this recipe, we look at configuring Fair Scheduler with pools instead of queues. This is for backwards compatibility. In Hadoop 1.X, Fair Scheduler was addressed with pools and it means the same as queues.

It is recommended to use queues, as this is quite standard across the board. But, for the sake of the readers, it is good to cover the concepts of pools.

Getting ready

To go through the recipe, complete the previous recipe and just modify the `fair-scheduler.xml` file to reflect pools.

How to do it...

1. Connect to the `master1.cyrus.com` master node in the cluster and switch as user `hadoop`.
2. Edit the allocation file `fair-scheduler.xml`, as shown in the following screenshot:

```
[hadoop@master1 hadoop]$ cat fair-scheduler.xml
<allocations>

<pool name="prod">
<minMaps>10</minMaps>
<minReduces>5</minReduces>
</pool>

<pool name="dev">
<minMaps>10</minMaps>
<minReduces>5</minReduces>
</pool>

</allocations>
```

3. Copy the `fair-scheduler.xml` file to all the nodes in the cluster and restart the YARN daemons.

4. Check the ResourceManager page to confirm whether the pools are visible or not, as shown in the following screenshot:

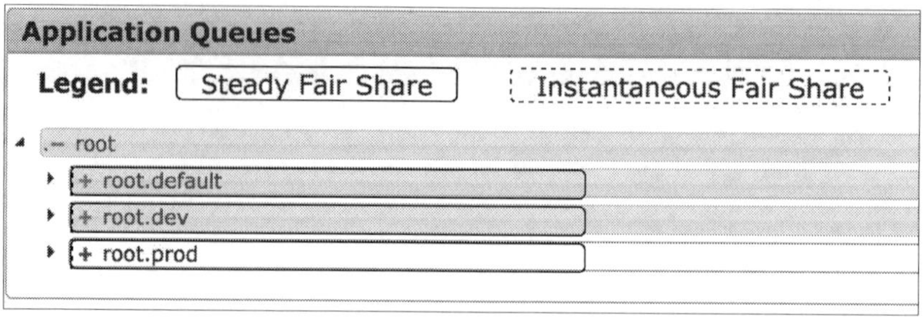

5. Submit a sample job such as `wordcount` as user `hadoop` and see the ResourceManager page, as shown in the following screenshot:

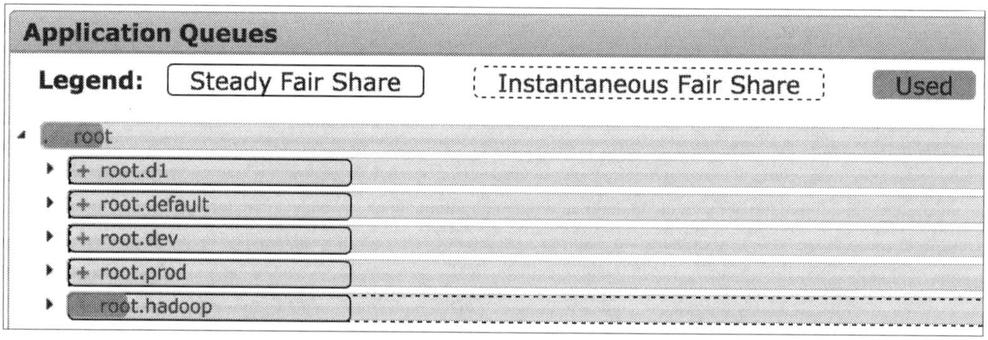

6. Test the same thing for the `d1` user, as shown in the following screenshot:

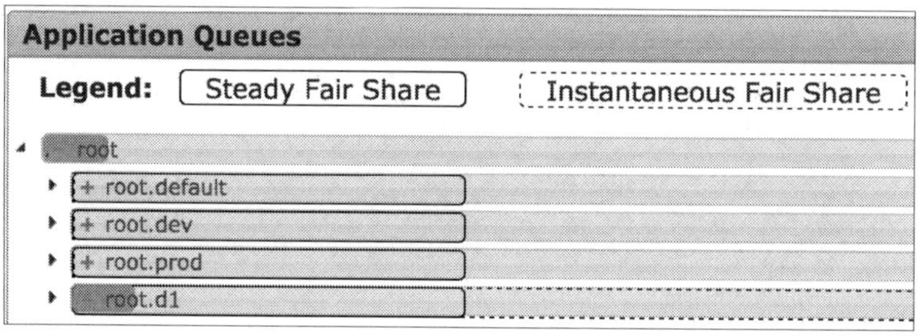

7. This is a very basic introduction to the pool configuration. In Hadoop 1.x, there was no YARN and hence no `yarn-site.xml` file. The configuration for the schedulers were made in the `mapred-site.xml` file using the parameter as follows:

```
<property>
    <name>mapred.jobtracker.taskScheduler</name>
    <value>org.apache.hadoop.mapred.FairScheduler</value>
</property>
```

   In Fair Scheduler, that mapping can be done between pool and queues using the following settings:

```
<property>
    <name>mapred.fairscheduler.poolnameproperty</name>
    <value>mapred.job.queue.name</value>
</property>
```

How it works...

Whenever a user submits a job, it goes to the pool allocated to it, after looking at the placement policy and ACLs. By default, create pool is true, so each user will get its own queue or pool.

The use of pools is deprecated and it is recommended to use queues for configuring the jobs. The intent of this recipe was to make users aware that pool was an old name for the queues in Fair Scheduler.

Configuring job queues

In this recipe, we will configure the job queue and allow users to submit jobs to the queues. In production, there might be many departments such as marketing, sales, and finance, sharing a cluster of resources and it is important to have the correct shares proportional to business and funding.

In the previous recipe, although the queues were setup, they were still not used. Queues were dynamically created for jobs submitted by specifying a queue. If no queue is specified, jobs are submitted to a queue by the name of the user who submitted the job. We will explore these a bit more in this recipe.

Getting ready

To complete the recipe, the user must have a running cluster with HDFS and YARN configured and must have completed the previous two recipes.

How to do it...

1. Connect to the `master1.cyrus.com` master node in the cluster and switch as user `hadoop`.
2. Edit the `fair-scheduler.xml` allocation file as shown next. Note that there is no user specified for any queue (within the `<queue>` tags) and also the queue policy is set to assign to default if no match happens:

```
<?xml version="1.0"?>
<allocations>
  <queue name="prod">
    <minResources>100 mb,0vcores</minResources>
    <maxResources>4000 mb,0vcores</maxResources>
    <maxRunningApps>20</maxRunningApps>
    <maxAMShare>0.2</maxAMShare>
    <weight>1.0</weight>
    <schedulingPolicy>fair</schedulingPolicy>
  </queue>

  <queue name="dev">
    <minResources>100 mb,0vcores</minResources>
    <maxResources>3000 mb,0vcores</maxResources>
    <maxAMShare>0.6</maxAMShare>
    <weight>1.0</weight>
    <schedulingPolicy>fair</schedulingPolicy>
  </queue>

  <user name="hadoop">
    <maxRunningApps>5</maxRunningApps>
  </user>

  <user name="d1">
    <maxRunningApps>1</maxRunningApps>
  </user>

  <user name="d2">
    <maxRunningApps>1</maxRunningApps>
  </user>
  <userMaxAppsDefault>5</userMaxAppsDefault>


  <queuePlacementPolicy>
      <rule name="specified" />
      <rule name="primaryGroup" create="false" />
```

```
        <rule name="nestedUserQueue">
        <rule name="secondaryGroupExistingQueue" create="false" />
        </rule>
        <rule name="default" queue="default"/>
    </queuePlacementPolicy>

</allocations>
```

3. Make sure to restart the YARN daemon when you make a change to the configurations. Later, we will talk about refreshing queues without restarting daemons.
4. Submit a simple `wordcount` job without specifying any queue, as user `hadoop`. See the command in the following screenshot:

```
[hadoop@jt1 hadoop]$ yarn jar /opt/cluster/hadoop/share/hadoop/mapre
duce/hadoop-mapreduce-examples-2.7.3.jar wordcount /file1.txt /out
```

5. Check the ResourceManager page to see, which queue the job got submitted to as shown in the following screenshot. Did it go to the `default` queue?

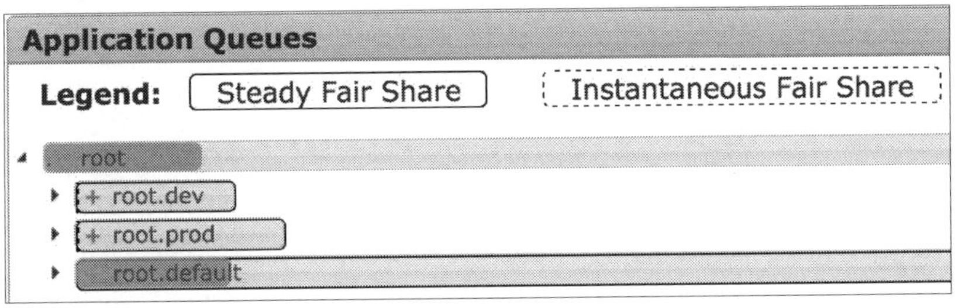

6. Now, edit the `fair-scheduler.xml` file and remove the `queuePlacementPolicy` tag.
7. Submit the same job again and check the ResourceManager page to see the status of the job. This time it goes to a new queue `hadoop`, as shown in the following screenshot:

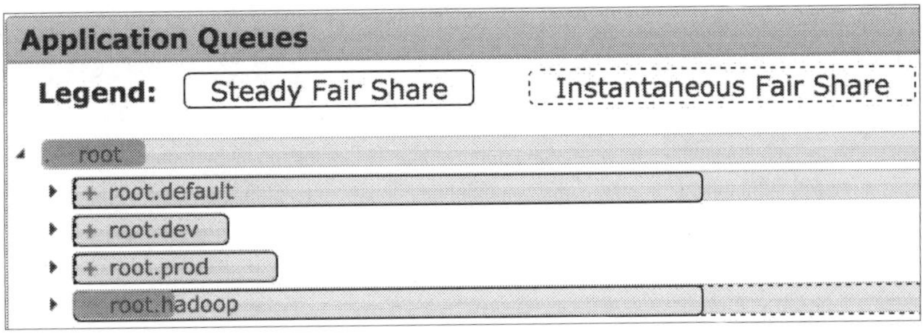

8. Now, once again, edit the `fair-scheduler.xml` file and add back the `queuePlacementPolicy` tag and submit a test job, but this time with a queue name as shown here:

```
$ yarn jar /opt/cluster/hadoop/share/hadoop/mapreduce/hadoop-mapreduce-examples-2.7.3.jar wordcount -D mapreduce.queue.name=prod /file1.txt /out2
```

9. This time the job got submitted as a `default` queue instead of `prod`, as shown in the following screenshot:

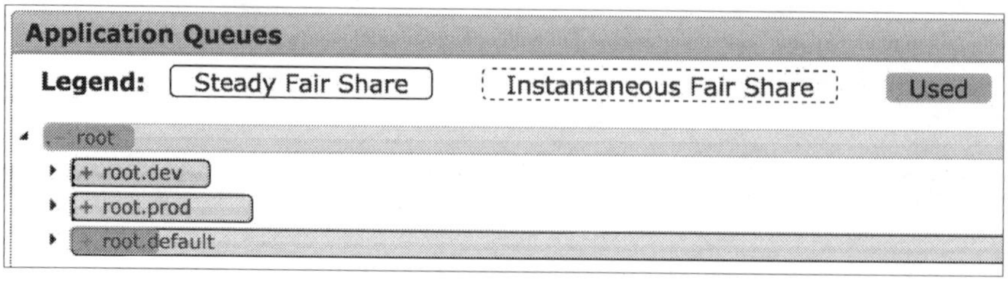

10. Now, let's submit a job to a queue which does not exist, as shown next — it should go to the `default` queue:

```
-D mapreduce.queue.name=sales
```

11. Now, edit the `fair-scheduler.xml` file again and remove the `queuePlacementPolicy` tag and submit the job again to a queue that does not exist:

```
-D mapreduce.queue.name=sales
```

12. This time it goes to the user who submitted the job, rather than to the default queue, as shown in the following screenshot:

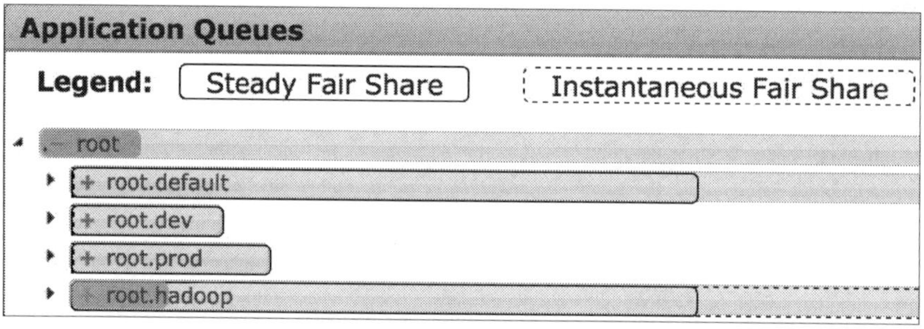

13. The preceding behavior is due to two parameters in `yarn-site.xml`, which are `true` by default. Change the values of the following parameters to `false`:

```
<property>
    <name>yarn.scheduler.fair.allow-undeclared-pools</name>
```

```
        <value>false</value>
    </property>
    <property>
        <name>yarn.scheduler.fair.user-as-default-queue</name>
        <value>false</value>
    </property>
```

14. Edit the `fair-scheduler.xml` file to include users `hadoop` and `d1` in the queues as shown next:

```
<?xml version="1.0"?>
<allocations>
  <queue name="prod">
    <aclAdministerApps>hadoop</aclAdministerApps>
    <aclSubmitApps>hadoop</aclSubmitApps>
    <minResources>1000 mb,0vcores</minResources>
    <maxResources>6000 mb,100vcores</maxResources>
    <maxRunningApps>20</maxRunningApps>
    <weight>1.0</weight>
    <schedulingPolicy>fair</schedulingPolicy>
  </queue>

  <queue name="dev">
  <aclAdministerApps>d1</aclAdministerApps>
  <aclSubmitApps>d1</aclSubmitApps>
  <minResources>1000 mb,0vcores</minResources>
  <maxResources>6000 mb,100vcores</maxResources>
  <maxRunningApps>20</maxRunningApps>
  <weight>1.0</weight>
  <schedulingPolicy>fair</schedulingPolicy>
  </queue>
</queue>
  <user name="hadoop">
    <maxRunningApps>5</maxRunningApps>
  </user>

  <user name="d1">
    <maxRunningApps>1</maxRunningApps>
  </user>

  <user name="d2">
    <maxRunningApps>1</maxRunningApps>
  </user>
  <userMaxAppsDefault>5</userMaxAppsDefault>
```

```
    <queuePlacementPolicy>
        <rule name="specified" />
        <rule name="primaryGroup" create="false" />
           <rule name="nestedUserQueue">
          <rule name="secondaryGroupExistingQueue" create="false"
/>
           </rule>
      <rule name="default" queue="default"/>
    </queuePlacementPolicy>
</allocations>
```

15. Now, submit job to the `prod` queue as user `hadoop`, using the following command:

    ```
    $ yarn jar /opt/cluster/hadoop/share/hadoop/mapreduce/hadoop-mapreduce-examples-2.7.3.jar wordcount -D mapreduce.job.queuename=prod /file1.txt /user/d1/out6
    ```

16. Visit the ResourceManager page to use the queue status as shown in the following screenshot:

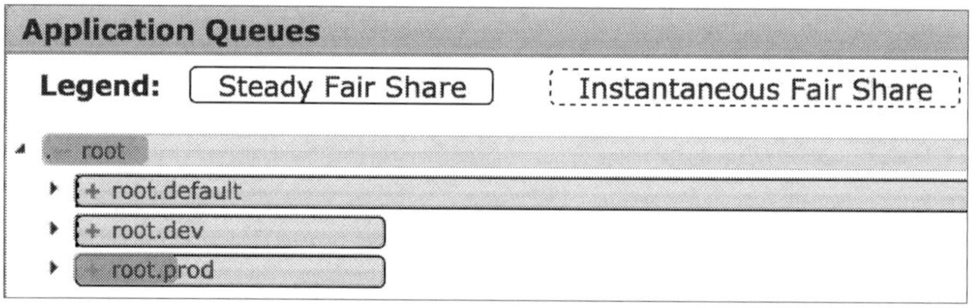

17. Now, submit the job as user `d1` and again visit the page to see the job running in the `dev` queue:

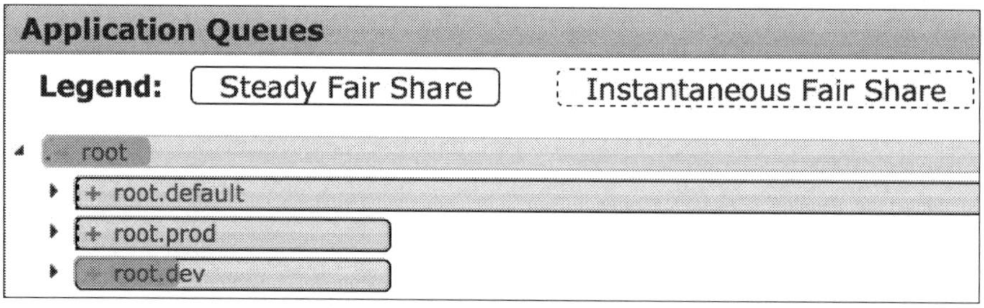

How it works...

Whenever a user submits a job, the queue policy is evaluated and it is submitted in the order of precedence. Make sure changes are made to the `yarn-site.xml`.

Presently, the queue is set up with a capacity of guarantee of 1000 MB for `prod` and 100 MB for `dev`. But, despite putting the ACLs as preceding, the users will be able to submit jobs to other queues. For example, the `d1` user can submit to the `prod` queue, because the `root` queue which is parent for all the queues has a wildcard, and the child inherits them.

See also

- The *Job queue ACLs* recipe

Job queue ACLs

In YARN, whenever a job is submitted, it is submitted either to a specified queue or default queue. This behavior has been explored in the last recipe. In this recipe, we will configure ACLs to block users from submitting jobs to other queues.

Getting ready

In order to get started, you will need a running cluster with HDFS and YARN set up properly and an understanding of the last recipe.

> This feature is not yet production ready and is scheduled to be a standard feature in Hadoop 2.9.0, but users can still play with it and test it. Users will not see much improvement for small jobs with very few jars or common code.

How to do it...

1. Connect to the `master1.cyrus.com` master node and switch as user `hadoop`.
2. Execute the command as shown next in the picture to see the queue ACLs. By default, users can see that `d1` has administrative and submit rights to all the queues:

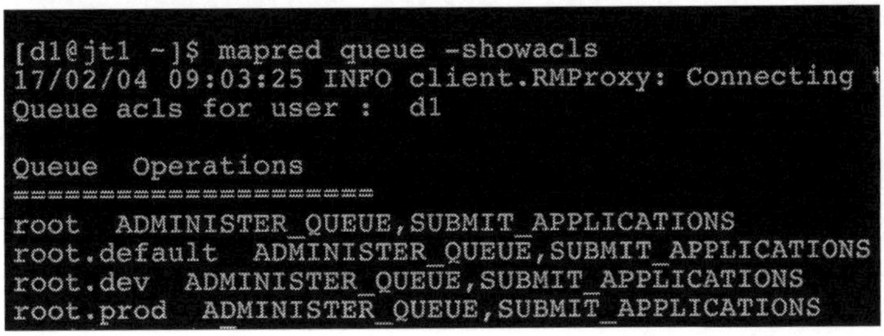

```
[d1@jt1 ~]$ mapred queue -showacls
17/02/04 09:03:25 INFO client.RMProxy: Connecting t
Queue acls for user :  d1

Queue  Operations
=====================
root  ADMINISTER_QUEUE,SUBMIT_APPLICATIONS
root.default  ADMINISTER_QUEUE,SUBMIT_APPLICATIONS
root.dev  ADMINISTER_QUEUE,SUBMIT_APPLICATIONS
root.prod  ADMINISTER_QUEUE,SUBMIT_APPLICATIONS
```

3. Edit the `fair-scheduler.xml` allocation file as shown next. Note the users specified for the specific queues (within the `<queue>` tags) and also that the `root` queue is being restrictive:

```
<?xml version="1.0"?>
<allocations>
<queue name="root">
<aclAdministerApps>hadoop</aclAdministerApps>
<aclSubmitApps> </aclSubmitApps>
  <queue name="prod">
    <aclAdministerApps>hadoop</aclAdministerApps>
    <aclSubmitApps>hadoop</aclSubmitApps>
    <minResources>1000 mb,0vcores</minResources>
    <maxResources>6000 mb,100vcores</maxResources>
    <maxRunningApps>20</maxRunningApps>
    <weight>1.0</weight>
    <schedulingPolicy>fair</schedulingPolicy>
  </queue>

  <queue name="dev">
  <aclAdministerApps>d1</aclAdministerApps>
  <aclSubmitApps>d1</aclSubmitApps>
  <minResources>1000 mb,0vcores</minResources>
  <maxResources>6000 mb,100vcores</maxResources>
  <maxRunningApps>20</maxRunningApps>
  <weight>1.0</weight>
  <schedulingPolicy>fair</schedulingPolicy>
  </queue>
</queue>
  <user name="hadoop">
    <maxRunningApps>5</maxRunningApps>
  </user>

  <user name="d1">
    <maxRunningApps>1</maxRunningApps>
  </user>

  <user name="d2">
    <maxRunningApps>1</maxRunningApps>
  </user>
  <userMaxAppsDefault>5</userMaxAppsDefault>


        <queuePlacementPolicy>
            <rule name="specified" />
            <rule name="primaryGroup" create="false" />
            <rule name="nestedUserQueue">
```

```
                <rule name="secondaryGroupExistingQueue"
create="false" />
            </rule>
            <rule name="default" queue="default"/>
          </queuePlacementPolicy>

</allocations>
```

4. Copy the file to all the nodes and restart the YARN daemons.
5. Execute the command as shown in the following screenshot to see the queue ACLs. You can see the changes in the queue ACLs now as shown in the following screenshot:

```
[d1@jt1 ~]$ mapred queue -showacls
17/02/04 09:10:12 INFO client.RMProxy: Connecting
Queue acls for user :  d1

Queue  Operations
=====================
root
root.default
root.dev  ADMINISTER_QUEUE,SUBMIT_APPLICATIONS
root.prod
```

6. Submit a job as the `d1` user to the `prod` and `dev` queues to test out the permissions. You will see an error as shown next, if `d1` submits a job to the `prod` queue:

```
17/02/04 09:12:31 INFO mapreduce.JobSubmitter: Cleaning up the stagin
job_1486179599793_0001
java.io.IOException: org.apache.hadoop.yarn.exceptions.YarnException:
0001 to YARN : User d1 cannot submit applications to queue root.prod
```

How it works...

Whenever a user submits a job, the queue ACLs are evaluated and if a user has rights to the queue, he can submit a job.

The important thing to keep in mind is that, if a user has administrative rights to a queue, he can definitely submit jobs to it. The administrator can only kill jobs or move and manage the jobs using the `yarn application -movetoqueue appID -queue targetQueueName` command.

This is a very basic introduction to Fair Scheduler and queueing and it could get quite complex with hierarchies and capacity assigned for different queues. You can explore the queue configuration settings.

See also

- The *Configure Capacity scheduler and Queue Mappings* recipe

Configuring Capacity Scheduler

Capacity Scheduler is mainly designed for multitenancy, where multiple organizations collectively fund the cluster based on the computing needs. There is an added benefit that an organization can access any excess capacity not being used by others. This provides elasticity for the organizations in a cost-effective manner.

Getting ready

For this recipe, you will again need a running cluster with YARN and HDFS configured in the cluster. Readers are recommended to read the previous recipes in this chapter to understand this recipe better.

In Hadoop 2.x, the default scheduler is **Capacity Scheduler** and it is enabled by default, unless modified explicitly as seen in the previous recipes where we have configured Fair Scheduler.

How to do it...

1. Connect to the `master1.cyrus.com` master node and switch as user `hadoop`.
2. Modify the `yarn-site.xml` file by changing the following parameter:

```
<property>
    <name>yarn.resourcemanager.scheduler.class</name>
    <value>org.apache.hadoop.yarn.server.resourcemanager.
scheduler.capacity.CapacityScheduler</value>
</property>
```

3. Remove any references to the Fair Scheduler allocations file, if any.
4. Copy the changes to all nodes in the cluster and restart the YARN daemons.
5. Access the ResourceManager page and verify that the default scheduler is set to Capacity Scheduler as shown in the following screenshot:

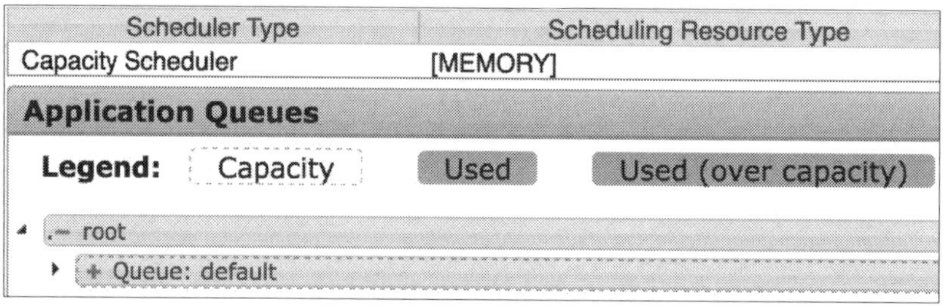

6. Edit `capacity-scheduler.xml`, to configure `prod and dev` queues and assign them shares as follows. Add the new queues and modify the `default` queue share, as it is a mandatory queue:

```
<property>
    <name>yarn.scheduler.capacity.root.queues</name>
    <value>default,prod,dev</value>
</property>

<property>
    <name>yarn.scheduler.capacity.root.default.capacity</name>
    <value>30</value>
    <description>This is the percentage of the total capacity
allocated to the default queue</description>
</property>

<property>
    <name>yarn.scheduler.capacity.root.prod.capacity</name>
    <value>50</value>
</property>

<property>
    <name>yarn.scheduler.capacity.root.dev.capacity</name>
    <value>20</value>
</property>
```

7. Configure the allowed usage percentage per queue as shown here:

```
<property>
    <name>yarn.scheduler.capacity.root.prod.user-limit-factor</
name>
    <value>1</value>
</property>

<property>
    <name>yarn.scheduler.capacity.root.dev.user-limit-factor</
name>
    <value>1</value>
</property>

<property>
    <name>yarn.scheduler.capacity.root.prod.maximum-capacity</
name>
    <value>100</value>
</property>

<property>
    <name>yarn.scheduler.capacity.root.dev.maximum-capacity</name>
    <value>100</value>
</property>
```

8. Change the state of the queue to be in running state:

```
<property>
    <name>yarn.scheduler.capacity.root.prod.state</name>
    <value>RUNNING</value>
</property>

<property>
    <name>yarn.scheduler.capacity.root.dev.state</name>
    <value>RUNNING</value>
</property>
```

9. Modify the queue ACLs and administrators of the queue:

```
<property>
    <name>yarn.scheduler.capacity.root.default.acl_submit_
applications</name>
    <value>*</value>
</property>

<property>
    <name>yarn.scheduler.capacity.root.prod.acl_submit_
applications</name>
    <value>*</value>
</property>

<property>
    <name>yarn.scheduler.capacity.root.dev.acl_submit_
applications</name>
     <value>*</value>
</property>

<property>
    <name>yarn.scheduler.capacity.root.default.acl_administer_
queue</name>
    <value>*</value>
</property>

<property>
    <name>yarn.scheduler.capacity.root.prod.acl_administer_queue</
name>
    <value>*</value>
</property>

<property>
    <name>yarn.scheduler.capacity.root.dev.acl_administer_queue</
name>
    <value>*</value>
</property>
```

10. Copy the `capacity-scheduler.xml` file across all nodes in the cluster and restart the YARN daemons.
11. Submit a test job to the `prod` queue as `d1` user, to test out the behavior and verify it on the ResourceManager page, as shown in the following screenshot:

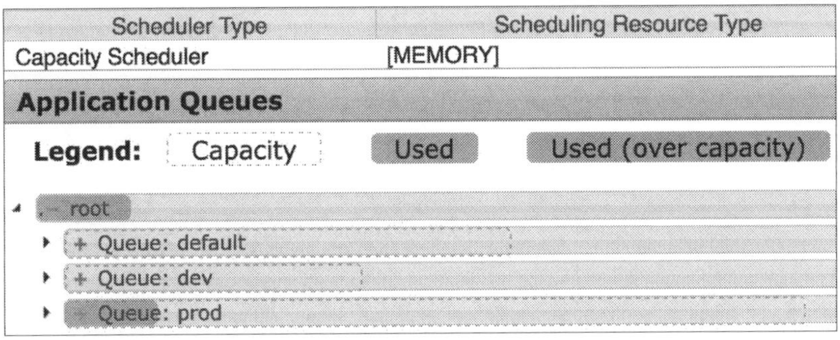

12. In the preceding configuration, we have changed only the required parameters and have left the defaults intact for `capacity-scheduler.xml`.

How it works...

In the preceding recipe, we configured Capacity Scheduler by setting up the `prod` and `dev` queues. We can have a child queue, called leaf queue, and jobs can only be submitted to leaf queues.

The total capacity of the cluster is 100% and is divided among queues totaling to 100%. If this is not correct, the ResourceManager will not start. Within each queue, the capacity used by each user can be controlled by user limit parameter.

See also

- The *Queue Mappings in Capacity Scheduler* recipe

Queuing mappings in Capacity Scheduler

In this recipe, we will be configuring users who can submit jobs to the queue and can also set rule for various job submissions.

Let's look at another use case where, if user `hadoop` submits a job, it should go to the `prod` queue and if any other users submits a job, it must go to `dev` queue. How can we set up something like this?

Getting ready

Make sure that the user has a running cluster with HDFS and YARN configured. It's best to have gone through at least the previous recipe.

How to do it...

1. Connect to the `master1.cyrus.com` Namenode and switch as user `hadoop`.
2. Edit the `capacity-scheduler.xml` allocation file as shown next:

```
<property>
    <name>yarn.scheduler.capacity.queue-mappings</name>
    <value>u:d1:dev,g:group1:default,u:hadoop:prod</value>
</property>
```

3. Make the preceding changes and copy the file across all nodes and restart the YARN daemons.
4. Whenever the `d1` user submits a job, it should go to the `dev` queue and for user `hadoop` to `prod` queue.
5. When a job is submitted to the cluster as user `hadoop` without specifying any queue as shown in the following command, the job will go to the `prod` queue:

```
$ yarn jar /opt/cluster/hadoop/share/hadoop/mapreduce/hadoop-mapreduce-examples-2.7.3.jar wordcount /file1.txt /out
```

6. Visit the ResourceManager to verify which queue the job got submitted to, as shown in the following screenshot, and that it is submitted to the `prod` queue:

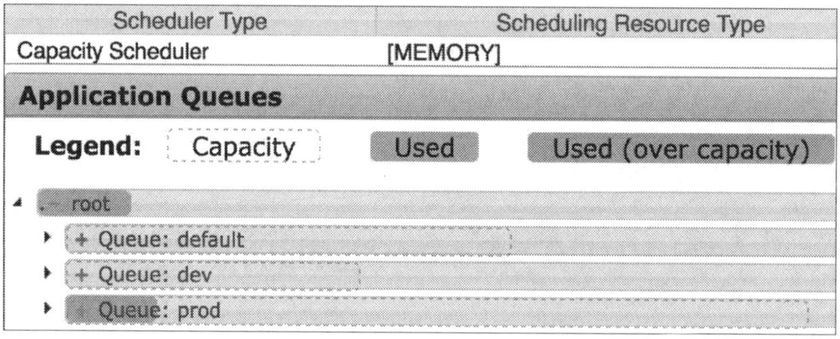

7. Now, edit the `capacity-scheduler.xml` file again to make the changes as shown next:

```
<property>
    <name>yarn.scheduler.capacity.queue-mappings</name>
    <value>u:%user:%user,u:user2:%primary_group</value>
</property>
```

8. The preceding configuration puts jobs into queues with usernames, and for user `user2`, it submits the job to the queue with the name of the primary group of the user.
9. Now, to submit job for user `hadoop` to the `prod` queue and all other jobs to the `dev` queue, we can use the following configuration:

```
<property>
    <name>yarn.scheduler.capacity.queue-mappings</name>
    <value>u:hadoop:prod,u:%user:dev</value>
</property>
```

How it works...

In this recipe, we have configured queue mappings, allowing us to classify where a job will go. The decision could be user-based, group-based, or exclude a match. In all the recipes, make sure that the permissions on the Hadoop configuration files are correct and synced across nodes.

In production or even with a cluster of more than 10 nodes, it becomes tedious to carry out changes and copy operation across nodes. Rather than carrying out changes manually, we use Puppet or Chef to push configuration changes across clusters. Puppet is bundled with the Bigtop, which is an infrastructure project for Hadoop deployment and configuration.

YARN and Mapred commands

In this recipe, we will cover a few of the important commands which can help with the administration of YARN.

Until now, after making any change to the configuration, we have restarted the YARN daemons. But, this is not always required if the parameters already exist in the configuration files. Updating the queue list and capacity can be done dynamically at run time. In this recipe, we will cover a few of the easy ways to make changes.

Getting ready

For this recipe, you will again need a running cluster with at least HDFS and YARN configured and have the queue setup as discussed in this chapter. It is recommended that users go through all the previous recipes in this chapter before following this particular recipe.

How to do it...

1. Connect to the `master1.cyrus.com` master node and switch as user `hadoop`.
2. The first thing is to list the queues configured using the following command:

```
$ mapred queue -list
```

3. The preceding command will list queues, along with their status as shown in the following screenshot:

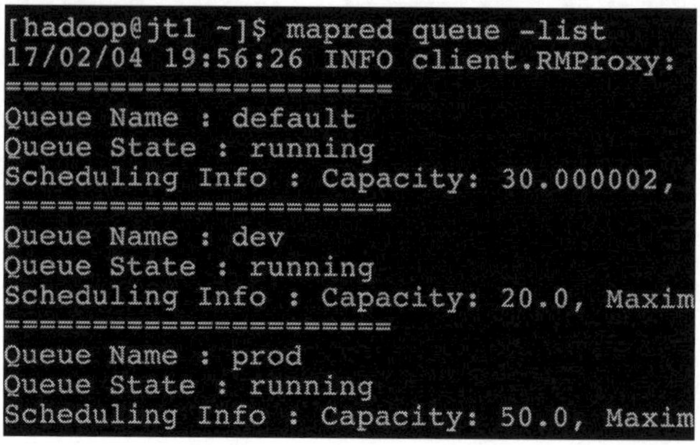
[hadoop@jt1 ~]$ mapred queue -list
17/02/04 19:56:26 INFO client.RMProxy:
======================
Queue Name : default
Queue State : running
Scheduling Info : Capacity: 30.000002,
======================
Queue Name : dev
Queue State : running
Scheduling Info : Capacity: 20.0, Maxim
======================
Queue Name : prod
Queue State : running
Scheduling Info : Capacity: 50.0, Maxim

4. To list the queue ACLs, use the following command:

   `$ mapred queue -showacls`

5. Now, the most important part of loading the changes is made to queue using the following command:

   `$ yarn rmadmin -refreshQueues`

6. The ACLs can be updated using the following command:

   `$ yarn rmadmin -refreshAdminAcls`

7. The Service ACLs can be refreshed using the following command:

   `$ yarn rmadmin -refreshServiceAcl`

8. The user to group mappings can also be updated using the following command:

   `$ yarn rmadmin -refreshUserToGroupsMappings`

How it works...

The preceding commands query the ResourceManager and fetch details on queues, users, groups, and ACLs. There are many other commands, which can be explored using the help option.

YARN label-based scheduling

In this recipe, we will configure YARN label-based scheduling. In a cluster, there can be a mixture of nodes with different configurations, some with more memory and CPU compared to other nodes in the cluster.

If we want to control which set of nodes a job executes, we need to assign labels to the nodes. A typical case could be that you want to run a Spark streaming job and want that to execute on nodes with high memory. For such a situation, we will configure the queue and assign a set of nodes for that, so that if a job is submitted to that queue, it executes on the nodes which have higher configuration in terms of memory and cores.

Getting ready

Make sure that the user has a running cluster with at least two Datanodes and YARN working perfectly. Users are expected to have a basic knowledge about queues in Hadoop, for which they can refer to the previous few recipes in this chapter.

How to do it...

1. Connect to the `master1.cyrus.com` master node and switch as user `hadoop`.
2. Create a directory on HDFS to store labels as follows:

```
$ hadoop fs -mkdir /node-labels
$ hadoop fs -chown -R Hadoop:hadoop /node-labels
$ hadoop fs -chmod -R 700 /node-labels
```

3. Edit the `yarn-site.xml` file to enable labels, as shown next:

```
<property>
    <name>yarn.node-labels.enabled</name>
    <value>true</value>
</property>
```

4. Edit the `yarn-site.xml` file to link it to the labels created in the first step. Make sure to give the absolute path to the directory:

```
<property>
    <name>yarn.node-labels.fs-store.root-dir</name>
    <value>hdfs://nn1.cluster1.com:9000/node-labels</value>
</property>
```

5. Save the changes and copy the file to all the nodes in the cluster and restart the daemons:

   ```
   $ yarn-stop.sh
   $ yarn-start.sh
   ```

6. Now, create labels for YARN using the following command:

   ```
   $ yarn rmadmin -addToClusterNodeLabels "memory"
   $ yarn cluster --list-node-labels
   ```

7. All labels are exclusive prior to Hadoop 2.8. Which means that a label can have only one rule for memory or CPU. We cannot have a shareable label, which is shown in the following command. But this will be supported soon:

   ```
   $ yarn rmadmin -addToClusterNodeLabels "memory(exclusive=true),cpu
   (exclusive=false)"
   ```

8. Assign labels to nodes using the following command:

   ```
   $ yarn rmadmin -replaceLabelsOnNode "dn1.cluster1.com=memory"
   ```

9. Now, the next step is to associate labels with the queues. For this, we will use the existing queues from the previous recipe and just make the changes for labels, as shown next. Edit the `capacity-scheduler.xml` file and add the following to it:

   ```
   <property>
       <name>yarn.scheduler.capacity.root.accessible-node-labels.
   memory.capacity</name>
       <value>100</value>
   </property>

   <property>
       <name>yarn.scheduler.capacity.root.prod.accessible-node-
   labels.memory.capacity</name>
       <value>100</value>
   </property>

   <property>
       <name>yarn.scheduler.capacity.root.prod.accessible-node-
   labels</name>
       <value>memory</value>
   </property>
   ```

10. After this, just refresh the queues using the following command:

    ```
    $ yarn rmadmin -refreshQueues
    ```

11. Verify the node status to make sure whether the node label has been assigned or not, as shown in the following screenshot:

```
[hadoop@jt1 hadoop]$ yarn node -status dn1.cluster1.com:57071
17/02/05 09:34:04 INFO client.RMProxy: Connecting to Resource
Node Report :
        Node-Id : dn1.cluster1.com:57071
        Rack : /default-rack
        Node-State : RUNNING
        Node-Http-Address : dn1.cluster1.com:8042
        Last-Health-Update : Sun 05/Feb/17 09:32:18:56IST
        Health-Report :
        Containers : 0
        Memory-Used : 0MB
        Memory-Capacity : 8192MB
        CPU-Used : 0 vcores
        CPU-Capacity : 8 vcores
        Node-Labels : memory
```

12. If no node label is specified for a child queue, it inherits the node label setting of its parent queue.

How it works...

Whenever a job is submitted to the `prod` queue, it will run on the nodes with the `memory` label. Node labels enable you to divide a cluster into subclusters, so that jobs can be run on nodes with specific characteristics. For example, you can use node labels to run memory-intensive jobs only on nodes with a larger amount of RAM.

If no node label is assigned to a queue, the applications submitted by the queue can run on any node without a node label, and applications that request labeled resources preempt nonlabeled applications on labeled nodes. Nonlabeled applications cannot preempt labeled applications running on labeled nodes.

YARN SLS

In this recipe, we will take a look at YARN simulator, which is useful to test and determine the load of YARN under various test conditions.

The YARN **Scheduler Load Simulator** (**SLS**) is such a tool, which can simulate large-scale YARN clusters and application loads in a single machine within a single JVM.

Getting ready

For this recipe, you will need a single machine with Hadoop installed. For this, readers can refer to the first chapter, where we have covered a single node cluster setup.

How to do it...

1. Connect to the `master1.cyrus.com` single node and switch as user `hadoop`.
2. The SLS is located at `$HADOOP_HOME/share/hadoop/tools/sls/`.
3. The SLS runs the simulator using the `sls-runner.xml` configuration file under `$HADOOP_HOME/etc/hadoop`.
4. A sample file is located at `$HADOOP_HOME/share/hadoop/tools/sls/sample-conf/sls-runner.xml`.
5. The `sls-runner.xml` file contains parameters to tune a number of threads, container memory, NM threads, and many other parameters or the choice of scheduler you want.
6. The simulator provides real-time metrics on web port `10001`.
7. To run the simulator, execute the command shown in the following screenshot:

```
[hadoop@jt1 hadoop]$ ./share/hadoop/tools/sls/bin/slsrun.sh --input-rumen=`pwd`/share/hadoop/tools/sls/sample-dat
a/2jobs2min-rumen-jh.json --output-dir=out_sim
17/02/05 10:08:03 INFO conf.Configuration: found resource core-site.xml at file:/opt/cluster/hadoop-2.7.3/etc/had
oop/core-site.xml
17/02/05 10:08:03 INFO security.Groups: clearing userToGroupsMap cache
17/02/05 10:08:03 INFO conf.Configuration: found resource yarn-site.xml at file:/opt/cluster/hadoop-2.7.3/etc/had
oop/yarn-site.xml
17/02/05 10:08:04 INFO event.AsyncDispatcher: Registering class org.apache.hadoop.yarn.server.resourcemanager.RMF
atalEventType for class org.apache.hadoop.yarn.server.resourcemanager.ResourceManager$RMFatalEventDispatcher
17/02/05 10:08:04 INFO security.NMTokenSecretManagerInRM: NMTokenKeyRollingInterval: 86400000ms and NMTokenKeyAct
ivationDelay: 900000ms
17/02/05 10:08:04 INFO security.RMContainerTokenSecretManager: ContainerTokenKeyRollingInterval: 86400000ms and
ontainerTokenKeyActivationDelay: 900000ms
17/02/05 10:08:04 INFO security.AMRMTokenSecretManager: AMRMTokenKeyRollingInterval: 86400000ms and AMRMTokenKey
ctivationDelay: 900000 ms
```

8. It writes many metrics, as shown in the following screenshot, which can be plotted using `gnuplot` or R Studio:

```
[hadoop@jt1 hadoop]$ ls -l out_sim/metrics/
total 356
-rw-rw-r-- 1 hadoop hadoop  2153 Feb  5 10:08 counter.scheduler.operation.allocate.csv
-rw-rw-r-- 1 hadoop hadoop  2153 Feb  5 10:08 counter.scheduler.operation.handle.APP_ADDED.csv
-rw-rw-r-- 1 hadoop hadoop  2153 Feb  5 10:08 counter.scheduler.operation.handle.APP_ATTEMPT_ADDED.csv
-rw-rw-r-- 1 hadoop hadoop  2153 Feb  5 10:08 counter.scheduler.operation.handle.APP_ATTEMPT_REMOVED.csv
-rw-rw-r-- 1 hadoop hadoop  2153 Feb  5 10:08 counter.scheduler.operation.handle.APP_REMOVED.csv
-rw-rw-r-- 1 hadoop hadoop  2153 Feb  5 10:08 counter.scheduler.operation.handle.CONTAINER_EXPIRED.csv
-rw-rw-r-- 1 hadoop hadoop  2153 Feb  5 10:08 counter.scheduler.operation.handle.CONTAINER_RESCHEDULED.csv
-rw-rw-r-- 1 hadoop hadoop  2356 Feb  5 10:08 counter.scheduler.operation.handle.csv
-rw-rw-r-- 1 hadoop hadoop  2153 Feb  5 10:08 counter.scheduler.operation.handle.DROP_RESERVATION.csv
-rw-rw-r-- 1 hadoop hadoop  2153 Feb  5 10:08 counter.scheduler.operation.handle.KILL_CONTAINER.csv
-rw-rw-r-- 1 hadoop hadoop  2153 Feb  5 10:08 counter.scheduler.operation.handle.NODE_ADDED.csv
-rw-rw-r-- 1 hadoop hadoop  2153 Feb  5 10:08 counter.scheduler.operation.handle.NODE_LABELS_UPDATE.csv
-rw-rw-r-- 1 hadoop hadoop  2153 Feb  5 10:08 counter.scheduler.operation.handle.NODE_REMOVED.csv
-rw-rw-r-- 1 hadoop hadoop  2153 Feb  5 10:08 counter.scheduler.operation.handle.NODE_RESOURCE_UPDATE.csv
-rw-rw-r-- 1 hadoop hadoop  2347 Feb  5 10:08 counter.scheduler.operation.handle.NODE_UPDATE.csv
-rw-rw-r-- 1 hadoop hadoop  2153 Feb  5 10:08 counter.scheduler.operation.handle.PREEMPT_CONTAINER.csv
-rw-rw-r-- 1 hadoop hadoop 14738 Feb  5 10:08 sampler.scheduler.operation.allocate.timecost.csv
-rw-rw-r-- 1 hadoop hadoop 14738 Feb  5 10:08 sampler.scheduler.operation.handle.APP_ADDED.timecost.csv
-rw-rw-r-- 1 hadoop hadoop 14738 Feb  5 10:08 sampler.scheduler.operation.handle.APP_ATTEMPT_ADDED.timecost.csv
-rw-rw-r-- 1 hadoop hadoop 14738 Feb  5 10:08 sampler.scheduler.operation.handle.APP_ATTEMPT_REMOVED.timecost.csv
-rw-rw-r-- 1 hadoop hadoop 14738 Feb  5 10:08 sampler.scheduler.operation.handle.APP_REMOVED.timecost.csv
```

How it works...

YARN simulator is designed to test YARN components and its behavior with a real-time metrics showing Vcores, threads per daemons, memory of containers, APP attempt, and kill event metrics. Make sure to stop all YARN daemons before running this test on the cluster, otherwise it will fail, with a ports already in use error.

6
Backup and Recovery

In this chapter, we will cover the following recipes:

- Initiating Namenode `saveNamespace`
- Using HDFS Image Viewer
- Fetching parameters which are in-effect
- Configuring HDFS and YARN logs
- Backing up and recovering Namenode
- Configuring Secondary Namenode
- Promoting Secondary Namenode to Primary
- Namenode recovery
- Namenode roll edits – Online mode
- Namenode roll edits – Offline mode
- Datanode recovery – Disk full
- Configuring NFS gateway to serve HDFS
- Recovering deleted files

Introduction

In this chapter, we will configure backup, restore processes, logs, and recovery using Secondary Namenode. Despite high availability, it is very important to back up data for adverse situations, irrespective of the notion of having a Secondary / backup node running and syncing constantly from the Primary node.

In a master-slave architecture, if the slave is syncing some data from the master and the data on the master gets corrupted, the slave will most likely pull the same corrupted data and now we will have two bad copies of the data. Although there are checks in place to account for corrupt data using checksums, it is still for production-critical data and so there must always be a business continuity or recovery plan.

Initiating Namenode saveNamespace

In our earlier recipes, we have configured the Hadoop cluster and have gone through various concepts on cluster operations. We saw that Namenode stores the metadata, which is a combination of the `fsimage` file and `edits` file and these two images are never merged by Namenode, unless it is restarted or there is some other node, such as Secondary Namenode, which does this. We will be covering Secondary Namenode in this chapter at a later stage.

Whenever the Namenode is started, it applies all the changes in the `edits` file to the `fsimage` file and starts with a clean `edits` file. Depending upon the size of the `edits` log, it could take a long time to start up Namenode and this adds to the total time a Namenode stays in the safemode. Safemode, as discussed in the earlier chapters, is not just a factor of `edits` file size, but also of the time taken to build up the bitmap, which is a mapping of blocks to the Datanodes.

> If the `edits` file cannot be applied to the `fsimage` file, the Namenode will not start.

In this recipe, we will see how to create a clean `fsimage` file, without stopping Namenode or using Secondary Namenode. It is good practice to keep the `fsimage` file clean and checkpointed to the latest changes as often as possible.

Getting ready

To step through the recipes in this chapter, make sure you have gone through the earlier recipes or at least have gone through the steps to install Hadoop cluster and understand the Namenode metadata.

How to do it...

1. Connect to the `master1` master node in the cluster and change to user `hadoop`.
2. Switch the Namenode to `safemode` and before doing that make sure that there are no critical jobs running in the cluster. In `safemode`, reads are unaffected but writes are blocked. Execute the following command:

   ```
   $ hdfs dfsadmin -safemode enter
   ```

3. Now, we will save the metadata of the cluster to make a consistent view with the help of the following command:

   ```
   $ hdfs dfsadmin -saveNamespace
   ```

   It will appear as shown in the following screenshot:

   ```
   [hadoop@master1 ~]$ hdfs dfsadmin -safemode enter
   Safe mode is ON
   [hadoop@master1 ~]$ hdfs dfsadmin -saveNamespace
   Save namespace successful
   ```

4. Now, switch back to the safe mode of the cluster using the following command:

   ```
   $ hdfs dfsadmin -savemode leave
   ```

In this recipe, we have put the Namenode into `safemode` and saved the metadata. Observe the changes in the sizes of the `edits` file, before and after the `saveNamespace` command.

How it works...

This method reduces the Namenode startup times, as it does not need to rebuild the entire metadata, which is a combination of namespace and bitmap (inodes structure) from the advertisements sent by the Datanodes. The namespace is persisted to disk and when we execute the preceding commands, it applies the `edits` to the `fsimage`. The bitmap is always stored only in the memory of the Namenode and when it is restarted, the entire space needs to be rebuilt. Depending upon the size of the cluster, that could take sufficient time, but the time to play the `edits` into `fsimage` is nullified by the preceding step. Also, a good practice is to roll the edits logs as shown in the following screenshot:

```
[hadoop@master1 ~]$ hdfs dfsadmin -rollEdits
Successfully rolled edit logs.
New segment starts at txid 132200
```

Using HDFS Image Viewer

It is important to understand how metadata of the Namenode is stored and what changes to the filesystem have been rolled into `fsimage` file. The `fsimage` file and `edits` file cannot be viewed using a `cat` or `vi` editor, but needs specialized tools to do so.

Hadoop, by default, comes with utilities to view the `fsimage` file and `edits` file and, in this recipe, we will cover how to use these tools.

Getting ready

To step through the recipe in this section, we need a Hadoop cluster set up and running. The reader is encouraged to understand the Namenode metadata and its location.

How to do it...

1. Connect to `master1.cyrus.com` master node in the cluster and switch to user `hadoop`.
2. Confirm the location of the Namenode metadata by looking into `hdfs-site.xml` file. There will be something similar to the following, which points to the location of metadata. We will see in a later recipe how to check the value of any parameter, without opening the configuration files. To know the location of where Namenode stores metadata, we can look at the section similar to the one shown as follows in the file `hdfs-site.xml`:

```
<property>
    <name>dfs.namenode.name.dir</name>
    <value>/data/namenode1</value>
</property>
```

3. Under the directory of Namenode metadata, you will see contents similar to the one shown in the following screenshot:

```
[hadoop@master1 ~]$ ls -l /data/namenode1/current/
total 1200
-rw-rw-r-- 1 hadoop hadoop 1048576 Mar 12 21:15 edits_inprogress_0000000000000132203
-rw-rw-r-- 1 hadoop hadoop   77888 Mar 12 21:01 fsimage_0000000000000132197
-rw-rw-r-- 1 hadoop hadoop      62 Mar 12 21:01 fsimage_0000000000000132197.md5
-rw-rw-r-- 1 hadoop hadoop   77888 Mar 12 21:03 fsimage_0000000000000132201
-rw-rw-r-- 1 hadoop hadoop      62 Mar 12 21:03 fsimage_0000000000000132201.md5
-rw-rw-r-- 1 hadoop hadoop       7 Mar 12 21:15 seen_txid
-rw-rw-r-- 1 hadoop hadoop     202 Mar 12 21:03 VERSION
```

4. Try to read the contents of the `fsimage` file and `edits` file by simply using the `cat` command. The output will be gibberish and does not make much sense.
5. In order to see the contents of `fsimage` file, use the following command:

```
$ hdfs oiv -i /data/namenode1/current/fsimage_xx -p XML -o fsimage.txt
```

6. The output of the preceding commands can have various file formats such as HTML or text. Users are recommended to explore the options.
7. Similarly, the contents of `edits` file can be seen using the following command:

```
$ hdfs oev -i /data/namenode/current/edits_xx -o edits.txt
```

How it works...

In this recipe, the preceding command allows user to read the contents of the metadata files and save it for future reference. We looked into ways to read the contents of the metadata files. This could be important in situations where we want to know what files have been checkpointed in the `fsimage` file and what are still in the `edits` file. The stats on these metadata files can be captured as shown in the following screenshot:

```
[hadoop@master1 current]$ hdfs oev -i edits_0000000000000000009-0000000000000000208 -o edits.txt -p stats
[hadoop@master1 current]$ head edits.txt
    VERSION                             : -63
    OP_ADD                          (   0): 33
    OP_RENAME_OLD                   (   1): 33
    OP_DELETE                       (   2): null
    OP_MKDIR                        (   3): null
    OP_SET_REPLICATION              (   4): null
    OP_DATANODE_ADD                 (   5): null
    OP_DATANODE_REMOVE              (   6): null
    OP_SET_PERMISSIONS              (   7): null
    OP_SET_OWNER                    (   8): null
```

To explore this better, copy any file to the HDFS filesystem and see whether it goes to the `edits` file and that, only when checkpointing happens, is it moved to `fsimage` file. You can parse the contents of the output files `fsimage.txt/edits.txt` using a simple Bash script to find the differences.

Fetching parameters which are in-effect

In this recipe, we look at how we can fetch the configured parameters in the Hadoop cluster, without going through the files.

The parameters are either default values, defined by files such as `hdfs-default.xml`, `core-default.xml`, `yarn-default.xml`, and so on, or defined explicitly in the configuration files such as `hdfs-site.xml`, `core-site.xml`, `mapred-site.xml`, and a few others. The default files are part of the packaged jars with the distribution, and any changes we make overrides them.

Getting ready

To step through the recipe, the user needs at least one node in the cluster and needs to make sure that the Hadoop environment variables are in place. It is not necessary to start any of the daemons in the cluster.

How to do it...

1. Connect to the `master1.cyrus.com` master node in the cluster and switch to user `hadoop`.

2. To find the value of any parameter, use the following command:

   $ hdfs getconf -confkey dfs.blocksize

   $ hdfs getconf -confkey dfs.replication

   $ hdfs getconf -confkey mapreduce.map.memory.mb

   $ hdfs getconf -confkey yarn.scheduler.maximum-allocation-mb

3. Using the preceding command, the user can fetch values for `yarn`, `mapreduce`, and `hdfs`.
4. Extract any of the default files from the JAR, to see all the available parameters for a particular component such as HDFS or YARN. This can be done using the steps shown in the following screenshot:

```
[hadoop@master1 ~]$ jar -ft $HADOOP_HOME/share/hadoop/hdfs/
hadoop-hdfs-2.7.2.jar | grep defaul
hdfs-default.xml
[hadoop@master1 ~]$ jar -ft $HADOOP_HOME/share/hadoop/hdfs/
hadoop-hdfs-2.7.2.jar | grep default
hdfs-default.xml
[hadoop@master1 ~]$ clear
[hadoop@master1 ~]$ jar -ft $HADOOP_HOME/share/hadoop/hdfs/
hadoop-hdfs-2.7.2.jar | grep default
hdfs-default.xml
[hadoop@master1 ~]$ jar -fx $HADOOP_HOME/share/hadoop/hdfs/
hadoop-hdfs-2.7.2.jar hdfs-default.xml
[hadoop@master1 ~]$ ls -l hdfs-default.xml
-rw-rw-r-- 1 hadoop hadoop 81867 May 16  2016 hdfs-default.
xml
```

How it works...

This is an easy method of knowing the value of any parameter in effect, as most parameters will be default and not show in the usual configuration files.

Often, the behavior of the cluster is not in accordance to the explicitly configured parameters which are just a minimal set of options from a list of hundreds of parameters. There are many inter-related configurations, which could be scripted without parsing files.

Configuring HDFS and YARN logs

In this recipe, we will configure logs for the HDFS and YARN, which is very important for troubleshooting and diagnosis of job failures.

For larger clusters, it is important to manage logs in terms of disk space usage, ease of retrieval, and performance. It is always recommended to store logs on separate hard disks and that too on RAIDed disks for performance. The disk thats used by Namenode or Datanodes for metadata or HDFS blocks must not be shared with for logs.

Getting ready

To complete the recipe, the user must have a running cluster with HDFS and YARN configured and have played around with *Chapter 1, Hadoop Architecture and Deployment* and *Chapter 2, Maintain Hadoop Cluster HDFS* to understand things better.

How to do it...

1. Connect to the `master1.cyrus.com` master node in the cluster and switch to user `hadoop`.
2. By default, the location of HDFS and YARN logs is defined by the settings `$HADOOP_HOME/logs` and `$YARN_LOG_DIR/logs` in file `hadoop-env.xml` and `yarn-env.sh`, respectively.
3. To change the location of logs, modify the `hadoo-env.sh` file and add the following line:

   ```
   export HADOOP_LOG_DIR=/var/log/hadoop
   ```

4. Make sure that the directory `/var/log/hadoop` is owned by the user `hadoop` and is on a separate disk for performance.
5. Copy the `hadoop-env.xml` file to all the nodes in the cluster and make sure that the log directory exists with correct permissions on all nodes.
6. For YARN, there is no need to do any changes as the parameter `YARN_LOG_DIR` points to `HADOOP_LOG_DIR` by default.
7. Restart the daemons on the cluster for changes to take effect.

This is a very basic log configuration for changing the log location. In addition to this, one can change the verbosity and the rotation policy of the logs using the `log4j.properties` file as discussed in the following steps:

1. The size of the logs and log policy handler can be defined, as shown in the following screenshot:

   ```
   # Rolling File Appender - cap space usage at 5gb.
   #
   hadoop.log.maxfilesize=256MB
   hadoop.log.maxbackupindex=20
   log4j.appender.RFA=org.apache.log4j.RollingFileAppender
   log4j.appender.RFA.File=${hadoop.log.dir}/${hadoop.log.file}

   log4j.appender.RFA.MaxFileSize=${hadoop.log.maxfilesize}
   ```

2. The log file naming convention is defined by the parameters as shown in the following screenshot:

```
# Pattern format: Date LogLevel LoggerName LogMessage
log4j.appender.RFA.layout.ConversionPattern=%d{ISO8601} %p %c: %m%n
# Debugging Pattern format
#log4j.appender.RFA.layout.ConversionPattern=%d{ISO8601} %-5p %c{2} (%F:%M(%L)) - %m%n
```

3. The log rotation policy can be defined as shown in the following screenshot:

```
# Rollover at midnight
log4j.appender.DRFA.DatePattern=.yyyy-MM-dd

log4j.appender.DRFA.layout=org.apache.log4j.PatternLayout
```

4. The user can enable Block Manager logs to track block changes, but this will generate too many logs on a large cluster. This can be done as shown in the following screenshot:

```
#
# HDFS block state change log from block manager
#
# Uncomment the following to suppress normal block state change
# messages from BlockManager in NameNode.
#log4j.logger.BlockStateChange=WARN
```

5. The user can enable security and audit logs for HDFS and MapReduce using the configuration, as shown in the following screenshot:

```
# hdfs audit logging
#
hdfs.audit.logger=INFO,NullAppender
hdfs.audit.log.maxfilesize=256MB
hdfs.audit.log.maxbackupindex=20
```

6. In addition to this, there can be many other settings for YARN Resource Manager application logs and HTTP server logs. The retention days can be configured to keep logs for a week or more.

How it works...

By default, the logging level is INFO, but it can be changed to **DEBUG**, **WARN**, and **CRIT**. However, one must be very careful while tuning the verbosity of logs, as sometimes too many logs can cause issues.

In addition to this, it is important to understand and configure YARN log aggregation as discussed in *Chapter 3, Maintain Hadoop Cluster – YARN and MapReduce*.

See also

- The *YARN log aggregation* recipe in *Chapter 3, Maintain Hadoop Cluster – YARN and MapReduce*

Backing up and recovering Namenode

In this recipe, we will look at how to backup and restore Namenode. As discussed previously, the importance of backup, despite having high availability, will cover some ways to restore the backup. The backup could be as simple as just a copy of the metadata to the other system and then copying it back on the new node and starting the Namenode process or using the import command to point to the backup location and executing the command to copy the contents to the right location with the right permissions.

Getting ready

For this recipe, you will again need a running cluster with HDFS configured in the cluster. Readers are recommended to read the previous recipes in this chapter to understand this recipe better.

How to do it...

1. Connect to the `master1.cyrus.com` master node and switch to user `hadoop`.
2. For backup, copy the contents of the directory pointed by `dfs.namenode.name.dir` to any other location, preferably outside the system. This could be doing a simple `scp` command across the machines or by using a mount point, imported as NFS share. For availability, it is recommended to have an external NFS share.
3. Mount the NFS export on the Namenode and ensure that it is owned by user `hadoop`.
4. Let's say that the directory name is mounted at `/data/backup`, which is an NFS export from the other system.
5. Now we have two options to write a backup to the location `/data/backup`. One is to use a simple recursive `cp` command or setup `rsync` between two directories.
6. The other recommended and usual way, is to use the comma-separated list of directories under `dfs.namenode.name.dir`. They are a good candidate to be used as a backup location in case of disaster.
7. In order to restore this to a new Namenode, we simply import the metadata from the backup location. Add the following lines to the `hdfs-site.xml` file:

```
<property>
    <name>fs.checkpoint.dir</name>
    <value>/data/backup</value>
</property>
```

8. Do not format the Namenode and make sure that the directories for Namenode metadata are empty, else the import will not work.
9. To import the backed-up metadata to the Namenode metadata location, execute the following command:

   ```
   $ hdfs namenode -importCheckpoint
   ```

10. The Namenode process will be automatically started after the import.
11. This method is a neat way of bootstrapping the Namenode, as quickly as possible, without loss of any data. See the following screenshot, for a glimpse of the output:

```
************************************************************/
17/03/14 06:55:57 INFO namenode.NameNode: registered UNIX signal handlers for [TERM, HUP, INT]
17/03/14 06:55:57 INFO namenode.NameNode: createNameNode [-importCheckpoint]
17/03/14 06:55:57 INFO impl.MetricsConfig: loaded properties from hadoop-metrics2.properties
17/03/14 06:55:57 INFO impl.MetricsSystemImpl: Scheduled snapshot period at 10 second(s).
17/03/14 06:55:57 INFO impl.MetricsSystemImpl: NameNode metrics system started
17/03/14 06:55:57 INFO namenode.NameNode: fs.defaultFS is hdfs://master1.cyrus.com:9000
```

How it works...

In the preceding recipe, we configured backup and restored it on a new node using the `import` command. Obviously, for Namenode restore to be successful, we need to configure network reachability, operating system stack, routing and, so on.

To reduce the switch over or failure time, there are spare machines preconfigured with the same IP, hostname, and so on, on standby to be in action ASAP.

It is very important to have the Namenode metadata stored on NFS, so as to recover it immediately by launching a new node and importing the metadata.

See also

- The *Namenode HA using shared storage* recipe in *Chapter 4, High Availability*.

Configuring Secondary Namenode

In this recipe, we will be configuring Secondary Namenode, which is a checkpointing node. In the very first recipe of this chapter, we say that it is critical to manage metadata and keep it clean as often as possible.

The Secondary Namenode can have multiple roles such as backup node, checkpointing node, and so on. The most common is the checkpointing node, which pulls the metadata from Namenode and also does merging of the `fsimage` and `edits` logs, which is called the check pointing process and pushes the rolled copy back to the Primary Namenode.

Getting ready

Make sure that the user has a running cluster with HDFS and has one more node to be used as Secondary. The `master2` node, from the *Namenode HA using shared storage* recipe in *Chapter 4, High Availability* can be used as a Secondary Namenode or Secondary Namenode can co-exist with the Primary Namenode.

When running Namenode HA, there is no need to run Secondary Namenode, as the standby Namenode will do the job.

How to do it...

1. Connect to the `master2.cyrus.com` Namenode and switch to user `hadoop`. If the user has not used this node initially, make sure it has Hadoop installed and have the configuration files copied from the Primary Namenode.
2. Edit the `hdfs-site.xml` configuration file and add the lines given in the next steps to the file. Firstly, specify the Primary Namenode webserver address:

```
<property>
    <name>dfs.http.address</name>
    <value>master1.cyrus.com:50070</value>
</property>
```

3. Now, add the Secondary Namenode webserver entry to the file as follows:

```
<property>
    <name>dfs.secondary.http.address</name>
    <value>master2.cyrus.com:50090</value>
</property>
```

4. Define the time period for the check point interval—defaults to 1 hour:

```
<property>
    <name>fs.checkpoint.period</name>
    <value>3600</value>
</property>
```

5. Now, define the directory, where the merge process will happen on the Secondary Namenode side as shown in the following command—make sure the directory is owned by the user `hadoop`:

```
<property>
    <name>fs.checkpoint.dir</name>
    <value>/data/secondary</value>
</property>
```

6. Now, configure a location for the edits logs on the Secondary node as shown here and make sure the ownership of the directory is correct:

```
<property>
    <name>fs.checkpoint.edits.dir</name>
    <value>/data/secedits</value>
</property>
```

7. Once the configurations are in place, execute the following command to make sure the Secondary Namenode can pull data from Primary Namenode:

```
$ hdfs secondarynamenode -checkpoint force
```

8. The preceding command with a `-force` option, will ask the secondary to pull metadata from Primary Namenode irrespective of the size of the `fsimage` and `edits` file or the number of transactions in the edit logs.
9. Once we are sure that the Secondary has been configured correctly, start the daemon on the Secondary Namenode, as shown in the screenshot below:

```
$ hadoop-daemon.sh start secondarynamenode
```

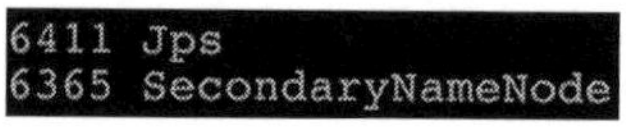
6411 Jps
6365 SecondaryNameNode

How it works...

In this recipe, we have configured the Secondary Namenode to fetch the `fsimage` and `edits` file from the Primary and merge them, and then push it back to the Primary Namenode.

The Secondary Namenode does check pointing based upon the size of the edits or the time period from last check point. Both of these parameters `fs.checkpoint.period` and `dfs.namenode.checkpoint.txns` are configurable.

In production, especially in Hadoop 2.x, we always prefer using HA and then have a Secondary node. HA and Secondary Namenode are mutually exclusive.

Promoting Secondary Namenode to Primary

In this recipe, we will cover how to promote Secondary Namenode to be Primary Namenode.

In production, Datanodes will never talk to the Secondary and only the Primary node knows about the data block mappings. In a non-HA setup, if the Primary Namenode fails, there will be outage, but we can still reduce the downtime by quickly promoting the Secondary to be Primary.

Getting ready

For this recipe, make sure you have completed the previous recipe on Secondary Namenode configuration and have a running Secondary Namenode.

How to do it...

1. Connect to the `master2.cyrus.com` master node and switch to user `hadoop`.
2. The first thing is to check the `seen_txid` file under location `/data/secondary/current/`, to make sure until what point is the Secondary in sync with Primary.
3. If the lag is high, it is important that the metadata is copied from the NFS mount of the Primary Namenode. That is the reason of having at least one Primary Namenode metadata directory mount on NFS.
4. Change the hostname and IP address of Secondary to be that of Primary. Edit the file `/etc/sysconfig/network` and change the hostname line as follows:

   ```
   HOSTNAME=master2.cyrus.com
     to
   HOSTNAME=master1.cyrus.com
   ```

5. Now, update the IP address of the secondary to be of the primary node. Edit the file `/etc/sysconfig/network-scripts/ifcfg-eth0` as follows:

   ```
   $ IPADDR=10.0.0.104
   ```

6. Save the changes and restart the network service using the following command:

   ```
   $ sudo /etc/init.d/network restart
   ```

7. Make sure that the hostname has been modified and the IP address updated, as shown in the following screenshot:

```
[ec2-user@master1 ~]$ hostname -f
master1.cyrus.com
[ec2-user@master1 ~]$ ifconfig
eth0      Link encap:Ethernet  HWaddr 0A:D3:E1:29:9D:97
          inet addr:10.0.0.104  Bcast:10.0.0.255  Mask:255.255.255.0
          inet6 addr: fe80::8d3:e1ff:fe29:9d97/64 Scope:Link
```

8. Update the `hdfs-site.xml` file to point to the metadata location directory for Primary Namenode. Refer to the *Configuring Secondary Namenode* recipe for more details.

   Now, we will consider the following code:

   ```
   <property>
       <name>fs.checkpoint.dir</name>
       <value>/data/secondary</value>
   </property>
   ```

And change it to the following:

```
<property>
    <name>dfs.namenode.name.dir</name>
    <value>/data/secondary</value>
</property>
```

9. Start the Namenode daemon and check the Namenode logs for updates.

How it works...

The reason for changing the DNS name and IP address of the Secondary to the Primary is to avoid changing the configuration on all the Datanodes in the cluster and the need to restart them.

Depending upon the consistency of the metadata kept by the Secondary, the new Namenode could be brought up either from the Secondary metadata save or the directory which is written directly by the Primary name to the NFS location.

Consider the following example:

```
<property>
    <name>dfs.namenode.name.dir</name>
    <value>/data/namenode1,/data/namenode2</value>
</property>
```

Here, `/data/namenode2` is a NFS exported mount point.

See also

- The *Namenode HA using shared storage* recipe in *Chapter 4, High Availability*.
- The *Namenode saveNamespace* recipe
- The *Namenode restore* recipe

Namenode recovery

In this recipe, we will cover how to recover Namenode from corrupted `edits` or `fsimage`. During the Namenode startup, the `edits` is check pointed into the `fsimage` image . What if the image is corrupted? Will the Namenode boot up?

In a worst-case scenario, it recovers as much data as possible and removes any corrupted entries from metadata so that the Namenode can start up.

Getting ready

For this recipe, make sure you have completed the recipe on Hadoop cluster setup, *Chapter 1, Hadoop Architecture and Deployment*, and have at least HDFS running perfectly.

How to do it...

1. Connect to the `master1.cyrus.com` master node and switch to user `hadoop`.
2. While attempting to start the Namenode, it just fails with bad or corrupted blocks and we have no way to bring the Namenode up.
3. Remember we cannot run `fsck` if Namenode is not running.
4. As a last resort, we will try to skip the missing or corrupted metadata and start the Namenode with a cleaner image.
5. To start the Namenode recover process, use the following command:

   ```
   $ hdfs namenode -recover
   ```

6. Namenode will prompt you, asking whether you are sure or not. Enter `yes` to continue.
7. It will prompt you with the option on what to do with the corrupt blocks, to skip them or abort the process.
8. Once the recovery process is complete, it reports the processed inodes, and the corrupted blocks are removed. Blocks here means the metadata blocks and if metadata is gone, there is no way to reach the data blocks. This is shown in the following screenshot:

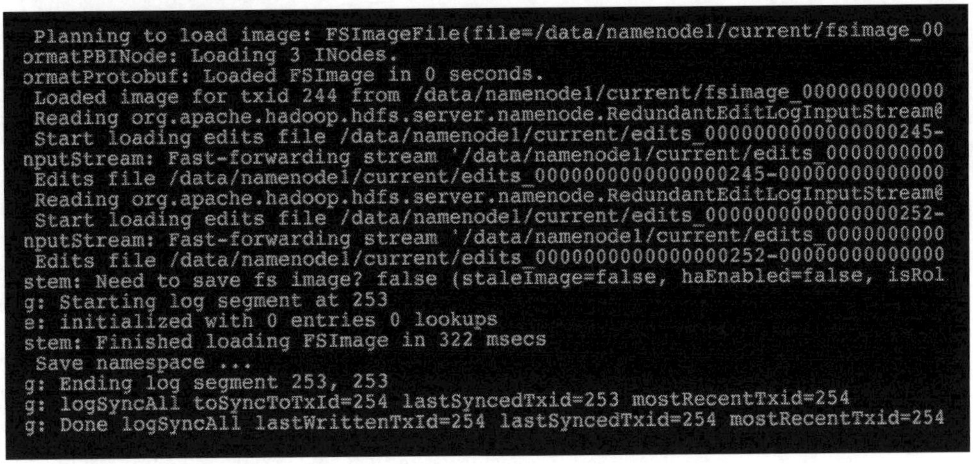
Planning to load image: FSImageFile(file=/data/namenode1/current/fsimage_00
ormatPBINode: Loading 3 INodes.
ormatProtobuf: Loaded FSImage in 0 seconds.
Loaded image for txid 244 from /data/namenode1/current/fsimage_000000000000
Reading org.apache.hadoop.hdfs.server.namenode.RedundantEditLogInputStream@
Start loading edits file /data/namenode1/current/edits_0000000000000000245-
nputStream: Fast-forwarding stream '/data/namenode1/current/edits_0000000000
Edits file /data/namenode1/current/edits_0000000000000000245-00000000000000
Reading org.apache.hadoop.hdfs.server.namenode.RedundantEditLogInputStream@
Start loading edits file /data/namenode1/current/edits_0000000000000000252-
nputStream: Fast-forwarding stream '/data/namenode1/current/edits_0000000000
Edits file /data/namenode1/current/edits_0000000000000000252-00000000000000
stem: Need to save fs image? false (staleImage=false, haEnabled=false, isRol
g: Starting log segment at 253
e: initialized with 0 entries 0 lookups
stem: Finished loading FSImage in 322 msecs
Save namespace ...
g: Ending log segment 253, 253
g: logSyncAll toSyncToTxId=254 lastSyncedTxid=253 mostRecentTxid=254
g: Done logSyncAll lastWrittenTxId=254 lastSyncedTxid=254 mostRecentTxid=254

9. Start the Namenode process and it should be all good to go. Give it some time to come out of safe mode and check for any missing blocks using the `fsck` commands.

How it works...

The recovery process is not recommended in production, as it is a last resort to recover data. It could be wise to skip few files and recover as much data as possible. It is always recommended to keep multiple copies of metadata, so that in case one copy gets corrupted, we can use the other copy to restore it.

Namenode roll edits – online mode

In this recipe, we will take a look at how to roll edits and keep the size of the metadata to a minimum. Over a period of time, the number of `edits` files grow and also the Namenode keeps old versions of `fsimage` file. In a large busy cluster, the edits files could be large, with each of about 1 GB.

This will utilize disk space on Namenode and can cause disk issues in the longer run of the cluster. Also, if the Secondary Namenode is not configured or is not working correctly, these `edits` files will be in large numbers, with each file of approximately 1 million transactions. Due to this, the Namenode start time will increase and Namenode might not even start if the memory is not sufficient to do the checkpoint operation.

Getting ready

For this recipe, make sure that you have completed the recipe on Hadoop cluster setup, *Chapter 1, Hadoop Architecture and Deployment*, and have at least HDFS running for a few hour with some data on HDFS.

How to do it...

1. Connect to the `master1.cyrus.com` master node and switch to user `hadoop`.
2. The location of the metadata directory is pointed by `dfs.namenode.name.dir`, which, in our case, is as shown in the following screenshot. We can see the directory is an NFS mount:

```
[hadoop@master1 ~]$ hdfs getconf -confkey dfs.namenode.name.dir
file:/data/namenode1,file:/data/namenode2
[hadoop@master1 ~]$ df -h | grep namenode
/dev/xvdb1              20G   47M   19G   1% /data/namenode1
filer.cyrus.com:/nfs_  7.8G  4.5G  3.3G  58% /data/namenode2
```

3. To safeguard the data, remove one of the metadata directories from the Namenode by modifying the `dfs.namenode.name.dir` parameter, to just have one directory. Restart the Namenode daemon.

4. Then do a listing on the contents of the directory and see that there are few `edits` files and `fsimage` files in the directory, as shown in the following screenshot. The users will have a different set of files:

```
[hadoop@master1 ~]$ hdfs getconf -confkey dfs.namenode.name.dir
file:/data/namenode1
[hadoop@master1 ~]$ ls -l /data/namenode1/current/
total 4120
-rw-rw-r-- 1 hadoop hadoop 1048576 Apr 14 01:15 edits_0000000000000000001-0000000000000000001
-rw-rw-r-- 1 hadoop hadoop 1048576 Apr 18 01:05 edits_0000000000000000002-0000000000000000002
-rw-rw-r-- 1 hadoop hadoop 1048576 Apr 18 01:10 edits_0000000000000000003-0000000000000000217
-rw-rw-r-- 1 hadoop hadoop 1048576 Apr 18 01:31 edits_inprogress_0000000000000000218
-rw-rw-r-- 1 hadoop hadoop     317 Apr 14 01:15 fsimage_0000000000000000000
-rw-rw-r-- 1 hadoop hadoop      62 Apr 14 01:15 fsimage_0000000000000000000.md5
-rw-rw-r-- 1 hadoop hadoop     317 Apr 18 01:05 fsimage_0000000000000000001
-rw-rw-r-- 1 hadoop hadoop      62 Apr 18 01:05 fsimage_0000000000000000001.md5
-rw-rw-r-- 1 hadoop hadoop       4 Apr 18 01:31 seen_txid
-rw-rw-r-- 1 hadoop hadoop     215 Apr 18 01:05 VERSION
```

5. We can see that there are three `edits` files, one `edits_inprogress` file, and two `fsimage` files with their checksum files. Notice the `edits` file sequence number, it is at `218` for in-progress `edits` file.
6. These `edits` files can grow big, as they keep up to 1 million transactions, which will be approximately 1 GB in size. We can roll these files manually to keep them small using the `hdfs dfsadmin -rollEdits` command, as shown in the following screenshot:

```
[hadoop@master1 ~]$ hdfs dfsadmin -rollEdits
Successfully rolled edit logs.
New segment starts at txid 221
[hadoop@master1 ~]$ ls -l /data/namenode1/current/
total 5148
-rw-rw-r-- 1 hadoop hadoop 1048576 Apr 14 01:15 edits_0000000000000000001-0000000000000000001
-rw-rw-r-- 1 hadoop hadoop 1048576 Apr 18 01:05 edits_0000000000000000002-0000000000000000002
-rw-rw-r-- 1 hadoop hadoop 1048576 Apr 18 01:10 edits_0000000000000000003-0000000000000000217
-rw-rw-r-- 1 hadoop hadoop 1048576 Apr 18 01:31 edits_0000000000000000218-0000000000000000218
-rw-rw-r-- 1 hadoop hadoop      42 Apr 18 01:36 edits_0000000000000000219-0000000000000000220
-rw-rw-r-- 1 hadoop hadoop 1048576 Apr 18 01:36 edits_inprogress_0000000000000000221
```

If you look at the preceding screenshot, the `edits` file is now at `221` for `edits` in progress. Notice that the `seen_txid` file keeps track of all the files it has seen.

Now the question is, can we remove the old `edits`? Can all the `edits` files from `edits` segment 001 to 220 be removed? Let's try that.

7. Move all the `edits` files, expect the one which is in progress, to another directory as shown in the following screenshot. Do not delete it:

```
[hadoop@master1 ~]$ mv /data/namenode1/current/edits_0000000000000000* ~/image_backup/
[hadoop@master1 ~]$ ls -l /data/namenode1/current/
total 1048
-rw-rw-r-- 1 hadoop hadoop 1048576 Apr 18 01:36 edits_inprogress_0000000000000000221
-rw-rw-r-- 1 hadoop hadoop     317 Apr 14 01:15 fsimage_0000000000000000000
-rw-rw-r-- 1 hadoop hadoop      62 Apr 14 01:15 fsimage_0000000000000000000.md5
-rw-rw-r-- 1 hadoop hadoop     317 Apr 18 01:05 fsimage_0000000000000000001
-rw-rw-r-- 1 hadoop hadoop      62 Apr 18 01:05 fsimage_0000000000000000001.md5
-rw-rw-r-- 1 hadoop hadoop       4 Apr 18 01:36 seen_txid
-rw-rw-r-- 1 hadoop hadoop     215 Apr 18 01:05 VERSION
```

8. Now, restart the Namenode and it will fail with a message as shown in the following screenshot. Why is the Namenode looking for transaction ID 2?

```
2017-04-18 01:41:45,012 INFO org.apache.hadoop.metrics2.impl.MetricsSystemImpl: NameNode metrics system sto
2017-04-18 01:41:45,012 INFO org.apache.hadoop.metrics2.impl.MetricsSystemImpl: NameNode metrics system shu
2017-04-18 01:41:45,012 ERROR org.apache.hadoop.hdfs.server.namenode.NameNode: Failed to start namenode.
java.io.IOException: Gap in transactions. Expected to be able to read up until at least txid 221 but unable
 txid 2
```

9. If we look at the position of `fsimage`, it is at `fsimage_0..001`. So, when the Namenode comes up, it looks for all the transaction IDs from its present `fsimage` position, which is 001 to `edits_in_progress` ID, which is 221 and it sees a gap, because we moved the `edits` files, and fails.
10. Now, move the `fsimage` files back and start the Namenode, and it will succeed.
11. Namenode has created a new `fsimage_00223` and all the `edits` are in tact as shown in the following screenshot:

```
[hadoop@master1 ~]$ ls -l /data/namenode1/current/
total 6184
-rw-rw-r-- 1 hadoop hadoop 1048576 Apr 18 01:58 edits_0000000000000000001-0000000000000000001
-rw-rw-r-- 1 hadoop hadoop 1048576 Apr 18 01:58 edits_0000000000000000002-0000000000000000002
-rw-rw-r-- 1 hadoop hadoop 1048576 Apr 18 01:58 edits_0000000000000000003-0000000000000000217
-rw-rw-r-- 1 hadoop hadoop 1048576 Apr 18 01:58 edits_0000000000000000218-0000000000000000218
-rw-rw-r-- 1 hadoop hadoop      42 Apr 18 01:58 edits_0000000000000000219-0000000000000000220
-rw-rw-r-- 1 hadoop hadoop 1048576 Apr 18 01:36 edits_0000000000000000221-0000000000000000221
-rw-rw-r-- 1 hadoop hadoop      42 Apr 18 02:00 edits_0000000000000000222-0000000000000000223
-rw-rw-r-- 1 hadoop hadoop 1048576 Apr 18 02:00 edits_inprogress_0000000000000000224
-rw-rw-r-- 1 hadoop hadoop     317 Apr 14 01:15 fsimage_0000000000000000000
-rw-rw-r-- 1 hadoop hadoop      62 Apr 14 01:15 fsimage_0000000000000000000.md5
-rw-rw-r-- 1 hadoop hadoop     317 Apr 18 01:05 fsimage_0000000000000000001
-rw-rw-r-- 1 hadoop hadoop      62 Apr 18 01:05 fsimage_0000000000000000001.md5
-rw-rw-r-- 1 hadoop hadoop    2389 Apr 18 02:00 fsimage_0000000000000000223
-rw-rw-r-- 1 hadoop hadoop      62 Apr 18 02:00 fsimage_0000000000000000223.md5
```

12. To save the Namespace, we can use the following commands:

```
$ hdfs dfsadmin -safemode enter

$ hdfs dfsadmin -saveNamespace

$ hdfs dfsadmin -safemode leave
```

13. This will manually roll the `edits` into the `fsimage` file without restarting the Namenode.

What if we now remove the old `edits` files? Will the Namenode work correctly? The directory is shown in following screenshot:

```
[hadoop@master1 ~]$ ls -l /data/namenode1/current/
total 6184
-rw-rw-r-- 1 hadoop hadoop 1048576 Apr 18 01:58 edits_0000000000000000001-0000000000000000001
-rw-rw-r-- 1 hadoop hadoop 1048576 Apr 18 01:58 edits_0000000000000000002-0000000000000000002
-rw-rw-r-- 1 hadoop hadoop 1048576 Apr 18 01:58 edits_0000000000000000003-0000000000000000217
-rw-rw-r-- 1 hadoop hadoop 1048576 Apr 18 01:58 edits_0000000000000000218-0000000000000000218
-rw-rw-r-- 1 hadoop hadoop      42 Apr 18 01:58 edits_0000000000000000219-0000000000000000220
-rw-rw-r-- 1 hadoop hadoop 1048576 Apr 18 01:36 edits_0000000000000000221-0000000000000000221
-rw-rw-r-- 1 hadoop hadoop      42 Apr 18 02:00 edits_0000000000000000222-0000000000000000223
-rw-rw-r-- 1 hadoop hadoop 1048576 Apr 18 02:00 edits_inprogress_0000000000000000224
-rw-rw-r-- 1 hadoop hadoop     317 Apr 14 01:15 fsimage_0000000000000000000
-rw-rw-r-- 1 hadoop hadoop      62 Apr 14 01:15 fsimage_0000000000000000000.md5
-rw-rw-r-- 1 hadoop hadoop     317 Apr 18 01:05 fsimage_0000000000000000001
-rw-rw-r-- 1 hadoop hadoop      62 Apr 18 01:05 fsimage_0000000000000000001.md5
-rw-rw-r-- 1 hadoop hadoop    2389 Apr 18 02:00 fsimage_0000000000000000223
-rw-rw-r-- 1 hadoop hadoop      62 Apr 18 02:00 fsimage_0000000000000000223.md5
```

14. Move all the `edits` except `edits_in_progress` and restart the Namenode. Now, the Namenode will start because `fsimage` is at position 223 and `edits_in_progress` is at 224. There is no gap, as shown in the following screenshot:

```
[hadoop@master1 ~]$ mv /data/namenode1/current/edits_0000000000000000* ~/image_backup/
[hadoop@master1 ~]$ ls -l /data/namenode1/current/
total 1056
-rw-rw-r-- 1 hadoop hadoop 1048576 Apr 18 02:00 edits_inprogress_0000000000000000224
-rw-rw-r-- 1 hadoop hadoop     317 Apr 14 01:15 fsimage_0000000000000000000
-rw-rw-r-- 1 hadoop hadoop      62 Apr 14 01:15 fsimage_0000000000000000000.md5
-rw-rw-r-- 1 hadoop hadoop     317 Apr 18 01:05 fsimage_0000000000000000001
-rw-rw-r-- 1 hadoop hadoop      62 Apr 18 01:05 fsimage_0000000000000000001.md5
-rw-rw-r-- 1 hadoop hadoop    2389 Apr 18 02:00 fsimage_0000000000000000223
-rw-rw-r-- 1 hadoop hadoop      62 Apr 18 02:00 fsimage_0000000000000000223.md5
```

Now, we need to understand why there are so many edits and `fsimage` files kept. The number of transactions kept in addition to what is required by Namenode to start is controlled by few parameters. This is done for HA Namenode to catch up in case of lags, but we can tune it using the parameters `dfs.namenode.num.extra.edits.retained` and `dfs.namenode.max.extra.edits.segments.retained`.

15. Let the Namenode run for some time and we can see that the number of `edits` files will grow, as shown in the following screenshot:

```
[hadoop@master1 ~]$ ls -l /data/namenode1/current/
total 6172
-rw-rw-r-- 1 hadoop hadoop 1048576 Apr 18 02:12 edits_0000000000000000224-0000000000000000224
-rw-rw-r-- 1 hadoop hadoop      42 Apr 18 02:12 edits_0000000000000000225-0000000000000000226
-rw-rw-r-- 1 hadoop hadoop 1048576 Apr 18 02:06 edits_0000000000000000227-0000000000000000227
-rw-rw-r-- 1 hadoop hadoop 1048576 Apr 18 02:15 edits_0000000000000000228-0000000000000000228
-rw-rw-r-- 1 hadoop hadoop 1048576 Apr 18 02:43 edits_0000000000000000229-0000000000000000229
-rw-rw-r-- 1 hadoop hadoop      42 Apr 18 02:50 edits_0000000000000000230-0000000000000000231
-rw-rw-r-- 1 hadoop hadoop     788 Apr 18 04:49 edits_0000000000000000232-0000000000000000241
-rw-rw-r-- 1 hadoop hadoop 1048576 Apr 18 04:49 edits_0000000000000000242-0000000000000000242
```

16. Connect to Namenode and modify the `hdfs-site.xml` file with the properties as follows:

```
<property>
    <name>dfs.namenode.num.extra.edits.retained</name>
    <value>4</value>
</property>
    <property>
    <name>dfs.namenode.max.extra.edits.segments.retained</name>
    <value>2</value>
</property>
```

17. Then, on Namenode execute the following commands to do the manual check point:

```
$ hdfs dfsadmin -safemode enter
$ hdfs dfsadmin -saveNamespace
$ hdfs dfsadmin -safemode leave
```

18. Take a look at the `edits` files and you will see that now the number of files retained is just 3, as shown in the following screenshot. Remember, this number could vary in your cluster, as this is not the number of `edit` files, but the number of transactions to keep. The default is, each `edit` can contain about 1 million transactions and the number of edit segments by default is 10,000:

```
[hadoop@master1 ~]$ ls -l /data/namenode1/current/
total 2080
-rw-rw-r-- 1 hadoop hadoop     788 Apr 18 04:49 edits_0000000000000000232-0000000000000000241
-rw-rw-r-- 1 hadoop hadoop 1048576 Apr 18 04:49 edits_0000000000000000242-0000000000000000242
-rw-rw-r-- 1 hadoop hadoop      42 Apr 18 04:52 edits_0000000000000000243-0000000000000000244
-rw-rw-r-- 1 hadoop hadoop 1048576 Apr 18 04:52 edits_inprogress_0000000000000000245
```

19. We should never be reducing this value that low in production; this is just for you guys to understand it's working. Keep it at about 500 segments

20. Next is to reduce the number of `fsimage` files, which, by default, is 2. To do that, we use the parameter in the `hdfs-site.xml` file as shown in the following code:

```
<property>
    <name>dfs.namenode.num.checkpoints.retained</name>
    <value>1</value>
</property>
```

21. Now, do a manual checkpoint using the `saveNamespace` command and confirm that there will just be one `fsimage` file with its checksum file.

How it works...

In this recipe, we learned how to control the number of files to keep in the `metastore` directory, and thus control the disk space. Remember, to do all these operations, Namenode must be running. The commands `rollEdits` or `saveNamespace` will not work if the Namenode daemon is not up.

What if the Namenode is not able to start? Then we cannot do all these tasks and get rid of the disk full issue on the Namenode. For that, we will have to use the offline mode, which is discussed in the next recipe.

The important thing to keep in mind is that, we didn't ever touched the other directory under `dfs.namenode.name.dir` and only played with `/data/namenode1`. In case, something went bad, we still have the data in `/data/namenode2`.

Namenode roll edits – offline mode

In this recipe, we will look at how to roll edits in offline mode. What if the Namenode disk is completely full and it is not able to start at all? We cannot use the process described in the precious recipe.

For this, we will use another Namenode, mount the NFS mount there, and perform the process there.

Getting ready

For this recipe, make sure you have completed the recipe on Hadoop cluster setup, *Chapter 1, Hadoop Architecture and Deployment*, and has one more node to use as just Namenode.

How to do it...

1. Connect to the `master1.cyrus.com` master node and switch to user `root`.
2. Unmount the NFS share, which is used as a directory to store the metadata as shown in the following screenshot:

```
[hadoop@master1 ~]$ hdfs getconf -confkey dfs.namenode.name.dir
file:/data/namenode1,file:/data/namenode2
[hadoop@master1 ~]$ df -h | grep namenode
/dev/xvdb1              20G   47M   19G   1% /data/namenode1
filer.cyrus.com:/nfs   7.8G  4.5G  3.3G  58% /data/namenode2
```

3. Again, we are keeping the other mount point `/data/namenode1` safe this time and just playing around with `/data/namenode2`.

4. Mount the NFS share on the `master2.cyrus.com` node using the following command:

   ```
   # mount -t nfs4 filer.cyrus.com:/nfs /mnt
   ```

5. On `master2`, create a directory owned by user `hadoop` named `/data/namenode`.
6. Now, the Namenode `master2`, makes an entry in `hdfs-site.xml` as follows:

   ```
   <property>
       <name>fs.checkpoint.dir</name>
       <value>/mnt</value>
   </property>
   <property>
       <name>dfs.namenode.name.dir</name>
       <value>/data/namenode</value>
   </property>
   ```

7. Execute the `import` command on the `master2` node as user `hadoop`, which is shown as follows. The assumption here is that the user has configured the `core-site.xml`, Java, and environment variables as discussed in *Installation methods* recipe in *Chapter 1, Hadoop Architecture and Deployment*.

   ```
   $ hdfs namenode -importCheckpoint
   ```

8. Namenode will read the contents of `/mnt` and import it into `/data/namenode`. Do not execute the Namenode format command on this node.
9. Now, on this node, we can do all the operations we discussed in the previous recipe and reduce the size of the metadata. The contents can be copied back to the same NFS mount point or to a new directory on the same NFS share.
10. Now, on the main Namenode, `master1`, remove the entry from `dfs.namenode.name.dir` for `/data/namenode1` and mount the NFS share back to `/data/namenode2`.
11. This way we are safeguarding the original metadata of Namenode `master1` and starting the Namenode.
12. Give it some time to stabilize and do the verification using `fsck`. Once everything is fine, we can add the second mount point `/data/namenode1` back after cleaning the old data on it.

How it works...

The recovery process here depicts a situation when the Primary Namenode is low on disk and also, as often happens, due to limited memory, the check pointing can take a very long time.

We can use a powerful node, with more memory and disk space to clean up the metadata and put it back on the main node. Follow the recommendations in the previous recipe to control the number of files and always keep the Namenode checkpoint healthy by having a secondary or a HA Namenode.

Datanode recovery – disk full

In this recipe, we will discuss on the process to recover the Datanode once it is low on disk space. Usually, Datanodes are assumed to fail in the cluster, but sometimes it is important to know how to recover in case of the disk being full.

This is a process which we have to perform when the replication factor is set to `1` and we have critical data to recover.

If the disk on the Datanode is bad and it cannot be read due to hardware issues such as controller failure, then we cannot follow this process. On the Datanode, which is low on disk space, we will add a new larger disk and mount it on the Datanode and start the Datanode daemon for the blocks that are available.

One thing we need to know here is that once we shutdown the Datanode, how quickly the Namenode sees it being removed from the cluster. Remember, we are not decommissioning the node, but trying to replace the disk and start the Datanode service back, without movement of blocks of the Datanode.

This could get tricky as the Namenode will see the Datanode not sending a heartbeat and it will mark it bad and start the replication process. But, this will not happen until 10 minutes 30 seconds by default. Only if we try to read blocks from the node that we removed from the cluster will there be failures, and then Namenode will update itself and start the replication process.

The best thing is to shutdown the Namenode in the cluster and then replace the disk on the Datanode. Do not confuse this with whether it is hot swappable disk or not. Here, the intention is to keep the data on the Datanode disk and, when we bring the Datanode back, it should simply join the cluster, without triggering replication or movement of blocks across the Datanodes.

If the Datanode disk is 100% full, Datanode will not start and hence we have to do this process. If the Datanode daemon can start on the node, we can run Hadoop balancer, to move data to other nodes in the cluster.

The process of shutting down Namenode, is not recommended in a busy cluster with critical jobs running.

Getting ready

For this recipe, make sure readers have completed the recipe on Hadoop cluster setup and have at least HDFS running perfectly. Users are expected to know how to create a filesystem and mount it under Linux.

How to do it...

1. Connect to the master and shutdown the Namenode if it is a busy cluster. Otherwise, the removal of the Datanode will trigger replication.
2. If the cluster is not busy and the changes of hitting the failed Datanode are minimal, keep the Namenode up.
3. Connect to the Datanode `dn1.cyrus.com`, assuming this is the node that is having a disk full for the Datanode directory and shutdown the server.
4. The disk is `/space/data1` on Datanode `dn1`.
5. Add a new disk, format it, and mount it to the directory `/space/data2`.
6. Copy the folder `/space/data1/current` to `/space/data2/` and ensure that the permissions are correct.
7. Modify the `hdfs-site.xml` file and change the data directory as follows:

```
<property>
    <name>dfs.datanode.data.dir</name>
    <value>/space/data2</value>
</property>
```

8. Start the Datanode daemons and you should be good to go.

How it works...

In the preceding process, the question is whether it is worth causing the cluster outage to do this process? But what if the replication was one and that Datanode is not starting up because the disk is full, then we have to do this for critical data.

We cannot add more Datanodes and bump up the replication and let the blocks make a copy on the new nodes, as the Datanode `dn1` will not start at all.

Configuring NFS gateway to serve HDFS

In this recipe, we will configure NFS server to export HDFS as a filesystem which can be mounted onto another system and the native operating system commands, such as `ls`, `cp`, and so, on will work efficiently.

As we have seen upto now, the HDFS filesystem is a filesystem which is not understood by Linux shell commands such, as `cp`, `ls`, and `mkdir`, and so the user must use Hadoop commands to perform file operations.

Getting ready

Make sure that the user has a running cluster with at least HDFS configured and working perfectly. Users are expected to have a basic knowledge about Linux and NFS server. The NFS Gateway supports NFSv3 and allows HDFS to be mounted as part of the client's local filesystem.

How to do it...

1. Connect to the `master1.cyrus.com` master node and switch to user `hadoop`.
2. The user running the NFS-gateway must be able to proxy all the users using the NFS mounts. Edit the `core-site.xml` file and add the configuration lines as shown here:

```
<property>
    <name>hadoop.proxyuser.nfsserver.groups</name>
    <value>*</value>
</property>
```

3. Edit the `core-site.xml` file to enable which nodes in the cluster can act as gateway nodes. If you want only Namenode to be the gateway, then enable it by specifying the host instead of a wildcard:

```
<property>
    <name>hadoop.proxyuser.nfsserver.hosts</name>
    <value>*</value>
</property>
```

4. Edit the `hdfs-site.xml` file to create a `tmp` directory for users to write data, as NFS clients reorders random writes. This directory stores, out-of-order writes, before writing to HDFS:

```
<property>
    <name>dfs.nfs3.dump.dir</name>
    <value>/tmp/.hdfs-nfs</value>
</property>
```

5. Tune the read and write buffer by adding the following lines to `hdfs-site.xml`:

```
<property>
     <name>dfs.nfs.rtmax</name>
     <value>1048576</value>
</property>

<property>
     <name>dfs.nfs.wtmax</name>
     <value>65536</value>
</property>
```

6. Control which hosts can mount the exports from the Hadoop cluster:

```
<property>
     <name>dfs.nfs.exports.allowed.hosts</name>
     <value>* rw</value>
</property>
```

7. Make sure that there is no operating system native NFS server or portmap service running on the master node, as shown in the following screenshot:

```
[hadoop@master1 hadoop]$ sudo service nfs stop
Shutting down NFS daemon:                                   [FAILED]
Shutting down NFS mountd:                                   [FAILED]
Shutting down NFS quotas:                                   [FAILED]
[hadoop@master1 hadoop]$ sudo service rpcbind stop
Stopping rpcbind:                                           [  OK  ]
```

8. Start the portmap service of the Hadoop using the following command, which needs root privileges:

```
# hadoop-daemon.sh start portmap
```

9. Make sure that the portmap service is up and running as shown in the following screenshot:

```
[root@master1 ~]# jps
7425 SecondaryNameNode
7889 Jps
7207 NameNode
7819 Portmap
```

10. Now, as user Hadoop start `mountd` and `nfsd` services using the following command:

```
$ hadoop-daemon.sh start nfs3
```

11. Make sure that the Namenode. Nfs3 service are up, as shown in the following screenshot:

```
[hadoop@master1 hadoop]$ jps
7425 SecondaryNameNode
7921 Nfs3
7207 NameNode
8009 Jps
```

12. Verify that all the services are up and running as shown in the following screenshot:

```
[hadoop@master1 hadoop]$ rpcinfo -p `hostname`
   program vers proto   port  service
    100005    3   udp   4242  mountd
    100005    1   tcp   4242  mountd
    100000    2   udp    111  portmapper
    100000    2   tcp    111  portmapper
    100005    3   tcp   4242  mountd
    100005    2   tcp   4242  mountd
    100003    3   tcp   2049  nfs
    100005    2   udp   4242  mountd
    100005    1   udp   4242  mountd
```

13. Verify that the HDFS namespace is exported and can be mounted as shown in the following screenshot:

```
[hadoop@master1 nfs]$ showmount -e `hostname`
Export list for master1.cyrus.com:
/ *
```

14. Mount the `nfs` export using the following command as user root:

    $ sudo mount -t nfs -o vers=3,proto=tcp,nolock master1.cyrus.com:/ /data/nfs

15. Change to the directory `/data/nfs` and the user can list the HDFS filesystem using the shell commands as shown in the following screenshot:

```
[hadoop@master1 hadoop]$ cd /data/nfs/
[hadoop@master1 nfs]$ ls -l
total 4
drwxr-xr-x 4 hadoop 2584148964 128 Mar  2 18:47 out
drwxr-xr-x 4 hadoop 2584148964 128 Mar  2 19:03 out1
drwxr-xr-x 2 hadoop 2584148964  64 Jan  5 04:11 projects
drwxr-xr-x 2 hadoop 2584148964  64 Jan  5 01:11 sharedcache
-rw-r--r-- 1 hadoop 2584148964  42 Mar  2 18:46 test
drwxrwxrwt 4 hadoop 2584148964 128 Feb  3 01:59 tmp
drwxrwxrwt 7 hadoop 2584148964 224 Feb  3 02:01 user
```

16. Copy any test file to the location `/data/nfs` and see whether it is visible in the HDFS filesystem. For this test, we can use the offline Image Viewer output file `fsimage.txt` as shown in the following screenshot:

```
[hadoop@master1 ~]$ hadoop fs -ls /
Found 4 items
drwxr-xr-x   - hadoop supergroup          0 2017-01-05 04:11 /projects
-rw-r--r--   1 hadoop supergroup         42 2017-03-02 18:46 /test
drwxrwxrwt   - hadoop supergroup          0 2017-02-03 01:59 /tmp
drwxrwxrwt   - hadoop supergroup          0 2017-02-03 02:01 /user
[hadoop@master1 ~]$ cp fsimage.txt /data/nfs/
[hadoop@master1 ~]$ hadoop fs -ls /
Found 5 items
-rw-rw-r--   1 hadoop supergroup          0 2017-03-14 22:01 /fsimage.txt
drwxr-xr-x   - hadoop supergroup          0 2017-01-05 04:11 /projects
-rw-r--r--   1 hadoop supergroup         42 2017-03-02 18:46 /test
drwxrwxrwt   - hadoop supergroup          0 2017-02-03 01:59 /tmp
drwxrwxrwt   - hadoop supergroup          0 2017-02-03 02:01 /user
```

How it works...

The NFS server which is bundled with the Hadoop distribution can be configured and enabled to serve the HDFS filesystem as an NFS export.

The advantage of this is that any system which supports NFS protocol in an organization can copy data to the HDFS in Hadoop cluster, without the need for a Hadoop client. This can be a use case for data backup to the Hadoop cluster as a data warehousing solution for legacy applications.

Recovering deleted files

In this recipe, we will look at how we can recover deleted files from the Hadoop cluster. What if the user deletes a critical file with the `-skipTrash` option? Can it be recovered?

This recipe, is more of a best effort to restore the files after deletion. When the delete command is executed, the Namenode updates its metadata in `edits` file and then fires the `invalidate` command to remove the blocks. If the cluster is very busy, the invalidation might take time and we can revoke the files. But, on an idle cluster, if we delete the files, Namenode will immediately fire the invalidate command in response to the Datanode heartbeat and as Datanode does not have any pending operations to do, it will delete the blocks.

Getting ready

Make sure that the user has a running cluster with at least HDFS configured and working perfectly.

How to do it...

1. Connect to the `master1.cyrus.com` master node and switch to user `hadoop`.
2. Create any file and copy it to HDFS. Then, delete that file using the `skipTrash` option as shown in the following screenshot:

```
[hadoop@master1 ~]$ hadoop fs -cat /test
This is test
[hadoop@master1 ~]$ hadoop fs -rm -skipTrash /test
Deleted /test
```

3. Now, immediately shutdown the Namenode using the following command. This needs to be done using the `master1.cyrus.com` master:

```
$ hadoop-daemon.sh stop namenode
```

4. Now, go the directory of the Namenode metastore and use the following command on the `edits` file which is in progress. The filename in user case will be different:

```
$ hdfs oev -i edits_inprogress_0000000000000000224 -o edits.xml
```

5. Open the `edits.xml` file and remove the entries for the delete operation. The xml file stores each record within the `<RECORD>` opening and `</RECORD` closing tags. The operation will be `OP_DELETE`, as shown in the following screenshot:

```
<RECORD>
  <OPCODE>OP_DELETE</OPCODE>
  <DATA>
    <TXID>252</TXID>
    <LENGTH>0</LENGTH>
    <PATH>/test</PATH>
    <TIMESTAMP>1492491267769</TIMESTAMP>
    <RPC_CLIENTID>34809cac-7e94-4881-a4d7-10c54d7aac1a</RPC_CLIENTID>
    <RPC_CALLID>1</RPC_CALLID>
  </DATA>
</RECORD>
```

6. Remove the entry from `RECORD` to `RECORD` for the delete operation. Usually, this will be at the end of the file, if there are no more operations done after the file delete operation.
7. Convert the file back into the binary format using the following command:

```
$ hdfs oev -i edits.xml -o edits_inprogress_0000000000000000224
-p binary
```

8. Start the Namenode process and check whether the file is back or not, as shown in the following screenshot:

```
[hadoop@master1 ~]$ hadoop-daemon.sh start namenode
starting namenode, logging to /opt/cluster/hadoop-2.8.0/logs/h
[hadoop@master1 ~]$ hadoop fs -ls /
Found 2 items
-rw-r--r--   3 hadoop hadoop         13 2017-04-18 04:53 /test
drwxr-xr-x   - hadoop hadoop          0 2017-04-18 01:10 /user
```

How it works...

The preceding recovery process is not recommended for production and it is always advisable to keep a backup of the `edits_in_progress` file. In a busy cluster, there might be many entries in the `edits` file and just removing the entry will not work, if there are transactions after the delete operation. Then, we will have to go through the Namenode recovery process and try our best to roll back if possible.

7

Data Ingestion and Workflow

In this chapter, we will cover the following topics:

- Hive server modes and setup
- Using MySQL for Hive metastore
- Operating Hive with ZooKeeper
- Loading data into Hive
- Partitioning and Bucketing in Hive
- Hive metastore database
- Designing Hive with credential store
- Configuring Flume
- Configure Oozie and workflows

Introduction

Firstly, let us understand what Apache Hive is. Apache Hive is a data warehousing infrastructure built on top of Hadoop that queries the data using SQL. The goal of Hive was to help existing SQL users quickly transition to Hadoop in dealing with structured data, without worrying about the complexities of the Hadoop framework.

In this chapter, we will configure the various methods of data ingestion. Most readers will be well acquainted with the databases and their usage. Databases are also an integral part of Hadoop, and play a very important role in storing, organizing, and retrieving data quickly.

Hadoop works with three types of database: NoSQL databases, such as HBase, warehousing solutions, such as Hive, and for storing metadata, it can use a traditional RDBMS, such as MySQL. In this chapter, we will cover the Hive warehouse and its modes of operation, along with other data ingestion tools, such as Flume, and workflow schedulers, such as Oozie.

Hive server modes and setup

In this recipe, we will look at how to setup a Hive server and use it to query the data stored in a distributed system.

Apache Hive is a client-side library that provides a warehouse solution, which enables representation of data on HDFS in a structure format and querying of it using SQL. The table definitions and mapping are stored in a metastore, which is a combination of a service and a database.

The Hive metastore can run in any of three modes: standalone, local metastore, and remote metastore mode. Standalone or embedded mode is not used in production as it limits the number of connections to just one, and everything runs inside a single JVM.

The Hive driver, metastore interface, and database are the three things that make the Hive connection. The default database is Derby, which is used in standalone mode. In production, an external JDBC-compliant database, such as MySQL, is used in place of Derby, as Derby supports only one client connection which would not be ideal case for a multi-user environment.

Getting ready

Before you go through the recipes in this chapter, make sure you have gone through the steps to install a Hadoop cluster with HDFS and YARN enabled. Although Hive can be installed on any node in the cluster, it is always a good practice to install it on an edge node in the cluster. If users do not have an extra node for an edge node, Hive can be setup on the master node.

How to do it...

1. Connect to the master node `edge1.cyrus.com` in the cluster and change to the `hadoop` user.
2. Make sure that the edge node can connect to the Hadoop cluster, and execute the following commands. Please refer to the *Setting Edge node HA* recipe in *Chapter 4, High Availability*:

```
$hadoop fs -ls /

$ yarn jar <path_to_jar>/hadoop-mapreduce-examples-2.7.2.jar pi 2
2
```

3. Change to the `/opt/cluster` directory. Download Apache Hive from the following link. Always use the stable release. If you want the MR, use Hive 1.x, because in Hive 2.x, tez is the default engine:

   ```
   $ wget mirror.ventraip.net.au/apache/hive/stable/apache-hive-
   1.2.1-bin.tar.gz
   ```

4. Now untar the Hive package as follows:

   ```
   $ tar -zxvf apache-hive-1.2.1-bin.tar.gz
   ```

5. Create a symlink to the Hive package as follows:

   ```
   $ ln -s apache-hive-1.2.1-bin hive
   ```

6. Update the environment variables as the `root` user, as shown in the following screenshot:

```
[root@edge1 ~]# cat /etc/profile.d/hadoopenv.sh
export HADOOP_HOME=/opt/cluster/hadoop
export HADOOP_MAPRED_HOME=$HADOOP_HOME
export HADOOP_COMMON_HOME=$HADOOP_HOME
export HADOOP_HDFS_HOME=$HADOOP_HOME
export YARN_HOME=$HADOOP_HOME
export HADOOP_CONF_DIR=$HADOOP_HOME/etc/hadoop
export YARN_CONF_DIR=$HADOOP_HOME/etc/hadoop
export HBASE_HOME=/opt/cluster/hbase
export JAVA_HOME=/usr/java/latest
export PATH=$PATH:/usr/local/scala/bin

export HIVE_HOME=/opt/cluster/hive
PATH=$HBASE_HOME/bin:$HIVE_HOME/bin:$HADOOP_HOME/bin
export PATH
```

7. Make the changes effective by executing the command as follows:

   ```
   # . /etc/profile.d/hadoopenv.sh
   ```

8. Execute the commands as shown in the following screenshot to see whether Hive is available in the path:

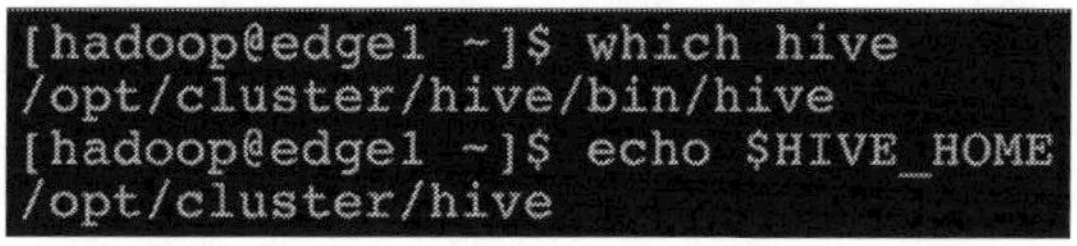

```
[hadoop@edge1 ~]$ which hive
/opt/cluster/hive/bin/hive
[hadoop@edge1 ~]$ echo $HIVE_HOME
/opt/cluster/hive
```

9. The Hive directory will look similar to the one shown in the following screenshot:

```
[hadoop@edge1 hive]$ pwd
/opt/cluster/hive
[hadoop@edge1 hive]$ ls -l
total 476
drwxr-xr-x 3 hadoop hadoop   4096 Oct 23 21:07 bin
drwxr-xr-x 2 hadoop hadoop   4096 Oct 25 11:41 conf
drwxr-xr-x 4 hadoop hadoop   4096 Jun 11  2016 examples
drwxr-xr-x 7 hadoop hadoop   4096 Oct 12 23:11 hcatalog
drwxr-xr-x 4 hadoop hadoop   4096 Aug 15  2016 lib
-rw-rw-r-- 1 hadoop hadoop  24754 Aug 26  2016 LICENSE
-rw-rw-r-- 1 hadoop hadoop    397 Aug 26  2016 NOTICE
-rw-rw-r-- 1 hadoop hadoop   4366 Aug 26  2016 README.txt
-rw-rw-r-- 1 hadoop hadoop 421129 Aug 26  2016 RELEASE_NOTES.txt
drwxr-xr-x 3 hadoop hadoop   4096 Jun 11  2016 scripts
```

10. Switch to the directory of the Hive extract `$HIVE_HOME/conf/`. Copy the file `hive-default.xml.template` to `hive-default.xml`.
11. You can leave the configuration parameters as default. It will create the directory structure on the HDFS `/user/hive/warehouse`. This is because of the setting in the file `hive-default.xml`, as shown in the following screenshot:

```
[hadoop@edge1 conf]$ grep warehouse hive-default.xml
    <name>hive.metastore.warehouse.dir</name>
    <value>/user/hive/warehouse</value>
```

12. Now execute the command `hive` and create any database, as shown in the following screenshot. You will see a directory structure created on the HDFS:

```
hive> create database test_hive_db;
OK
Time taken: 0.141 seconds
hive> quit;
[hadoop@edge1 ~]$ hadoop fs -ls /user/hive/warehouse
Found 1 items
drwxr-xr-x   - hadoop hadoop          0 2017-04-19 01:12 /user/hive/warehouse/test_hive_db.db
```

13. This is the embedded mode; you can see a database created in the present working directory, as shown in the following screenshot:

```
[hadoop@edge1 conf]$ ls -l metastore_db/
total 28
-rw-rw-r-- 1 hadoop hadoop    4 Mar 21 21:13 dbex.lck
-rw-rw-r-- 1 hadoop hadoop   38 Mar 21 21:13 db.lck
drwxrwxr-x 2 hadoop hadoop 4096 Mar 21 21:09 log
-rw-rw-r-- 1 hadoop hadoop  608 Mar 21 21:09 README_DO_NOT_TOUCH_FILES.txt
drwxrwxr-x 2 hadoop hadoop 4096 Mar 21 21:09 seg0
-rw-rw-r-- 1 hadoop hadoop  931 Mar 21 21:09 service.properties
drwxrwxr-x 2 hadoop hadoop 4096 Mar 21 21:13 tmp
```

14. Now try to start the `hiveserver2` and try connecting to it, as shown in the following screenshot:

```
[hadoop@edge1 conf]$ hive --service hiveserver2&
[1] 24549
[hadoop@edge1 conf]$ jps
24692 Jps
24549 RunJar
```

15. Try executing the command `hive` and see what happens. You will see the following error:

```
Caused by: java.sql.SQLException: Failed to start database 'metastore_db' with class loader sun.misc.Launc
pClassLoader@214c265e, see the next exception for details.
        at org.apache.derby.impl.jdbc.SQLExceptionFactory.getSQLException(Unknown Source)
        at org.apache.derby.impl.jdbc.SQLExceptionFactory40.wrapArgsForTransportAcrossDRDA(Unknown Source)
        ... 74 more
Caused by: java.sql.SQLException: Another instance of Derby may have already booted the database /opt/clus
ache-hive-1.2.1-bin/conf/metastore_db.
        at org.apache.derby.impl.jdbc.SQLExceptionFactory.getSQLException(Unknown Source)
        at org.apache.derby.impl.jdbc.SQLExceptionFactory40.wrapArgsForTransportAcrossDRDA(Unknown Source)
        at org.apache.derby.impl.jdbc.SQLExceptionFactory40.getSQLException(Unknown Source)
        at org.apache.derby.impl.jdbc.Util.generateCsSQLException(Unknown Source)
```

How it works...

In the preceding recipe, we configured the Hive server to run in default mode, which is the embedded mode. The inbuilt database **Derby** is used in the preceding case, and only one session can be active at a time.

The Derby database is stored locally on the node, where the Hive client resides, thus limiting the number of clients that have a consistent view of the data. This is never used in production. We do not need to start the Hive server; the moment we execute the Hive command, the client/driver is started.

Using MySQL for Hive metastore

The preceding configuration is the embedded mode configuration, which is not production ready and should not be used.

Now, we will enable the metastore to connect to an external MySQL database and scale to multiple connections. This will be the local metastore mode.

The assumption here is that the readers know the basics of MySQL user management and can assign grants.

How to do it...

1. Clean up the old databases by either dropping from Hive or simply cleaning the warehouse location. Note: this should never be done in production. This is shown in the following screenshot:

```
[hadoop@edge1 conf]$ rm -rf metastore_db
[hadoop@edge1 conf]$ rm derby.log
[hadoop@edge1 conf]$ clear
[hadoop@edge1 conf]$ hadoop fs -ls /user/hive/warehouse/
Found 1 items
drwxr-xr-x   - hadoop supergroup          0 2017-03-21 21:13 /user/hive/warehouse
/test_hive_db.db
[hadoop@edge1 conf]$ hadoop fs -rm -r /user/hive/warehouse/test_hive_db.db
```

2. Now, firstly, we need to install the MySQL server on any node in the cluster or outside the Hadoop cluster. In our case, we will install it on the master node `master1.cyrus.com`:

```
# yum install mysql-server -y
# /etc/init.d/mysqld start
# chkconfigmysql on
```

3. Make sure that the firewall on the master node allows the connection to port `3306` from the Edge node in the cluster. It is better to allow it to connect from all nodes in the cluster, which is required when we configure Oozie later.
4. Firstly, you need to setup a password for the MySQL server and connect locally from the node where it is installed, and then setup user grants.
5. Connect to MySQL and create a user named `hadoop`, which will be used to connect from the Hive client:

```
mysql> CREATE USER 'hadoop'@'%' IDENTIFIED BY 'hadoop';
mysql> GRANT ALL PRIVILEGES ON hive_db.* TO 'hadoop'@'%';
```

6. Now change to the `$HIVE_HOME/conf` directory and create a file `hive-site.xml` with the following configuration:

```
<configuration>
<property>
    <name>hive.metastore.local</name>
    <value>true</value>
</property>
<property>
    <name>javax.jdo.option.ConnectionURL</name>
    <value>jdbc:mysql://master1.cyrus.com:3306/hive_db?createDatab
aseIfNotExist=true</value>
</property>
```

7. Now, let's specify the username and password strings for the connection, as follows:

```
<property>
    <name>javax.jdo.option.ConnectionUserName</name>
    <value>hadoop</value>
</property>

<property>
    <name>javax.jdo.option.ConnectionPassword</name>
    <value>hadoop</value>
</property>
</configuration>
```

8. Now we have to install the MySQL JDBC driver for Hive to connect to MySQL. Download the driver from `https://dev.mysql.com/downloads/connector/j/5.1.html`, extract the JAR, and copy it to the location `$HIVE_HOME/lib`, as follows:

```
$ tar -xzvfmysql-connector-java-5.1.39.tar.gz
$ cpmysql-connector-java-5.1.39/mysql-connector-java-5.1.39-bin.
jar hive/lib/
```

9. Now start the `hiveserver2` and connect to it, as shown in the following screenshot:

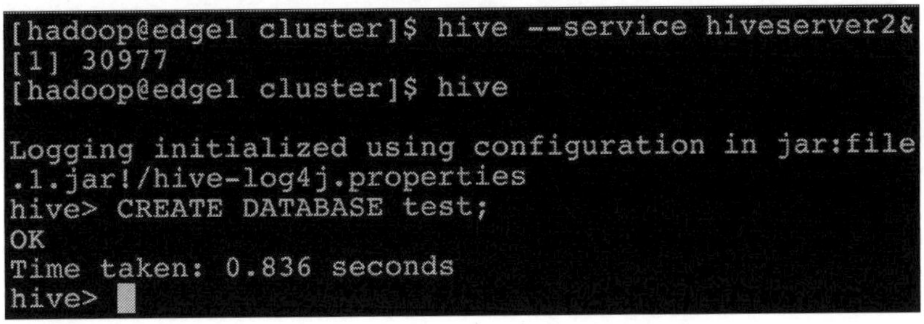

```
[hadoop@edge1 cluster]$ hive --service hiveserver2&
[1] 30977
[hadoop@edge1 cluster]$ hive

Logging initialized using configuration in jar:file
.1.jar!/hive-log4j.properties
hive> CREATE DATABASE test;
OK
Time taken: 0.836 seconds
hive>
```

10. For each database created, a directory with the extension `.db` is created on HDFS, as shown in the following screenshot:

```
[hadoop@edge1 ~]$ hadoop fs -ls /user/hive/warehouse/
Found 1 items
drwxr-xr-x   - hadoop supergroup          0 2017-03-21
22:20 /user/hive/warehouse/test.db
```

11. Connect to the MySQL server from the edge node to see the database created, as shown in the following screenshot:

```
[hadoop@edge1 ~]$ mysql -u hadoop -h master1.cyrus.com -p
Enter password:
Welcome to the MySQL monitor.  Commands end with ; or \g.
Your MySQL connection id is 18
Server version: 5.5.54 MySQL Community Server (GPL)

Copyright (c) 2000, 2016, Oracle and/or its affiliates. All rights reserved.

Oracle is a registered trademark of Oracle Corporation and/or its
affiliates. Other names may be trademarks of their respective
owners.

Type 'help;' or '\h' for help. Type '\c' to clear the current input statement.

mysql> show databases;
+--------------------+
| Database           |
+--------------------+
| information_schema |
| hive_db            |
| mysql              |
| performance_schema |
| test               |
+--------------------+
5 rows in set (0.00 sec)
```

12. To enable a remote metastore mode, we need to enable the metastore URL and start the metastore service on the respective node. Add the following line to the `hive-site.xml` file and start the metastore daemon:

```
<property>
    <name>hive.metastore.uris</name>
    <value>thrift://localhost:9083</value>
</property>
```

13. Start the Hive metastore interface:

```
$ hive --service metastore&
```

How it works...

In the preceding recipe, we configured the Hive server to use MySQL for a persistent store. Now, the metadata can be shared irrespective of where the client is launched from and can query the MySQL for information about the tables and their data location mappings on HDFS. We can have a common MySQL store for multiple clusters, but for this the storage must be on S3 as an external table. Instead of MySQL, we can use Postgres, MSSQL, or Oracle as a metastore database.

Throughout the process, HDFS must be healthy and YARN must be configured to run MapReduce when we need to import data into Hive. We can use the hive client or a beeline client to connect to `hiveserver2`, as shown in the following screenshot:

```
[hadoop@edge1 ~]$ beeline
Beeline version 1.2.1 by Apache Hive
beeline> !connect jdbc:hive2://localhost:10000 hadoop hadoop
Connecting to jdbc:hive2://localhost:10000
Connected to: Apache Hive (version 1.2.1)
Driver: Hive JDBC (version 1.2.1)
Transaction isolation: TRANSACTION_REPEATABLE_READ
0: jdbc:hive2://localhost:10000> show databases;
+----------------+--+
| database_name  |
+----------------+--+
| default        |
| test           |
| testdb         |
+----------------+--+
3 rows selected (0.158 seconds)
```

In the upcoming recipes, we will see how we can upload data. We will also look at other Hive concepts, such as Partitioning and Bucketing.

Operating Hive with ZooKeeper

It is important to configure high availability in production so that if one of the `hiveserver2` fails, the others can respond to client requests. This can be achieved by using the ZooKeeper discovery mechanism to point the clients to the active Hive servers.

Secondly, to enable concurrency, it is important to run the table manager, which is a lock manager. Both these features require setting up the ZooKeeper ensemble and configuring the Hive clients to use it.

Getting ready

To progress through the recipe in this section, we need a ZooKeeper ensemble running. Please refer to *Chapter 4, High Availability* for details of how to configure ZooKeeper clients. Secondly, users must have completed the previous recipe *Using MySQL for Hive metastore*.

How to do it...

1. Connect to the edge node `edge1.cyrus.com` in the cluster and switch to the `hadoop` user.
2. Modify the `hive-site.xml` file and enable the table manager by using the properties as follows. This is for concurrency:

```
<property>
     <name>hive.support.concurrency</name>
     <value>true</value>
</property>

<property>
     <name>hive.zookeeper.quorum</name>
     <value>master1.cyrus.com,edge1.cyrus.com, rt1.cyrus.com</
value>
</property>

<property>
     <name>hive.zookeeper.client.port</name>
     <value>2181</value>
</property>

<property>
     <name>hive.server2.support.dynamic.service.discovery</name>
     <value>true</value>
</property>

<property>
     <name>hive.server2.zookeeper.namespace</name>
     <value>hiveserver2</value>
</property>
```

3. Now start the `hiveserver2` on whichever nodes you want to run it. Connect to the Hive server using the ZooKeeper discovery, as follows:

```
beeline>!connect jdbc:hive2://master1.cyrus.com:2181,edge1.
cyrus.com:2181,rt1.cyrus.com:2181/;serviceDiscoveryMode=zooKeeper;
zooKeeperNamespace=hiveserver2
```

How it works...

In the preceding recipe, we used ZooKeeper discovery to find the active Hive server and connect to it, rather than specifying any one particular Hive server instance. The ZooKeeper namespace string is `hiveserver2`, which can be any string. This is the namespace that is maintained by the ZooKeeper and queried by the Hive clients. Please explore the ZooKeeper namespace `hiveserver2` directory for details.

Loading data into Hive

In this recipe, we look at how we can import data into Hive and also how we can point it to existing data using an external table.

The data store formats for Hive can be text, ORC and parquet, as well as a few other formats. Each one has its advantages in terms of compression, performance, space utilization and memory overheads.

Getting ready

To progress through the recipe, you must have completed the recipe *Using MySQL for Hive metastore*. There are many examples of each type of Hive distribution at `$HIVE_HOME/examples`.

How to do it...

1. Connect to the edge node `edge1.cyrus.com` in the cluster and switch to the `hadoop` user.
2. Connect by either using Hive or the beeline client and import the data by creating a table as shown in the following screenshot:

```
hive> use test;
OK
Time taken: 0.015 seconds
hive> CREATE TABLE pokes (foo INT, bar STRING);
OK
Time taken: 0.199 seconds
hive> LOAD DATA LOCAL INPATH './hive/examples/files/kv1.txt' INTO TABLE pokes;
Loading data to table test.pokes
Table test.pokes stats: [numFiles=1, totalSize=5812]
OK
Time taken: 0.473 seconds
```

3. Now take a look at the HDFS warehouse location. You will see a file named `kv1.txt` copied there, as shown in the following screenshot:

```
[hadoop@master1 ~]$ hadoop fs -ls /user/hive/warehouse/
Found 1 items
drwxr-xr-x   - hadoop supergroup          0 2017-03-22
03:53 /user/hive/warehouse/test.db
[hadoop@master1 ~]$ hadoop fs -ls /user/hive/warehouse/
test.db/pokes/
Found 1 items
-rwxr-xr-x   2 hadoop supergroup       5812 2017-03-22
03:53 /user/hive/warehouse/test.db/pokes/kv1.txt
```

4. Describe the table `pokes` and look at the data, as shown in the following screenshot. What if you `cat` the `kv1.txt` file directly? Is it field delimited?

```
hive> desc pokes;
OK
foo                         int
bar                         string
Time taken: 0.067 seconds, Fetched: 2 row(s)
hive> select * from pokes limit 5;
OK
238     val_238
86      val_86
311     val_311
27      val_27
165     val_165
Time taken: 0.262 seconds, Fetched: 5 row(s)
```

5. The default delimiter is control-A, which is ASCII01 and can be seen in the following screenshot:

```
[hadoop@master1 ~]$ hadoop fs -cat /user/hive/warehous
e/test.db/pokes/kv1.txt | head -1 | tr -d "\n" | od -A
n -t dC
   50   51   56    1  118   97  108   95   50   51   5
6
```

Now, what if the data is already in HDFS and needs to be imported into Hive? This can happen when the data size is huge. If this were to happen, instead of importing it, just point the Hive external table to it.

The Hive external table is not managed by Hive, so whenever we drop a table from Hive, the data is not deleted from HDFS. This is true only for external tables, which are explained in the following sections.

1. Now, let's drop the table from Hive using the following command. This will delete the data from HDFS:

   hive> drop table pokes;

   $ hadoop fs -ls /user/hive/warehouse/test.db/

```
hive> use test;
OK
Time taken: 0.71 seconds
hive> drop table pokes;
Moved: 'hdfs://master1.cyr
.com:9000/user/hadoop/.Tra
OK
Time taken: 0.467 seconds
```

2. Once the table has been dropped, just copy the file to the HDFS location as shown in the following screenshot:

```
hive> !hadoop fs -ls /user/hive/warehouse/test.db/;
hive> !hadoop fs -put /opt/cluster/hive/examples/fi
les/kv1.txt /user/hive/warehouse/test.db/;
hive> !hadoop fs -ls /user/hive/warehouse/test.db/;
Found 1 items
-rw-r--r--   2 hadoop supergroup       5812 2017-03
-22 04:23 /user/hive/warehouse/test.db/kv1.txt
```

3. Now create an external table and point it to the location by using the following command:

```
hive> CREATE external TABLE pokes (foo INT, bar STRING) ROW FORMAT
DELIMITED LINES TERMINATED BY '\n' stored as textfile location '/
user/hive/warehouse/test.db/';
```

4. Now, even if we drop this table, the data is still retained in the HDFS. This is useful if we want to use the same data from multiple components, such as MapReduce, Spark, Hive, and so on.

How it works...

In this recipe, we uploaded data into Hive by using the `load` command. Note that we used the keyword `LOCAL` as the file was on a non-HDFS system; if the file were on HDFS, we could use the same import as `LOAD DATA INPATH'./examples/files/kv1.txt' OVERWRITE INTO TABLE pokes;`. The actual data is on HDFS. The metastore database is in MySQL, and whenever we query Hive, it contacts the metastore database to get the table location and details, and returns the results.

The storage mechanism of the schema/metadata information in the MySQL database is fascinating, and will be covered in a later recipe.

See also

- The *Hive metastore database* recipe

Partitioning and Bucketing in Hive

In this recipe, we will look at Partitioning and Bucketing concepts in Hive. Partitioning is a scheme by which we reduce the amount of a dataset to be queried for a result.

For example, let's say we keep a record of the entire population in a Hive table, and when someone asks for a person's details, we query it based on the name and gender. This will take a lot of time, as it has to go though many records. Instead, a better approach would be to partition it by country and then query only the specific subset of records. In the RDBMS world, this is known as sharding. Partitioning lets you organize the data in a logical fashion and skip all but the data you need.

Bucketing is a concept of hashing, and based, upon the principle of hashing, it places the data into various buckets, which are themselves files. In simple terms, it is clustering the columns in a group set so as to reduce the number of partitions. Having a large number of partitions is also a bottleneck.

Getting ready

To complete the recipe, you must have a running cluster with HDFS and YARN configured, and must have completed the recipe *Loading data into Hive* recipe.

How to do it...

1. Connect to the edge node `edge1.cyrus.com` in the cluster and switch to the `hadoop` user.
2. Connect to the Hive prompt and create a partitioned table with the following commands:

```
hive> CREATE TABLE invites (foo INT, bar STRING) PARTITIONED BY
(ds STRING);
```

```
hive> LOAD DATA LOCAL INPATH'./hive/examples/files/kv2.txt'
OVERWRITE INTO TABLE invites PARTITION (ds='2008-08-15');
```

```
hive> LOAD DATA LOCAL INPATH'./examples/files/kv3.txt' OVERWRITE
INTO TABLE invites PARTITION (ds='2008-08-08');
```

3. This will create subdirectories based upon the partition key, as shown in the following screenshot:

```
hive> !hadoop fs -ls /user/hive/warehouse/test.db/invites;
Found 2 items
drwxr-xr-x   - hadoop supergroup          0 2017-03-22 05:
25 /user/hive/warehouse/test.db/invites/ds=2008-08-08
drwxr-xr-x   - hadoop supergroup          0 2017-03-22 05:
25 /user/hive/warehouse/test.db/invites/ds=2008-08-15
```

4. Query the data specific to a date and only that subdirectory will be read, as shown in the following screenshot:

```
hive> explain select * from invites where ds='2008-08-08';
OK
STAGE DEPENDENCIES:
  Stage-0 is a root stage

STAGE PLANS:
  Stage: Stage-0
    Fetch Operator
      limit: -1
      Processor Tree:
        TableScan
          alias: invites
          Statistics: Num rows: 2 Data size: 216 Basic stats: COMPLETE Column stats: NONE
          Select Operator
            expressions: foo (type: int), bar (type: string), '2008-08-08' (type: string)
            outputColumnNames: _col0, _col1, _col2
            Statistics: Num rows: 2 Data size: 216 Basic stats: COMPLETE Column stats: NONE
            ListSink

Time taken: 0.074 seconds, Fetched: 17 row(s)
```

Partitions are good if all are of the same size and if they are few in number, which is not always practical. For example, tables depicting populations that are partitioned by country cannot be of the same size, as different countries will have different populations.

Instead of creating too many partition files, why not cluster them by state and partition them by country? Set `hive.enforce.bucketing=true` to configure Hive to create the specified number of buckets. The table creates a statement that will include the following:

```
partitioned by (country varchar(64))
clustered by (state) sorted by (city) into 32 buckets stored as
sequencefile;
```

1. Create a very simple `emp` table as shown in the following screenshot:

```
hive> select * from emp;
OK
1       Amit    Programmer      50000   A
2       Gopal   Programmer      50000   B
3       Ankit   Marketing       60000   A
4       Harry   Programmer      50000   C
5       Kapil   Programmer      50000   C
6       Saket   Lead    12000   A
7       Karan   Lead    12000   B
8       Anju    Engineer        45000   B
9       Nan     Programmer      50000   A
10      Andy    Manager 40000   A
11      Anil    Manager 40000   B
12      Ratish  Marketing       60000   B
13      Marry   Manager 40000   A
14      Lamma   Engineer        45000   A
15      Catty   Ceo     100000  B
16      Arthi   Manager 40000   B
17      Pawan   Engineer        45000   B
18      Jogi    Programmer      50000   B
19      Andrew  Engineer        45000   A
20      Sandeep Cto     100000  A
Time taken: 0.495 seconds, Fetched: 20 row(s)
```

2. The schema of the table `emp` is as follows:

```
hive>descemp;
OK
employeeidint
firstnamestring
designation         string
salary              int
department          string
```

3. Now create a table with buckets using the following command:

```
hive> create table emp_bucket (EmployeeIDInt,FirstNameString,
DesignationString,SalaryInt,Department String) clustered by
(department) into 3 buckets row format delimited fields terminated
by ",";
```

4. Enable the bucket by setting the parameter as follows. This is mandatory, otherwise the number of buckets will not be configured:

```
hive> set hive.enforce.bucketing=true;
```

5. Now import the `emp` data in the bucketed table using the following command:

```
hive> from emp insert into table emp_bucket
select employeeid,firstname,designation,salary,department;
```

6. The data is bucketed into three buckets, as shown in the following screenshot, thus segregating it into smaller datasets clustered by department:

```
hive> !hadoop fs -ls /user/hive/warehouse/test.db/emp_bucket;
Found 3 items
-rwxr-xr-x   2 hadoop supergroup        224 2017-03-22 06:31 /user/
hive/warehouse/test.db/emp_bucket/000000_0
-rwxr-xr-x   2 hadoop supergroup         54 2017-03-22 06:31 /user/
hive/warehouse/test.db/emp_bucket/000001_0
-rwxr-xr-x   2 hadoop supergroup        224 2017-03-22 06:31 /user/
hive/warehouse/test.db/emp_bucket/000002_0
```

How it works...

In this recipe, we explored the concepts of the *Partitioning and Bucketing in Hive* recipe, where a number of records are segregated into smaller sets for quick retrieval. Unlike partitioned columns, bucketed columns are part of the table definitions.

See also

- The *Hive metastore database* recipe

Hive metastore database

In this recipe, we will look at the MySQL database that is used as a metastore database. It is important to understand how the Hive-managed tables are depicted by metadata, and how the metadata database is queried to find the location of tables and their partitions.

Getting ready

For this recipe, you must have completed the *Partitioning and Bucketing in Hive* recipe and have a basic understanding of MySQL commands and SQL query syntax.

How to do it...

1. Connect to the MySQL server from any node in the cluster using the following command:

   ```
   $ mysql -u hadoop -h master1.cyrus.com -p
   ```

2. The username and password can be found in the `hive-site.xml` file.
3. Switch to the Hive metastore database, which in our case is `hive_db`. There are many tables in the databases that together constitute metadata for the tables.
4. The `VERSION` table stores information about the schema version, as shown in the following screenshot:

```
mysql> select * from VERSION;
+--------+----------------+------------------------------------+
| VER_ID | SCHEMA_VERSION | VERSION_COMMENT                    |
+--------+----------------+------------------------------------+
|      1 | 1.2.0          | Set by MetaStore hadoop@10.0.0.52  |
+--------+----------------+------------------------------------+
1 row in set (0.00 sec)
```

5. The `TBLS` table stores information about the tables, as shown in the following screenshot. It is this table that marks it as a managed or an external table:

```
mysql> select * from TBLS limit 2;
+--------+-------------+-------+------
------------+-------+-----------+-----
-+-----------+---------------+--------
------------+--------------------+
| TBL_ID | CREATE_TIME | DB_ID | LAST_A
CCESS_TIME | OWNER  | RETENTION | SD_ID
 | TBL_NAME | TBL_TYPE          | VIEW_EXP
ANDED_TEXT | VIEW_ORIGINAL_TEXT |
+--------+-------------+-------+------
------------+-------+-----------+-----
-+-----------+---------------+--------
------------+--------------------+
|     11 |  1490157004 |     6 |
          0 | hadoop |         0 |     11
 | pokes     | EXTERNAL_TABLE | NULL
            | NULL                |
|     12 |  1490157098 |     6 |
          0 | hadoop |         0 |     12
```

6. The table `SDS` stores the location and the input/output formats.
7. The table `DBS` stores the databases as shown in the following screenshot:

```
mysql> select * from DBS;
+-------+-----------------------+------------------------------------------------------------
+---------+------------+------------+
| DB_ID | DESC                  | DB_LOCATION_URI
NAME    | OWNER_NAME | OWNER_TYPE |
+-------+-----------------------+------------------------------------------------------------
+---------+------------+------------+
|     1 | Default Hive database | hdfs://master1.cyrus.com:9000/user/hive/warehouse
 default | public     | ROLE       |
|     6 | NULL                  | hdfs://master1.cyrus.com:9000/user/hive/warehouse/test.db
| test    | hadoop     | USER       |
```

8. The table `PARTITIONS` store the partition information, as shown in the following screenshot:

```
mysql> select * from PARTITIONS;
+---------+-------------+------------------+---------------+-------+--------+
| PART_ID | CREATE_TIME | LAST_ACCESS_TIME | PART_NAME     | SD_ID | TBL_ID |
+---------+-------------+------------------+---------------+-------+--------+
|       1 |  1490160309 |                0 | ds=2008-08-15 |    17 |     16 |
|       2 |  1490160349 |                0 | ds=2008-08-08 |    18 |     16 |
+---------+-------------+------------------+---------------+-------+--------+
2 rows in set (0.00 sec)
```

9. The aforementioned tables are queried in conjunction to retrieve the table location, the partitions of a table, and other details.

10. To find the list of table locations, the query shown in the following screenshot is used:

```
mysql> select TBLS.TBL_NAME,SDS.LOCATION
    -> from SDS,TBLS
    -> where TBLS.SD_ID = SDS.SD_ID;
+------------+---------------------------------------------------------------------+
| TBL_NAME   | LOCATION                                                            |
+------------+---------------------------------------------------------------------+
| pokes      | hdfs://master1.cyrus.com:9000/user/hive/warehouse/test.db            |
| pokes1     | hdfs://master1.cyrus.com:9000/user/hive/warehouse/test.db            |
| invites    | hdfs://master1.cyrus.com:9000/user/hive/warehouse/test.db/invites    |
| emp        | hdfs://master1.cyrus.com:9000/user/hive/warehouse/emp                |
| emp_bucket | hdfs://master1.cyrus.com:9000/user/hive/warehouse/test.db/emp_bucket |
+------------+---------------------------------------------------------------------+
5 rows in set (0.00 sec)
```

11. Similarly, the table partition locations can be listed as shown in the following screenshot:

```
mysql> select TBLS.TBL_NAME,PARTITIONS.PART_NAME,SDS.LOCATION
    -> from SDS,TBLS,PARTITIONS
    -> where PARTITIONS.SD_ID = SDS.SD_ID
    -> and TBLS.TBL_ID=PARTITIONS.TBL_ID
    -> order by 1,2;
+----------+---------------+-----------------------------------------------
------------------------------------+
| TBL_NAME | PART_NAME     | LOCATION
                                    |
+----------+---------------+-----------------------------------------------
------------------------------------+
| invites  | ds=2008-08-08 | hdfs://master1.cyrus.com:9000/user/hive/
warehouse/test.db/invites/ds=2008-08-08 |
| invites  | ds=2008-08-15 | hdfs://master1.cyrus.com:9000/user/hive/
warehouse/test.db/invites/ds=2008-08-15 |
```

How it works...

In the preceding recipe, we looked at retrieving information from the MySQL database and finding details about the Hive table location, partitions, and so on.

In production, this metastore is critical, and must be backed up by using the best practices of MySQL. To do this, either setup a MySQL master-slave setup or take periodic backups of the MySQL database.

See also

- The *Chapter 8, Performance Tuning*

Designing Hive with credential store

In this recipe, we will be configuring the Hive credential store and using authentication for beeline clients to connect and have access control.

This is supported in Hive beeline clients. The authentication by default is **PAM**, which is a pluggable authentication module, but Hive can have its own credential store.

Getting ready

Make sure that you have completed the *Using MySQL for Hive metastore* recipe for this section and that you understand the basic Linux user management.

How to do it...

1. Connect to the edge node`edge1.cyrus.com` and switch to the `hadoop` user.
2. Edit the `hive-site.xml` file and add the following lines to it:

```
<property>
    <name>hive.server2.enable.doAs</name>
    <value>false</value>
</property>

<property>
    <name>hive.users.in.admin.role</name>
    <value>root</value>
</property>

<property>
    <name>hive.security.metastore.authorization.manager</name>
    <value>org.apache.hadoop.hive.ql.security.authorization.Stora
geBasedAuthorizationProvider,org.apache.hadoop.hive.ql.security.
authorization.MetaStoreAuthzAPIAuthorizerEmbedOnly</value>
</property>

<property>
    <name>hive.security.authorization.manager</name>
    <value>org.apache.hadoop.hive.ql.security.authorization.
plugin.sqlstd.SQLStdConfOnlyAuthorizerFactory</value>
</property>
```

3. Create a new file `hiveserver2-site.xml`, with the following contents:

```
<property>
    <name>hive.security.authorization.manager</name>
    <value>org.apache.hadoop.hive.ql.security.authorization.
plugin.sqlstd.SQLStdHiveAuthorizerFactory</value>
</property>

<property>
    <name>hive.security.authenticator.manager</name>
    <value>org.apache.hadoop.hive.ql.security.
SessionStateUserAuthenticator</value>
</property>

<property>
    <name>hive.conf.restricted.list</name>
    <value>hive.security.authorization.enabled,hive.security.
authorization.manager,hive.security.authenticator.manager</value>
</property>
```

4. Now restart `hiveserver2`, and then connect using the beeline client, as shown in the following screenshot:

```
0: jdbc:hive2://localhost:10000> !connect jdbc:hive2://localhost:10000
Connecting to jdbc:hive2://localhost:10000
Enter username for jdbc:hive2://localhost:10000: root
Enter password for jdbc:hive2://localhost:10000:
Connected to: Apache Hive (version 2.1.0-amzn-0)
Driver: Hive JDBC (version 2.1.0-amzn-0)
16/09/30 05:54:28 [main]: WARN jdbc.HiveConnection: Request to set autoCommit
autoCommit=false.
Transaction isolation: TRANSACTION_REPEATABLE_READ
```

5. Now set the `ADMIN` role as shown in the following screenshot:

```
1: jdbc:hive2://localhost:10000> set role ADMIN;
INFO  : Compiling command(queryId=hive_20160930055431_53dc8cdd-4d7f-40a2-b7c4-f55c7f508307): set role ADMIN
INFO  : Semantic Analysis Completed
INFO  : Returning Hive schema: Schema(fieldSchemas:null, properties:null)
INFO  : OK
```

6. Check the roles that we created by using the command as shown in the following screenshot:

```
1: jdbc:hive2://localhost:10000> show roles;
INFO  : Compiling command(queryId=hive_20160930055456_3c6578ed-d7c0-4a40-9f36-9ab0fa6c47cf): show roles
INFO  : Semantic Analysis Completed
INFO  : Returning Hive schema: Schema(fieldSchemas:[FieldSchema(name:role, type:string, comment:from deserializer)], properties:null)
INFO  : Completed compiling command(queryId=hive_20160930055456_3c6578ed-d7c0-4a40-9f36-9ab0fa6c47cf); Time taken: 0.005 seconds
INFO  : Concurrency mode is disabled, not creating a lock manager
INFO  : Executing command(queryId=hive_20160930055456_3c6578ed-d7c0-4a40-9f36-9ab0fa6c47cf): show roles
INFO  : Starting task [Stage-0:DDL] in serial mode
INFO  : Completed executing command(queryId=hive_20160930055456_3c6578ed-d7c0-4a40-9f36-9ab0fa6c47cf); Time taken: 0.021 seconds
INFO  : OK
+-----------+--+
|   role    |
+-----------+--+
| admin     |
| public    |
+-----------+--+
```

7. Create a role `src_role_wadmin` as shown in the following screenshot:

```
1: jdbc:hive2://localhost:10000> create role src_role_wadmin;
INFO  : Compiling command(queryId=hive_20160930055525_f0d362be-cbb5-42c9-9a8b-dee1711d848b): create role src_role_wadmin
INFO  : Semantic Analysis Completed
INFO  : Returning Hive schema: Schema(fieldSchemas:null, properties:null)
INFO  : Completed compiling command(queryId=hive_20160930055525_f0d362be-cbb5-42c9-9a8b-dee1711d848b); Time taken: 0.003 seconds
INFO  : Concurrency mode is disabled, not creating a lock manager
INFO  : Executing command(queryId=hive_20160930055525_f0d362be-cbb5-42c9-9a8b-dee1711d848b): create role src_role_wadmin
INFO  : Starting task [Stage-0:DDL] in serial mode
INFO  : Completed executing command(queryId=hive_20160930055525_f0d362be-cbb5-42c9-9a8b-dee1711d848b); Time taken: 0.021 seconds
INFO  : OK
No rows affected (0.039 seconds)
```

8. Now grant the `hadoop` user the preceding role by using the command shown in the following screenshot:

```
1: jdbc:hive2://localhost:10000> grant  src_role_wadmin to user hadoop with admin option;
INFO  : Compiling command(queryId=hive_20160930055542_fb363fa1-39de-45d2-835f-80ad4610d40
hadoop with admin option
INFO  : Semantic Analysis Completed
INFO  : Returning Hive schema: Schema(fieldSchemas:null, properties:null)
INFO  : Completed compiling command(queryId=hive_20160930055542_fb363fa1-39de-45d2-835f-8
seconds
```

9. Verify the role grant for the `hadoop` user as shown in the following screenshot:

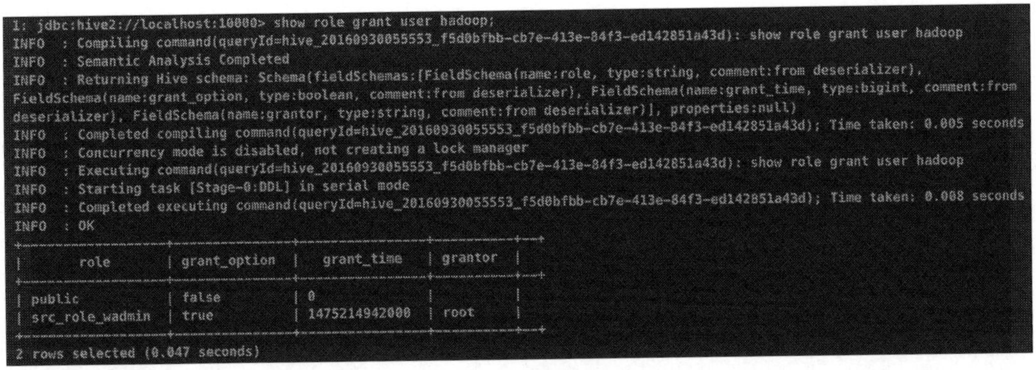

```
1: jdbc:hive2://localhost:10000> show role grant user hadoop;
INFO  : Compiling command(queryId=hive_20160930055553_f5d0bfbb-cb7e-413e-84f3-ed142851a43d): show role grant user hadoop
INFO  : Semantic Analysis Completed
INFO  : Returning Hive schema: Schema(fieldSchemas:[FieldSchema(name:role, type:string, comment:from deserializer), FieldSchema(name:grant_option, type:boolean, comment:from deserializer), FieldSchema(name:grant_time, type:bigint, comment:from deserializer), FieldSchema(name:grantor, type:string, comment:from deserializer)], properties:null)
INFO  : Completed compiling command(queryId=hive_20160930055553_f5d0bfbb-cb7e-413e-84f3-ed142851a43d); Time taken: 0.005 seconds
INFO  : Concurrency mode is disabled, not creating a lock manager
INFO  : Executing command(queryId=hive_20160930055553_f5d0bfbb-cb7e-413e-84f3-ed142851a43d): show role grant user hadoop
INFO  : Starting task [Stage-0:DDL] in serial mode
INFO  : Completed executing command(queryId=hive_20160930055553_f5d0bfbb-cb7e-413e-84f3-ed142851a43d); Time taken: 0.008 seconds
INFO  : OK
+------------------+---------------+----------------+----------+--+
|       role       | grant_option  |   grant_time   | grantor  |
+------------------+---------------+----------------+----------+--+
| public           | false         | 0              |          |
| src_role_wadmin  | true          | 1475214942000  | root     |
+------------------+---------------+----------------+----------+--+
2 rows selected (0.047 seconds)
```

10. Verify the principal `src_role_wadmin` as shown in the following screenshot:

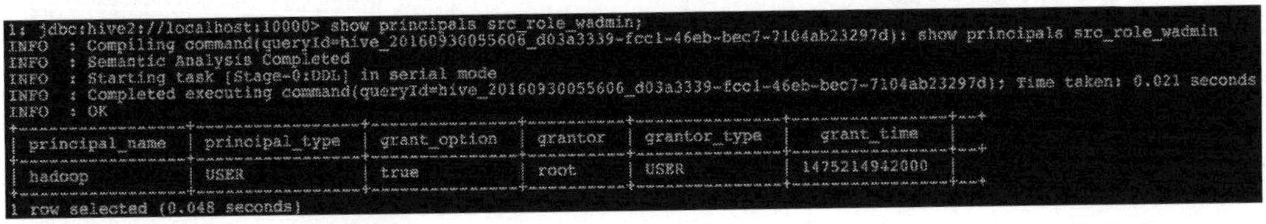

```
1: jdbc:hive2://localhost:10000> show principals src_role_wadmin;
INFO  : Compiling command(queryId=hive_20160930055606_d03a3339-fcc1-46eb-bec7-7104ab23297d): show principals src_role_wadmin
INFO  : Semantic Analysis Completed
INFO  : Starting task [Stage-0:DDL] in serial mode
INFO  : Completed executing command(queryId=hive_20160930055606_d03a3339-fcc1-46eb-bec7-7104ab23297d); Time taken: 0.021 seconds
INFO  : OK
+-----------------+-----------------+---------------+----------+---------------+----------------+--+
| principal_name  | principal_type  | grant_option  | grantor  | grantor_type  |   grant_time   |
+-----------------+-----------------+---------------+----------+---------------+----------------+--+
| hadoop          | USER            | true          | root     | USER          | 1475214942000  |
+-----------------+-----------------+---------------+----------+---------------+----------------+--+
1 row selected (0.048 seconds)
```

How it works...

In this recipe, we have configured the credential store for Hive, which enables users to control access in a granular way, and can assign roles for admin tasks.

Configuring Flume

In this recipe, we will cover how to configure Flume for data ingestion. Flume is a general tool that consumes a log stream or Twitter feeds.

In any organization, we might have hundreds of web servers serving web pages, and we may need to quickly parse these logs for ads targeting or triggering events. These Apache web server logs can be streamed to Flume, from where they can be constantly uploaded to HDFS for processing.

In simple terms, Flume is a distributed, reliable, and efficient way of collecting and aggregating data into HDFS. It has the concepts of Flume agents, channels, and sinks, which together make a robust system. There can be multiple sources, channels, and output paths like a file system on a non-HDFS or HDFS filesystem, or being used by other consumers downstream.

Getting ready

For this recipe, make sure that you have completed the Hadoop cluster setup recipe and have at least a healthy HDFS. Flume can be installed on any node in the cluster, but it is good practice to install it on a gateway node.

Make sure that the source from which Flume consumes data is reachable, and that firewall rules are in place for it to work.

How to do it...

1. Connect to the edge node `edge1.cyrus.com` and switch to the `hadoop` user.
2. For simplicity, we are installing the Apache web server on edge node, but it can be any node. On most CentOS distros it is installed by default:

   ```
   # yum install httpd -y
   # chkconfighttpd on
   # service httpd restart
   ```

3. The Flume agent needs to be installed on all nodes that need to send data. In production, we will have a rsyslogd running in remote logging mode, and all servers will be sending logs to a centralized server. This single centralized server has a Flume agent installed that sends it to HDFS.
4. Download a Flume-stable package and update the Flume environment variable as follows:

   ```
   $wgethttp://apache.uberglobalmirror.com/flume/1.7.0/apache-flume-1.7.0-bin.tar.gz
   $ tar -xzvf apache-flume-1.7.0-bin.tar.gz
   $ ln -s apache-flume-1.7.0-bin flume
   ```

5. Firstly, configure a source agent by creating a file with any name. We will call it `flume-source-agent.conf`, and it will have the following contents:

   ```
   source_agent.sources = apache_server
   source_agent.sources.apache_server.type = exec
   source_agent.sources.apache_server.command = tail -f /var/log/httpd/access_log
   source_agent.sources.apache_server.batchSize = 1
   source_agent.sources.apache_server.channels = memoryChannel
   source_agent.sources.apache_server.interceptors = itimeihostitype
   ```

6. The command `tail -f /var/log/httpd/access_log` is consuming Apache logs and sending to the Flume target.
7. Define host interceptor for Apache server logs. These are specific to log type:

```
http://flume.apache.org/FlumeUserGuide.html#timestamp-interceptor

source_agent.sources.apache_server.interceptors.itime.type =
timestamp

# http://flume.apache.org/FlumeUserGuide.html#host-interceptor

source_agent.sources.apache_server.interceptors.ihost.type = host

source_agent.sources.apache_server.interceptors.ihost.useIP =
false

source_agent.sources.apache_server.interceptors.ihost.hostHeader =
host
```

8. Define the source sink and channel as shown in the following screenshot. The host where this host will advertise its data is specified using the host syntax:

```
# http://flume.apache.org/FlumeUserGuide.html#static-interceptor
source_agent.sources.apache_server.interceptors.itype.type = static
source_agent.sources.apache_server.interceptors.itype.key = log_type
source_agent.sources.apache_server.interceptors.itype.value = apache_access_combined

# http://flume.apache.org/FlumeUserGuide.html#memory-channel
source_agent.channels = memoryChannel
source_agent.channels.memoryChannel.type = memory
source_agent.channels.memoryChannel.capacity = 100

## Send to Flume Collector on Hadoop Node
# http://flume.apache.org/FlumeUserGuide.html#avro-sink
source_agent.sinks = avro_sink
source_agent.sinks.avro_sink.type = avro
source_agent.sinks.avro_sink.channel = memoryChannel
source_agent.sinks.avro_sink.hostname = 192.168.1.99
source_agent.sinks.avro_sink.port = 4545
```

9. Now configure the target agent using the following configuration. Create a field with any name — we are using `flume-trt-agent.conf` — and add the following lines to it:

```
#http://flume.apache.org/FlumeUserGuide.html#avro-source
collector.sources = AvroIn
collector.sources.AvroIn.type = avro
collector.sources.AvroIn.bind = 0.0.0.0
collector.sources.AvroIn.port = 4545
collector.sources.AvroIn.channels = mc1mc2

## Channels ##
## Source writes to 2 channels, one for each sink
```

```
collector.channels = mc1mc2
#http://flume.apache.org/FlumeUserGuide.html#memory-channel

collector.channels.mc1.type = memory
collector.channels.mc1.capacity = 100

collector.channels.mc2.type = memory
collector.channels.mc2.capacity = 100

## Sinks ##
collector.sinks = LocalOutHadoopOut
```

10. Writing to the local filesystem is the way to multiplex the output to different destinations:

```
## Write copy to Local Filesystem
#http://flume.apache.org/FlumeUserGuide.html#file-roll-sink
collector.sinks.LocalOut.type = file_roll
collector.sinks.LocalOut.sink.directory = /var/log/flume-ng
collector.sinks.LocalOut.sink.rollInterval = 0
collector.sinks.LocalOut.channel = mc1
```

11. Write to a file on HDFS with the output format as text:

```
## Write to HDFS
#http://flume.apache.org/FlumeUserGuide.html#hdfs-sink
collector.sinks.HadoopOut.type = hdfs
collector.sinks.HadoopOut.channel = mc2
collector.sinks.HadoopOut.hdfs.path = /user/hadoop/flume-channel/%{log_type}/%y%m%d
collector.sinks.HadoopOut.hdfs.fileType = DataStream
collector.sinks.HadoopOut.hdfs.writeFormat = Text
collector.sinks.HadoopOut.hdfs.rollSize = 0
collector.sinks.HadoopOut.hdfs.rollCount = 10000
collector.sinks.HadoopOut.hdfs.rollInterval = 600
```

12. Once these changes have been saved, start the Flume source and target the agents. These can be on the same node or on different nodes. Usually, the source agent will run on the web server and the target of a host, such as an edge node, with access to HDFS.

13. Start the Flume agent with the following commands:

```
$ flume-ng agent -c conf -f flume/conf/flume-tgt-agent.conf -n collector

$ flume-ng agent -c conf -f flume/conf/flume-source-agent.conf -n source_agent
```

14. Verify the HDFS location to see whether or not the logs are written.

How it works...

Flume can be configured to consume from different sources, and can write to multiple targets with different file formats. For Twitter, we need to have an app account with credential tokens setup to access the streams. The configuration of the source agent will be something like the following for keywords, such as elections, voting, rankings, and so on:

```
# Naming the components on the current agent.
TwitterAgent.sources = Twitter
TwitterAgent.channels = MemChannel
TwitterAgent.sinks = HDFS

# Describing/Configuring the source: - Source is where the data is
generated or a producer of data. Sink is the destination of data, it
could be memory, disk or another consumer.
TwitterAgent.sources.Twitter.type = org.apache.flume.source.twitter.
TwitterSource
TwitterAgent.sources.Twitter.consumerKey = Your OAuth consumer key
TwitterAgent.sources.Twitter.consumerSecret = Your OAuth consumer
secret
TwitterAgent.sources.Twitter.accessToken = Your OAuth consumer key
access token
TwitterAgent.sources.Twitter.accessTokenSecret = Your OAuth consumer
key access token secret
TwitterAgent.sources.Twitter.keywords = elections, voting, ranking
```

Configure Oozie and workflows

In this recipe, we will configure the Oozie workflow engine and look at some examples of scheduling jobs using the Oozie workflow.

Oozie is a scheduler to manage Hadoop jobs, with the ability to make decisions on the conditions or states of previous jobs or the presence of certain files.

Getting ready

Make sure that you have completed the recipe of Hadoop cluster configuration with the edge node configured. HDFS and YARN must be configured and healthy before starting this recipe.

How to do it...

1. Connect to the edge node `edge1.cyrus.com` and switch to the `hadoop` user.

2. Download the Oozie source package, untar it, and build it:

```
$ tar -xzvfoozie-4.1.0.tar.gz
$ cd oozie-4.1.0
```

3. Edit the file `pom.xml` to make it suitable for the Java version and the Hadoop version. Change the fields according to the version of Java used. For Hadoop 2.x, it must be version 2.3.0:

```
<targetJavaVersion>1.8</targetJavaVersion>
<hadoop.version>2.3.0</hadoop.version>
<hbase.version>0.94.2</hbase.version>
<hcatalog.version>0.13.1</hcatalog.version>
```

4. Make sure that Maven is setup and installed, and that the Java path is setup correctly, as shown in the following screenshot:

[hadoop@rt1 ~]$ mvn -version
Apache Maven 3.3.9 (bb52d8502b132ec0a5a3f4c09453c07478323dc5; 2015-11-10T16:41:47+00:00)
Maven home: /opt/apache-maven-3.3.9
Java version: 1.8.0_101, vendor: Oracle Corporation
Java home: /usr/java/jdk1.8.0_101/jre
Default locale: en_US, platform encoding: UTF-8
OS name: "linux", version: "4.9.20-10.30.amzn1.x86_64", arch: "amd64", family: "unix"

5. For the purposes of the build, we are using a machine with decent memory and disk space, as it needs to download dependencies. Change to the `bin` directory as shown in the following screen shot and execute the command `./mkdistro.sh -DskipTests -X`:

[root@rt1 oozie-4.1.0]# pwd
/data/oozie-build/oozie-4.1.0
[root@rt1 oozie-4.1.0]# cd bin/
[root@rt1 bin]# ls -l mkdistro.sh
-rwxr-xr-x 1 hadoop hadoop 2358 Dec 5 2014 mkdistro.sh

6. Once the build is complete, you will see a distro created under `distro/target/`, as shown in the following screenshot:

[root@rt1 oozie-4.1.0]# ls distro/target/
antrun maven-archiver oozie-4.1.0-distro.tar.gz tomcat
archive-tmp oozie-4.1.0-distro oozie-distro-4.1.0.jar

7. Copy or extract this `oozie-4.1.0-distro.tar.gz` distro to the location of the Hadoop installation of the edge node:

```
$ tar -zxvfoozie-4.1.0-distro.tar.gz -C /opt/cluster/
$ ln -s oozie-4.1.0-distro oozie
```

8. Update the `/etc/profile.d/hadoopenv.sh` file to include the following Oozie variables. This can be added to `.bash_profile` as well the `hadoop` user.

```
export OOZIE_HOME=/opt/cluster/oozie
PATH=$OOZIE_HOME/bin:$PATH
```

9. Create a `libext` directory, as follows:

```
$ mkdir /opt/cluster/oozie/libext
```

10. Now copy all the Hadoop JAR files into the preceding folder from the following build path, the build path where the Maven build was done:

```
./oozie-4.1.0/hadooplibs/target/oozie-4.1.0-hadooplibs/
oozie-4.1.0/hadooplibs/hadooplib-2.3.0.oozie-4.1.0/*
```

11. Download `ext-2.2.zip`. This is required for the Web UI. This can be found in many locations. Just search for it and download the ZIP file.
12. Copy the preceding downloaded ZIP file `ext-2.2.zip` to the`/libext` folder as shown in the following screenshot:

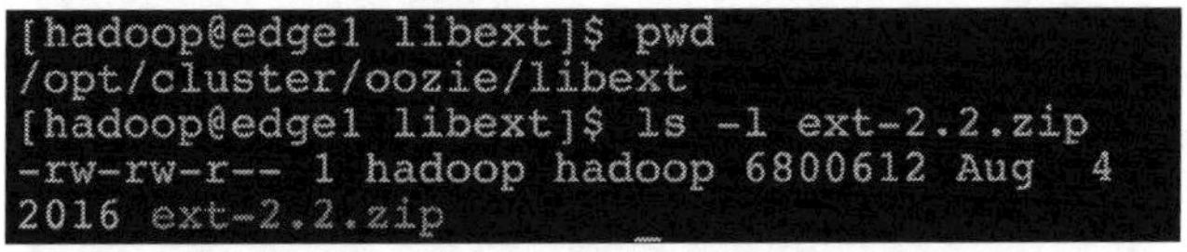
[hadoop@edge1 libext]$ pwd
/opt/cluster/oozie/libext
[hadoop@edge1 libext]$ ls -l ext-2.2.zip
-rw-rw-r-- 1 hadoop hadoop 6800612 Aug 4
2016 ext-2.2.zip

13. Make sure that the Oozie environment is setup correctly. Verify using the following screenshot:

[hadoop@edge1 ~]$ which oozie-setup.sh
/opt/cluster/oozie/bin/oozie-setup.sh
[hadoop@edge1 ~]$ which oozie
/opt/cluster/oozie/bin/oozie

14. Now you need to prepare the Oozie war as shown in the following screenshot:

[hadoop@edge1 ~]$ oozie-setup.sh prepare-war
setting CATALINA_OPTS="$CATALINA_OPTS -Xmx1024m"
setting OOZIE_CONFIG_FILE=oozie-site.xml
setting OOZIE_LOG=${OOZIE_HOME}/logs
setting OOZIE_HTTP_PORT=11000
setting OOZIE_HTTP_HOSTNAME=`hostname -f`
setting JAVA_HOME=/usr/java/latest

15. Once the Oozie war build is complete, you will see a message similar to the one shown in the following picture:

```
INFO: Adding extension: /opt/cluster/oozie/libext/s
INFO: Adding extension: /opt/cluster/oozie/libext/x
INFO: Adding extension: /opt/cluster/oozie/libext/x
INFO: Adding extension: /opt/cluster/oozie/libext/x
INFO: Adding extension: /opt/cluster/oozie/libext/x
INFO: Adding extension: /opt/cluster/oozie/libext/z

New Oozie WAR file with added 'ExtJS library, JARs'
oozie-server/webapps/oozie.war


INFO: Oozie is ready to be started
```

16. Edit the `core-site.xml` file to add the following properties to it:

```
<property>
 <name>hadoop.proxyuser.oozie.hosts</name>
 <value>*</value>
</property>

<property>
 <name>hadoop.proxyuser.oozie.groups</name>
 <value>*</value>
</property>
```

17. Edit the `oozie-site.xml` file to point to the Hadoop configuration directory, as shown in the following screenshot:

```
<property>
    <name>oozie.service.HadoopAccessorService.hadoop.configurations</name>
    <value>*=/opt/cluster/hadoop/etc/hadoop</value>
```

18. Edit the `oozie-site.xml` file to point to the library path, as shown in the following screenshot:

```
<name>oozie.service.WorkflowAppService.system.libpath</name>
<value>hdfs://master1.cyrus.com:9000/user/${user.name}/share/lib</value>
```

19. Now create a `sharelib` directory on HDFS by using the following command:

    `$ oozie-setup.shsharelib create -fs hdfs://master1.cyrus.com:9000`

20. Now create an Oozie database by installing a MySQL server, if not already installed. Refer to the *Hive metastore with MySQL* recipe for reference.

21. Edit the `oozie-site.xml` file to add connection strings for the MySQL database as follows:

```
<property>
    <name>oozie.service.JPAService.jdbc.driver</name>
    <value>com.mysql.jdbc.Driver</value>
</property>

<property>
    <name>oozie.service.JPAService.jdbc.url</name>
    <value>jdbc:mysql://master1.cyrus.com:3306/OOZIEDB</value>
</property>

<property>
    <name>oozie.service.JPAService.jdbc.username</name>
    <value>hadoop</value>
</property>

<property>
    <name>oozie.service.JPAService.jdbc.password</name>
    <value>Axxx</value>
</property>
```

22. Make sure to copy MySQL JAR to the `libext` folder to enable Oozie to connect to MySQL. For details on obtaining the JDBC driver, please refer to *Hive metastore with MySQL* recipe.
23. Connect to the MySQL server and create an empty database named `OOZIEDB`, as shown in the following screenshot:

```
mysql> create database OOZIEDB;
Query OK, 1 row affected (0.01 sec)

mysql> quit;
Bye
```

24. Save the preceding file and initialize the database using the following command:

```
$ oooziedb.sh create -sqlfileoozie.sql -run
```

25. Once the database is initialized, it will give an output as shown in the following screenshot:

```
[hadoop@edge1 conf]$ ooziedb.sh create -sqlfile oozie.sql -run
  setting CATALINA_OPTS="$CATALINA_OPTS -Xmx1024m"
  setting OOZIE_CONFIG_FILE=oozie-site.xml
  setting OOZIE_LOG=${OOZIE_HOME}/logs
  setting OOZIE_HTTP_PORT=11000
  setting OOZIE_HTTP_HOSTNAME=`hostname -f`
  setting JAVA_HOME=/usr/java/latest

Validate DB Connection
DONE
Check DB schema does not exist
DONE
Check OOZIE_SYS table does not exist
DONE
Create SQL schema
DONE
Create OOZIE_SYS table
DONE

Oozie DB has been created for Oozie version '4.1.0'


The SQL commands have been written to: oozie.sql
```

26. Now that the Oozie is setup correctly, it is time to start it using the command:

    $ oozied.sh start

27. Execute the command as shown in the following picture to see the available sharedLibs:

```
[hadoop@edge1 ~]$ oozie admin -shareliblist -oozie http://edge1.cyrus
.com:11000/oozie
[Available ShareLib]
hive
distcp
mapreduce-streaming
oozie
hcatalog
sqoop
pig
```

We can submit jobs using our examples as a starting point. To run a MapReduce wordcount, simply modify the respective `job.properties` and `workflow.xml` files. Workflow defines the order of execution, environment variables, and system configuration parameters like Namenode, and Resourcemanager. Job coordinator defines the conditions under which the job execution should be done, at what frequency and which jobs must be chained or resolve dependencies. The contents of the files are shown in the following screenshot:

```
[hadoop@edge1 examples]$ pwd
/opt/cluster/oozie/examples
[hadoop@edge1 examples]$ cat apps/map-reduce/job.properties
nameNode=hdfs://master1.cyrus.com:9000
jobTracker=master1.cyrus.com:9003
queueName=default
examplesRoot=examples
```

The input and output information is provided by the `workflow.xml` file, and it has a sample example to read data from the `oozie/examples/input-data/`. The directory structure is shown in the following screenshot:

```
[hadoop@edge1 examples]$ ls -l
total 12
drwxr-xr-x 24 hadoop hadoop 4096 Aug  2  2016 apps
drwxrwxr-x  4 hadoop hadoop 4096 Aug  4  2016 input-data
drwxr-xr-x  3 hadoop hadoop 4096 Dec  5  2014 src
[hadoop@edge1 examples]$ ls -l input-data/
total 8
drwxrwxr-x 3 hadoop hadoop 4096 Aug  4  2016 rawLogs
drwxrwxr-x 2 hadoop hadoop 4096 Aug  4  2016 text
[hadoop@edge1 examples]$ ls -l input-data/text/
total 4
-rw-r--r-- 1 hadoop hadoop 1409 Dec  5  2014 data.txt
```

To execute this example set, make the aforementioned necessary changes and copy the `example` directory to the user's home directory on HDFS:

`$ hadoop fs -put examples /user/hadoop/`

`$ oozie job -oozie http://edge1.cyrus.com:11000/oozie -config examples/apps/map-reduce/job.properties -run`

`$ oozie job -info 0000000-160804094152598-oozie-hado-W`

To avoid being given this long path, setup the `OOZIE_URL` in `.bash_profile` as:

```
export OOZIE_URL=http://edge1.cyrus.com:11000/oozie
```

Now we can execute commands like the following:

```
$ oozie job -config examples/apps/map-reduce/job.properties -run
```

How it works...

In the preceding recipe, we looked at the steps to configure the Oozie server, and learned how to run or schedule a job using Oozie.

Oozie can be used to schedule MapReduce, Spark, and Hive jobs, and is the most widely used scheduler in the Hadoop world. There are a lot more details about job configuration and workflow properties, such as dependency graphs, output formats, event trigger-based run, and many others. We can check the status using either the Oozie Web UI or the command line `oozie admin -oozie http://edge1.cyrus.com:11000/oozie -status`.

8
Performance Tuning

In this chapter, we will cover the following recipes:

- Tuning the operating system
- Tuning the disk
- Tuning the network
- Tuning HDFS
- Tuning Namenode
- Tuning Datanode
- Configuring YARN for performance
- Configuring MapReduce for performance
- Hive performance tuning
- Benchmarking Hadoop cluster

In this chapter, we will configure a Hadoop cluster with different parameters and see its effect on performance. There is no one way of doing things and if a particular setting works on one cluster, it does not necessarily mean that it will work for the other cluster with different hardware or work load.

> This being a recipe book, we will not be covering a lot of theory, but it is recommended to build a background on the things we are going to do in this chapter, rather than simply changing the values.

As stated initially, the performance may vary from one system to another and in many cases, it is just context. When someone says that the system is slow, what does it mean? Slower than what? Is it slow in initial response or has the query execution time increased?

Are you doing a comparison on the same dataset? Many times, users will not realize that the data or the format has changed, which could impact the execution time of the job. It is important to note that it is not the performance that has changed in this case, as it is bound to perform that way with the increased dataset. The question should be, is it performing optimally for that dataset under the given environment?

Tuning the operating system

In Hadoop, we mostly use Linux-based operating systems, so the settings we talk about will be restricted to any Linux-based systems.

The first important thing to consider is making sure that the hardware is optimal with latest drivers for motherboard components and the right kind of memory modules with matching bus speed. The BIOS settings are tuned to be optimal like disable power saving mode, VT flag enabled, 64-bit architecture, the right cabling for disk enclosures (**Just a bunk of disks** (**JBOD**)). Multiple CPUs with at least a quad core per CPU socket and high bandwidth bonded interface cards. Racks with support for 1U or 2U servers, with rack top switches which can support network traffic from a large Hadoop cluster.

The hardware configuration will vary according to the Hadoop components like whether it is a Namenode, Datanode, HBase master, or region server. Also, whether the work load is I/O intensive or CPU intensive. There will always be a race between right performance and optimal cost.

Getting ready

To step through the recipes in this chapter, make sure you have at least one node with CentOS 6 and above installed. It does not matter which flavor of Linux you choose, as long as you are comfortable with it.

The same settings apply to all the nodes in the cluster. In larger setups, this is done by prebaking the OS images with the desired configurations and then provisioning the nodes from a common server. Another strategy is to use a configuration management tool like **Puppet** to push the changes during the installation of each node.

How to do it...

1. Connect to a node, which at a later stage will be used to install Hadoop. We are using the node `master1.cyrus.com`.
2. Make sure to switch to root user or have `sudo` privileges.

3. Change the process and file limit for each user with which the service will run, like `hdfs`, `mapred`, `hbase`, `hadoop`, and `yarn`. This can be done by editing the `/etc/security/limits.conf` file and adding the following lines:

```
hdfs    -       nofile          50000
hdfs    -       noproc          35000
hadoop      -nofile             50000
hadoop      -     noproc         35000
mapred    -     nofile                  50000
mapred      -     noproc         35000
```

4. The preceding numbers after `noproc` states the number of processes allowed for that user and the number after `nofile` is the total number of open files that particular user can have.
5. Change the system wide open file limit by changing the file `/etc/sysctl.conf` file as follows. The error `Java.io.FileNotFoundException` (too many open files) is related to this setting:

```
fs.file-max = 600000
```

6. Then make the changes effective by using the command `sysctl -p`.
7. Now, disable the swapping to disk in the `/etc/sysctl.conf` file with the following parameter. This does not truly mean a disable of swap, but it is a balance between swapping the anonymous page cache and file page caches:

```
vm.swappiness = 0
```

8. Then make the changes effective by using the command `sysctl -p`.
9. Disable **transparent huge pages** (**THP**) as this will cause CPU spikes due to memory compaction in an attempt to have contiguous memory allocation. This can be done by editing the `/etc/sysctl.conf` file and adding the following line:

```
vm.nr_hugepages = 0
```

10. The preceding can be done at runtime by using the following commands:

```
echo never > /sys/kernel/mm/transparent_hugepage/enabled
echo never > /sys/kernel/mm/transparent_hugepage/defrag
```

11. To check whether the THP is disabled, we can use the commands as shown in the following screenshot:

```
[root@master1 ~]# egrep 'trans|thp' /proc/vmstat
nr_anon_transparent_hugepages 0
thp_fault_alloc 0
thp_fault_fallback 0
thp_collapse_alloc 0
thp_collapse_alloc_failed 0
thp_split 0
thp_zero_page_alloc 0
thp_zero_page_alloc_failed 0
[root@master1 ~]# grep -i HugePages_Total /proc/meminfo
HugePages_Total:       0
```

12. Next is to tune the shared memory segment size and the total shared segment memory by changing the parameters below in the `/etc/sysctl.conf` file The parameter `kernel.shmmax` is the maximum size a shared segment can be; it makes sense to keep it at the maximum size of memory on the system. The parameter `kernel.shmall` defines the total size of the shared space, which is in pages (page size is 4 Kbytes):

```
kernel.shmmax = 68719476736 (In bytes)
kernel.shmall = 4294967296 (In Pages)
```

13. To verify the preceding values in a more user-friendly way, we can use the command shown in the following screenshot:

```
[root@master1 ~]# ipcs -lm

------ Shared Memory Limits --------
max number of segments = 4096
max seg size (kbytes) = 67108864
max total shared memory (kbytes) = 17179869184
min seg size (bytes) = 1
```

14. We need to monitor the system with tools like `top`, `vmstat`, and `htop` to see how the settings have made a difference. The following screenshot shows the output of `vmstat` to check for disk swap usage:

```
[root@master1 ~]# vmstat 2
procs -----------memory---------- ---swap-- --
 r  b   swpd   free   buff  cache   si   so
 0  0      0 15762084  22284 185072    0    0
 0  0      0 15761944  22292 185092    0    0
 0  0      0 15761944  22292 185132    0    0
 0  0      0 15761944  22292 185164    0    0
 0  0      0 15761944  22300 185192    0    0
 0  0      0 15761820  22300 185224    0    0
```

15. To see the number of open files for a process, we can use the command shown in the following screenshot:

```
[hadoop@master1 ~]$ jps
3424 NameNode
3666 SecondaryNameNode
3834 Jps
[hadoop@master1 ~]$ lsof -p 3424 | wc -l
595
```

16. We can see the status of a process, like its state, CPU assigned to it, huge table pages, threads, and so on with the following command:

```
$ cat /proc/<PID>/status
Example:
$ cat /proc/3424/status
Name:  java
State: S (sleeping)
HugetlbPages:        0 kB
Threads:     46
Cpus_allowed: 7fff
```

Another important part of OS tuning is keeping the install as light as possible. Do the bare minimal install and remove packages and libraries that are not used.

How it works...

In the preceding recipe, we configured kernel parameters to optimize the memory and process utilization, which are very critical to the operating system health.

The changes can be made at runtime or using persistent changes to the respective files. These changes must to be thoroughly tested by simulating the actual work load in testing or staging clusters.

See also

- It is recommended to read through the entire *Chapter 8, Performance Tuning*, as tuning is inter-related to many things like memory, disk, network, and the Hadoop stack itself.

Tuning the disk

In this recipe, we will tune the disk drives to give the optimal performance. For I/O bound workloads like sorting, indexing, data movement disks, and network play an important role and need to be addressed in the right manner.

The workload conditions on a Datanode will be different from that of a Namenode or that of a database running a MySQL metastore. The changes mentioned in the following recipe are valid for all nodes, unless explicitly mentioned otherwise.

Getting ready

To step through the recipe in this section, we need at least one node to test and to make the configuration first, and the same can be applied to nodes within the same categories of master nodes or Datanodes. It is recommended to read *Chapter 10, Cluster Planning*, to get an idea about the cluster layout.

How to do it...

1. Connect to a node which at a later stage will be used to install Hadoop. We are using the node, `master1.cyrus.com`.
2. Switch to `root` user or have `sudo` privileges.
3. Make sure that you have different hard disks for OS, logs, and Hadoop metadata or data blocks.
4. In the case of Namenode, the OS disk must be RAID 1, preferably using the hardware RAID controller.

5. For Namenode, use two separate disks for storing metadata. Disk size should be around 1 TB per disk.
6. For Datanodes, the OS disk does not need to be in RAID. There could be multiple disk drives for data node storage, each disk mounted on a separate mount point.
7. Firstly, do a read performance test on the disks to be used in the nodes, by using the following command. The read must be at least around 80 MB/sec, if not use a faster disk:

```
# hdparm -t --direct /dev/sdb
Timing buffered disk reads: 358 MB in 3.00 seconds = 119.16 MB/sec
```

8. Test cached read timings as below, it should be greater than 5 GB/sec:

```
# hdparm -T /dev/sdb
/dev/sdb:
Timing cached reads:   20404 MB in 2.00 seconds = 10214.66 MB/sec
```

9. Next, disable the reserved space on the disks to be used as metadata or data disk by using the following command. The default is 5% reserved for root, which for a 1 TB disk, means 46 GB per disk. Do this for each disk in the cluster:

```
# tune2fs -m 0 /dev/sdX
```

10. Mount the disks with `noatime` and `ext4`, as shown in the following screenshot. Otherwise, it will write to disk, even what you just did was read. It is interesting to consider the XFS filesystem:

```
/dev/xvdb1 on /data/namenode1 type ext4 (rw,noatime,data=ordered)
/dev/xvdc1 on /data/namenode2 type ext4 (rw,noatime,data=ordered)
```

11. The disk mount paths must be short and branching to just one level. This is shown in the following screenshot. Longer names will be an issue in larger clusters:

```
/dev/xvdb1          20G   51M   19G   1% /space/d1
/dev/xvdc1          20G   58M   19G   1% /space/d2
/dev/xvdd1          20G   63M   19G   1% /space/d3
```

12. Once the mount points are done, test them for write speed using the following command:

```
# dd if=/dev/zero of=/space/d1/test.img conv=fdatasyncbs=512
count=1k
```

13. Make sure that the disks used in a single Datanode are from the same manufacturer. This is to do with the disk geometry alignment.
14. Make sure the disk I/O scheduler is `cfq`, as it is suitable for most workloads. Change this to `noop` if using virtualized hosts:

```
# cat /sys/block/sda/queue/scheduler
# echo noop> /sys/block/sda/queue/scheduler
```

15. Change the disk queue length as, by default, it is just 128. This can be done as follows:

```
# cat /sys/block/sda/queue/nr_requests
# echo 500 > /sys/block/sda/queue/nr_requests
```

16. Never use LVM for disks in the Hadoop cluster as it will degrade performance.

How it works...

In the preceding recipe, we looked at the options to tune disks for performance by changing the filesystem type, parameters, space, and disk layout structure. As post jobs in Hadoop are disk I/O bound, we will see a significant difference in performance by optimizing parameters.

The disk block size can also be tuned for performance and better utilization of space. By default, the block size is equal to the page size of 4 Kb (group of 8 blocks).

Tuning the network

In this recipe, we will look at tuning the network for better performance. This recipe is very much limited to the operating system parameters and not the optimization of routers or switches.

Getting ready

To step through the recipe in this section, we need at least one node to test and to make the configuration changes, and the same can be applied to all the nodes in the cluster.

How to do it...

1. Connect to a node which at a later stage will be used to install Hadoop. We are using the node `master1.cyrus.com`.
2. Switch as user `root` or have `sudo` privileges.
3. Edit the `/etc/sysctl.conf` file to tune parameters which affect the network performance. The parameters shown in the next steps need to be changed in this file.
4. Change the port range by adding the following line:

   ```
   net.ipv4.ip_local_port_range = 1024 65535
   ```

5. Enable TCP socket reuse and recycle by using the following line:

   ```
   net.ipv4.tcp_tw_recycle = 1
   net.ipv4.tcp_tw_reuse = 1
   ```

6. Tune the SYN backlog queue by adjusting the following values. This is for legitimate half open connections. Adjust `net.core.netdev_max_backlog`, rather than increasing `tcp_max_syn_backlog`, as follows:

   ```
   net.ipv4.tcp_max_syn_backlog = 4096
   net.core.netdev_max_backlog = 2000
   ```

7. Change the send and receive socket buffer size by using the below settings. By default, 16 MB is more than enough per socket:

   ```
   net.core.rmem_max = 16777216
   net.core.wmem_max = 16777216
   ```

8. Prevent SYN flood by controlling the half open connections by using the following parameter:

   ```
   net.ipv4.tcp_syncookies = 1
   ```

9. Increase the listening queue length, as this will help in communication between nodes. By default, this is just set to 1024 and can be changed as follows:

   ```
   net.core.somaxconn = 4096
   ```

10. Always keep some memory free for network traffic and not cause OOM. This can be done by reserving free memory. The default is 64 MB; increase this on systems with large memory:

    ```
    vm.min_free_kbytes = 67584
    ```

11. Enable jumbo frames on the Ethernet network by changing the MTU from 1500 to 9000 bytes. But for this, devices like switches and routers must support jumbo frames:

    ```
    # echo "MTU=9000">> /etc/sysconfig/network-scripts/ifcfg-eth0
    ```

12. Disable responses to broadcast by using the following value:

    ```
    net.ipv4.icmp_echo_ignore_broadcasts = 1
    ```

13. Enable route verification, unless you are using a specialized hardware for multi-pathing or direct server return:

    ```
    net.ipv4.conf.all.rp_filter = 1
    ```

14. Disable IPv6, till it becomes an industry standard for Hadoop by using the following. This can also be passed in the Java opts options:

    ```
    net.ipv6.conf.all.disable_ipv6=1
    net.ipv6.conf.default.disable_ipv6=1
    ```

15. Enable `nscd` to cache DNS resolutions, but cache only DNS and passwords.
16. The JVM also caches the DNS resolutions and it can cause issues if DNS records a change, especially in long running jobs. It is better to set TTL in the, `$JAVA_HOME/jre/lib/security/java.security` file as follows:

    ```
    networkaddress.cache.ttl=60
    ```

17. The preceding can also be set per application by using something like `java.security.Security.setProperty("networkaddress.cache.ttl" , "60");`
18. Also, enable selective acknowledgement for TCP packets by using the following settings:

    ```
    # echo 'net.ipv4.tcp_sack = 1'>> /etc/sysctl.conf
    ```

19. Increase the count of `inotify` watcher to listen to more directories for changes by using the parameter `fs.inotify.max_user_watches = 65536`.
20. After making all the changes make sure to commit by using `sysctl -p`.

How it works...

In the preceding recipe, we modified the `sysctl` parameters for tuning network connections. Always try these in non-production clusters to see their impact. Once you understand what these do, then only apply in the production setup.

> It is good to read about TCP/IP connection details and how memory plays a role. It is important to keep the system patched with the latest stable releases and plug any performance gaps which could affect performance and security.

Tuning HDFS

In the previous few recipes, we tuned the operating system, disks, and network setting for the installation of Hadoop.

In this recipe, we will tune HDFS for best performance. As stated initially, the HDFS read/write performance on a node with a slow disk and resource constraints will be slower compared to a node having a faster disk, CPU, and RAM. Tuning is always a layered approach, tuning each layer in conjunction to come to a final result.

Getting ready

To complete the recipe, the user must have a running cluster with HDFS and YARN setup. Users can refer to *Chapter 1, Hadoop Architecture and Deployment*, on installation details.

The assumption here is that the user is well familiar with HDFS concepts and knows its layout. Please read the *Tuning the disk* recipe, as HDFS will be a pseudo-file system of a native EXT4 or XFS filesystem.

How to do it...

1. Connect to the Namenode `master1.cyrus.com` and switch to user `hadoop`.
2. Edit the file `hdfs-site.xml` and change the HDFS block size to be 128 MB, as follows:

   ```
   <property>
   <name>dfs.blocksize</name>
   <value>134217728</value>
   </property>
   ```

3. Adjust the replication factor according to the number of nodes in the cluster. If the number of nodes are greater than ten, then keep replication to three, else reduce it to two:

   ```
   <property>
   <name>dfs.replication</name>
   <value>3</value>
   </property>
   ```

4. The replication count must never be greater than the number of nodes in the cluster, or else clients will not be able to close the files.
5. The maximum number of items a directory can contain is controlled by the parameter `dfs.namenode.fs-limits.max-directory-items`.
6. Control the smallest block that a file can have. This limits a file with many small blocks. This is done by the following parameter:

   ```
   dfs.namenode.fs-limits.min-block-size = 1048576
   ```

7. Tune the largest file size that can be created on HDFS by limiting the maximum blocks per file by using the following parameter:

   ```
   dfs.namenode.fs-limits.max-blocks-per-file = 1048576
   ```

8. Always prefer more disks, rather than having larger disks for distribution.
9. Never, ever increase the minimum block replication count from the default value of 1. This is defined by the following parameter:

   ```
   dfs.namenode.replication.min
   ```

10. The important thing to note here is that the block replication is different from job file replication, which is defaulted to 10. Files like `job.xml`, JARs build the dist cache and must be available for localization. This is controlled by the following parameter in the `mapred-site.xml` file:

    ```
    mapreduce.client.submit.file.replication
    ```

How it works...

We can check the value for any parameter in the cluster by using the command shown in the following screenshot:

```
[root@master1 ~]# hdfs getconf -confkey dfs.blocksize
134217728
[root@master1 ~]# hdfs getconf -confkey dfs.replication
1
```

HDFS is not a native filesystem, it is just an abstraction in which each HDFS block is actually a file on EXT4. So, for a 128 MB HDFS block, (128 MB/64 Kbytes) = 32 k blocks on a native filesystem.

Tune HDFS is a broader term in which Namenode and Datanodes must be optimized for performance, which is covered in the next few recipes.

Tuning Namenode

In this recipe, we will look at tuning Namenode by making some important configuration changes. Namenode is more CPU and memory bound and must run on hardware with multi-core CPU and large memory to accommodate the entire namespace.

We will look at parameters only for the Namenode, which in production will come into effect in conjunction with HDFS and Datanode parameters, discussed in this chapter.

Getting ready

To complete the recipe, the user must have a running cluster with HDFS and YARN setup. Users can refer to *Chapter 1, Hadoop Architecture and Deployment,* for installation details.

The assumption here is that the user is well familiar with Namenode functionality and can edit and restart services for changes to be effective.

> It is recommended that users explore the load characteristics of Namenode and understand its memory usage, thread count, and GC cycle.

How to do it...

1. Connect to the master node `master1.cyrus.com` and switch to the `hadoop` user.

   The first thing to make sure is the number of directory paths for Namenode metadata. It should not be more than two, as the metadata is synced to all the disks specified under the parameter `dfs.namenode.name.dir`:

   ```
   <property>
   <name>dfs.namenode.name.dir</name>
   <value>file:/data/namenode1,file:/data/namenode2</value>
   </property>
   ```

2. If using NFS share as one of the preceding directories, make sure to tune NFS server and client to high throughput. We can tune `rsize=65536` and `wsize=65536`, depending upon the network bandwidth.
3. The preceding setting will make sense only if we increase the MTU size, as discussed in the previous recipe.

4. The default NFS server thread count is 8, and for a busy Namenode, it must be increased to a higher value, like 20. This can be done in the/`etc/sysconfig/nfs` file by adding the following parameter:

   ```
   RPCNFSDCOUNT=20
   ```

5. As Namenode stores the entire metadata in memory, it is important to calculate the head space correctly. The recommendation is 1 GB of memory for every 1 million files, where each file is of 2 blocks. This current usage can be calculated by using the following formula:

   ```
   $ hdfs oiv -p XML -printToScreen -i /data/namenode1/current/
   fsimage_0000000000000026487 | egrep"block|inode" | wc -l |
   awk'{printf"Objects=%d : Suggested Xms=%0dmXmx=%0dm\n", $1, (($1 /
   1000000 )*1024), (($1 / 1000000 )*1024)}'
   ```

6. Estimating the Namenode memory based on cluster size:

   ```
   Block size = 128MB
   Each Node present 20TB of Disk space
   Total number of nodes in cluster = 1000 nodes

   Calculations:
   150 bytes per object
   Total Blocks = (20TB x 1000)/128MB
   = 163840000 blocks
   Adjusting for replication factor, which is 3 by default. As each
   replicated block just takes about 16 bytes in memory of namenode.
   163840000/3 = 54613333 x 150 + (16 bytes X 54613333)
      = 8192000000 + 873813328 = 8.44 GB
   ```

7. The Namenode heap can be configured by editing the `hadoop-env.sh` file and adding the following line:

   ```
   export HADOOP_NAMENODE_HEAPSIZE=8192
   ```

8. If the heap memory is not sufficient, restarting a Namenode with a large `edits` file and inodes to load will take a long time to start.
9. Adjust the Namenode handler count by using the following configuration in the `hdfs-site.xml` file:

   ```
   <property>
   <name>dfs.namenode.handler.count</name>
   <value>60</value>
   </property>
   ```

10. The value of handler count should be capped at 240 max, irrespective of the size of the cluster. Each thread takes about 5 MB of memory, which needs to be accounted for in addition to the above memory calculations.

11. In larger clusters, when Datanodes start, they advertise their blocks using block reports, which could overwhelm the Namenode. This can be controlled by introducing a delay with a random number and spreading the block reports over a period of delayed time. This can be done by using the following parameter in the `hdfs-site.xml` file:

```
<property>
<name>dfs.blockreport.initialDelay</name>
<value>10</value>
</property>
```

12. It is a good practice to let the Namenode stabilize in a cluster with more than 1000 nodes and give it more time in safe mode by using the following parameter; this is in milliseconds:

```
<property>
<name>dfs.namenode.safemode.extension</name>
<value>50000</value>
</property>
```

13. In case you have to co-host the Namenode and Datanode directory on the same disk, it is good to reserve some space for Namenode metadata by using the parameter `dfs.namenode.resource.du.reserved`.
14. In case we have to decommission a Datanode with large disks, it is important to increase the number of blocks to process per decommission interval. This should be increased to a high number if you have Datanodes with large storage capacity:

```
<property>
<name>dfs.namenode.decommission.blocks.per.interval</name>
<value>500000</value>
</property>
```

15. If decommissioning many nodes at a time, then decrease the preceding value to avoid network congestion.
16. To track the decommissioning Datanodes, Namenode consumes additional memory and the number of nodes that it tracks at a time should be controlled if the number of nodes to decommission at a time is very large. This is configured by using the following configuration:

```
<property>
<name>dfs.namenode.decommission.max.concurrent.tracked.nodes</
name>
<value>500000</value>
</property>
```

17. It is very important to protect the production Namenode from accidental format. It is a good practice to disable formatting of the Namenode by using the following parameter:

```
<property>
<name>dfs.namenode.support.allow.format</name>
<value>false</value>
</property>
```

18. For JVM, it is recommended to use the `-XX:+UseConcMarkSweepGC` algorithm for garbage collection.

There's more...

We can look into the heap usage pattern by using the command shown in the following screenshot:

```
[hadoop@master1 ~]$ jmap -heap 3424
Attaching to process ID 3424, please wait...
Debugger attached successfully.
Server compiler detected.
JVM version is 25.92-b14

using thread-local object allocation.
Parallel GC with 4 thread(s)

Heap Configuration:
   MinHeapFreeRatio         = 0
   MaxHeapFreeRatio         = 100
   MaxHeapSize              = 2147483648 (2048.0MB)
   NewSize                  = 88080384 (84.0MB)
   MaxNewSize               = 715653120 (682.5MB)
   OldSize                  = 176160768 (168.0MB)
   NewRatio                 = 2
   SurvivorRatio            = 8
   MetaspaceSize            = 21807104 (20.796875MB)
   CompressedClassSpaceSize = 1073741824 (1024.0MB)
   MaxMetaspaceSize         = 17592186044415 MB
   G1HeapRegionSize         = 0 (0.0MB)
```

See also

- The *Tuning Datanode* recipe

Tuning Datanode

In this recipe, we will look at tuning the Datanode by making some important configuration changes. Datanodes are mostly I/O bound, but can have a varied workload for HBase region servers. The network throughout the disks must be tuned for optimal performance.

We will look at parameters only for the Datanode, which in production will come into effect in conjunction with HDFS and Namenode parameters, discussed earlier in this chapter.

Getting ready

For this recipe, you will again need a running cluster and have at least the HDFS daemons running in the cluster.

How to do it...

1. Connect to the master node `master1.cyrus.com` and switch to user `hadoop`.
2. The `hdfs-site.xml` file will remain the same in the cluster. Each of the Namenode and Datanode daemons will read its respective parameters, ignoring the others.
3. Tune the Datanode handler count by using the following configuration in the `hdfs-site.xml` file:

```
<property>
<name>dfs.datanode.handler.count</name>
<value>40</value>
</property>
```

4. If the Datanodes have large disks, it is important to increase the threads to transfers in and out. This is really useful while doing a decommission on Datanodes with huge disks. If using HBase, this number should be set much higher:

```
<property>
<name>dfs.datanode.max.transfer.threads</name>
<value>8192</value>
</property>
```

5. For Datanodes with multiple disks, increase the thread count for volume scans. This can be done as follows:

```
<property>
<name>dfs.datanode.directoryscan.threads</name>
<value>2</value>
</property>
```

6. It is important to cap the bandwidth usage for the Datanode balancer in peak time by using the following property. This is in bytes per second per Datanode:

```
<property>
<name>dfs.datanode.balance.bandwidthPerSec</name>
<value>1048576</value>
</property>
```

7. On a Datanode with many disks, it is not wise for just a single disk going bad to mark the entire Datanode as bad. We can control the number of volumes that can be tolerated as bad. This value should be equal to the number of *data disks -1*. For a Datanode with 20 data disks, the following configuration could be used:

```
<property>
<name>dfs.datanode.failed.volumes.tolerated</name>
<value>19</value>
</property>
```

8. On a Datanode, we can have disks of different capacities. How should the usage of these disk be managed? Should it be round robin or the disk which has the most space available that is used? This can be configured by using the following properties:

```
<property>
<name>dfs.datanode.fsdataset.volume.choosing.policy</name>
<value>org.apache.hadoop.hdfs.server.datanode.fsdataset.
AvailableSpaceVolumeChoosingPolicy</value>
</property>

<property>
<name>dfs.datanode.available-space-volume-choosing-policy.
balanced-space-threshold</name>
<value>10737418240</value>
</property>

<property>
<name>dfs.datanode.available-space-volume-choosing-policy.
balanced-space-preference-fraction</name>
<value>0.75f</value>
</property>
```

9. It is important to understand the above, as always targeting the least used disk will cause a bottleneck on the disk controller.
10. Another important parameter is the Datanode heap memory. If the Datanode has a large number of blocks, then we have to bump up the heap memory by making an entry in the `Hadoop-env.sh` file as shown below:

    ```
    export HADOOP_DATANODE_HEAPSIZE=4096
    ```

How it works...

In this recipe, we tuned Datanodes for better performance by adjusting various parameters. Always remember that these parameters are interlinked with many others on the node. Increasing memory for one might starve the other.

In addition to the preceding, we can also bypass the stale Datanodes to safe socket timeouts by enabling parameters such as `dfs.namenode.avoid.read.stale.datanode` and `dfs.namenode.avoid.write.stale.datanode`.

See also

- The *Tuning Namenode* recipe
- The *Tuning HDFS* recipe
- The *Configuring YARN for performance* recipe

Configuring YARN for performance

Another important component to tune is the YARN framework. Until now, we have concentrated on the HDFS/storage layer, but we need to tune the scheduler and compute the layer as well.

In this recipe, we will see which important properties to take care of and how they can be optimized. To get a picture of the YARN layout and to correlate things better, please refer to the following diagram:

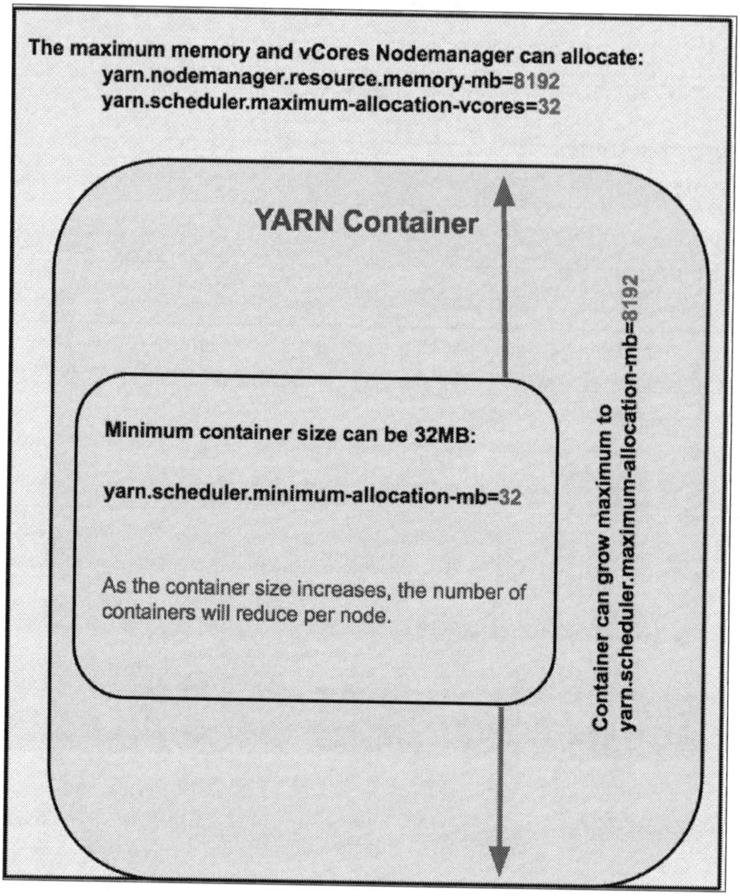

Getting ready

Make sure that the user has a running cluster with HDFS and YARN configured. The user must be able to execute HDFS and YARN commands. Please refer to *Chapter 1, Hadoop Architecture and Deployment,* for Hadoop installation and configuration.

How to do it...

1. Connect to the Namenode `master1.cyrus.com` and switch to the `hadoop` user.
2. The important file for this recipe is `yarn-site.xml` and all the parameters in the following steps will be part of it.
3. The memory on the system after accounting for the operating system, any daemons like Namenode or Datanodes, and HBase regions servers is represented as being available to YARN for scheduling. The maximum memory available for Nodemanager to allocate is configured as follows:

```
<property>
<name>yarn.nodemanager.resource.memory-mb</name>
<value>8192</value>
</property>
```

4. The maximum memory that can be allocated to a container cannot be greater than what is presented by the preceding Nodemanager. This is configured by using the property as follows. This is also how big the container can be, this being the upper bound:

```
<property>
<name>yarn.scheduler.maximum-allocation-mb</name>
<value>8192</value>
</property>
```

5. Memory must always be allocated as a whole number of a smallest allocation unit, which is shown as follows:

```
<property>
<name>yarn.scheduler.minimum-allocation-mb</name>
<value>32</value>
</property>
```

6. The **Application master** (**AM**) is per application and also needs resources to run and execute the containers of a job. The memory for AM is defined by the following configuration:

```
<property>
<name>yarn.app.mapreduce.am.resource.mb</name>
<value>1536</value>
</property>
```

7. To control the maximum number of applications that can run concurrently in the cluster, we modify the following configuration. By default, this value is just 1 percent, not allowing other applications to run:

```
<property>
<name>yarn.scheduler.capacity.maximum-am-resource-percent</name>
<value>0.3</value>
</property>
```

8. The next step is to tune the vCores available per node for the containers. This can be configured by using the following settings:

```
<property>
<name>yarn.scheduler.maximum-allocation-vcores</name>
<value>32</value>
</property>

<property>
<name>yarn.scheduler.minimum-allocation-vcores</name>
<value>1</value>
</property>
```

9. Check and tune for virtual memory for any container and make sure that it does not exceed more than a certain ratio of physical memory:

```
<property>
<name>yarn.nodemanager.vmem-check-enabled</name>
<value>true</value>
</property>

<property>
<name>yarn.nodemanager.vmem-pmem-ratio</name>
<value>2.1</value>
</property>
```

10. Tune the Resourcemanager and Nodemanager heap size using the `yarn-env.sh` file as shown as follows:

```
export YARN_NODEMANAGER_HEAPSIZE=2048
export YARN_RESOURCEMANAGER_HEAPSIZE=4096
```

11. Tune the YARN Java options to prefer IPv4 and use the following settings:

```
YARN_OPTS="$YARN_OPTS -server -Djava.net.preferIPv4Stack=true
-XX:+UseConcMarkSweepGC"
```

12. Make sure that you do not schedule containers on Datanodes which have already reached a threshold of disk usage, which is 90% by default. The important parameter is `yarn.nodemanager.disk-health-checker.max-disk-utilization-per-disk-percentage`.
13. If the disks are quite large, for example a 4 TB disk, 10%, which is 400 GB, would still be a significant amount of free disk space to run jobs on the node, rather than marking it as dead.
14. In large clusters with thousands of jobs, it is important to optimize Resourcemanager tracker, scheduler, and client thread count as shown below:

```
<property>
<name>yarn.resourcemanager.scheduler.client.thread-count</name>
<value>30</value>
</property>

<property>
<name>yarn.resourcemanager.resource-tracker.client.thread-count</
name>
<value>20</value>
</property>

<property>
<name>yarn.resourcemanager.client.thread-count</name>
<value>20</value>
</property>
```

15. For Nodemanager it is important to tune container manager and localization thread counts as follows:

```
<property>
<name>yarn.nodemanager.container-manager.thread-count</name>
<value>20</value>
</property>

<property>
<name>yarn.nodemanager.localizer.fetch.thread-count</name>
<value>10</value>
</property>
```

16. It is not necessary that increasing the thread count will improve performance, as it could have a negative impact for resource issues.
17. After making all the changes, copy the file to all nodes in the cluster and restart the daemons.

How it works...

In the preceding recipe, we looked at YARN memory composition and how we can optimize the allocations making sure that we do not fragment the memory available to YARN per node. If we ask for a mapper with 2048 MB of memory, then *2048/32 = 64* YARN memory units will be allocated. On the other hand, if the request is for, say, 2310 MB per mapper, then 2310 is not divisible by 32, so it will be rounded to the next whole number, 2336, which is divisible by 32. This creates more resource ask than is actually required.

We can use the command `jstat -gcPID` for details of GC of a process and its utilization.

Configuring MapReduce for performance

In this recipe, we will touch upon MapReduce parameters and see how we can optimize them.

Getting ready

For this recipe, you will again need a running cluster with HDFS and YARN. Users must have completed the recipe *Configuring YARN for performance* recipe.

How to do it...

1. Connect to the master node `master1.cyrus.com` and switch to the `hadoop` user.
2. The file where these changes will be made is `mapred-site.xml`.
3. The first thing to adjust is to sort the buffer according to the HDFS block size. It must always be greater than the value of `dfs.blocksize`. This can be configured as follows:

```
<property>
<name>mapreduce.task.io.sort.mb</name>
<value>200</value>
</property>
```

4. The next value to tune is the number of streams to merge while sorting. This many file handles will be open per mapper:

```
<property>
<name>mapreduce.task.io.sort.factor</name>
<value>24</value>
</property>
```

5. Another important thing to take care of is not to co-locate the Mapred temp location on the disk where Datanode blocks are. This can be done by using the configuration as follows, where `/space/tmp` should be a separate mount point:

```
<property>
<name>mapreduce.cluster.local.dir</name>
<value>/space/tmp</value>
</property>
```

6. We need to tune the mapper memory according to the data size and type. For example, if my mapper loads the complete non-splittable file, it needs more memory:

```
<property>
<name>mapreduce.map.memory.mb</name>
<value>2048</value>
</property>
```

7. Similarly, the general rule for reducer is that it should have twice the memory of a mapper:

```
<property>
<name>mapreduce.reduce.memory.mb</name>
<value>4096</value>
</property>
```

8. The JVM heap space for both mapper and reducer should be about 80% of the respective mapper and reduce memory as follows:

```
<property>
<name>mapreduce.map.java.opts</name>
<value>-Xmx1664m</value>
</property>

<property>
<name>mapreduce.reduce.java.opts</name>
<value>-Xmx3328m</value>
</property>
```

9. Navigate to the directory `/opt/cluster/hadoop/etc/hadoop`.
10. Edit the `hdfs-site.xml` file and add the following configuration:

```
<property>
<name>dfs.storage.policy.enabled</name>
<value>true</value>
</property>
```

11. The mapper output files are served by the node on which mapper ran, using the task tracker HTTP threads. If this number is 40, it means that it will fetch data from 40 HTTP threads and serve 40 reducers at a time. This is a minimum value:

```
<property>
<name>mapreduce.tasktracker.http.threads</name>
<value>60</value>
</property>
```

12. Now, on the reducer side during the shuffle phase, the mapper output needs to be fetched and this can be done in parallel as follows:

```
<property>
<name>mapreduce.reduce.shuffle.parallelcopies</name>
<value>10</value>
</property>
```

13. In addition to the preceding, a fetcher is assigned by doing a group by host, so all mappers on a node are assigned to it in one go, limited to a hard-coded value of 20 mapper outputs to a single fetcher.
14. Compress the job output to save on the data to be copied across nodes. This can be done by using the following properties:

```
<property>
<name>mapreduce.map.output.compress</name>
<value>true</value>
</property>

<property>
<name>mapreduce.output.fileoutputformat.compress.type</name>
<value>BLOCK</value>
</property>

<property>
<name>mapreduce.map.output.compress.codec</name>
<value>org.apache.hadoop.io.compress.SnappyCodec</value>
</property>
```

15. There is no significant reason for using more than one vCore per Mapper or Reducer:

```
<property>
<name>mapreduce.map.cpu.vcores</name>
<value>1</value>
</property>

<property>
<name>mapreduce.reduce.cpu.vcores</name>
<value>1</value>
</property>
```

16. It is important to tune what share of the Reducer memory will be used to store map outputs during shuffle. By default, this value is 70% of the Reducer heap size, which is good for most cases. If the Reducer heap size is small, reduce this value to avoid OOM errors:

```
<property>
<name>mapreduce.reduce.shuffle.input.buffer.percent</name>
<value>0.70</value>
</property>
```

17. There is a slight overhead in initializing the JVMs for tasks and it makes sense to reuse the JVM for different tasks. But, if enabled to be re-used infinitely during the job life cycle, it can result in memory leak for long running larger jobs. The recommended value is to set it to a reasonable re-use count as follows:

```
<property>
<name>mapreduce.job.jvm.numtasks</name>
<value>10</value>
</property>
```

18. So, in the preceding, after 10 tasks, re-use the JVM. The JVM will be destroyed and a new one will be created, cleaning memory.

19. Another parameter to consider is the Reducer slow start, which controls when a Reducer phase starts. The Reducer can start early to start the copy operation, but the Reducer execution cannot start till all Mappers are done. By default, they start when 5% of Mappers are done. So, for a job with 4000 Mappers, only after 200 Mappers are completed, all the Reducers will be started, it could be 1,000 Reducers, causing resource contention for Mappers.

20. Sometimes, on a cluster with many Mappers, this could cause a dead lock between the Mapper's and Reducer's resource allocation asks. Reducers will be occupying the containers which otherwise could have been used by Mappers, but the Mapper phase cannot finish as there are no free resources available to launch them:

```
<property>
<name>mapreduce.job.reduce.slowstart.completedmaps</name>
<value>0.20</value>
</property>
```

How it works...

In the preceding recipe, we saw the important parameters to look for while tuning the MapReduce jobs.

All these calculations will vary if we are running Spark, HBase, and so on nodes. The important thing to note here is that the parameters like `mapreduce.map.memory.mb` or `mapreduce.reduce.memory.mb`, and so on must all be multiples of the `yarn.scheduler.minimum-allocation-mb`.

Hive performance tuning

In this recipe, we will cover Hive tuning by touching upon some important parameters. Hive is a data warehousing solution which runs on top of Hadoop, as discussed in *Chapter 7, Data Ingestion and Workflow*. Please refer to it for installation and configuration of Hive.

Getting ready

Make sure that the user has a running cluster with Hive installed and configured to run with the ZooKeeper ensemble. Users can refer to *Chapter 7, Data Ingestion and Workflow* on Hive, for configuring that.

How to do it...

1. Connect to the Edge node `client1.cyrus.com` and switch to the `hadoop` user.
2. If you have followed the previous recipes, Hive is installed at `/opt/cluster/hive` on the Edge node.
3. The first thing is to tune the JVM heap used, when Hive is started by the shell as shown in the following screenshot, to the file `hive-env.sh` file:

```
# if [ "$SERVICE" = "cli" ]; then
#   if [ -z "$DEBUG" ]; then
#     export HADOOP_OPTS="$HADOOP_OPTS -XX:NewRatio=12 -Xms10m -XX:MaxHeapFreeRatio=40 -XX:MinHeapFreeRatio=15 -XX:+UseParNewGC -XX:-UseGCOverheadLimit"
#   else
#     export HADOOP_OPTS="$HADOOP_OPTS -XX:NewRatio=12 -Xms10m -XX:MaxHeapFreeRatio=40 -XX:MinHeapFreeRatio=15 -XX:-UseGCOverheadLimit"
#   fi
# fi
```

4. Configure the local Hive scratch space on a separate disk by using the following configuration:

```
<property>
<name>hive.exec.local.scratchdir</name>
<value>/space/scratch</value>
</property>
```

5. It is good to enable Hive compression to save on the data size, but there will be an overhead in terms of CPU cycles:

```
<property>
<name>hive.exec.compress.output</name>
<value>false</value>
</property>
```

6. Hive runs MapReduce at the backend and by default, each Reducer works on 256 MB of data. Increase this for larger datasets by using the following parameter. This will adjust the parallelism:

```
<property>
<name>hive.exec.reducers.bytes.per.reducer</name>
<value>256000000</value>
</property>
```

7. Disable speculative execution for Hive, as it can result in duplicate data. It is enabled by default:

```
<property>
<name>hive.mapred.reduce.tasks.speculative.execution</name>
<value>false</value>
</property>
```

8. Increase the metastore handler count by increasing the threads for filesystem operations as follows:

```
<property>
<name>hive.metastore.fshandler.threads</name>
<value>40</value>
</property>
```

9. Bump up the threads pool for the thrift server. This should be done only for heavy workloads and large client connections. This will reduce the initial client response:

```
<property>
<name>hive.metastore.server.min.threads</name>
<value>400</value>
</property>
```

10. The MapReduce mode is deprecated in the most recent Hive releases and it is recommended to see Tez as an execution engine. This can be done as shown in the following screenshot:

hive> set hive.execution.engine=tez;
hive> set hive.execution.engine;
hive.execution.engine=tez

11. Capture the GC metrics for the Hive job by enabling `hive.tez.exec.print.summary=true`.
12. Always use storage optimized formats for large datasets. Use the file formats as ORC, parquet rather than simple text files.
13. If we are doing a `JOIN` on two tables, then the larger table must be specified second in the `JOIN` statement. This is to avoid loading the larger table into memory and causing **Out Of Memory** (**OOM**).
14. Enable bucketing for a large dataset with partitions, by using `hive.enforce.bucketing=true`.
15. To optimize processing rows in a group, rather than processing one row at a time, enable vectorization in Tez. This can be done with the setting, `hive.vectorized.execution.enabled=true`.
16. Reduce the session timeouts for Hive `server2`, when running concurrent queries by using the following parameters:

```
hive.server2.idle.operation.timeout=3200000
hive.server2.idle.session.timeout=12000000
```

17. Limit the number of partitions for a query to be not more than 1000 partitions. This can be done by filtering the partitions using the `hive.metastore.limit.partition.request` parameter. This forces the Hive user to optimize their queries for tables with large partitions. What's the point of having partitions if a user query touches all of the partitions?
18. Avoid wide tables when possible. This means that the number of columns must be as small as possible, especially in parquet format, as larger columns will have a high memory footprint.

There's more...

1. Instead of typing the `set` commands on the Hive prompt, the user can create a `.hiverc` file in the home directory with the required settings as follows:

```
set hive.execution.engine=tez;
set hive.cli.print.current.db=true;
set hive.cbo.enable=true;
set hive.compute.query.using.stats=true;
```

2. It is a good practice to analyze tables and gather statistics for performance evolutions and better query plans as shown in the following screenshot. These statistics are used for query optimization only if `hive.cbo.enable` and `hive.compute.query.using.stats` is set to `true`:

```
hive> analyze table emp_hive compute statistics;
Query ID = hadoop_20170407204933_1d837d35-a987-4626-9b83-2bc7b16d4a7d
Total jobs = 1
Launching Job 1 out of 1
```

3. It is a good practice to analyze tables and gather statistics for performance evolutions and better query.

4. To check the raw data size, the number of files per table, or storage parameters, use the command as shown in the following screenshot:

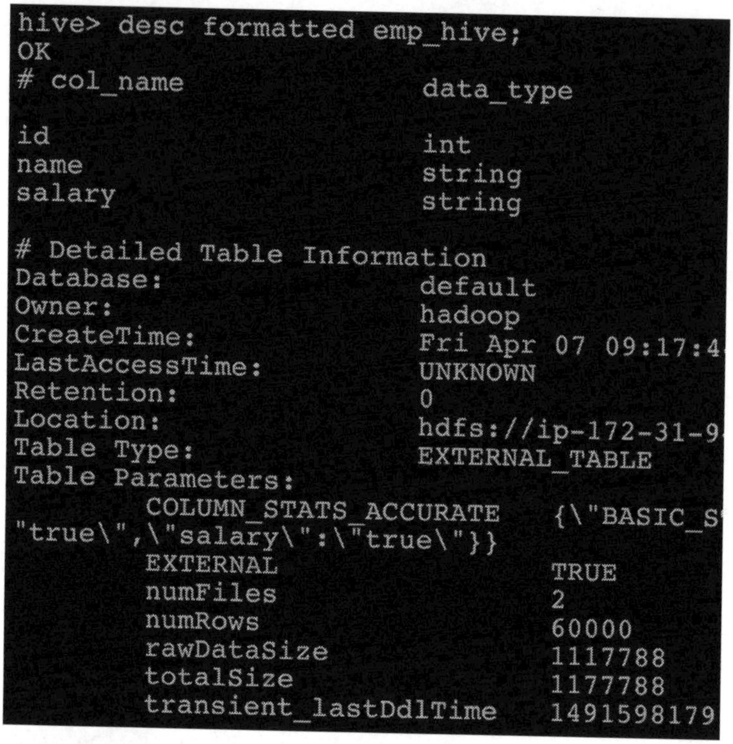

```
hive> desc formatted emp_hive;
OK
# col_name                data_type

id                        int
name                      string
salary                    string

# Detailed Table Information
Database:                 default
Owner:                    hadoop
CreateTime:               Fri Apr 07 09:17:4
LastAccessTime:           UNKNOWN
Retention:                0
Location:                 hdfs://ip-172-31-9
Table Type:               EXTERNAL_TABLE
Table Parameters:
        COLUMN_STATS_ACCURATE    {\"BASIC_S
"true\",\"salary\":\"true\"}}
        EXTERNAL                 TRUE
        numFiles                 2
        numRows                  60000
        rawDataSize              1117788
        totalSize                1177788
        transient_lastDdlTime    1491598179
```

How it works...

The optimizations we discussed are in addition to writing optimized queries. It is the responsibility of the SQL developer to write optimized queries, and stringent checks must be in place on the infrastructure to disallow badly written queries.

All connected components must be tuned for the services to work correctly. For example, if Hive is using ZooKeeper quorum for connections and ZooKeeper is timing out, it is important to tune the ZooKeeper parameters like `maxClientCnxns` or `export JVMFLAGS="-Xmx2048m` in the `$ZOOKEEEPER_HOME/conf/java.env` file.

Benchmarking Hadoop cluster

It is important to benchmark so as to have a baseline to do comparisons after making changes. In this recipe, we will look at some of the benchmarks which can help to profile the changes committed.

Before running any tests for the changed parameters, make sure to enable verbose logging and also enable GC logs for all the components by using `-verbose:gc -XX:+PrintGCDetails -XX:+PrintGCTimeStamps -XX:+PrintGCDateStamps -Xloggc:${LOG_DIR}/gc-{component}.log-$(date +'%Y%m%d%H%M')`.

Getting ready

Make sure that the user has a running cluster with HDFS and YARN fully functional in a multi-node cluster.

All these tests must be run first without making any changes to the cluster and then optimizing parameters, discussed in the preceding recipes, and again running the benchmarking test.

How to do it...

Connect to the Edge node `client1.cyrus.com` or master node and change to the `Hadoop` user.

All test output will be written to the location `/bencharks` on HDFS, under respective test directories.

Benchmark 1--Testing HDFS with TestDFSIO

This is a read/write test for HDFS by stress testing HDFS to test Namenode and Datanodes for any bottlenecks in terms of network or disk I/O.

1. The tool to be used for this can be invoked by using the following command. The JAR might be different in your case, depending upon the Hadoop version:

    ```
    $ hadoop jar hadoop-mapreduce-client-jobclient-2.7.2-tests.jar
    ```

2. Execute the command with the options as follows. This will write 100 files, with each file of 1 GB:

    ```
    $ hadoop jar hadoop-mapreduce-client-jobclient-2.7.2-tests.
    jarDFSCIOTest -write -nrFiles 10 -fileSize 1000
    ```

3. After the run, make a note of the file written at the`/benchmarks/TestDFSIO/io_write`.
4. Now run the read test with the same parameters as the preceding:

    ```
    $ hadoop jar hadoop-mapreduce-client-jobclient-2.7.2-tests.
    jarDFSCIOTest -read -nrFiles 10 -fileSize 1000
    ```

5. Take a note of the metrics written to the file. We will refer to them again after making changes discussed in the tuning sections and running all the tests again.

Benchmark 2--Stress testing Namenode

This is a read/write test for HDFS by stress testing HDFS to test Namenode and Datanodes for any bottlenecks in terms of network and disk I/O.

1. The tool to be used for this can be invoked by using the following command:

```
$ hadoop jar hadoop-mapreduce-client-jobclient-2.7.2-tests.
jarnnbench -operation create_write -blockSize 67108864
```

2. Run the preceding command with different block size and bytes to write:

```
nnbench -operation create_write -blockSize 134217728 -
bytesToWrite 10000
```

Benchmark 3--MapReduce testing by generating small files

This is a good test for JVM reuse by doing multiple runs.

1. The tool to be used for this can be invoked by using the following command:

```
$ hadoop jar hadoop-mapreduce-client-jobclient-2.7.2-tests.
jarmrbench -numRuns 10 -maps 100 -reduces 100 -inputLines 1
```

2. Do the second run with a large number of input lines and more Reducers:

```
mrbench -numRuns 10 -maps 1000 -reduces 1000 -inputLines 100000
```

3. Test by running with just one Reducer:

```
mrbench -numRuns 10 -maps 1000 -reduces 1 -inputLines 100000
```

Benchmark 4--TeraGen, TeraSort, and TeraValidate benchmarks

This is the most common test for benchmarking Hadoop clusters. It generates large data and then sorts it and validates it.

1. The first step is to generate the data by using the following command. It generates 100 byte rows of that count:

   ```
   $ hadoop jar hadoop-mapreduce-example.jarteragen 10000000000 /
   teraout
   ```

2. The next step is to sort the data by using the following command:

   ```
   $ hadoop jar hadoop-mapreduce-example.jarterasort /teraout /sorted
   ```

3. The last step is to validate the sorted data by using the following command:

   ```
   $ hadoop jar hadoop-mapreduce-example.jarteravalidate /sorted /
   validated
   ```

There's more...

1. We can look into tapping into the JMX to look at various metrics emitted by each of the components. For this, we have to enable JMX for that particular service by editing the environment files like `yarn-env.sh or hadoop-env.sh` for YARN and HDFS daemons respectively. This is shown in the following screenshot for Namenode. In addition to this, the performance can also be monitored by using Ganglia:

```
export HADOOP_NAMENODE_OPTS="-Dcom.sun.management.jmxremote
-Dcom.sun.management.jmxremote.password.file=$HADOOP_CONF_DIR/jmxremote.password
-Dcom.sun.management.jmxremote.authenticate=false
-Dcom.sun.management.jmxremote.ssl=false
-Dcom.sun.management.jmxremote.port=8004 $HADOOP_NAMENODE_OPTS"
```

2. The file `$HADOOP_CONF_DIR/jmxremote.password`, even though empty, must exist and it can also contain a username and password for authentication if enabled by `com.sun.management.jmxremote.authenticate=true`. In this case, we have disabled authentication by setting it to `false`.

3. Once the respective daemon is started, the port specified by "`om.sun.management.jmxremote.port=8004`, will start listening, as shown in the following screenshot:

```
[hadoop@nn1 ~]$ sudo netstat -tlpn | grep 8004
tcp        0      0 0.0.0.0:8004                0.0.0.0:*
           LISTEN      2846/java
```

4. We can connect to it by using the command `hdfs jmxget -server localhost -port 8004 -service Namenode`, as shown in the following screenshot:

```
[hadoop@nn1 ~]$ hdfs jmxget -server localhost -port 8004 -service NameNode
init: server=localhost;port=8004;service=NameNode;localVMUrl=null
Create RMI connector and connect to the RMI connector serverservice:jmx:rmi
```

5. Another way of connecting to JMX is by using JConsole as shown in the following screenshot:

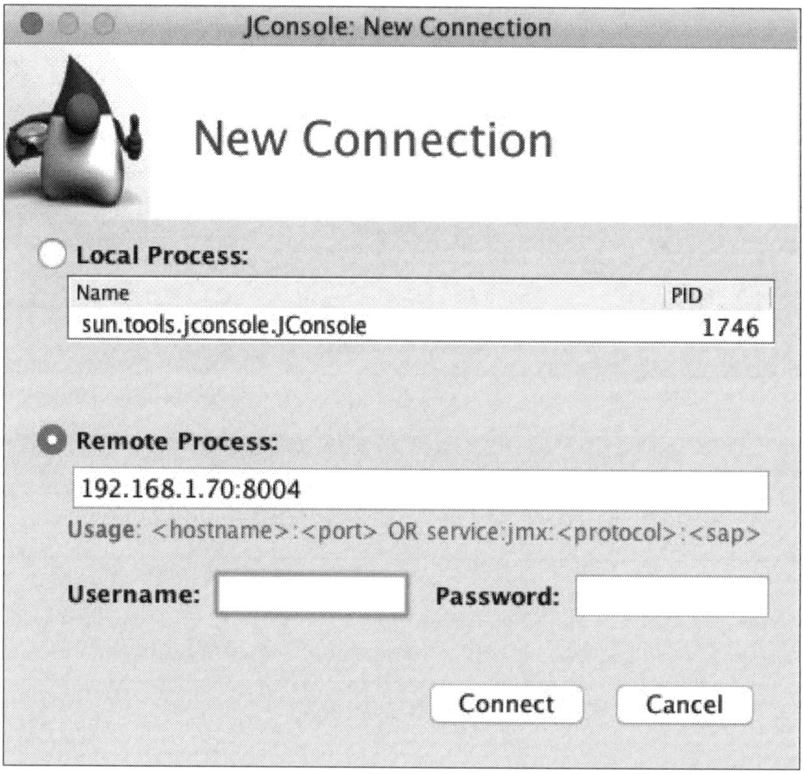

6. We can see various metrics for Namenode heap, CPU utilization, number of threads, and so on. This is shown in the following screenshot:

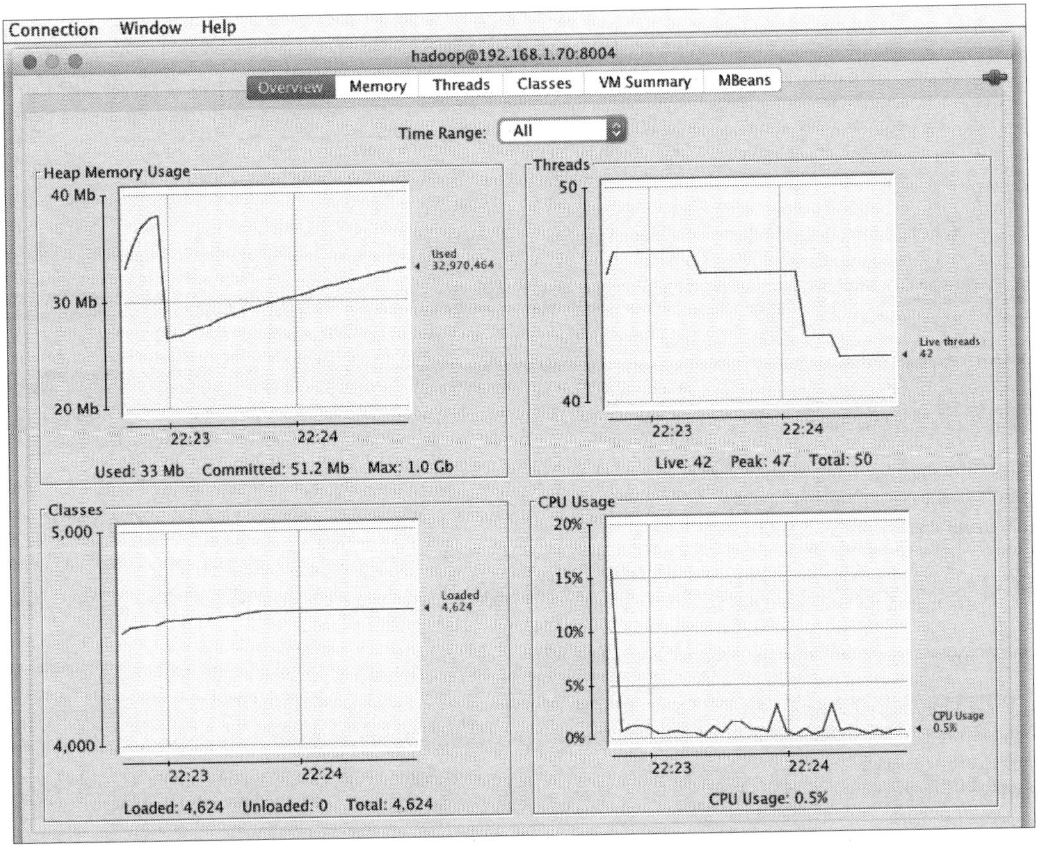

7. We can closely monitor each of these metrics, for example, how much memory is utilized during the Namenode startup as shown in the following screenshot:

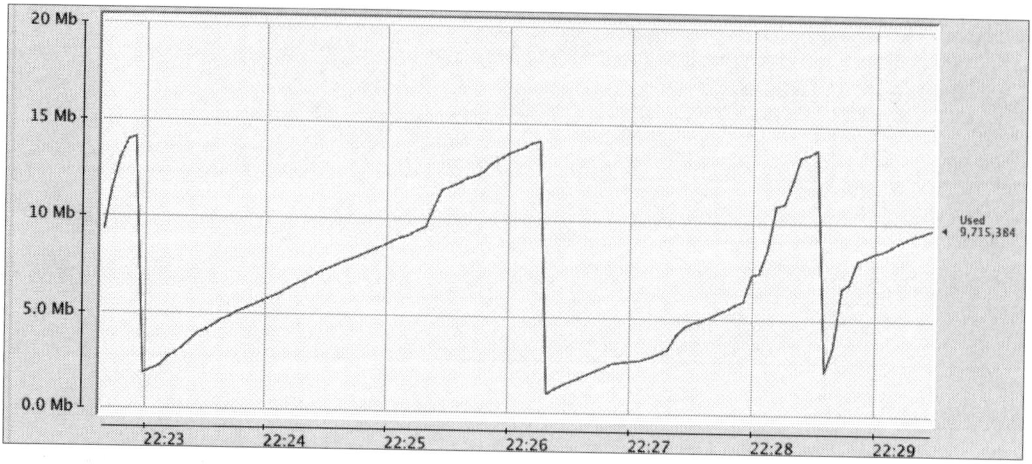

How it works...

We need to run the preceding tests multiple times by making a few changes at a time and then noting down the metrics in terms of time, data sizes, spills to disk, and memory usage pattern. Also, look into the logs which we enabled for tracking any GC events and timeouts.

It is recommended to setup Ganglia on the cluster before doing any of these tests and then do the comparative study on the metrics. One of the examples of monitoring is to track network bandwidth between nodes using tools like `ntop`. In the following screenshot, we can see the traffic characteristics between Namenode and Datanodes for `mrbench` benchmarking test:

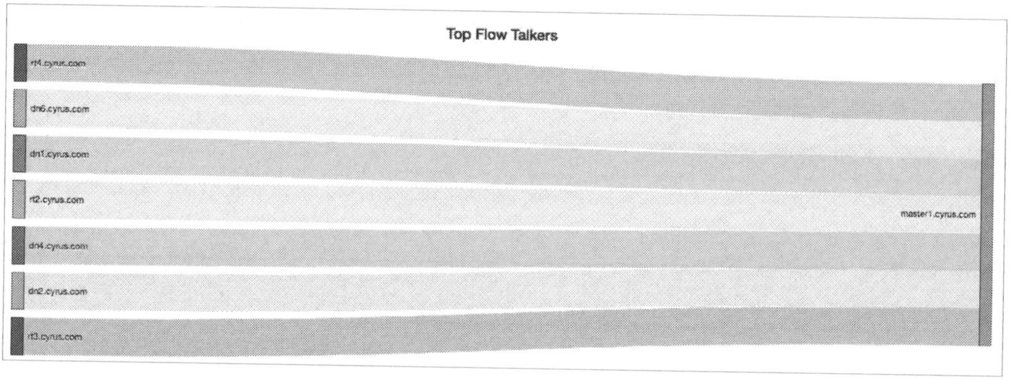

8. We can look at granular details in terms of connections, memory, and packet drops. The following screenshot shows the application master on node `rt2.cyrus.com` talking to different nodes and also fetching details from Namenode:

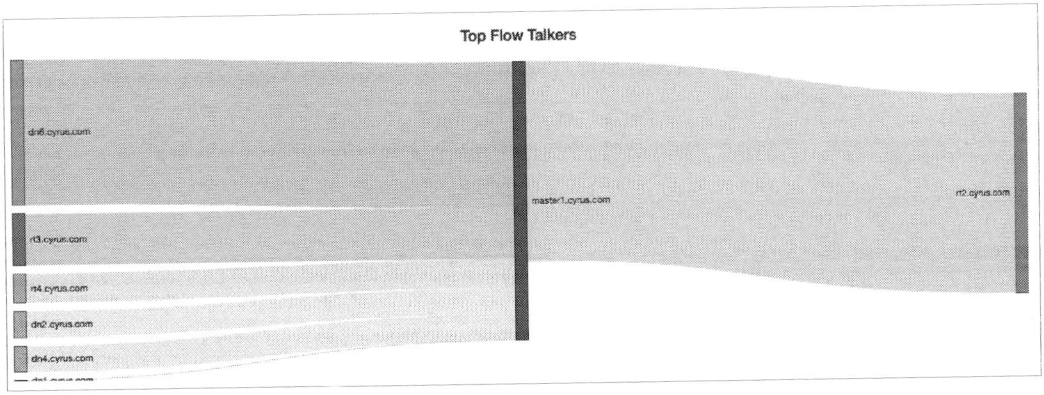

9. The optimizations we discussed here are in addition to writing optimized queries. It is the responsibility of the SQL developer to write optimized queries and stringent checks must be in place on the infrastructure to disallow badly written queries.

9

HBase Administration

In this chapter, we will cover the following recipes:

- Setting up single node HBase cluster
- Setting up multi-node HBase cluster
- Inserting data into HBase
- Integration with Hive
- HBase administration commands
- HBase backup and restore
- Tuning HBase
- HBase upgrade
- Migrating data from MySQL to HBase using Sqoop

Introduction

Apache HBase is a non-relational distributed, scalable key-value data store. It provides random read/write, real-time access to HDFS.

In this chapter, we will configure the various modes of the HBase cluster. In simple terms, it is a Hadoop database based on column families with massive scale. The important thing to note is that having a column family does not make it column oriented or NoSQL. There is a common misconception, where many refer to HBase as a column-oriented database even though it isn't, and secondly, a column-oriented database is not necessarily a NoSQL database.

In this chapter, we will cover the HBase cluster configuration, backup, restore, and upgrade processes.

Setting up single node HBase cluster

In this recipe, we will see how to set up an HBase single node cluster and its components. Apache HBase works on the basis of client server architecture with an HBase master and slaves known as region servers. The HBase master can be co-located with the Namenode, but it is recommended to run it on a dedicated node. The region servers will run on Datanodes.

In this recipe, we are just setting up a single node HBase cluster with the HBase master, a region server running on a single node with Namenode, and Datanode daemons.

Getting ready

Before going through the recipes in this chapter, make sure you have gone through the steps to install the Hadoop cluster with HDFS and YARN enabled. We need a single node for this recipe, so make sure you choose a node with decent configuration.

We are using a standalone ZooKeeper in this recipe or you can point it to the already configured ZooKeeper ensemble from the previous *Hive with ZooKeeper* recipe in *Chapter 7, Data Ingestion and Workflow*.

How to do it...

1. Connect to the `master1.cyrus.com` master node in the cluster and change to the user `hadoop`.
2. Download a stable release from the following link:

   ```
   $ wget apache.uberglobalmirror.com/hbase/stable/hbase-1.1.5-bin.
   tar.gz
   ```

3. Now untar the HBase package as shown:

   ```
   $ tar -zxvf hbase-1.1.5-bin.tar.gz -C /opt/cluster/
   ```

4. Change to the directory `/opt/cluster` and create a symlink as shown next:

   ```
   $ ln -s hbase-1.1.5-bin hbase
   ```

5. Update the environment variables to user `root`, as shown in the following screenshot:

```
export HBASE_HOME=/opt/cluster/hbase
PATH=$OOZIE_HOME/bin:$SPARK_HOME/bin:$SPARK_HOME/sbin:
$HBASE_HOME/bin:$HIVE_HOME/bin:$HADOOP_HOME/bin/:$HADO
OP_HOME/sbin/:$JAVA_HOME/bin/:$PATH
```

6. Make the changes effective by executing the following command:

```
# . /etc/profile.d/hadoopenv.sh
```

7. Execute the commands as shown in the following screenshot to see whether HBase is available in the path:

```
[hadoop@master1 ~]$ which hbase
/opt/cluster/hbase/bin/hbase
[hadoop@master1 ~]$ echo $HBASE_HOME
/opt/cluster/hbase
```

8. The `hbase` directory will look similar to the one shown in the following screenshot:

```
[hadoop@master1 cluster]$ ls -l hbase/
total 384
drwxr-xr-x  4 hadoop hadoop   4096 Mar 29 09:00 bin
-rw-r--r--  1 hadoop hadoop 183633 Mar 29 09:00 CHANGES.txt
drwxr-xr-x  2 hadoop hadoop   4096 Mar 29 09:00 conf
drwxr-xr-x 12 hadoop hadoop   4096 Mar 29 09:00 docs
drwxr-xr-x  7 hadoop hadoop   4096 Mar 29 09:00 hbase-webapps
-rw-r--r--  1 hadoop hadoop    261 Mar 29 09:00 LEGAL
drwxr-xr-x  3 hadoop hadoop   4096 Mar 29 09:00 lib
-rw-r--r--  1 hadoop hadoop 140387 Mar 29 09:00 LICENSE.txt
-rw-r--r--  1 hadoop hadoop  34474 Mar 29 09:00 NOTICE.txt
-rw-r--r--  1 hadoop hadoop   1477 Mar 29 09:00 README.txt
```

9. Switch to the directory of `hbase` extract `$HBASE_HOME/conf/` and edit the `hbase-site.xml` file, shown as follows:

```
<property>
    <name>hbase.rootdir</name>
    <value>file:///home/hadoop/hdata</value>
</property>

<property>
    <name>hbase.zookeeper.property.dataDir</name>
    <value>/home/hadoop/zookeeper</value>
</property>
```

10. You can leave the other configuration parameters at default. Create directories `/home/hadoop/zookeeper` and `/home/hadoop/hdata` with correct permissions.

11. Start the Datanode daemon on the node, so that a region server can start up there, as shown in the following screenshot:

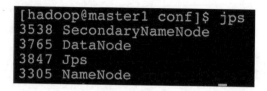

```
[hadoop@master1 conf]$ jps
3538 SecondaryNameNode
3765 DataNode
3847 Jps
3305 NameNode
```

12. This is a not a production setup and is used only for the Dev environment to test code. The Datanode daemon will create a directory structure under the `tmp` directory, as we have not explicitly defined it in `hdfs-site.xml`.
13. The `$HBASE_HOME/conf/regionservers` file will contain the entry `localhost` by default.
14. Now, start the HBase cluster either by using the `hbase-start.sh` command or you can start the master and regions servers using `hbase-daemon.sh start master`. The services will be shown as in the following screenshot:

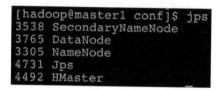

```
[hadoop@master1 conf]$ jps
3538 SecondaryNameNode
3765 DataNode
3305 NameNode
4731 Jps
4492 HMaster
```

15. The HBase master web UI can be accessed on port `16010`, as shown in the following screenshot:

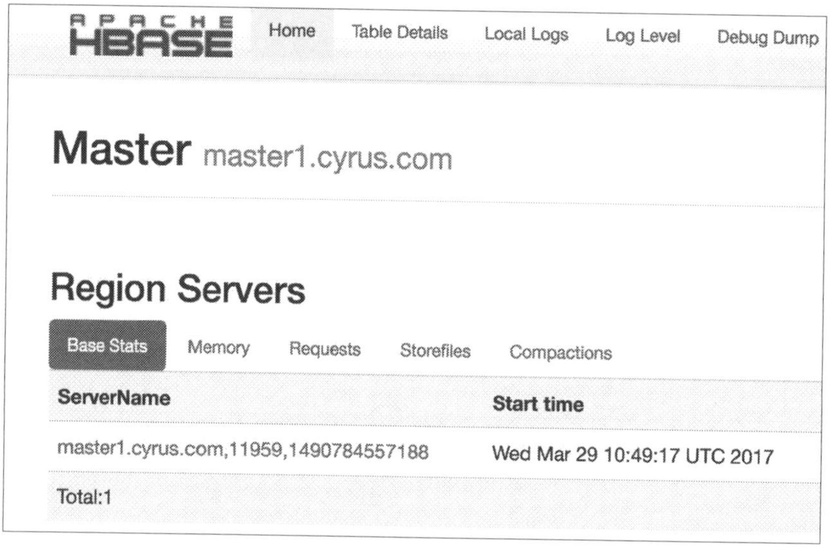

16. The user can verify the servers running in the HBase cluster either through the web UI or with the command, as shown in the following screenshot:

```
[hadoop@master1 ~]$ echo "status" | hbase shell
SLF4J: Class path contains multiple SLF4J bindings.
SLF4J: Found binding in [jar:file:/opt/cluster/hbas
ticLoggerBinder.class]
SLF4J: Found binding in [jar:file:/opt/cluster/hado
ar!/org/slf4j/impl/StaticLoggerBinder.class]
SLF4J: See http://www.slf4j.org/codes.html#multiple_
SLF4J: Actual binding is of type [org.slf4j.impl.Lo
HBase Shell; enter 'help<RETURN>' for list of suppo
Type "exit<RETURN>" to leave the HBase Shell
Version 1.1.5, r239b80456118175b340b2e562a5568b5c74

status
1 servers, 0 dead, 2.0000 average load
```

How it works...

In this recipe, we configured the HBase standalone cluster with ZooKeeper running locally on the node—HBase manages the ZooKeeper. This setup is a single point of failure and must not be used for critical data.

The HBase master holds system tables, which are metadata and namespace tables, as shown in the following screenshot:

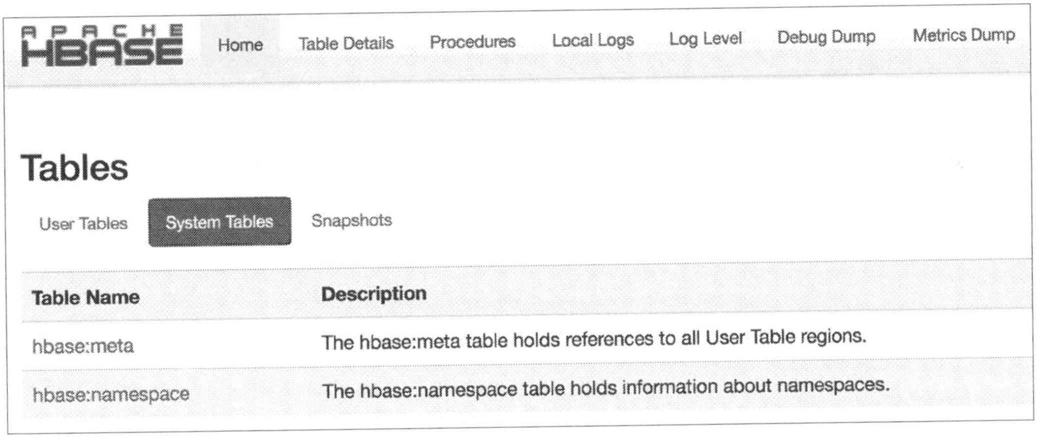

The HBase master passes the preceding information to the ZooKeeper and the clients connect to ZooKeeper to fetch the details about which region is served by which server.

Setting up multi-node HBase cluster

In this recipe, we will configure an HBase fully distributed cluster with ZooKeeper quorum formed by three nodes. This is the recommended configuration for the production environment.

Getting ready

The user is expected to complete the previous recipe and must have completed the recipes for setting up Hive with ZooKeeper. In this recipe, we will be using the already configured ZooKeeper ensemble.

How to do it...

1. Connect to the `master1.cyrus.com` master node in the cluster and change to the user `hadoop`.
2. Stop any daemons running from the previous HBase recipe.
3. Make sure the HBase package is downloaded, extracted, and the environment variables are set up as discussed in the previous recipe.
4. To confirm the setup, execute the commands as shown in the following screenshot:

```
[hadoop@master1 ~]$ which hbase
/opt/cluster/hbase/bin/hbase
[hadoop@master1 ~]$ echo $HBASE_HOME
/opt/cluster/hbase
```

5. Edit the `hbase-site.xml` file, as shown here:

```
<property>
     <name>hbase.master</name>
     <value>master1.cyrus.com:60000</value>
</property>

<property>
     <name>hbase.rootdir</name>
     <value>hdfs://master1.cyrus.com:9000/hbase</value>
</property>

<property>
     <name>hbase.cluster.distributed</name>
     <value>true</value>
</property>

<property>
```

```
        <name>hbase.zookeeper.quorum</name>
        <value>master1.cyrus.com,edge1.cyrus.com,rt1.cyrus.com</value>
    </property>

    <property>
        <name>hbase.zookeeper.property.clientPort</name>
        <value>2181</value>
    </property>
```

6. Now edit the region server file to include the names of the nodes where the region server will run. This is shown in the following screenshot:

```
[hadoop@master1 conf]$ cat regionservers
rt1.cyrus.com
rt2.cyrus.com
rt3.cyrus.com
```

7. Now create a file named `backup-masters` with the name of the server, where HBase standby master will run, as shown in the following screenshot:

```
[hadoop@master1 conf]$ cat backup-masters
rt4.cyrus.com
[hadoop@master1 conf]$
```

8. Disable the ZooKeeper to be managed by HBase by editing the `hbase-env.sh` file and adding `export HBASE_MANAGES_ZK=false`.
9. Copy the `HBase` directory on the nodes where the HBase standby server and regions servers will run.
10. Make sure that the Namenode and Datanode daemons are running on all nodes, which will act as region servers.
11. Make sure the ZooKeeper is running and is healthy, as shown in the following screenshot:

```
edge1.cyrus.com,master1.cyrus.com (2)
Mode: follower
rt1.cyrus.com
Mode: leader
```

12. Start the HBase cluster with the `start-hbase.sh` command. Once the services are up, visit the HBase master web UI on port `16010` and you will see the services as shown in the following screenshot:

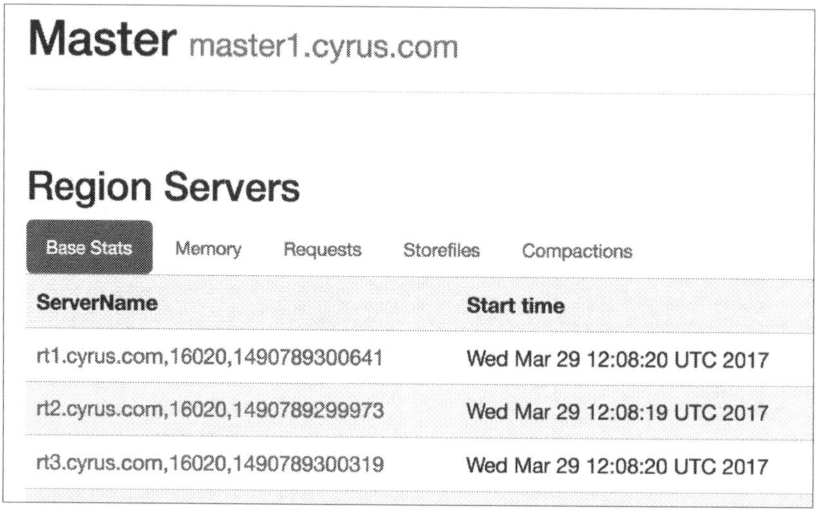

13. To test the HBase standby server, just kill the Active HBase master and you will see a failure to the backup master. The backup master is shown in the following screenshot:

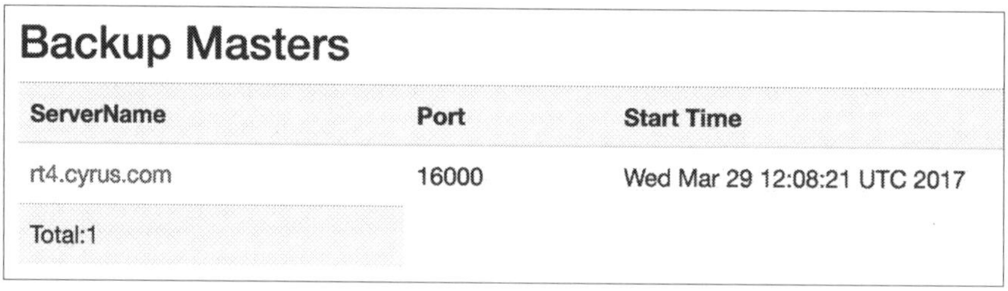
Backup Masters
ServerName
Port
Start Time
rt4.cyrus.com
16000
Wed Mar 29 12:08:21 UTC 2017
Total:1

How it works...

In this recipe, we configured an HBase distributed cluster to run with an external ZooKeeper ensemble. The moment HBase master is started, it will create HBase meta and namespace. The region servers will register with the HBase master and that information is stored in ZooKeeper for further reference.

For all the steps listed earlier, HDFS must be healthy and Namenode must not be in safemode, else HBase will not be able to create the HBase root directory.

In the upcoming recipes, we will see how we can upload data and backup HBase data.

Inserting data into HBase

In this recipe, we will insert data into HBase and see how it is stored. The syntax for import data is not similar to SQL, as there are no select or insert statements. To insert data, we use put and scan for select.

Getting ready

Before going through the recipe in this section, make sure you have completed the previous recipe, *Setting up multi-node HBase cluster*.

How to do it...

1. Connect to the `master1.cyrus.com` master node in the cluster and switch to the user `hadoop`.
2. Connect to the HBase shell using the `hbase shell` command. You can connect to the shell in interactive mode or script it.
3. Create a table as shown in the following screenshot:

```
hbase(main):001:0> create 'test', 'cf'
0 row(s) in 2.4290 seconds

=> Hbase::Table - test
```

4. Insert data using the commands shown in the following screenshot:

```
hbase(main):002:0> put 'test', 'row1', 'cf:1', 'value1'
0 row(s) in 0.1140 seconds

hbase(main):003:0> put 'test', 'row2', 'cf:2', 'value2'
0 row(s) in 0.0100 seconds
```

5. You can list the tables and scan a table, as shown in the following screenshot:

```
hbase(main):004:0> list
TABLE
test
1 row(s) in 0.0100 seconds

=> ["test"]
hbase(main):005:0> scan 'test'
ROW                           COLUMN+CELL
 row1                         column=cf:1, timestamp=1490824460000, value=value1
 row2                         column=cf:2, timestamp=1490824484973, value=value2
2 row(s) in 0.0300 seconds
```

6. Commands can be passed in non-interactive mode, as shown in the following screenshot:

```
$ echo "scan 'test'" | hbase shell
$ echo "put 'test', 'r3', 'cf:3', 'val3'" | hbase shell
```

7. We can use the `get` command to fetch individual values, as shown in the following screenshot:

```
hbase(main):008:0> get 'test', 'row1'
COLUMN                            CELL
 cf:1                             timestamp=1490824460000, value=value1
1 row(s) in 0.0250 seconds
```

We can also use Java API or Python to insert data into HBase. HBase is a widely-used database with a warehousing layer on top of it like the Hive or Phoenix interface.

How it works...

In this recipe, we inserted data into an HBase table using simple `put` and `get` commands. Each cell in HBase has multiple versions that can be changed using the `alter` command `alter 'test', { NAME => 'row1', VERSIONS => 5 }` and many other things, which we will see in the upcoming sections.

Integration with Hive

In this recipe, we look at how we can integrate Hive with HBase and use Hive to perform all the data operations.

You will have realized from the previous recipe that it gets cumbersome to perform queries using just the native HBase commands.

Getting ready

Before going through the recipe, you must have completed the *Hive metastore using MySQL* recipe in *Chapter 7, Data Ingestion and Workflow,* and the *Setting up multi-node HBase cluster* recipe.

How to do it...

1. Connect to the `edge1.cyrus.com` edge node in the cluster and switch to the user `hadoop`.
2. We will create an external Hive table and point it to the HBase using the ZooKeeper ensemble.

3. Create a table in HBase if it is not there already, as shown next:

```
hbase> create 'hivetable', 'ratings'
put 'hivetable', 'row1', 'ratings:userid', 'user1'
put 'hivetable', 'row1', 'ratings:bookid', 'book1'
put 'hivetable', 'row1', 'ratings:rating', '1'
```

4. Connect either using a hive or beeline client and map by creating a table, as shown next:

```
CREATE EXTERNAL TABLE hbasehive_table
(key string, userid string,bookid string,rating int)
STORED BY 'org.apache.hadoop.hive.hbase.HBaseStorageHandler'
WITH SERDEPROPERTIES
("hbase.columns.mapping" = ":key,ratings:userid,ratings:bookid,rat
ings:rating")
TBLPROPERTIES ("hbase.table.name" = "hivetable");
```

5. The preceding command maps the Hive external table to the HBase. If you have completed the *Hive with ZooKeeper* recipe in *Chapter 7*, *Data Ingestion and Workflow*, you will be able to do this from `edge1.cyrus.com`, as the ZooKeeper ensemble will point to the HBase without the need to have an HBase client on the edge node. The command is shown in the following screenshot:

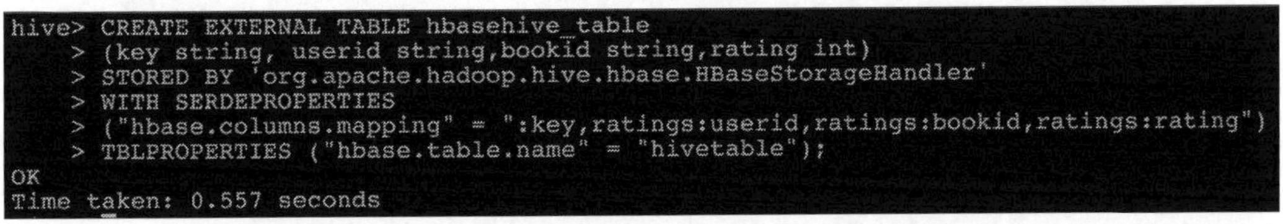
hive> CREATE EXTERNAL TABLE hbasehive_table
> (key string, userid string,bookid string,rating int)
> STORED BY 'org.apache.hadoop.hive.hbase.HBaseStorageHandler'
> WITH SERDEPROPERTIES
> ("hbase.columns.mapping" = ":key,ratings:userid,ratings:bookid,ratings:rating")
> TBLPROPERTIES ("hbase.table.name" = "hivetable");
OK
Time taken: 0.557 seconds

6. Now query the `HBase` table using the Hive query, as shown in the following screenshot:

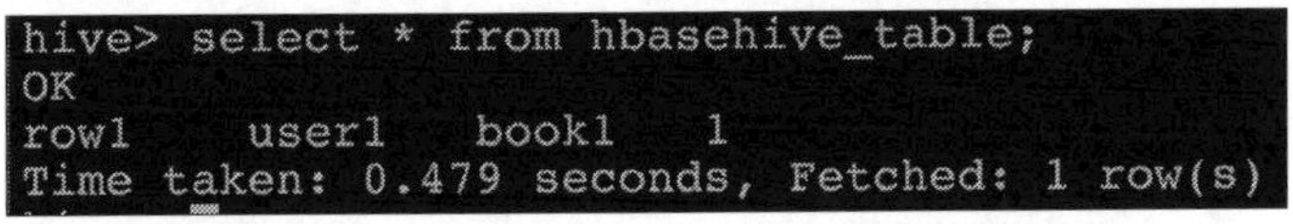
hive> select * from hbasehive_table;
OK
row1 user1 book1 1
Time taken: 0.479 seconds, Fetched: 1 row(s)

How it works...

In this recipe, we uploaded data into HBase using the `put` command. Then, we mapped it from Hive by creating an external table.

It is interesting to understand how the schema/metadata information is stored in the MySQL database, so query the MySQL metastore to see the arrangement of the tables and its mappings, as shown in the following screenshot:

```
mysql> select TBLS.TBL_NAME,SDS.LOCATION from SDS,TBLS where SDS.SD_ID = '3
1' and TBLS.TBL_ID='31';
+------------------+--------------------------------------------------------------
-----------+
| TBL_NAME         | LOCATION
          |
+------------------+--------------------------------------------------------------
-----------+
| hbasehive_table | hdfs://master1.cyrus.com:9000/user/hive/warehouse/hbase
hive_table |
+------------------+--------------------------------------------------------------
-----------+
1 row in set (0.00 sec)

mysql> select * from TBLS where TBLS.TBL_ID='31';
+--------+-------------+-------+------------------+--------+-----------+---
---+-----------------+------------------+--------------------+-----------
------+
| TBL_ID | CREATE_TIME | DB_ID | LAST_ACCESS_TIME | OWNER  | RETENTION | SD
_ID | TBL_NAME        | TBL_TYPE         | VIEW_EXPANDED_TEXT | VIEW_ORIGINAL
_TEXT |
+--------+-------------+-------+------------------+--------+-----------+---
---+-----------------+------------------+--------------------+-----------
------+
|     31 |  1490827021 |     1 |                0 | hadoop |         0 |
 31 | hbasehive_table | EXTERNAL_TABLE | NULL               | NULL
      |
+--------+-------------+-------+------------------+--------+-----------+---
---+-----------------+------------------+--------------------+-----------
```

See also

- The *HBase administration commands* recipe

HBase administration commands

In this recipe, we will look at HBase administration commands, which are very useful for troubleshooting and managing the cluster.

Being an HBase administrator in a company, one needs to perform backup, recovery, troubleshooting, tuning, and many other complex things. It is good to know about the commands to make intuitive decisions.

Getting ready

To complete the recipe, you must have a running HBase cluster and must have completed the *Setting up HBase multi-node cluster* recipe.

How to do it...

1. Connect to the `master1.cyrus.com` master node in the cluster and switch to the user `hadoop`. Note that we can connect to any node in the cluster or use HBase client for connections.
2. Connect to the HBase shell prompt and execute the commands shown in the next few steps to get familiar with HBase:

```
$ hbase shell
  hbase> list
  hbase> version
  hbase> whoami
```

3. We can drop the column family or disable a table as shown next. Do not execute these on production database, unless you know what you are doing:

```
  hbase> alter 'test', 'delete' => 'f1'
  hbase> disable 'test'
  hbase> disable_all 'cb.*'
  hbase> is_disabled 'test'
  hbase> exists 'test'
```

4. Change the size of the region to 128 MB:

```
  hbase> alter 'test', MAX_FILESIZE => '134217728'
```

5. Find the HBase cluster details, online/offline regions, and the number of region servers:

```
  hbase> status
  hbase> status 'summary'
  hbase> status 'detailed'
```

6. You can enable `in_memory` and block cache, as shown here:

```
  hbase> create 't1', {NAME => 'f1', VERSIONS => 1, TTL =>
2592000, BLOCKCACHE => true}
  hbase> create 't1', {NAME => 'f1', CONFIGURATION => {'hbase.
hstore.blockingStoreFiles' => '10'}}
  hbase> alter 't1', 'f1', {NAME => 'f2', IN_MEMORY => true}
```

7. Hfile management and verification is done using the following command and the output is shown in the upcoming screenshot:

   $ hbase hfile -b -f hdfs://master1.cyrus.com:9000/hbase/data/hbase/meta/1588230740/info/1490fbeea3454da4a2913822144fd554

```
2017-03-29 23:23:16,871 INFO  [main] hfile.CacheConfig: CacheC
onfig:disabled
Block Index:
size=1
key=hivetable,,1490827001115.b635d3534fe0393b753ceaf20e66320a.
/info:regioninfo/1490827000989/Put
  offset=0, dataSize=829
```

8. We can start rest and thrift servers using the HBase interface commands.
9. Similar to the filesystem check utility, we have `hbck` to fix any consistency issues in HBase, as shown in the following screenshot:

   $ hbase hbck

```
Summary:
Table hbase:meta is okay.
    Number of regions: 1
    Deployed on:  rt2.cyrus.com,16020,1490789299973
Table hivetable is okay.
    Number of regions: 1
    Deployed on:  rt3.cyrus.com,16020,1490789300319
Table test is okay.
    Number of regions: 1
    Deployed on:  rt1.cyrus.com,16020,1490789300641
Table hbase:namespace is okay.
    Number of regions: 1
    Deployed on:  rt1.cyrus.com,16020,1490789300641
0 inconsistencies detected.
Status: OK
```

10. To fix any other inconsistencies, `hbase hbck` is a great tool for repairing unassigned, incorrectly assigned, or multiply assigned regions:

    $ hbase hbck -fixAssignments

11. Sometimes hbase metadata may have entries for regions that is not present in HDFS or vice versa. To fix this issue, we can use the following command:

    $ hbase hbck -fixMeta

12. To create Hfiles for new empty regions on the filesystem, ensure that the new regions are consistent:

    $ hbase hbck -repairHoles

13. To repair a region directory that is missing a region metadata file (the region info file), use the following command:

```
$ hbase hbck -fixHdfsOrphans
```

14. Check all Hfiles by opening them to make sure they are valid:

```
$ hbase hbck -checkCorruptHFiles
```

15. A really good and quick way to check the health of the region servers and what regions are online is to visit the HBase master Web UI.

16. For HBase Admin API use `HBaseAdmin` and `HTableDescriptor` classes under the `org.apache.hadoop.hbase.client` package.

How it works...

In this recipe, we explored the HBase administration commands to better manage the cluster. In the upcoming recipe, we will explore HBase tuning and see what things we can do to improve the performance.

See also

- The *Tuning HBase* recipe

HBase backup and restore

In this recipe, we will look at HBase backup and restore. We have discussed in the Namenode high availability section about the importance of backup, despite having HA. We will look at ways to take snapshots and restore it.

Getting ready

For this recipe, you must have completed the *Setting up multi-node Hbase cluster* recipe and have a basic understanding of the backup principles.

How to do it...

1. Connect to the `master1.cyrus.com` HBase master node and switch to the user `hadoop`.
2. Execute the following command to take a snapshot of a particular table. In this case, the table name is `test`:

```
$ hbase snapshot create -n test_30march -t test
```

3. To list the snapshots, connect the HBase shell as shown in the following screenshot:

```
hbase(main):002:0* list_snapshots
SNAPSHOT                    TABLE + CREATION TIME
 test_30march               test (Thu Mar 30 00:00:55 +0000 2017)
1 row(s) in 0.1720 seconds

SNAPSHOT                    TABLE + CREATION TIME
 test_30march               test (Thu Mar 30 00:00:55 +0000 2017)
1 row(s) in 0.0050 seconds
```

4. We can restore the snapshot using the following command—the table must be disabled for the restore:

```
hbase> disable 'test_30march'
hbase> restore_snapshot 'test_30march'
```

5. To clone the table, we can restore it to a new table. This is good way of testing and retaining the old table without modifying the original table:

```
hbase> clone_snapshot 'test_30march', 'newtable'
```

6. The snapshot can be exported to an HDFS location or on S3 using the following command:

```
$ hbase snapshot export -snapshot snapshotName -copy-to hdfs://
namenode:9000/folder -mappers 2
$ hbase snapshot export -snapshot snapshotName -copy-to s3://
bucketName/folder -mappers 2
```

7. To restore the snapshots, we can use the `export` command by interchanging the paths as we have done here:

```
$ hbase snapshot export -copy-from s3://bucket/folder -snapshot
snapshotName -copy-to hdfs://namenode:9000/hbase
```

8. We can use the `CopyTable` command to copy the entire table using the following command:

```
$ hbase org.apache.hadoop.hbase.mapreduce.CopyTable --peer.
adr=dstClusterZK:2181:/hbase --new.name=newtable test
```

How it works...

In this recipe, we looked at the steps required to perform backup and restore it. Snapshot is a light method of backing up as it only copies the metadata and not the actual blocks.

It is good practice to keep HBase backup on AWS S3 or point the HBase root directly to AWS S3. By doing that, you can create a new cluster by just pointing to the same HBase root.

You should take note of the fact that although HBase might be snapshot-enabled, that is oblivious to the Namenode. For HDFS snapshots, the snapshotted directory cannot be deleted but in case of HBase, we can delete the HBase root, despite it having the snapshots, as shown in the following screenshot:

```
[hadoop@master1 ~]$ hadoop fs -ls /hbase/.hbase-snapshot
Found 2 items
drwxr-xr-x   - hadoop supergroup          0 2017-03-30 0
0:00 /hbase/.hbase-snapshot/.tmp
drwxr-xr-x   - hadoop supergroup          0 2017-03-30 0
0:00 /hbase/.hbase-snapshot/test_30march
```

Tuning HBase

In this recipe, we will look at HBase tuning and some things to keep in mind. This is not an exclusive list of things to do, but it is a good starting point.

You are recommended to read through *Chapter 8, Performance Tuning*, before going through the tuning aspects of HBase cluster. It will give you a better insight into tuning the operating system, network, disk, and so on.

Getting ready

Make sure that you have completed the *Setting up multi-node HBase cluster* recipe for this section and understand the basic Linux commands.

How to do it...

1. Connect to the `master1.cyrus.com` master node and switch to the user `hadoop`.
2. Edit the `hbase-env.sh` file and add the following lines to it to tune the heap as per the work load:

   ```
   export HBASE_HEAPSIZE=1G
   export HBASE_OFFHEAPSIZE=1G
   ```

3. We can tune the Java GC algorithm. The default is marked sweep and if the GC times is high, this should be changed to Parallel GC:

   ```
   export HBASE_OPTS="-XX:+UseConcMarkSweepGC"
   ```

4. If we are using Java 8, then the PermSize option is no longer valid. Remove `PermSize` and `MaxPermSize` from both master and regions server settings:

   ```
   export HBASE_MASTER_OPTS="$HBASE_MASTER_OPTS -XX:PermSize=128m
   -XX:MaxPermSize=128m"
   ```

5. Tune the regions server handler count to be equal to the number of CPU vCores in `hbase-stie.xml`:

```
<property>
    <name>hbase.regionserver.handler.count</name>
    <value>64</value>
</property>
```

6. Modify the HStore file size to tune the size for better writes.

```
<property>
    <name>hbase.hregion.max.filesize</name>
    <value>1073741824</value>
</property>
```

7. Tune Hbase blockcache using the `hfile.block.cache.size` parameter, which is 40% of JVM Heap by default.
8. To optimize read performance, increase `hfile.block.cache.size` and decrease `hbase.regionserver.global.memstore.upperLimit`, especially when RAM is a constraint of the node.
9. It is important to tune how often the memstore flush happens to the disk. This will impact the minor compactions and disk I/O:

```
<property>
    <name>hbase.hregion.memstore.flush.size</name>
    <value>134217728</value>
</property>
```

10. It is important to control the memstore runaway during spikes, by controlling the `hbase.hregion.memstore.block.multiplier` parameter.

How it works...

Too frequent flushes can affect read performance and bring additional load to the cluster. Every time Memstore flush happens, one HFile is created for each CF.

HLog (WAL) Size and Memstore Flush can be found on regions servers and when WAL grows very big, it may take a lot of time to replay it. For that reason, there are certain limits for WAL size, which when reached can cause Memstore to flush. Flushing Memstores decreases WAL, as we don't need to keep WAL edits that were written to Hfiles (persistent store). This is configured by `hbase.regionserver.hlog.blocksize` and `hbase.regionserver.maxlogs`.

HBase upgrade

In this recipe, we will cover how to upgrade to the latest stable release, which at the time of writing this recipe is version 1.2.5.

In any organization, it is important to keep it patched and updated to the latest release to address any bug fixes and issues.

But upgrading is not always that easy, as it may involve downtime and one version might not support the old metadata structure. An example of this is the old Hfile v1 format.

Getting ready

For this recipe, make sure you have an HBase cluster running and that you understand the regions and its communication.

How to do it...

1. Connect to the `master1.cyrus.com` master node and switch to the user `hadoop`.
2. Before performing any upgrades, it is important to verify that we have backup in place and that the cluster is in a consistent state.
3. Download the latest HBase release, as we did initially and update the symlink to point to the new version, as shown here:

   $ unlink hbase

   $ ln -s hbase-1.2.5-bin hbase

4. Do the same on all the nodes in the cluster so that they all are pointing to the latest release.
5. On Master, we must check for any incompatibility and see whether there are any old Hfiles using the command shown in the following screenshot:

   $ hbase upgrade -check

```
2017-03-30 01:37:11,713 INFO  [main] util.HFileV1Detector: Result:

2017-03-30 01:37:11,713 INFO  [main] util.HFileV1Detector: Tables Processed:
2017-03-30 01:37:11,713 INFO  [main] util.HFileV1Detector: Count of HFileV1: 0
2017-03-30 01:37:11,713 INFO  [main] util.HFileV1Detector: Count of corrupted files: 0
2017-03-30 01:37:11,713 INFO  [main] util.HFileV1Detector: Count of Regions with HFileV1: 0
2017-03-30 01:37:11,815 INFO  [main] migration.UpgradeTo96: No HFileV1 found.
```

6. The preceding command will check for any corrupted files, WALs, Hfiles, metadata, and so on.
7. To verify any corrupted files or incompatible files, use the command to check a specific directory path:

   ```
   $ hbase upgrade --check --dir /hbase/data
   ```

8. If we find any old version 1 Hfiles, we can do a forceful major compaction to convert them to version 2, using the `hbase> major_compact 'usertable'` command.
9. Once we have verified that everything is fine, do a graceful shutdown of the HBase cluster using the following command:

   ```
   $ stop-hbase.sh
   ```

10. Make sure ZooKeeper is running. In our case, it is external, so it will not shut down with the preceding command.
11. Now execute he HBase upgrade using the `hbase upgrade -execute` command.
12. Verify the new HBase version using the `hbase version` command.

How it works...

In this recipe, we have upgraded the HBase version to the latest stable release. After upgrade is successful, make sure to verify the tables and connections. It is good practice to go through the logs in order to catch any anomalies in the process and fix them early.

Migrating data from MySQL to HBase using Sqoop

In this recipe, we will cover how to migrate data from MySQL to HBase. This could be a very common use case in any organization that has been using RDMS and wants to move to HBase.

An important thing to understand here is that the intent of migration is not a replacement for the traditional RDBMS system, but to complement it.

To do this operation we will be using Sqoop to import data from RDBMS to Hadoop. The destination could be the HDFS filesystem, Hive, or HBase.

Getting ready

Before going through the recipe, you must have completed the *Hive metastore using MySQL* recipe in *Chapter 7, Data Ingestion and Workflow*, and the *Setting up multi-node HBase cluster* recipe. Make sure the services for HBase, YARN, and HDFS are running as shown in the following screenshot:

```
[hadoop@master1 hadoop]$ jps
10401 ResourceManager
9749 HMaster
10616 Jps
9163 NameNode
3630 QuorumPeerMain
```

How to do it...

1. Connect to the `edge1.cyrus.com` edge node and switch to the user `hadoop`.
2. Although you can do these steps on any node, all clients are installed on the edge nodes.
3. Firstly, we need to download the latest stable release of Sqoop from the apache site and untar it under `/opt/cluster`, using the following commands:

   ```
   $ wget apache.uberglobalmirror.com/sqoop/1.4.6/sqoop-1.4.6.bin__hadoop-2.0.4-alpha.tar.gz
   ```

   ```
   $ tar -xzvf sqoop-1.4.6.bin__hadoop-2.0.4-alpha.tar.gz -C /opt/cluster
   ```

4. Now create a symlink as we have done in all our previous recipes:

   ```
   $ ln -s sqoop-1.4.6.bin__hadoop-2.0.4-alpha sqoop
   ```

5. Update the environment variable for Sqoop in file `/etc/profile.d/hadoopenv.sh` with the following lines:

   ```
   export SQOOP_HOME=/opt/cluster/sqoop
   PATH=$PATH:$QOOP_HOME/bin
   Export PATH
   ```

6. Make the environment variable effective by executing the following command:

   ```
   $ source /etc/profile.d/hadoopenv.sh
   ```

7. Now copy the MySQL driver JAR `mysql-connector-java-5.1.39-bin.jar` to the directory `sqoop/lib/`. Please refer to section *Hive metastore using MySQL* recipe in *Chapter 7, Data Ingestion and Workflow*.

8. Connect to MySQL, which we have setup in the recipe *Hive metastore using MySQL* recipe in *Chapter 7* and create a test table as shown as follows:

```
mysql> CREATE TABLE emp(emp_id VARCHAR(10), name VARCHAR(20), salary VARCHAR(20));
Query OK, 0 rows affected (0.00 sec)
```

9. Insert some data into the `emp` table as shown in the following screenshot:

```
mysql> insert into emp(emp_id,name,salary) values('1','Am1','10000');
Query OK, 1 row affected (0.00 sec)

mysql> insert into emp(emp_id,name,salary) values('2','Am2','10000');
Query OK, 1 row affected (0.00 sec)
```

10. Now connect to HBase shell and create an empty table, which will be used to store the data imported from MySQL, using the command as shown in the following screenshot:

```
hbase(main):001:0> create 'test','emp_records'
0 row(s) in 8.4690 seconds

=> Hbase::Table - test
```

11. Then use the `sqoop` command as shown to import the table:

```
$ sqoop import --connect jdbc:mysql://ip-172-31-9-226.ec2.
internal:3306/test --driver com.mysql.jdbc.Driver --username hive
--password xxxxxx --table emp --hbase-table test --column-family
emp_records --hbase-row-key emp_id -m 1
```

12. In the preceding command, we have used the same user `hive`, which we used for importing data in the Hive recipe. Whichever user we use, must have the MySQL grant on the database to read the tables and import records.

13. Connect to the HBase shell using the command `hbase shell` and use the records imported as shown in the following screenshot:

```
hbase(main):002:0> scan 'test'
ROW                          COLUMN+CELL
 1                           column=emp_records:name, timestamp=1494498684358, value=Am1
 1                           column=emp_records:salary, timestamp=1494498684358, value=10000
 2                           column=emp_records:name, timestamp=1494498684358, value=Am2
 2                           column=emp_records:salary, timestamp=1494498684358, value=10000
 3                           column=emp_records:name, timestamp=1494498684358, value=Am3
 3                           column=emp_records:salary, timestamp=1494498684358, value=10000
3 row(s) in 0.1310 seconds
```

This is a very basic operation of importing data from any RDBMS and we can schedule regular imports and build a data lake or a warehouse solution with Hive integration to query HBase as discussed in the Integration with Hive recipe.

10
Cluster Planning

In this chapter, we will cover the following recipes:

- Disk space calculations
- Nodes needed in the cluster
- Memory requirements
- Sizing the cluster as per SLA
- Network design
- Estimating the cost of the Hadoop cluster
- Hardware and software options

Introduction

In this chapter, we will look at cluster planning and some of the important aspects of cluster utilization.

Although this is a recipe book, it is good to have an understanding on the Hadoop cluster layout, network components, operating system, disk arrangements, and memory. We will try to cover some of the fundamental concepts on cluster planning and a few formulas to estimate the cluster size.

Let's say we are ready with our big data initiative and want to take the plunge into the Hadoop world. The first few of the primary concerns is what size cluster do we need? How many nodes and what configurations? What will be the roadmap in terms of the software/application stack, what will be the initial investment? What hardware to choose, whether to go with the vanilla Hadoop distribution or to go with vendor-specific Hadoop distributions.

There are no straightforward answers to these or any magic formulas. Many times, these decisions are influenced by market statistics, or by an organizational trust with a particular brand. Going with a vanilla version, such as Apache Hadoop, will have its own pros and cons.

It will be up to the user to patch any bugs, issues, or wait for the community release. How big will the team be, can we find the right people for the job? Many of these questions cannot be answered until we take the plunge and start using it and, over a period of time, we can adjust it according to the feedback we get from different data points.

Disk space calculations

In this recipe, we will calculate the disk storage needed for the Hadoop cluster. Once we know what our storage requirement is, we can plan the number of nodes in the cluster and narrow down on the hardware options we have.

The intent of this recipe is not to tune performance, but to plan for capacity. Users are encouraged to read *Chapter 9, HBase Administration* on optimizing the Hadoop cluster.

Getting ready

To step through the recipe in this section, we need a Hadoop cluster set up and running. We need at least the HDFS configured correctly. It is recommended to complete the first two chapters before starting with this recipe.

How to do it...

1. Connect to the `master1.cyrus.com` master node in the cluster and switch to the user `hadoop`.
2. On the master node, execute the following command:

   ```
   $ hdfs dfsadmin -report
   ```

   This command will give you an understanding about how the storage in the cluster is represented. The total cluster storage is a summation of storages from each of the Datanodes. Observe the number of nodes in the cluster and the storage for each Datanode.

3. You may have noticed that the storage of the master nodes such as Namenode, Resourcemanager, Secondary Namenode, and so on are not added to the total storage available, unless the user is running Datanode daemons on them.

4. To calculate the disk storage needed on the cluster, we will use the formula derived in the next few points. The storage needed is based on the assumption that we are going onboard a project starting with 500 TB of data and taking into account its growth over a period of 6 months. If the initial onboarding data size is very small, then our cluster could be much smaller.

5. Let's say the starting data size is 500 TB with a growth of 5 TB per month and the retention period of data is 3 months, we plan for 6 months of cluster growth:

   S = Size of data (500 TB)

   G = Growth rate per month (5 TB)

   R = Replication (default 3)

   r = Retention period (3 months)

   D = Delta for temp space (30%)

   P = Plan time period (6 months)

   C = Total disk space needed

   $C = S * R + G * P + G * r + D (S * R * 0.3)$

   $C = 1500 TB + 5*6 + 5 * 3 + (450 TB)$

   $C = 1500 + 30 + 30 + 450$

   $C = 2PB$

6. This is the storage needed in the cluster, without taking into account compression, which will save some space, but increase CPU cycles.

7. The growth rate is taken as a constant here, but in reality, it will vary. The growth rate is defined by *Growth rate = (present - past)/past*.

8. So, in our case, the rate is very low = *(1505 - 1500)/1500 = 0.0033*, as we boarded an existing project, which had a lot of historical data, but less growth rate.

9. Login to any of the Datanodes in the cluster we configured in the initial chapters and look at the disk layout. It is recommended to have separate data disks as specified by `dfs.datanode.data.dir` and the operating system:

   ```
   $ df -h
   ```

10. Each of the Datanodes will have a disk configured just for logs and intermediate outputs. Take a look at the parameters `mapreduce.task.tmp.dir` and `mapreduce.cluster.local.dir` and also the location of the logs, as discussed in *Chapter 6, Backup and Recovery*.

How it works...

In the preceding recipe, we have looked at the storage requirements for a cluster. The total disk space needed is a summation of the storage for the actual data on the cluster, logs and temp space, and operating system disk requirements.

The preceding scenario could be an example of using the Hadoop cluster for a warehouse, from which the data can be a filtered or extracted. These requirements will vary, depending on whether the user runs HBase or Hive frameworks.

The performance aspects are explained in *Chapter 8, Performance Tuning*, where the impact of disk arrangements on performance will be discussed.

Nodes needed in the cluster

In this recipe, we will look at the number of nodes needed in the cluster based upon the storage requirements.

From the initial *Disk space calculations* recipe, we estimated that we need about 2 PB of storage for our cluster. In this recipe, we will estimate the number of nodes required for running a stable Hadoop cluster.

Getting ready

To step through the recipe, the user needs to have understood the Hadoop cluster daemons and their roles. It is recommended to have a cluster running with healthy HDFS and at least two Datanodes.

How to do it...

1. Connect to the `master1.cyrus.com` master node in the cluster and switch to the user `hadoop`.
2. Execute the command as shown here to see the Datanodes available and the disk space on each node:

   ```
   $ hdfs dfsadmin -report
   ```

3. From the preceding command, we can tell the storage available per node, but we cannot tell the number of disks that make up that storage. Refer to the following screenshot for details:

```
Name: 10.0.0.75:50010 (dn6.cyrus.com)
Hostname: dn6.cyrus.com
Rack: /rack6
Decommission Status : Normal
Configured Capacity: 63007739904 (58.68 GB)
DFS Used: 73728 (72 KB)
Non DFS Used: 3409612800 (3.18 GB)
DFS Remaining: 59598053376 (55.51 GB)
DFS Used%: 0.00%
DFS Remaining%: 94.59%
```

4. Login to a Datanode `dn6.cyrus.com` and execute the following command:

   $ hdfs getconf -confkey dfs.datanode.data.dir

The following screenshot shows the disk layout that accounts for the total storage projected from that particular Datanode. Observe the three disks, each of 20 GB, that make up the total storage per node:

```
[hadoop@dn6 ~]$ hdfs getconf -confkey dfs.datanode.data.dir
file:/space/d1,file:/space/d2,file:/space/d3
[hadoop@dn6 ~]$ df -h
Filesystem      Size  Used Avail Use% Mounted on
/dev/xvda1      7.8G  2.2G  5.5G  29% /
devtmpfs        3.9G   88K  3.9G   1% /dev
tmpfs           3.9G     0  3.9G   0% /dev/shm
/dev/xvdb1       20G   44M   19G   1% /space/d1
/dev/xvdc1       20G   44M   19G   1% /space/d2
/dev/xvdd1       20G   44M   19G   1% /space/d3
```

5. All these are separate disks and not just separate mount points. This is done for performance and also for utilizing the entire disks, as shown in the following screenshot:

```
/dev/xvdb1 on /space/d1 type ext4 (rw,noatime,data=ordered)
/dev/xvdc1 on /space/d2 type ext4 (rw,noatime,data=ordered)
/dev/xvdd1 on /space/d3 type ext4 (rw,noatime,data=ordered)
```

6. Now, let's calculate the number of nodes needed in the cluster:

   N = Total nodes required in the cluster

   Nm = Number of master nodes in the cluster

   Ns = Number of Datanodes nodes in the cluster

   D = Disks per nodes

   Sd = Size of each disk

   Cn = Storage capacity per node *(D * Sd)*

   C = Storage required, as calculated in the previous recipe (2 PB)

F = Datanode failure rate (10%)

Nm = 2 (Master Namenode and secondary Namenode only; if HA, then account for ZooKeeper and journal nodes as well)

D = 20 (Number of disks per `slave/Datanode`. This is excluding 1 disk for OS, 2 disks for `logs/tmp` space)

Sd = 4 TB (Each disk is of 4 TB, with no reserved space for root)

To calculate the total number of nodes in the cluster:

N = Nm + Ns

*Ns = C / (Sd * D) = 2000 TB/ (20 * 4) = 2000/80 = 25 nodes*

N = 2 + 25 + 2.5 (Failure rate) = 30 nodes

N = 30 nodes

How it works...

Here, we made an assumption that the Datanodes are not running HBase region servers or any other service daemons, which might need storage or any other compute engine or frameworks such as YARN.

The preceding calculation is a raw calculation, not taking into account the work load, memory requirements, and the cost of having 23 disks per server. The cost of a single 4 TB disk versus the cost of two 2 TB disks. The storage is just a JBOD and not any special raided disks.

The preceding cluster sizing will change with memory requirements as well. Please read the next recipe before making any conclusions.

See also

- The *Memory requirements* recipe

Memory requirements

In this recipe, we will look at the memory requirements per node in the cluster, especially looking at the memory on Datanodes as a factor of storage.

Despite having large clusters with many Datanodes, it is of not much use if the nodes do not have sufficient memory to serve the requests. A Namenode stores the entire metadata in the memory and also has to take care of the block reports sent by the Datanodes in the cluster. The larger the cluster, the larger will be the block reports, and the more resources a Namenode will require.

The intent of this recipe is not to tune it for memory, but to give an estimate on the memory required per node.

Getting ready

To complete this recipe, the user must have completed the *Disk space calculations* recipe and the *Nodes needed in the cluster* recipe. For better understanding, the user must have a running cluster with HDFS and YARN configured and must have played around with *Chapter 1, Hadoop Architecture and Deployment* and *Chapter 2, Maintaining Hadoop Cluster HDFS*.

How to do it...

1. Connect to the `master1.cyrus.com` master node in the cluster and switch to the user `hadoop`.
2. The memory requirements on a node will be a factor of the memory required by the OS, and the memory required per daemon running on that node.
3. By default, the memory used by Hadoop daemons is defined by properties in `$HADOOP_HOME/etc/hadoop/hadoop-env.sh` and `$YARN_HOME/etc/hadoop/yarn-env.sh` in the `hadoop-env.sh` and `yarn-env.sh` files respectively. This is shown in the following screenshot:

```
[hadoop@master1 hadoop]$ cat hadoop-env.sh | grep HEAPSIZE
export HADOOP_HEAPSIZE=2048
#export HADOOP_NAMENODE_INIT_HEAPSIZE=""
[hadoop@master1 hadoop]$ cat yarn-env.sh | grep HEAPSIZE
# YARN_HEAPSIZE=1000
if [ "$YARN_HEAPSIZE" != "" ]; then
  JAVA_HEAP_MAX="-Xmx""$YARN_HEAPSIZE""m"
#export YARN_RESOURCEMANAGER_HEAPSIZE=1000
#export YARN_TIMELINESERVER_HEAPSIZE=1000
#export YARN_NODEMANAGER_HEAPSIZE=1000
```

4. In addition to this, the number of mappers, reducers, and containers on a node will also be a factor of the memory on a node. Explore the following parameters to get a feel of these factors:

```
$ hdfs getconf -confkey mapreduce.map.memory.mb
$ hdfs getconf -confkey mapreduce.reduce.memory.mb
$ hdfs getconf -confkey yarn.app.mapreduce.am.resource.mb
$ hdfs getconf -confkey yarn.app.mapreduce.am.resource.mb
$ hdfs getconf -confkey yarn.scheduler.maximum-allocation-mb
```

5. Each of the Datanodes will run a Datanode daemon and Nodemanager daemon at the minimal.

6. A Namenode will run the Namenode daemon, whose memory requirements will be approximately 1 GB for every 1 million files or 2 million objects on HDFS. Refer to *Chapter 8, Performance Tuning* for details.
7. The Datanode daemon memory will be a factor of the Datanode handler count, the block report size, and transfer threads. For the details on the handler count, and so on, refer to *Chapter 8, Performance Tuning*.

Minimal memory required per Datanode:

Datanode daemon memory = 1 GB

Nodemanager memory = 1 GB

Mapper memory = 1 GB

HDFS block size =128 MB

Hot data = 4 TB per node

In the previous recipe, we estimated 80 TBs per node, let's assume out of which only 4 TBs is hot data, which needs to be worked upon.

To process 32,768 splits in parallel (4 TB/block size), we need at least 32,768 * mapper memory = 32 TB memory per node, which is neither feasible nor practical.

So, we run mapper waves, dividing the number of maps into stages and running, say, 128 mappers per node in parallel. So, it means we need 128 GB of memory per Datanode, running 256 waves of 128 mappers.

1. What about reducers? Although reducers do not start until all the mappers are done, the copy/shuffle phase starts much early. Look at the `mapreduce.job.reduce.slowstart.completedmaps` parameter for details.
2. So, reducers will also occupy containers, downloading mapper output, and hence can cause deadlock, if constrained on resources.
3. Also, running 256 waves of mappers will take a very long time. Does each Datanode have 256 vCores?

The answer to this will be mostly *No*, as 256 cores per node are not economical, though it's possible using GPUs which can support thousands of cores.

Now, how can we improve this in terms of cost and time?

If we reduce the number of mappers per wave, the time will increase drastically; otherwise, the cost will be very high.

The preceding estimate on the number of nodes will change now due to memory and costing.

Revised estimate

Now, let's calculate the number of Datanodes needed in the cluster after memory accounting:

Ns = Number of slave nodes in the cluster

D = Disks per nodes

Sd = Size of each disk

Cn = Storage capacity per node (*D * Sd*)

C = Storage required, as calculated in the previous recipe (2 PB)

F = Datanode failure rate (10%)

D = 20 (Number of disks per slave/Datanode; this is excluding one disk for OS, two disks for logs/`tmp` space)

Sd = 2 TB (Each disk is of 2 TB, with no reserved space for `root`)

To calculate the total number of Datanodes in the cluster:

*Ns = C / (Sd * D) = 2000 TB/ (20 * 2) = 2000/40 = 50 nodes*

Ns = 50 + 5(Failure rate) = 55 nodes

Ns = 55 nodes

Now, the hot data per node will be almost halved, reducing the memory and CPU requirements. Now, the estimated value will be approximately 64 GB of memory with 64 vCores, running the same number of waves.

Now, the resource requirements have gone down, but not the time of execution, as the number of mappers have reduced but the number of nodes have increased.

We have to again revisit our thought process, and why not increase the number of Datanodes to be six times, that is, 300 nodes? This will be manageable in terms of resource requirements per node and much more spread out, reducing the number of waves.

For Namenode memory requirements take a look at the *HDFS tuning* recipe in *Chapter 8, Performance Tuning*.

How it works...

As we discussed, the estimates should not be just based upon storage of memory or CPU. It is a constant feedback system, which will ask to scale the Hadoop cluster horizontally rather them making each node more powerful.

See also

- *Tuning the Disk* recipe in *Chapter 8, Performance Tuning*

Sizing the cluster as per SLA

In this recipe, we will look at how service-level agreements can impact our decision to size the clusters. In an organization, there will be multitenant clusters, which are funded differently by business units and ask for a guarantee for their share.

A good thing about YARN is that multiple users can run different jobs such as MapReduce, Hive, Pig, HBase, Spark, and so on. While YARN guarantees what it needs to start a job, it does not control how the job will finish. Users can still step on each other and cause an impact on SLAs.

Getting ready

For this recipe, the users must have completed the *Memory requirements* and *Nodes needed in the cluster* recipes. It is good to have a running cluster with HDFS and YARN to run quick commands for reference. It is also good to understand the scheduler recipes covered in *Chapter 5, Schedulers*.

How to do it...

1. Connect to the `master1.cyrus.com` master node and switch to the user `hadoop`.
2. Run a `teragen` and `terasort` on the cluster using the following command:

   ```
   $ hadoop jar mapreduce/hadoop-mapreduce-examples-2.7.2.jar teragen 100000 /bench
   ```

   ```
   $ hadoop jar mapreduce/hadoop-mapreduce-examples-2.7.2.jar terasort /bench /out
   ```

3. Increase the cluster size by adding a few more Datanodes and run the tests again. Note the difference in the times of the runs.
4. In the previous recipe, we saw that sizing the cluster to a greater number of nodes, improves on the execution time by reducing the number of waves of mappers and reducers. The more the number of nodes, the more will be the parallelism, as the number of tasks that can be run simultaneously will increase.
5. Configure the queues as discussed in *Chapter 5, Schedulers* and run benchmarking tests per queue to estimate the SLA.

How it works...

In the preceding recipe, we tried to estimate the cluster sizing according to the SLA and saw that increasing the size of the luster will reduce the SLA.

See also

- The *Disk Space requirements* recipe
- The *Memory requirements* recipe

Network design

In this recipe, we will be looking at the network design for the Hadoop cluster and what things to consider for planning a Hadoop cluster.

Getting ready

Make sure that the user has a running cluster with HDFS and YARN and has at least two nodes in the cluster.

How to do it...

1. Connect to the `master1.cyrus.com` Namenode and switch to the user `hadoop`.
2. Execute the commands as follows to check for the link speed and other network option modes:

   ```
   $ ethtool eth0
   $ iftop
   $ netstat -s
   ```

3. Always have a separate network for Hadoop traffic by using VLANs.
4. Ensure the DNS resolution works for both forward and reverse lookup.
5. Run a caching-only DNS within the Hadoop network, which caches records for faster resolution.
6. Consider NIC teaming or binding for better performance.
7. Use dedicated core switches and rack top switches.
8. Consider having static IPs per node in the cluster.
9. Disable IPv6 for all nodes and just use IPv4.
10. Increasing the size of the cluster will mean more connections and more data across nodes. Ensure nodes have high speed Ethernet cards.

11. Enable jumbo frames to `MTU=9000` under `/etc/sysconfig/network-scripts/ifcfg-eth0` for each node.
12. Ensure that the port speeds on the switches match with the nodes.
13. Make sure rack awareness is enabled and configured correctly.
14. Use network monitoring tools such as `iftop` and `bmon` to track bandwidth and connection states.

How it works...

It is very important to segregate the network for Hadoop cluster and try to keep the hops to minimum. If we put the streaming servers in the network where the Hadoop cluster runs, it will overwhelm the network and impact the performance.

Estimating the cost of the Hadoop cluster

In this recipe, we will estimate the costing for the Hadoop cluster and see what factors to a take into account. The exact figures can vary according to the hardware and software choices.

The Hadoop cluster is a combination of servers, network components, power consumption, man hours to maintain it, software license costs, and cooling costs.

How to do it...

In this recipe, there is nothing to execute or do by logging into the cluster, but it is more of an estimation which will be governed by the following mentioned factors.

Each server in the Hadoop cluster will at least fall into three categories: Master nodes, Datanodes, and Edge nodes.

Costing master nodes: Intensive on memory and CPU, but need less of disk space.

- Two OS disks in Raid 1 configuration
- Two disks for logs and two disks for Namenode metadata
- At least two network cards bounded together with minimum 1 Gbps
- RAM 128 GB, higher if the HBase master is co-located on a Namenode
- CPU cores per master
- Redundant power supply units

Costing slave nodes: Intensive on memory and disk.

- Redundant power supply units
- One disk for OS, no need for RAID on Datanodes

- 20 disks for data blocks
- Two disks for logs and `tmp` space
- Disk enclosures (JBOD enclosures), as 24 disks cannot fit inside a server encasing
- At least two NIC cards per Datanode
- RAM 96 to 128 GM per node
- CPU Cores 16 to 32 cores

Costing edge nodes: Intermediate on-memory and CPU.

- Two to three edge nodes behind a load balancer
- One disk for OS
- Two disks for logs and `tmp` space
- The user directory is scalable as the mount can be from Hadoop HDFS as NFS export
- RAM 64 GB
- The intent is to not execute anything on edge nodes, but just stage them to run on the cluster

Costing network components, racks, power supply, and cooling:

- Rack top switch costs, depending upon the number of ports per switch
- The number of servers that can go into a rack and the rack top switch support for the number of ports
- Aggregation, backbone switches, and routers
- Cooling needs for the entire cluster
- Power needs for the cluster
- Real estate for the data center

Costing manpower and skill set: This implies the cost of the team to manage the Hadoop cluster and keep the light on. Hadoop skills are expensive in the market and the engineer cost could easily be a few hundred thousand dollars yearly.

How it works...

The cost of running a Hadoop cluster includes all the factors mentioned earlier and as a practice we say that the cost is a few thousand dollars per node per year. So, if a business approaches you for a cost estimate, we will say that it is $10k per node per engineer as an example.

Hardware and software options

In this recipe, we will discuss the hardware and software option to take account of while considering the Hadoop cluster.

There are many vendors for hardware and software and the options can be overwhelming. But some important things which must be taken into account are as follows:

1. Run benchmark tests on different hardware examples from HP, IBM, or Dell and compare them for the throughput per unit cost.
2. What is the roadmap for the hardware you choose? How long will the vendor support it?
3. Every year, the new hardware will be a better value for compute per unit. What will be the buyback strategy for the old hardware? Will the vendor take back the old hardware and give the new hardware at discounted rates?
4. Does the hardware have tightly coupled components, which could be difficult to replace in isolation?
5. What software options does the user have in terms of vendors? Should we go for HDP, Cloudera, or Mapr distribution or use the Apache Hadoop distribution.
6. **Total cost of ownership** (**TCO**) should take into account all the factors discussed in the previous recipe. Apache Hadoop may initially look like a very economical option, but what about the cost of building your support engineering teams to handle that.
7. What is the release cycle for the Hadoop stack? Is it stable or rapid with an intent to have the latest software?
8. Always have multiple environments such as Dev, Staging, and Prod to rollout the changes in a systematic way and catch the errors and capacity issues before they hit production.

How it works...

It is important to evaluate and understand the various options we have at hand, rather than going with the flow in the media. Each use case can be different and various companies implement it based on their experiences with a vendor or sometimes not having many options, due to lockup in terms of hardware or software stacks.

Many large organizations just pump in old spare hardware into Hadoop clusters and publish benchmarking results, but it does not mean that it is the best option.

11
Troubleshooting, Diagnostics, and Best Practices

In this chapter, we will cover the following recipes:

- Namenode troubleshooting
- Datanode troubleshooting
- Resourcemanager troubleshooting
- Diagnose communication issues
- Parse logs for errors
- Hive troubleshooting
- HBase troubleshooting
- Hadoop best practices

Introduction

In this chapter, we will look at best practices and troubleshooting techniques for various components of Hadoop. The same can be used to troubleshoot any other service or application.

With distributed systems and the scale at which Hadoop operates, it can become cumbersome to troubleshoot it. In production, most will use log management and parsing tools such as Splunk and a combination of Ganglia, Nagios, or other tools for monitoring and alerting.

In this chapter, we will build the basics of troubleshooting skills and how we can quickly look for keywords, which will point the users to common errors in the Hadoop cluster. Users are encouraged to read this chapter after reading *Chapter 8, Performance Tuning*, to better relate and understand the recipes in this chapter.

Namenode troubleshooting

In this recipe, we will see how to find issues with Namenode and resolve them. As this is a recipe book, we will keep the theory to a minimum, but users must understand the moto behind the commands and how the mentioned tools work.

Getting ready

To step through the recipes in this chapter, make sure you have gone through the steps to install Hadoop cluster with HDFS and YARN enabled. Make sure to use Multi-node Hadoop cluster for better understanding and troubleshooting practice.

It is assumed that the user has basic knowledge about networking fundamentals, Linux commands, and filesystem.

How to do it...

Scenario 1: Namenode not starting due to permission issues on the `Namenode` directory.

1. Connect to the `master1.cyrus.com` master node in the cluster and change to user `hadoop`.
2. Try to write a `test` file to the location using the following command. If it succeeds, then the permissions are fine:

   ```
   $ touch /data/namenode1/test
   ```

3. Otherwise, make sure the permission of the directory pointed by `dfs.namenode.name.dir` is owned by the correct user. The user could be either `hadoop` or `hdfs`. Also, the directory permission should be `755`, as shown in the following screenshot:

   ```
   [hadoop@master1 ~]$ ls -ld /data/namenode*
   drwxr-xr-x 3 hadoop hadoop 4096 Mar 29 08:57 /data/namenode1
   drwxr-xr-x 3 hadoop hadoop 4096 Mar 29 08:57 /data/namenode2
   ```

4. Make sure the disks used for the store are mounted read / write. This can be checked using the mount command as shown in the following screenshot:

```
/dev/xvdb1 on /data/namenode1 type ext4 (rw,noatime,data=ordered)
/dev/xvdc1 on /data/namenode2 type ext4 (rw,noatime,data=ordered)
/dev/xvdd1 on /var/log/hadoop type ext4 (rw,noatime,data=ordered)
```

5. Also make sure that the `log` directory is writeable and owned by the correct user.

Scenario 2: Namenode not formatting and service not starting.

1. The Namenode, by default, will bind to port `8020` and the `Namenode` directory will be pointed by the `hadoop.tmp.dir/dfs/name` parameter. This is not a good practice for production, as the Linux `tmp` directory is scheduled for regular cleanup.
2. We change the location explicitly by modifying the `core-site.xml` file with the `fs.defaultFS` parameter.
3. Make sure the parameter is pointing to the correct host and a valid free port. This is shown in the following screenshot:

```
<property>
<name>fs.defaultFS</name>
<value>hdfs://master1.cyrus.com:9000</value>
```

4. Make sure the user executes the Namenode format command with the user who has permissions to write to the directory pointed by `dfs.namenode.name.dir`.
5. Make sure `JAVA_HOME` is in the PATH variable and the minimum Java version installed is 1.7. This is shown in the following screenshot:

```
[hadoop@master1 cluster]$ which java
/usr/java/latest/bin/java
[hadoop@master1 cluster]$ java -version
java version "1.8.0_92"
```

6. Make sure that the root volume is not full, else it can give strange errors on JVM shared memory, as shown in the following screenshot:

```
[hadoop@master1 ~]$ jps
Java HotSpot(TM) 64-Bit Server VM warning: Insufficient space for shared memory file:
   14730
Try using the -Djava.io.tmpdir= option to select an alternate temp location.
```

7. The preceding error is due to the disk getting full. We can see that in the following screenshot:

```
[hadoop@master1 ~]$ df -h
Filesystem      Size  Used Avail Use% Mounted on
/dev/xvda1      7.8G  7.8G     0 100% /
devtmpfs        7.9G   84K  7.9G   1% /dev
tmpfs           7.9G     0  7.9G   0% /dev/shm
```

8. Another very common reason seen is the user acknowledging with a small case y, rather than Y while formatting. Make sure to read each prompt carefully, as shown in the following screenshot:

```
17/04/03 00:00:35 INFO namenode.FSNamesystem: Retry cache will use 0.
iry time is 600000 millis
17/04/03 00:00:35 INFO util.GSet: Computing capacity for map NameNode
17/04/03 00:00:35 INFO util.GSet: VM type       = 64-bit
17/04/03 00:00:35 INFO util.GSet: 0.029999999329447746% max memory 1.
17/04/03 00:00:35 INFO util.GSet: capacity      = 2^16 = 65536 entrie
Re-format filesystem in Storage Directory /data/namenode1 ? (Y or N)
```

Scenario 3: Namenode service not starting due to port bind issue or open file descriptors.

1. The Namenode needs to bind to a port specified in the `core-site.xml` file under the `fs.defaultFS` parameter. By default, this port is `8020`. Make sure whichever port it uses (`9000`, in our case), it is not used by any other service on the node, as shown in the following screenshot:

```
[hadoop@master1 cluster]$ sudo netstat -tlpn | grep 9000
tcp        0      0 10.0.0.104:9000         0.0.0.0:*               LISTEN
```

2. We can find the open file descriptors used by any service using the following command:

   ```
   $ lsof | awk '{print $3}' | sort | uniq -c | sort -nr
   ```

   This gives us an idea of whether we should bump up the value or not.

3. To increase the file descriptors, edit the `/etc/security/limits.conf` file and change it for the user `hadoop`. The default limit of 1024, is very low.
4. Make sure the DNS resolution is working and look in the logs for any errors like `HostException` or `NoRouteToHostException`.
5. Mostly in production, the Namenode will have multiple host adaptors / network cards. Make sure you configure the right IP for the interface.

Scenario 4: Namenode remains in safe mode for ever.

1. Namenode remains in **Safe mode** until a certain percentage of blocks can be received by the Namenode, defined by `dfs.namenode.safemode.threshold-pct`.
2. This can be due to missing Datanodes, resulting in corrupted data blocks. We can force the Namenode out of safe mode using the following command:

   ```
   $ hdfs dfsadmin -safemode leave
   ```

3. The corrupted files use the following command and then the blocks can be found by mapping the files to blocks:

   ```
   $ hdfs fsck / | egrep -v '^\.+$' | grep -v eplica
   $ hdfs fsck /corrupt_file -locations -blocks -files
   ```

4. The corrupted files can be deleted using the following command:

   ```
   $ hdfs fsck -delete
   ```

5. Make sure the disk space for the metastore is sufficient and the files `fsimage` and `edits` can be accommodated on-disk. There should an approximate margin for the edits roll to take place.
6. Datanodes do not have the same version file as Namenode, so they cannot join the cluster and hence, Namenode remains in the same mode.
7. Always, refer the logs to find the errors, it will always point to an error. Refer the *Backup and Restore* section for any steps to recover Namenode from backup.

How it works...

In this recipe, we looked at common Namenode errors and ways to solve them. All this needs to be looked at in conjunction with all the recipes in this chapter, whether they are about Datanode or communication channels.

See also

- The *Hadoop best practices* recipe

Datanode troubleshooting

In this recipe, we will look at some of the common issues with Datanode and how to resolve them.

Getting ready

The user is expected to complete the previous recipe and must have completed the *Setting up multi-node HBase cluster* recipe in *Chapter 9, HBase Administration*. In this recipe, we will be using the already configured Hadoop cluster.

How to do it...

Scenario 1: Datanode not starting due to permission issues on the `Datanode` directory specified by `dfs.datanode.data.dir`:

1. Connect to the `dn1.cyrus.com` master node in the cluster and change to user `hadoop`.
2. Try to write a `test` file to the location using the following command:

   ```
   $ touch /space/dn1/test
   ```

   If it succeeds, then the permissions are fine.

3. Otherwise, make sure the permissions of the directories pointed by `dfs.datanode.data.dir` are owned by the correct user. This is shown in the following screenshot:

```
<property>
    <name>dfs.datanode.data.dir</name>
    <value>file:/space/d1,file:/space/d2,file:/space/d3</value>
</property>
```

4. The user could be `hadoop` or `hdfs`. Also, the directory permission is `755` for the top directory, as shown in the following screenshot:

   ```
   drwxr-xr-x 5 hadoop hadoop 4096 May 17  2016 /space/
   [hadoop@dn1 ~]$ ls -ld /space/d*
   drwx------ 3 hadoop hadoop 4096 Apr  3 00:14 /space/d1
   drwx------ 3 hadoop hadoop 4096 Apr  3 00:14 /space/d2
   drwx------ 3 hadoop hadoop 4096 Apr  3 00:14 /space/d3
   ```

   The permissions of the subdirectory will be automatically adjusted by the Datanode daemon. It makes it more restrictive, but if the permissions of the directories are more restrictive than what is defined by the `dfs.datanode.data.dir.perm` parameter, then it fails with an error.

5. Make sure the disks used for the store are mounted read / write. This can be checked using the mount command, as shown in the following screenshot:

```
/dev/xvdb1 on /space/d1 type ext4 (rw,noatime,data=ordered)
/dev/xvdc1 on /space/d2 type ext4 (rw,noatime,data=ordered)
/dev/xvdd1 on /space/d3 type ext4 (rw,noatime,data=ordered)
```

6. Also, make sure that the `log` directory is writeable and owned by the correct user.

7. Make sure `JAVA_HOME` is in the PATH and the minimum version is 1.7. This is shown in the following screenshot:

```
[hadoop@master1 cluster]$ which java
/usr/java/latest/bin/java
[hadoop@master1 cluster]$ java -version
java version "1.8.0_92"
```

Scenario 2: Datanode daemon not starting due to port binding issues.

1. The Datanode, by default, will bind to port `50010` and the `Datanode` directory will be pointed by the `hadoop.tmp.dir/dfs/data` parameter. This is not a good practice for production, as the Linux `tmp` directory is scheduled for regular cleanup.
2. Make sure that the port is free and available for the Datanode to bind. The import ports are `50010` and `50075`. These must be available for Data RPC and HTTP connections, as shown in the following screenshot:

```
[hadoop@dn1 ~]$ netstat -tlpn
(Not all processes could be identified, non-owned process info
 will not be shown, you would have to be root to see it all.)
Active Internet connections (only servers)
Proto Recv-Q Send-Q Local Address               Foreign Address
tcp        0      0 0.0.0.0:5679                0.0.0.0:*
tcp        0      0 0.0.0.0:111                 0.0.0.0:*
tcp        0      0 0.0.0.0:22                  0.0.0.0:*
tcp        0      0 0.0.0.0:26905               0.0.0.0:*
tcp        0      0 127.0.0.1:25                0.0.0.0:*
tcp        0      0 0.0.0.0:50010               0.0.0.0:*
tcp        0      0 0.0.0.0:50075               0.0.0.0:*
```

3. Make sure that this Datanode was not part of another cluster, as the `VERSION` file will be different and Namenode will keep shutting down the Datanodes.
4. Also, make sure the disk usage is below the default threshold of 90%, else those nodes will be excluded from the cluster.
5. Make sure the hostname used for the Datanode is resolvable and unique.
6. It is mandatory to have both forward and reverse lookup working, else Namenode will not let the Datanodes register with it.
7. Can Datanode connect to Namenode? Make sure you do this using `telnet` to the Namenode port, as shown in the following screenshot:

```
[hadoop@master1 cluster]$ telnet master1.cyrus.com 9000
Trying 10.0.0.104...
Connected to master1.cyrus.com.
Escape character is '^]'.
```

We will have to test the communication between nodes to make sure they are reachable and can talk to each other. We will look at this in the next recipe.

How it works...

In this recipe, we verified that the Datanode is healthy and we looked at ways to troubleshoot it. Refer to the logs to find any errors, which might not be obvious.

See also

- The *Hadoop best practices* recipe.

Resourcemanager troubleshooting

In this recipe, we will look at common Resourcemanager issues and how these can be addressed.

Getting ready

To step through the recipe in this section, make sure the users have completed the *Setting up multi-node HBase cluster* recipe in *Chapter 9, HBase Administration*.

How to do it...

Scenario 1: Resourcemanager daemon not starting.

1. The Resourcemanager, by default, will bind to port `80030` to `80033` and `8088`. These ports can be configured in the `yarn-site.xml` file and you should make sure these are unique and not used by any other service. In our labs, we used the ports as shown in the following screenshot:

```
<property>
<name>yarn.resourcemanager.resource-tracker.address</name>
<value>master1.cyrus.com:9001</value>
</property>

<property>
<name>yarn.resourcemanager.scheduler.address</name>
<value>master1.cyrus.com:9002</value>
</property>

<property>
<name>yarn.resourcemanager.address</name>
<value>master1.cyrus.com:9003</value>
</property>
```

2. The listening ports can be seen by using the following command:

```
$ netsta -tlpn
```

3. Look into the logs for any **Bind Errors** and make sure the hostname is resolvable. Check for both forward and reverse lookup:

```
$ nslookup <resource_manager_host>
```

4. On Node Manager, the import ports are `8040`, `8041`, and `8042`. These are used for scheduling, localization, and so on. So, on Datanodes, in addition to the Datanode ports, all these ports must be listening.
5. Make sure the `log` directory is writeable for Resourcemanager logs.
6. The disk space on the root volume and the volume of Resourcemanager install must have sufficient disk space available at all times.
7. Make sure `JAVA_HOME` is in the PATH and the minimum version is 1.7.

How it works...

In the preceding recipe, we looked at how we can narrow down the issues related to Resourcemanager and quick ways to resolve them.

See also

- The *Hadoop best practices* recipe

Diagnose communication issues

In this recipe, we will look at how to troubleshoot communication issues between nodes and how we can quickly find common errors.

Getting ready

To step through the recipe, the user must have completed the *Setting up multi-node HBase cluster* recipe in *Chapter 9, HBase Administration* and have gone through the previous recipes in this chapter. It is good to have a basic knowledge of the DNS and TCP communication.

How to do it...

1. Connect to the `master1.cyrus.com` master node in the cluster and switch to user `hadoop`.

2. The first thing is to check which connections are already established to the nodes. This can be seen with the following command, as shown here:

```
[hadoop@master1 cluster]$ netstat -tp
(Not all processes could be identified, non-owned process info
 will not be shown, you would have to be root to see it all.)
Active Internet connections (w/o servers)
Proto Recv-Q Send-Q Local Address               Foreign Address              State       PID/Program
tcp        0      0 master1.cyrus.co:cslistener dn3.cyrus.com:gprs-data      ESTABLISHED 17263/java
tcp        0      0 master1.cyrus.co:cslistener dn2.cyrus.com:31448          ESTABLISHED 17263/java
tcp        0      0 master1.cyrus.co:cslistener dn6.cyrus.com:47486          ESTABLISHED 17263/java
tcp        0      0 master1.cyrus.co:cslistener dn1.cyrus.com:11774          ESTABLISHED 17263/java
tcp        0      0 master1.cyrus.co:cslistener dn4.cyrus.com:52050          ESTABLISHED 17263/java
tcp        0      0 master1.cyrus.co:cslistener dn5.cyrus.com:36028          ESTABLISHED 17263/java
tcp        0      0 master1.cyrus.co:cslistener rt1.cyrus.com:15594          ESTABLISHED 17263/java
tcp        0      0 master1.cyrus.co:cslistener rt2.cyrus.com:41914          ESTABLISHED 17263/java
tcp        0      0 master1.cyrus.co:cslistener rt3.cyrus.com:40890          ESTABLISHED 17263/java
```

3. Check the reachability of nodes in the cluster using the following commands and also ensure reverse lookup for each host in the cluster:

   $ ping master1.cyrus.com

   $ ping dn1.cyrus.com

   $ nslookup "IP of Namenode, RM and Datanodes"

4. If there is a reachability issue, check for firewall rules on any intermediate network devices or on the host it uses, using the following command:

   $ sudo ipbales -L

   $ sudo Iptable -F

5. It is not a good practice to disable the firewall, but to isolate the issue, we can disable and test. Then, enable each respective port needed.
6. Make sure each node has a unique hostname and resolve to the correct IP on the host. Else, this can cause strange behavior and it would be difficult to resolve.
7. Look at the logs of the Master nodes to observe the communication about nodes. This can be seen in the logs, as shown in the following screenshot:

```
[hadoop@master1 cluster]$ tail -5f hadoop/logs/hadoop-hadoop-namenode-master1.cyrus.com.log
2017-04-03 01:55:41,769 INFO BlockStateChange: BLOCK* processReport: discarded non-initial block report from Da
tanodeRegistration(10.0.0.38:50010, datanodeUuid=15c07c2a-0227-4733-b05d-c272bfc280c0, infoPort=50075, infoSecu
rePort=0, ipcPort=50020, storageInfo=lv=-56;cid=CID-58e5f718-1bb0-4a03-ab11-3a6f368d81d2;nsid=880609571;c=0) be
cause namenode still in startup phase
```

8. The instructions given in the preceding step need to be repeated for Datanodes and Resourcemanager. Test one component at a time.
9. Another common mistake is copying the file from one node to another and not changing node-specific parameters such as data directory location, hostname, and so on.

10. Another important tool to look at the open files associated with a process is `lsof -p <pid>`, as shown in the following screenshot:

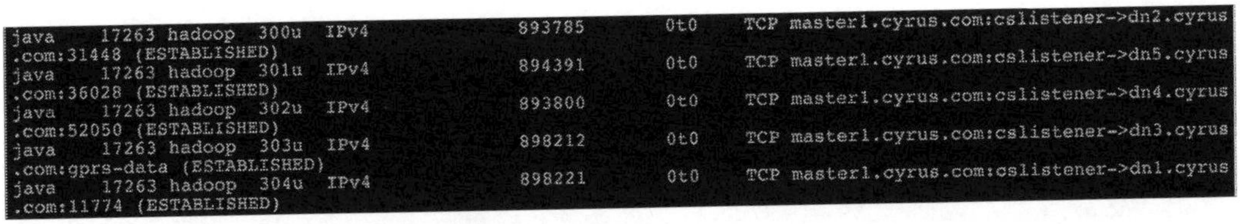

```
java     17263 hadoop  300u  IPv4              893785      0t0    TCP master1.cyrus.com:cslistener->dn2.cyrus
.com:31448 (ESTABLISHED)
java     17263 hadoop  301u  IPv4              894391      0t0    TCP master1.cyrus.com:cslistener->dn5.cyrus
.com:36028 (ESTABLISHED)
java     17263 hadoop  302u  IPv4              893800      0t0    TCP master1.cyrus.com:cslistener->dn4.cyrus
.com:52050 (ESTABLISHED)
java     17263 hadoop  303u  IPv4              898212      0t0    TCP master1.cyrus.com:cslistener->dn3.cyrus
.com:gprs-data (ESTABLISHED)
java     17263 hadoop  304u  IPv4              898221      0t0    TCP master1.cyrus.com:cslistener->dn1.cyrus
.com:11774 (ESTABLISHED)
```

11. The preceding command shows the JAR loaded, the sockets associated, and data directories being read or locked, as shown in the following screenshot:

```
java     17263 hadoop  279uW  REG                 202,17       23      15 /data/namenode1/in_use.lock
java     17263 hadoop  280u   unix 0xffff8803f85e1400       0t0  891726 socket
java     17263 hadoop  281uW  REG                 202,33       23      15 /data/namenode2/in_use.lock
java     17263 hadoop  282u   REG                 202,17  1048576    8751 /data/namenode1/current/edits_inprogres
s_0000000000000024829
java     17263 hadoop  283u   REG                 202,33  1048576    8751 /data/namenode2/current/edits_inprogres
s_0000000000000024829
```

12. Look at the memory utilization of daemons using the `jmap -heap <pid>` command, as shown in the following screenshot — they are running fine in our case:

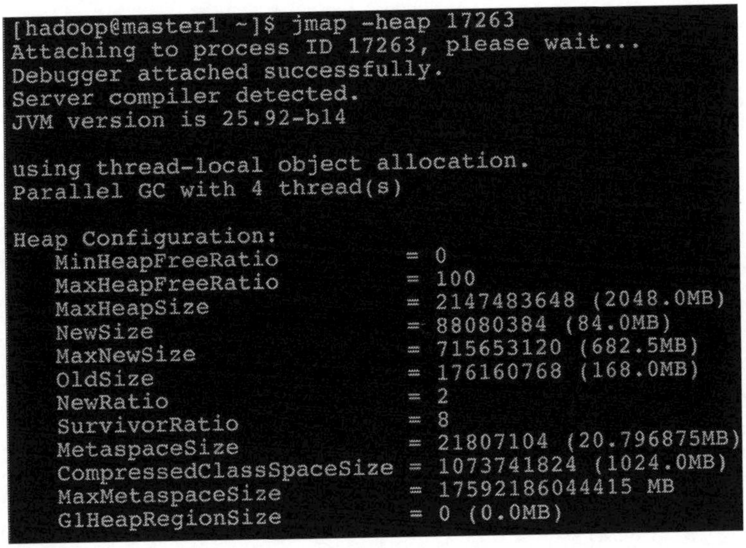

```
[hadoop@master1 ~]$ jmap -heap 17263
Attaching to process ID 17263, please wait...
Debugger attached successfully.
Server compiler detected.
JVM version is 25.92-b14

using thread-local object allocation.
Parallel GC with 4 thread(s)

Heap Configuration:
   MinHeapFreeRatio         = 0
   MaxHeapFreeRatio         = 100
   MaxHeapSize              = 2147483648 (2048.0MB)
   NewSize                  = 88080384 (84.0MB)
   MaxNewSize               = 715653120 (682.5MB)
   OldSize                  = 176160768 (168.0MB)
   NewRatio                 = 2
   SurvivorRatio            = 8
   MetaspaceSize            = 21807104 (20.796875MB)
   CompressedClassSpaceSize = 1073741824 (1024.0MB)
   MaxMetaspaceSize         = 17592186044415 MB
   G1HeapRegionSize         = 0 (0.0MB)
```

13. To check the packets coming on an interface, we can use the following command:

    tcpdump -i eth0

14. If there are any packet drops, run `tracert` to figure out the path to the destination and see where it drops.

How it works...

In this recipe, we looked at how we can troubleshoot network issues and common ports to be open for the communication. In an organization, we may need to engage the network team to help us diagnose these kinds of issues, as we may not have access to firewalls or routers.

Parse logs for errors

In this recipe, we will look at how to parse logs and quickly find errors. There are job logs, which are aggregated on HDFS, logs which include daemon logs, system logs, and so on.

We will look at some keywords and commands to find the errors in logs.

Getting ready

To complete the recipe, the user must have a running Hadoop cluster, must have completed the *Setting up multi-node HBase cluster* recipe in *Chapter 9, HBase Administration*, and know Bash or Perl/Python scripting basics.

How to do it...

1. Connect to the `edge1.cyrus.com` node in the cluster and switch to user `hadoop`. However, we can connect to any node in the cluster from which we can access the logs.
2. The location of the YARN logs on the cluster is exported as NFS export and mounted at location `/logs/hadoop` on the Edge node. Refer to the *HDFS as NFS export* recipe.
3. All the other logs, such as system and daemon logs, from the cluster are exported to the location `/logs/system`.
4. If the user is not from a Linux system background and does not know how to perform the preceding step, you can use the commands on individual nodes.
5. Switch to directory `/logs` and execute the command hence shown forth.
6. Check for input records processed by a job by using the following command:

   ```
   $ for i in $(find . -type f -name "*.log");do grep 'INPUT_RECORDS_
   PROCESSED' $i; done
   ```

7. Find the decommissioning nodes in the cluster. This will be in the Resourcemanager logs and can be found by the following command:

   ```
   $ for i in $(find . -type f -name "*");do grep  'org.apache.
   hadoop.hdfs.server.blockmanagement.DecommissionManager' $i;done
   ```

8. Look for any memory errors in the cluster YARN logs:

```
$ for i in $(find . -type f -name "*.log");do grep -l 'java.lang.OutOfMemoryError' $i;done
$ for i in $(find . -type f -name "*.log");do grep -l 'allocate memory' $i;done
$ for i in $(find . -type f -name "*.log");do grep 'org.apache.hadoop.util.JvmPauseMonitor' $i;done
```

9. The important keywords to look for disk related issues or blacklisted nodes are listed below. These can be passed to `for loop` to filter the given keywords.

```
'local-dirs are bad'
'hdfs.BlockMissingException'
'Removing stale replica from location'
'java.io.FileNotFoundException'
'Not enough space to cache'
'BLACKLIST'
```

10. To find the job failures and the reason for these failures, we can use the following keywords, which can be passed to the `for loop`:

```
'org.apache.hadoop.mapreduce.jobhistory.JobUnsuccessfulCompletion'
'org.apache.hadoop.mapreduce.jobhistory.TaskFailed'
'org.apache.hadoop.security.AccessControlException'
'Shell$ExitCodeException'
```

11. To find which reducer fetcher is assigned to which mapper, we can use the following code:

```
$ for i in $(find . -type f -name "*.log");do grep 'fetcher#1' $i;done
```

12. To find which node the Application master was launched in, we can use the following code:

```
$ for i in $(find . -type f -name "*.log");do grep -l 'appMasterHost' $i;done
```

13. To look into the system logs for any memory usage or other errors, we can parse `/var/log/messages` on each node or command as follows — change to directory `/var/log` and execute on each of the nodes:

```
$ for i in $(find . -type f -name "*.log");do grep 'packets pruned from receive queue' $i;done
```

How it works...

In this recipe, we looked at the important keywords which can help to quickly find issues and help troubleshoot complex issues.

Hive troubleshooting

In this recipe, we will look at Hive troubleshooting steps and important keywords in the logs, which can help us to identify issues.

Getting ready

For this recipe, the user must have completed the *Operating Hive with ZooKeeper* recipe in *Chapter 7, Data Ingestion and Workflow* and have a basic understanding of database connectivity.

How to do it...

1. Connect to the `edge1.cyrus.com` Edge node and switch to user `hadoop`.
2. The Hive query logs location is defined by `hive.querylog.location` and the Hive `server2` logs is defined by `hive.server2.logging.operation.log.location`.
3. As an example, if I try to query a table that does not exist, we can see the errors in the Hive log, as shown in the following screenshot:

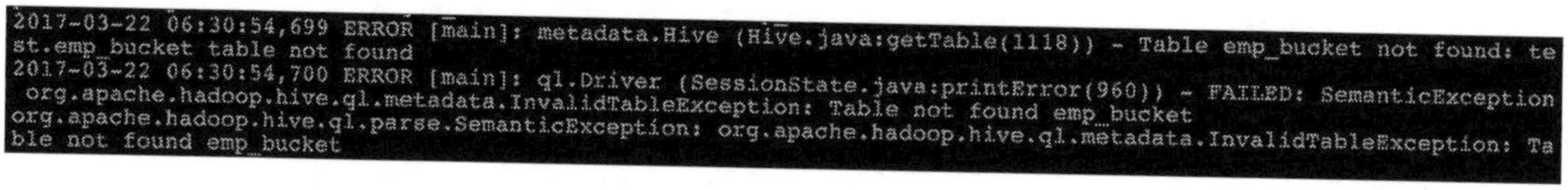

```
2017-03-22 06:30:54,699 ERROR [main]: metadata.Hive (Hive.java:getTable(1118)) - Table emp_bucket not found: te
st.emp_bucket table not found
2017-03-22 06:30:54,700 ERROR [main]: ql.Driver (SessionState.java:printError(960)) - FAILED: SemanticException
 org.apache.hadoop.hive.ql.metadata.InvalidTableException: Table not found emp_bucket
org.apache.hadoop.hive.ql.parse.SemanticException: org.apache.hadoop.hive.ql.metadata.InvalidTableException: Ta
ble not found emp_bucket
```

4. Make it a good habit to read logs to troubleshoot, as logs will give hints about errors.
5. Make sure Hive is able to connect to the Hive metastore. To verify this, first connect manually, as shown here:

   $ mysql -u Hadoop -h master1.cyrus.com -p

6. Make sure the user used in Hive Hadoop has grants to make changes in the Hive metastore. The grants for the user are shown in the following screenshot:

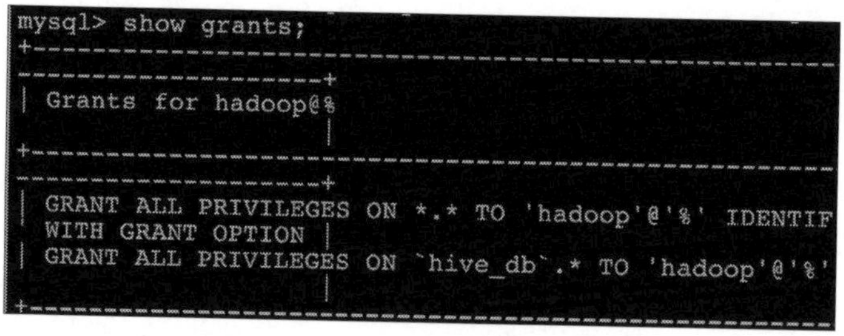

```
mysql> show grants;
+-----------------------------------------------------------------
-----------------------+
| Grants for hadoop@%
                       |
+-----------------------------------------------------------------
-----------------------+
| GRANT ALL PRIVILEGES ON *.* TO 'hadoop'@'%' IDENTIF
 WITH GRANT OPTION |
| GRANT ALL PRIVILEGES ON `hive_db`.* TO 'hadoop'@'%'
                       |
+-----------------------------------------------------------------
```

The `hadoop` user must have full access to the Hive DB.

7. Often, the user will be able to query Hive, but unable to write if the MySQL permissions for that user are not correct.
8. If the user `hadoop` has read/write permissions and he tries to do an **insert with overwrite** operation, he will be disallowed, as the user does not have the delete permission. Overwrite in Hive is a delete operation followed by a write operation, so the user must have delete permission.
9. If you are not able to connect to the MySQL server, then it is a connectivity issue. Check the firewall, listening port for MySQL `3306`, for connectivity issues.
10. To isolate the issue, first check the connection with simple Hive CLI and then with Beeline.
11. Make sure that the permission of the Hive warehouse is correct and the users who write to it can do the operations. Also, the permissions of the Hadoop `/tmp` must be write-enabled for Hive users, as shown in the following screenshot:

```
[hadoop@edge1 cluster]$ hadoop fs -ls /user/hive/
Found 1 items
drwxrwxr-x   - hadoop supergroup          0 2017-03-29 22:37 /user/hive/warehouse
[hadoop@edge1 cluster]$ hadoop fs -ls /tmp
Found 4 items
drwx------   - hadoop supergroup          0 2017-03-18 23:34 /tmp/hadoop-yarn
drwxr-xr-x   - hadoop supergroup          0 2017-03-29 10:49 /tmp/hbase-hadoop
drwx-wx-wx   - hadoop supergroup          0 2017-03-21 21:09 /tmp/hive
drwxrwxrwt   - hadoop supergroup          0 2017-03-18 23:36 /tmp/logs
```

12. Make sure the `VERSION` table in MySQL Hive metastore exists, else you can see DataNucleolus errors. The table is as shown in the following screenshot:

```
mysql> select * from VERSION;
+--------+----------------+------------------------------------+
| VER_ID | SCHEMA_VERSION | VERSION_COMMENT                    |
+--------+----------------+------------------------------------+
|      1 | 1.2.0          | Set by MetaStore hadoop@10.0.0.52 |
+--------+----------------+------------------------------------+
1 row in set (0.00 sec)
```

13. Some of the common keywords to look for in logs are as follows:

'org.apache.hive.service.cli.HiveSQLException: Session does not exist'

'Trying to connect to metastore'

'ERROR org.apache.hadoop.hive.ql.Driver'

'as metastore is getting bypassed'

14. Once we start the Hive `server2` using the command `hive --service hiveserver2`, we can see the connections to MySQL, as shown in the following screenshot:

```
[hadoop@edge1 cluster]$ lsof -Pan -p 14839 -i
COMMAND   PID   USER    FD   TYPE DEVICE SIZE/OFF NODE NAME
java    14839 hadoop  390u  IPv4  42827      0t0  TCP 10.0.0.52:61606->10.0.0.104:3306 (ESTABLISHED)
java    14839 hadoop  391u  IPv4  44061      0t0  TCP 10.0.0.52:61608->10.0.0.104:3306 (ESTABLISHED)
java    14839 hadoop  392u  IPv4  44064      0t0  TCP 10.0.0.52:61614->10.0.0.104:3306 (ESTABLISHED)
java    14839 hadoop  393u  IPv4  44065      0t0  TCP 10.0.0.52:61616->10.0.0.104:3306 (ESTABLISHED)
```

15. Make sure the ZooKeeper ensemble is up and running, as shown in the following screenshot — the nodes must either be in leader or follower state:

```
[hadoop@edge1 cluster]$ zkServer.sh status
ZooKeeper JMX enabled by default
Using config: /opt/cluster/zoo/bin/../conf/zoo.cfg
Mode: follower
```

16. Refer to the *Hive server modes and setup* recipe in *Chapter 7, Data Ingestion and Workflow* to understand the details about setup, which will help you understand the layout of things better.

How it works...

In the preceding recipe, we looked at steps to troubleshoot Hive and some keywords we can look into in order to quickly find errors in logs.

You can go through *Chapter 8, Performance Tuning* to understand things that make a difference to the system.

See also

- The *Hive performance tuning* recipe in *Chapter 8, Performance Tuning*
- The *Hive metastore database* recipe in *Chapter 7, Data Ingestion and Workflow*

HBase troubleshooting

In this recipe, we will look at HBase troubleshooting and how to identify some of the common issues in the HBase cluster.

Getting ready

Make sure that the user has completed the *Setting up multi-node HBase cluster* recipe in *Chapter 9, HBase Administration* for this section, and the assumption is that HDFS and YARN are working fine. Refer to previous recipes to troubleshoot any issues with the Hadoop cluster, before starting troubleshooting of HBase.

How to do it...

1. Connect to the `master1.cyrus.com` master node and switch to user `hadoop`.
2. Firstly, make sure ZooKeeper is up and the ensemble is healthy, as shown in the following screenshot — this is only if an external ZooKeeper is used:

```
[hadoop@edge1 cluster]$ zkServer.sh status
ZooKeeper JMX enabled by default
Using config: /opt/cluster/zoo/bin/../conf/zoo.cfg
Mode: follower
```

3. Rather than starting the entire cluster in one go, start each component one-by-one. Start `hbase` master using the following command:

   `$ hbase-daemon.sh start master`

4. Quickly check which nodes and services the HBase master is talking to. In the following screenshot, we can see connections to ZooKeeper, Namenode, and its RPC port:

```
[hadoop@master1 log]$ lsof -Pan -p 18438 -i
COMMAND   PID   USER   FD   TYPE DEVICE SIZE/OFF NODE NAME
java    18438 hadoop  395u  IPv6 906688      0t0  TCP 10.0.0.104:16000 (LISTEN)
java    18438 hadoop  439u  IPv6 912196      0t0  TCP 10.0.0.104:57894->10.0.0.52:2181 (ESTABLISHED)
java    18438 hadoop  441u  IPv6 912199      0t0  TCP *:16010 (LISTEN)
java    18438 hadoop  448u  IPv6 910115      0t0  TCP 10.0.0.104:17252->10.0.0.4:2181 (ESTABLISHED)
java    18438 hadoop  449u  IPv6 915480      0t0  TCP 10.0.0.104:15554->10.0.0.104:9000 (ESTABLISHED)
java    18438 hadoop  459u  IPv6 915408      0t0  TCP 10.0.0.104:57996->10.0.0.52:2181 (ESTABLISHED)
java    18438 hadoop  463u  IPv6 915411      0t0  TCP 10.0.0.104:57998->10.0.0.52:2181 (ESTABLISHED)
```

5. The first thing to check is whether Namenode is out of safe mode. As can be seen in the logs, HBase master is waiting for it, as shown in the following screenshot:

```
[hadoop@master1 log]$ tail -10f /opt/cluster/hbase/logs/hbase-hadoop-master-master1.cyrus.com.log
2017-04-03 05:57:21,826 INFO  [master1:16000.activeMasterManager] util.FSUtils: Waiting for dfs to exit safe mo
de...
2017-04-03 05:57:31,829 INFO  [master1:16000.activeMasterManager] util.FSUtils: Waiting for dfs to exit safe mo
de...
```

6. The next thing to check for is the directory on HDFS that has the right permissions, as shown in the following screenshot:

```
[hadoop@master1 log]$ hadoop fs -ls /hbase
Found 9 items
drwxr-xr-x   - hadoop supergroup          0 2017-03-30 00:00 /hbase/.hbase-snapshot
drwxr-xr-x   - hadoop supergroup          0 2017-03-29 23:28 /hbase/.tmp
drwxr-xr-x   - hadoop supergroup          0 2017-04-02 23:41 /hbase/MasterProcWALs
drwxr-xr-x   - hadoop supergroup          0 2017-03-29 12:11 /hbase/WALs
drwxr-xr-x   - hadoop supergroup          0 2017-03-29 22:25 /hbase/archive
drwxr-xr-x   - hadoop supergroup          0 2017-03-29 12:11 /hbase/data
-rw-r--r--   1 hadoop supergroup         42 2017-03-29 12:11 /hbase/hbase.id
-rw-r--r--   1 hadoop supergroup          7 2017-03-29 12:11 /hbase/hbase.version
drwxr-xr-x   - hadoop supergroup          0 2017-04-02 23:22 /hbase/oldWALs
```

7. The next thing is to start the region servers and see whether they talk to the master or not. The logs will be similar to the ones shown in the following screenshot:

```
2017-04-03 06:02:56,968 INFO  [master1:16000.activeMasterManager] master.ServerManager: W
aiting for region servers count to settle; currently checked in 0, slept for 4511 ms, exp
ecting minimum of 1, maximum of 2147483647, timeout of 4500 ms, interval of 1500 ms.
2017-04-03 06:02:58,471 INFO  [master1:16000.activeMasterManager] master.ServerManager: W
aiting for region servers count to settle; currently checked in 0, slept for 6015 ms, exp
ecting minimum of 1, maximum of 2147483647, timeout of 4500 ms, interval of 1500 ms.
```

8. Then start the regions servers using the following command:

```
$ hbase-daemons.sh --config "${HBASE_CONF_DIR}" \
--hosts "${HBASE_REGIONSERVERS}" start regionserver
```

9. Check for hostname resolution and host reachability for each host using the `ping` and `tracert` commands.
10. Visit the HBase master Web UI on port `16010` and see the status of the cluster, the regions available, and the region servers.
11. Check HBase master logs for assignments and regions initialized, as shown next in the logs:

```
2017-04-03 06:15:15,753 INFO  [master1:16000.activeMasterManager] master.Assignment
Manager: Bulk assigning done
2017-04-03 06:15:15,756 INFO  [master1:16000.activeMasterManager] master.Assignment
Manager: Joined the cluster in 196ms, failover=false
2017-04-03 06:15:15,812 INFO  [master1:16000.activeMasterManager] master.HMaster: M
aster has completed initialization
```

12. Remember to go through the *HBase cluster* recipe and understand the setup and the `hbck` commands to fix HBase consistency issues.
13. Look for the GC logs to figure out frequent flushes and errors.

How it works...

In this recipe, we looked at troubleshooting steps for HBase and how quickly we can find key points. The keywords such as `master.RegionStates` or `Offlined` can help to quickly narrow down errors.

Hadoop best practices

In this section, we will cover some of the common best practices for the Hadoop cluster in terms of log management and troubleshooting tools.

These are not from a tuning perspective, but to make things easier to troubleshoot and diagnose.

Things to keep in mind:

1. Always enable logs for each daemon that runs in the Hadoop cluster. Keep the logging level to INFO and, when needed, change it to DEBUG. Once the troubleshooting is done, revert to level INFO.
2. Implement log rotation and retention polices to manage the logs.
3. Use tools such as Nagios to alert for any errors in the cluster before it becomes an issue.
4. Use log aggregation and analysis tools such as Splunk to parse logs.
5. Never co-locate the logs disk with other data disks in the cluster.
6. Use central configuration management systems such as Puppet or Chef to maintain consistent configuration across the cluster.
7. Schedule a benchmarking job to run every day on the cluster and proactively predict any bottlenecks. This can be done using Jenkins and the tests run in off peak hours.
8. Always keep at least 20% disk space available on all nodes in the cluster and implement alerts if that is breached.
9. Archive logs older than a week and move them to a Splunk or any other custom log collecting cluster.
10. Do not overload servers with too many components and always do a wise segregation. Never use HBase master on a Namenode or a ZooKeeper on a node with a slow disk.
11. Make sure that the DNS resolution works both ways for all nodes in the cluster.
12. It is good to have a caching-only server for Hadoop clusters, if not a separate DNS server.

13. Tune the timeout wisely, as it can cause many issues, ranging from too many connections to memory errors. See the performance chapter for more details.
14. Keep the cluster patched to the latest stable releases and run the bare minimum of services needed for operation on the cluster.
15. Always run an NTP server in the Hadoop cluster for time synchronization. This will help in making a correct timeline of events in logs.

How it works...

In this chapter, we looked at some of the common errors and how we can fix them. There are many other errors that are common in production, which are related to the scale at which things operate. Some of these common issues are a large number of partitions in Hive causing performance issues, HBase regions offline or corrupt, and memory tuning. This is an ever-evolving technology, with lots to learn every day. Explore things and always ask why they worked, not just why they did not.

12
Security

In this chapter, we will cover the following recipes:

- Introduction
- Encrypting disk using LUKS
- Configuring Hadoop users
- HDFS encryption at Rest
- Configuring SSL in Hadoop
- In-transit encryption
- Enabling service level authorization
- Securing ZooKeeper
- Configuring auditing
- Configuring Kerberos server
- Configuring and enabling Kerberos for Hadoop

Introduction

In this chapter, we will configure Hadoop cluster to run in secure mode and enable authentication, authorization, and secure transit data. By default, Hadoop runs in nonsecure mode with no access control on data blocks or service-level access. We can run all the Hadoop daemons with a single user `hadoop`, without worrying about security and which daemons access what.

In addition to this, it is important to encrypt the disk, HDFS data at rest, and also to enable Kerberos for the authentication of service access. By default, a HDFS block can be accessed by any map or reduce task, but when Kerberos is enabled all this access is verified.

> Each directory, whether it is on HDFS or local disk must have the right permissions and should only allow the permissions which are necessary to run the service and not any more. Refer to the following link for recommended permissions on each directory in Hadoop:
>
> `https://hadoop.apache.org/docs/r2.7.2/hadoop-project-dist/hadoop-common/SecureMode.html#Permissions_for_both_HDFS_and_local_fileSystem_paths`

The data transfer between nodes, whether it is over RPC, shuffle phase, or over HTTP can be secured. In this chapter, we will look at many of the previously discussed aspects of securing Hadoop.

Encrypting disk using LUKS

Before we even start with Hadoop, it is important to secure at the operating system and network level. It is expected of the users to have prior knowledge for securing Linux and networks, and in this recipe, we will only look at disk encryption.

It is good practice to encrypt the data disk, so that even if they are stolen, the data is safe. The entire disk can be encrypted or just the disk where critical data resides.

Getting ready

To step through the recipes in this chapter, make sure you have at least one node with CentOS 6 and above installed. It does not matter which flavor of Linux you choose, as long as you are comfortable with it. Users must have prior knowledge of Linux installation and basic commands. The same settings apply to all the nodes in the cluster.

How to do it...

1. Connect to a node, which at a later stage will be used to install Hadoop or configured as a Namenode or Datanode data disk. We are using the `nn1.cluster1.com` node.
2. Make sure you switch to user `root` or you must have `sudo` privileges.
3. The first thing is to install the `cryptosetup` package using the following command:

   ```
   # yum install cryptsetup -y
   ```

4. Choose the partition you want to encrypt, such as `/dev/sdb1`. This will be used to store the Namenode metadata.

5. Initialize the partition with `cryptosetup` using the command shown in the following screenshot. Make sure you remember the password you use in this step:

```
[root@nn1 ~]# cryptsetup --verbose --verify-passphrase luksFormat /dev/sdb1

WARNING!
========
This will overwrite data on /dev/sdb1 irrevocably.

Are you sure? (Type uppercase yes): YES
```

6. You can verify the LUKS details for a partition using the command shown in the following screenshot:

```
[root@nn1 ~]# cryptsetup luksDump /dev/sdb1
LUKS header information for /dev/sdb1

Version:        1
Cipher name:    aes
Cipher mode:    xts-plain64
Hash spec:      sha1
Payload offset: 4096
MK bits:        256
MK digest:      64 ac 54 cd 94 48 e4 e7 86 7c b6 49 43 92 3b 63 9b 25 9c 9a
MK salt:        98 d2 f9 5d 61 6c c0 34 19 92 59 87 54 82 b7 05
                0c 7d d0 a4 8f 67 aa 6a d0 6a 1f c7 9c 9b 5b 88
MK iterations:  55625
UUID:           a25bfe03-541d-4e1a-a34b-7061c6141282

Key Slot 0: ENABLED
        Iterations:             218057
        Salt:                   b5 d5 89 55 98 7e cf ab 6f 26 c8 76 ea 5a ba fa
                                fb 34 d6 15 d5 94 61 05 2f 34 58 cd 86 47 c5 46
        Key material offset:    8
        AF stripes:             4000
```

7. Now we will open the encrypted partition and it will be mapped under `/dev/mapper/sdb1`. This can be done using the following command:

```
# cryptsetup luksOpen /dev/sdb1 sdb1
```

8. The preceding command will prompt you for a password and will be available and can be seen using the following command:

```
# fdisk -l
```

9. Create a new file system on it and mount it by using the following commands. Perform the same steps for all the mount points that you might have:

```
# mkfs.ext4 /dev/mapper/sdb1
# mount /dev/mapper/sdb1 /data/namenode1
# mount /dev/mapper/sdc1 /data/namenode2
```

10. To automatically mount these volumes, we need to create a file with random numbers and add it to the LUKS system, as shown by the commands in the following screenshot:

```
# dd if=/dev/urandom of=/root/keyfile bs=1024 count=4
# chmod 0400 /root/keyfile
# cryptsetup luksAddKey /dev/sdb1 /root/keyfile
```

11. Now we need to obtain the LUKS UUID using the following commands. Note down the UUID it shows:

    # cryptsetup luksUUID /dev/sdb1

12. Then, add the cryto key and UUID mapping in the `/etc/crypttab` file, as shown here:

    sdb1 /dev/disk/by-uuid/a25bfe03-541d-4e1a-a34b-7061c6141282 /root/key.sdb1 luks

13. Finally, update the `/etc/fstab` file to make the mounts permanent. This is shown in the following screenshot:

```
/dev/mapper/sdb1        /data/namenode          ext4    defaults        0 0
/dev/mapper/sdc1        /data/namenode1         ext4    defaults        0 0
```

14. Adjust the permissions on the mount point, as per the user running the HDFS daemons.
15. Repeat the steps for all the nodes in the cluster.

How it works...

In this recipe, we configured LUKS for the disks. Here, we have encrypted only the disk which will be used for Hadoop, either for Namenode or Datanodes. But, the entire root volume can be encrypted and the encryption passed to the boot loader to unlock the volume.

If the disk is to be replaced, securely wipe it and close it using the `cryptsetup luksClose sdb1` command.

Once the disks are encrypted, set up Hadoop as discussed in the installation chapter or follow the next recipe to secure it further.

See also

- The *HDFS encryption at Rest* recipe

Configuring Hadoop users

In this recipe, we will configure users to run Hadoop services so as to have better control of access by daemons.

In all the recipes so far, we have configured all services/daemons, whether it's HDFS, YARN, or Hive to run with user `hadoop`. This is not the right practice for production clusters as it would be difficult to control services in a fine and granular manner.

It is recommended to segregate services to run with different users, for example, HDFS daemons as `hdfs:hadoop`, YARN daemons as `yarn:hadoop`, and other services such as Hive or HBase with their own respective users.

Getting ready

To step through the recipe in this section, we need a Hadoop cluster already configured and it is assumed that users are aware about Hadoop installation and configuration. Refer to *Chapter 1, Hadoop Architecture and Deployment* for the installation and configuration of a Hadoop cluster. In this recipe, we are just separating daemons to run with different users, rather than them all running with user ID `hadoop`.

How to do it...

1. Connect to a node that is master in the Hadoop cluster. We are using the `nn1.cluster1.com` node.
2. Switch to user root or you must have `sudo` privileges.
3. Create users using the following command and make them members of the already existing group `hadoop`:

   ```
   # useradd hdfs -G hadoop
   # useradd yarn -G hadoop
   # useradd mapred -G hadoop
   ```

4. Make sure the same users are added to all the nodes in the cluster. When we say the same users, it means that their user IDs must be the same as well.
5. Configure a super group for Hadoop by editing the `hdfs-site.xml` file with the settings shown in the following screenshot:

   ```
   <property>
       <name>dfs.permissions.superusergroup</name>
       <value>hadoop</value>
   </property>
   ```

6. Make sure the permissions for the directories pointed by `dfs.namenode.data.dir` and `dfs.datanode.data.dir` are as shown in the following screenshot:

```
[root@nn1 ~]# chown hadoop:hadoop /data
[root@nn1 ~]# chown -R hdfs:hadoop /data/namenode
[root@nn1 ~]# ls -ld /data/namenode
drwxr-xr-x 2 hdfs hadoop 4096 Apr 11 04:36 /data/namenode
```

7. Now switch to user `hdfs` and format Namenode using the command shown here:

   $ sudo su - hdfs

   $ hdfs namenode -format

8. Once the format of the Namenode is done, make sure the directory permissions are correct, as shown in the following screenshot:

```
[hdfs@nn1 ~]$ id
uid=1006(hdfs) gid=1006(hdfs) groups=1006(hdfs),1003(hadoop)
[hdfs@nn1 ~]$ ls -ld /data
drwxr-xr-x 5 hadoop hadoop 52 Oct 22 16:22 /data
[hdfs@nn1 ~]$ ls -ld /data/namenode
drwxr-xr-x 3 hdfs hdfs 4096 Apr 11 04:48 /data/namenode
[hdfs@nn1 ~]$ ls -ld /data/namenode/current
drwxrwxr-x 2 hdfs hdfs 4096 Apr 11 04:48 /data/namenode/current
```

9. Make respective changes on all other nodes, such as Datanodes in the cluster, and start the HDFS daemon after setting ssh keys for user `hdfs`. Refer to *Chapter 1, Hadoop Architecture and Deployment* for steps on how to do that.

10. The Namenode and Datanode daemons will now run with user `hdfs`, as can be seen in the following screenshot:

```
[hdfs@nn1 ~]$ ps -ef | grep namenode
hdfs      1952     1  5 17:55 pts/0    00:00:05 /usr/java/latest/bin/java -Dproc_namenode -Xmx1000m -Djava.net.
preferIPv4Stack=true -Dhadoop.log.dir=/opt/cluster/hadoop-2.7.3/logs -Dhadoop.log.file=hadoop.log -Dhadoop.home
.dir=/opt/cluster/hadoop-2.7.3 -Dhadoop.id.str=hdfs -Dhadoop.root.logger=INFO,console -Djava.library.path=/opt/
cluster/hadoop-2.7.3/lib/native -Dhadoop.policy.file=hadoop-policy.xml -Djava.net.preferIPv4Stack=true -Djava.n
et.preferIPv4Stack=true -Djava.net.preferIPv4Stack=true -Dhadoop.log.dir=/opt/cluster/hadoop-2.7.3/logs -Dhadoo
p.log.file=hadoop-hdfs-namenode-nn1.cluster1.com.log -Dhadoop.home.dir=/opt/cluster/hadoop-2.7.3 -Dhadoop.id.st
r=hdfs -Dhadoop.root.logger=INFO,RFA -Djava.library.path=/opt/cluster/hadoop-2.7.3/lib/native -Dhadoop.policy.f
ile=hadoop-policy.xml -Djava.net.preferIPv4Stack=true -Dcom.sun.management.jmxremote -Dcom.sun.management.jmxre
mote.password.file=/opt/cluster/hadoop/etc/hadoop/jmxremote.password -Dcom.sun.management.jmxremote.authenticat
e=false -Dcom.sun.management.jmxremote.ssl=false -Dcom.sun.management.jmxremote.port=8004 -Dhadoop.security.log
ger=INFO,RFAS -Dhdfs.audit.logger=INFO,NullAppender -Dcom.sun.management.jmxremote -Dcom.sun.management.jmxremo
te.password.file=/opt/cluster/hadoop/etc/hadoop/jmxremote.password -Dcom.sun.management.jmxremote.authenticate=
false -Dcom.sun.management.jmxremote.ssl=false -Dcom.sun.management.jmxremote.port=8004 -Dhadoop.security.logge
r=INFO,RFAS -Dhdfs.audit.logger=INFO,NullAppender -Dcom.sun.management.jmxremote -Dcom.sun.management.jmxremote
.password.file=/opt/cluster/hadoop/etc/hadoop/jmxremote.password -Dcom.sun.management.jmxremote.authenticate=fa
lse -Dcom.sun.management.jmxremote.ssl=false -Dcom.sun.management.jmxremote.port=8004 -Dhadoop.security.logger=
INFO,RFAS -Dhdfs.audit.logger=INFO,NullAppender -Dhadoop.security.logger=INFO,RFAS org.apache.hadoop.hdfs.serve
r.namenode.NameNode
```

11. Make sure the `logs` and `temp` directory have the correct permissions to write logs. Test by uploading a file to HDFS, as shown in the following screenshot. Notice that the super group is now `hadoop`:

```
[hdfs@nn1 ~]$ hadoop fs -put test /
[hdfs@nn1 ~]$ clear
[hdfs@nn1 ~]$ hadoop fs -ls /
Found 1 items
-rw-r--r--   2 hdfs hadoop         20 2017-04-11 05:14 /test
```

12. Similarly, for YARN, we will start Resourcemanager and Nodemanagers with user `yarn`.
13. Make sure any log locations and YARN `temp` directory are owned by user `yarn`.
14. Start the YARN daemons using the following commands after setting ssh keys for user `yarn`:

```
$ sudo su - yarn
$ start-yarn.sh
```

15. Make sure you can see the Nodemanagers register with the Resourcemanager, as shown in the following screenshot:

```
[yarn@jt1 ~]$ yarn node -list
17/05/16 18:02:27 INFO client.RMProxy: Connecting to ResourceManager at jt1.cluster1.com/192.168.1.69:9003
Total Nodes:4
         Node-Id             Node-State Node-Http-Address       Number-of-Running-Containers
dn1.cluster1.com:46217          RUNNING dn1.cluster1.com:8090                              0
dn4.cluster1.com:54162          RUNNING dn4.cluster1.com:8090                              0
dn2.cluster1.com:52476          RUNNING dn2.cluster1.com:8090                              0
dn3.cluster1.com:59942          RUNNING dn3.cluster1.com:8090                              0
```

16. Execute a test job such as wordcount to make sure the cluster is working fine. You should be able to run the job successfully with `hadoop`, `hdfs`, and `yarn` users.
17. Later on, we can give finer control on what each of the users can do.
18. One thing to make a note of is that the `jps` command will show only the daemon running for that user. For example, if you are logged in as user `yarn`, then only Resourcemanager or Nodemanager daemons will be shown. To see all processed, use `jps` as the root user.

How it works...

In this recipe, we have segregated the daemons to run with individual users. Similarly, we can set up users for Hive, HBase, MapReduce, and so on and control access.

All the users are part of a common group, so that they can access each others' areas. Any job executed needs to access HDFS, so it must be able to read and write. This is achieved by adding all the users to a common group, which in our case is `hadoop`.

HDFS encryption at Rest

In this recipe, we will look at transparent HDFS encryption, which is encryption of data at rest. A typical use case could be a cluster used by a financial domain and others within a company using HDFS to store critical data.

The concept involves **Key Management Server** (**KMS**), which provides keys and encryption zones that secure data using the key. To access data, we need the key and data from the encrypted zone that cannot be moved to nonencrypted zones without a proper key.

Getting ready

To step through the recipe in this section, we need Hadoop cluster configured with HDFS at least. The changes can be done on one node and then the modified files copied across all nodes in the cluster.

How to do it...

1. Connect to the master node in the cluster; we are using the `nn1.cluster1.com` node.
2. Switch to user `hadoop` or `root` and make all the changes, as shown in the following steps.
3. Edit the file `/opt/cluster/hadoop/etc/hadoop/core-site.xml` and enable the KMS store by adding the following lines.

```
<property>
    <name>hadoop.security.key.provider.path</name>
    <value>kms://http@nn1.cluster1.com:16000/kms</value>
</property>
```

4. Edit the `hdfs-site.xml` file and make the changes shown here:

```
<property>
    <name>dfs.encryption.key.provider.uri</name>
    <value>kms://http@nn1.cluster1.com:16000/kms</value>
</property>
```

5. Copy the modified files across all the nodes in the cluster and restart the HDFS daemons.
6. Edit the `/opt/cluster/hadoop/etc/hadoop/kms-env.sh` file and adjust the KMS `temp` directory. Make sure the location is writable by user `hdfs` or whichever user is starting Namenode:

```
export KMS_TEMP=${KMS_HOME}/temp
```

7. The `KMS_HOME` is, by default, the same as the Hadoop home. The user can change it to whatever he desires.
8. Make sure that the Tomcat configuration files under `share/hadoop/kms/tomcat/conf` are readable by the user running the HDFS daemons, which in our case is `hdfs`.

9. Now, start the KMS service using the command shown in the following screenshot:

```
[hdfs@nn1 ~]$ kms.sh start
Using CATALINA_BASE:   /opt/cluster/hadoop/share/hadoop/kms/tomcat
Using CATALINA_HOME:   /opt/cluster/hadoop/share/hadoop/kms/tomcat
Using CATALINA_TMPDIR: /opt/cluster/hadoop/share/hadoop/kms/tomcat/temp
Using JRE_HOME:        /usr/java/latest
Using CLASSPATH:       /opt/cluster/hadoop/share/hadoop/kms/tomcat/bin/bootstrap.jar
Using CATALINA_PID:    /tmp/kms.pid
```

10. Make sure `openssl-devel` is installed on all nodes in the cluster:

    # yum install openssl-devel -y

11. Verify that we can connect to the KMS store using the following command:

    $ hadoop key list

12. Create a key using the command shown in the following screenshot. We can specify the key length, cipher, and description as well to the command:

```
[hdfs@nn1 ~]$ hadoop key create key1
key1 has been successfully created with options Options{cipher='AES/CTR/NoPadding', bitLength=128
null', attributes=null}.
KMSClientProvider[http://nn1.cluster1.com:16000/kms/v1/] has been updated.
```

13. Create an encrypted zone using the commands shown in the following screenshot:

```
[hdfs@nn1 ~]$ hadoop fs -mkdir /secure_zone
[hdfs@nn1 ~]$ hdfs crypto -createZone -keyName key1 -path /secure_zone
Added encryption zone /secure_zone
```

14. We can list the zones using the commands shown in the following screenshot:

```
[hdfs@nn1 ~]$ hdfs crypto -listZones
/secure_zone  key1
```

15. We can add files by copying them to the encrypted zones, as shown in the following screenshot:

```
[hdfs@nn1 ~]$ hadoop fs -cp /test /secure_zone
[hdfs@nn1 ~]$ hadoop fs -ls /
Found 2 items
drwxr-xr-x   - hdfs hadoop          0 2017-04-11 18:48 /secure_zone
-rw-r--r--   2 hdfs hadoop         20 2017-04-11 18:47 /test
[hdfs@nn1 ~]$ hadoop fs -ls /secure_zone
Found 1 items
-rw-r--r--   2 hdfs hadoop         20 2017-04-11 18:48 /secure_zone/test
```

16. It is important to back up the `keystore` file as, without it, we cannot access the data. By default, the `keystore` file and its crc will be in the home directory of the user, as shown in the following screenshot:

```
[hdfs@nn1 ~]$ ls -la .kms.keystore.crc
-rwx------ 1 hdfs hdfs 20 Apr 11 18:31 .kms.keystore.crc
[hdfs@nn1 ~]$ ls -l kms.keystore
-rwx------ 1 hdfs hdfs 1116 Apr 11 18:31 kms.keystore
```

17. If the KMS service is stopped, we cannot access any of the secure zones, as can be seen in the following screenshot:

```
[hdfs@nn1 ~]$ kms.sh stop
Using CATALINA_BASE:   /opt/cluster/hadoop/share/hadoop/kms/tomcat
Using CATALINA_HOME:   /opt/cluster/hadoop/share/hadoop/kms/tomcat
Using CATALINA_TMPDIR: /opt/cluster/hadoop/share/hadoop/kms/tomcat/temp
Using JRE_HOME:        /usr/java/latest
Using CLASSPATH:       /opt/cluster/hadoop/share/hadoop/kms/tomcat/bin/b
Using CATALINA_PID:    /tmp/kms.pid
[hdfs@nn1 ~]$ hadoop fs -cat /secure_zone/test
cat: Connection refused
```

18. We can have multiple secure zones with the same or different keys, as shown in the following screenshot:

```
[hdfs@nn1 ~]$ hdfs crypto -listZones
/secure_zone   key1
/secure_zone2  key2
```

19. We can move data across different secure zones, as long as the keys for both source and destination zones exist in the `keystore` file. This is shown in the following screenshot:

```
[hdfs@nn1 ~]$ hadoop fs -cp /secure_zone/test /secure_zone2/
[hdfs@nn1 ~]$ hadoop fs -ls /secure_zone2/
Found 1 items
-rw-r--r--   2 hdfs hadoop         20 2017-04-11 19:22 /secure_zone2/test
```

20. KMS keys are cached both at the server and client end. The server is KMS and the client in this case is Namenode. The cache at the server side can be controlled by editing the `kms-site.xml` file as follows:

```
<property>
    <name>hadoop.kms.cache.enable</name>
    <value>true</value>
```

```
</property>

<property>
    <name>hadoop.kms.cache.timeout.ms</name>
    <value>600000</value>
</property>

<property>
    <name>hadoop.kms.current.key.cache.timeout.ms</name>
    <value>30000</value>
</property>
```

21. Control the cache at the Namenode by editing `core-site.xml` as follows:

```
<property>
    <name>hadoop.security.kms.client.encrypted.key.cache.size</
name>
    <value>500</value>
</property>

<property>
    <name>hadoop.security.kms.client.encrypted.key.cache.low-
watermark</name>
    <value>0.3</value>
</property>

<property>
    <name>hadoop.security.kms.client.encrypted.key.cache.num.
refill.threads</name>
    <value>2</value>
</property>

<property>
    <name>hadoop.security.kms.client.encrypted.key.cache.expiry</
name>
    <value>43200000</value>
</property>
```

How it works...

In this recipe, we configured KMS to provide keys for encrypting data on HDFS. The process depicts how we can create secure zones and then move the data across. Sometimes, while moving data from encrypted to unencrypted zones, we may get CRC verification errors, as the underlying blocks will be different. These CRC checks can be skipped using `-skipcrccheck` command.

Another important thing to note while using encrypted zones in Hive is to make sure the hive scratch directory is within the encrypted zones, else the job will fail while doing a move during the final stage of the job.

> KMS can be integrated with Kerberos for authentication. By default, the authentication method is simple.

Configuring SSL in Hadoop

In this recipe, we will configure SSL for Hadoop services. We can configure SSL for Web UI, WebHDFS, YARN, shuffle phase, RPC, and so on. The important components for enabling SSL are certificates, keystore, and truststore. These must individually be kept secure and safe.

We can have SSL single or two-way, but the preferred method is a single way in which the clients validate the server's identity. Using 2-way SSL increases latency and involves configuration overhead.

Getting ready

To complete this recipe, the user must have a running cluster with HDFS and YARN setup. The users can refer to *Chapter 1, Hadoop Architecture and Deployment* for installation details.

The assumption here is that the user is very familiar with HDFS concepts and knows its layout, and is also familiar with how SSL works, with experience of creating SSL certificates. For this recipe, we will be using self-signed certificates, but for production it is recommended to use a proper CA-signed certificate.

How to do it...

1. Connect to the `nn1.cluster1.com` Namenode and switch to user `hadoop`.

2. Create a directory on each node in the cluster to store certificates. This directory should have the minimum access permissions and only be allowed to be read by the group `hadoop`:

   ```
   $ mkdir -p /opt/cluster/security/certs
   $ mkdir -p /opt/cluster/security/jks
   ```

3. The first step is to create a self-signed certificate and a `keystore` file by using the commands, as shown in the following screenshot.

```
[hadoop@nn1 keys]$ keytool -genkey -alias nn1.cluster1.com -keyalg rsa -ke
ysize 1024 -dname "CN=nn1.cluster1.com,OU=hadoop,O=Netxillon,L=Sydney,ST=N
SW,C=AU" -keypass hadoop@123 -keystore nn1-keystore.jks -storepass hadoop@
123
[hadoop@nn1 keys]$ ls -l
total 4
-rw-rw-r-- 1 hadoop hadoop 1410 Apr 11 22:10 nn1-keystore.jks
```

   This needs to be done for each host in the cluster.

4. This can be scripted out to generate keys for each host, as shown in the following command:

   ```
   $ for i in {dn1,dn2,dn3,dn4,jt1};do keytool -genkey -alias ${i}.
   cluster1.com -keyalg rsa -keysize 1024 -dname "CN=${i}.cluster1.co
   m,OU=hadoop,O=Netxillon,L=Sydney,ST=NSW,C=AU" -keypass hadoop@123
   -keystore ${i}-keystore.jks -storepass hadoop@123; done
   ```

5. Next, we will export the certificate's public key for each host, as shown in the following screenshot. We can use a simple for loop to generate the keys for all hosts. The command used within the for loop is `keytool -export -alias ${i}.cluster1.com -keystore ${i}-keystore.jks -rfc -file ${i}.crt -storepass hadoop@123`:

```
[hadoop@nn1 keys]$ for i in {nn1,dn1,dn2,dn3,dn4,jt1};do keytool -export
 -alias ${i}.cluster1.com -keystore ${i}-keystore.jks -rfc -file ${i}.cr
t -storepass hadoop@123; done
Certificate stored in file <nn1.crt>
Certificate stored in file <dn1.crt>
Certificate stored in file <dn2.crt>
Certificate stored in file <dn3.crt>
Certificate stored in file <dn4.crt>
Certificate stored in file <jt1.crt>
```

6. Keep the password the same for the keypass and storepass to avoid any prompts while starting a service.

7. Now we will import the preceding exported key into the trust store using the `keytool -import -noprompt -alias ${i}.cluster1.com -file ${i}.crt -keystore ${i}-truststore.jks -storepass hadoop@123` command in a loop, as shown in the following screenshot:

```
[hadoop@nn1 keys]$ for i in {nn1,dn1,dn2,dn3,dn4,jt1};do keytool -import
 -noprompt -alias ${i}.cluster1.com -file ${i}.crt -keystore ${i}-trusts
tore.jks -storepass hadoop@123; done
Certificate was added to keystore
Certificate was added to keystore
Certificate was added to keystore
Certificate was added to keystore
Certificate was added to keystore
Certificate was added to keystore
```

8. Create a single trust store file from all the preceding store keys using the `keytool -import -noprompt -alias ${i}.cluster1.com -file ${i}.crt -keystore truststore.jks -storepass hadoop@123` command. This is shown in the following screenshot:

```
[hadoop@nn1 keys]$ for i in {nn1,dn1,dn2,dn3,dn4,jt1};do keytool -import
 -noprompt -alias ${i}.cluster1.com -file ${i}.crt -keystore truststore.
jks -storepass hadoop@123; done
Certificate was added to keystore
Certificate was added to keystore
Certificate was added to keystore
Certificate was added to keystore
Certificate was added to keystore
Certificate was added to keystore
```

9. Now we need to copy the `truststore.jks` and `${i}-keystore.jks` and `${i}-truststore.jks` files to the respective nodes in the cluster. This is shown in the following screenshot:

```
[hadoop@nn1 keys]$ cp truststore.jks /opt/cluster/security/jks/
[hadoop@nn1 keys]$ cp nn1-truststore.jks /opt/cluster/security/certs/host-truststore.jks
[hadoop@nn1 keys]$ cp nn1-keystore.jks /opt/cluster/security/certs/host-keystore.jks
```

10. Copy `truststore.jks` and the other files across nodes, as shown in the following screenshot:

```
[hadoop@nn1 keys]$ for i in {dn1,dn2,dn3,dn4,jt1}; do scp truststore.jks ${i}.cluster1.com:/opt/c
luster/security/jks/; done
truststore.jks                                              100% 4058     4.0KB/s   00:00
truststore.jks                                              100% 4058     4.0KB/s   00:00
truststore.jks                                              100% 4058     4.0KB/s   00:00
truststore.jks                                              100% 4058     4.0KB/s   00:00
truststore.jks                                              100% 4058     4.0KB/s   00:00
[hadoop@nn1 keys]$ for i in {dn1,dn2,dn3,dn4,jt1}; do scp ${i}-truststore.jks ${i}.cluster1.com:/
opt/cluster/security/certs/host-truststore.jks; done
dn1-truststore.jks                                          100%  703     0.7KB/s   00:00
dn2-truststore.jks                                          100%  703     0.7KB/s   00:00
dn3-truststore.jks                                          100%  703     0.7KB/s   00:00
dn4-truststore.jks                                          100%  703     0.7KB/s   00:00
jt1-truststore.jks                                          100%  703     0.7KB/s   00:00
[hadoop@nn1 keys]$ for i in {dn1,dn2,dn3,dn4,jt1}; do scp ${i}-keystore.jks ${i}.cluster1.com:/op
t/cluster/security/certs/host-keystore.jks; done
dn1-keystore.jks                                            100% 1410     1.4KB/s   00:00
dn2-keystore.jks                                            100% 1410     1.4KB/s   00:00
dn3-keystore.jks                                            100% 1410     1.4KB/s   00:00
dn4-keystore.jks                                            100% 1408     1.4KB/s   00:00
jt1-keystore.jks                                            100% 1409     1.4KB/s   00:00
```

11. Verify the host `keystore` file and trust stores using the following command:

    $ keytool -list -v -keystore /opt/cluster/security/certs/host-keystore.jks

    $ keytool -list -v -keystore /opt/cluster/security/certs/host-truststore.jks

12. It is recommended to keep the filenames the same across the nodes, so as to have a common `ssl-client.xml` and `ssl-server.xml` file across the cluster.
13. Adjust the permission of the directory `/opt/cluster/secure` to be accessible by group `hadoop` and not writable, as shown in the following screenshot:

```
[root@repo ~]# clush -g all -b "ls -ld /opt/cluster/security"
---------------
dn[1-4].cluster1.com,jt1.cluster1.com (5)
---------------
drwxr-xr-x 4 hadoop hadoop 28 Apr 16 07:36 /opt/cluster/security
---------------
nn1.cluster1.com
---------------
drwxr-xr-x 4 hadoop hadoop 28 Apr 11 22:05 /opt/cluster/security
```

Now it is time to change the Hadoop configuration file to make the preceding configuration effective.

The files that need to be adjusted are `core-site.xml`, `hdfs-site.xml`, `ssl-client.xml`, `ssl-server.xml` and `yarn-site.xml`.

14. Edit `core-site.xml` to add the following lines on each node in the cluster:

```
<property>
    <name>hadoop.rpc.protection</name>
    <value>privacy</value>
</property>
```

15. Edit `hdfs-site.xml` to add the following lines on each node in the cluster:

```
<property>
    <name>dfs.webhdfs.enabled</name>
    <value>true</value>
</property>

<property>
    <name>dfs.https.enable</name>
    <value>true</value>
</property>

<property>
    <name>dfs.http.policy</name>
    <value>HTTPS_ONLY</value>
</property>

<property>
    <name>dfs.namenode.https-address</name>
    <value>nn1.cluster1.com:50470</value>
</property>
```

16. Add the following code according to the hostname on each of the Datanodes in the cluster:

```
<property>
    <name>dfs.datanode.https.address</name>
    <value>dn1.cluster1.com:50475</value>
</property>
```

17. Edit `yarn-site.xml` as shown next for all the nodes in the cluster:

```
<property>
    <name>yarn.http.policy</name>
    <value>HTTPS_ONLY</value>
</property>

<property>
    <name>yarn.resourcemanager.webapp.https.address</name>
    <value>jt1.cluster1.com:8089</value>
```

```
</property>

<property>
    <name>yarn.nodemanager.webapp.https.address</name>
    <value>0.0.0.0:8090</value>
</property>
```

18. Now configure `ssl-server.xml` on each node in the cluster, as shown next:

```
<configuration>

<property>
    <name>ssl.server.truststore.type</name>
    <value>jks</value>
</property>

<property>
    <name>ssl.server.truststore.location</name>
    <value>/opt/cluster/security/certs/host-truststore.jks</value>
</property>

<property>
    <name>ssl.server.truststore.password</name>
    <value>hadoop@123</value>
</property>

<property>
    <name>ssl.server.truststore.reload.interval</name>
    <value>10000</value>
</property>

<property>
    <name>ssl.server.keystore.type</name>
    <value>jks</value>
</property>

<property>
```

```
        <name>ssl.server.keystore.location</name>
        <value>/opt/cluster/security/certs/host-keystore.jks</value>
    </property>

    <property>
        <name>ssl.server.keystore.password</name>
        <value>hadoop@123</value>
    </property>

    <property>
        <name>ssl.server.keystore.keypassword</name>
        <value>hadoop@123</value>
    </property>

    </configuration>
```

19. Now configure `ssl-client.xml` on each node in the cluster, as shown next:

```
    <property>
        <name>ssl.client.truststore.type</name>
        <value>jks</value>
    </property>

    <property>
        <name>ssl.client.truststore.location</name>
        <value>/opt/cluster/security/jks/truststore.jks</value>
    </property>

    <property>
        <name>ssl.client.truststore.password</name>
        <value>hadoop@123</value>
    </property>
```

20. Once the services are started, try to access the Web UI at port `50470`, as shown in the following screenshot. As it is a self-signed certificate, you will see a warning message:

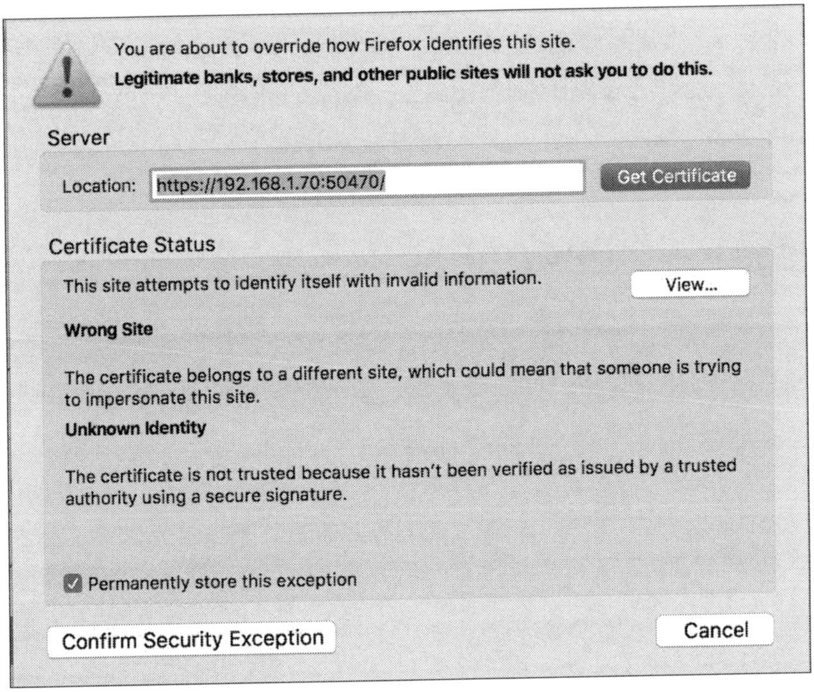

21. Accept the certificate and you will see the Namenode Web UI, as shown in the following screenshot:

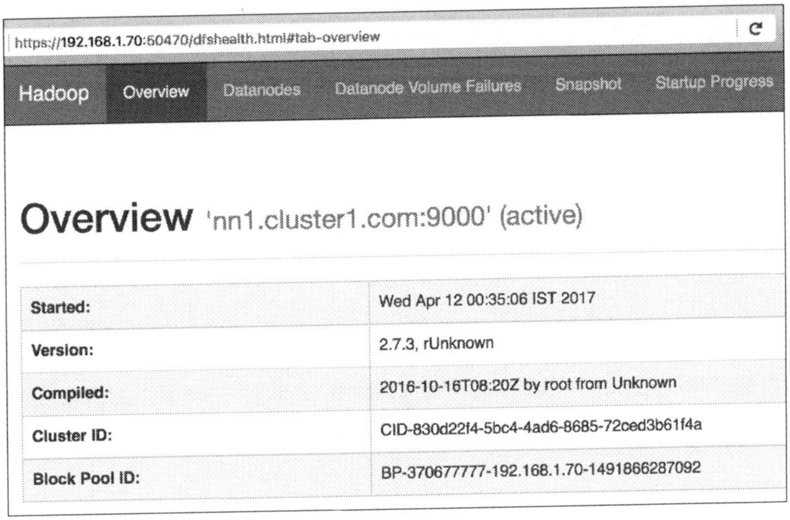

22. Save the changes, copy the files across the cluster, and restart the services.
23. Make sure that the Datanodes are up and taking to the Namenode, as shown in the following screenshot:

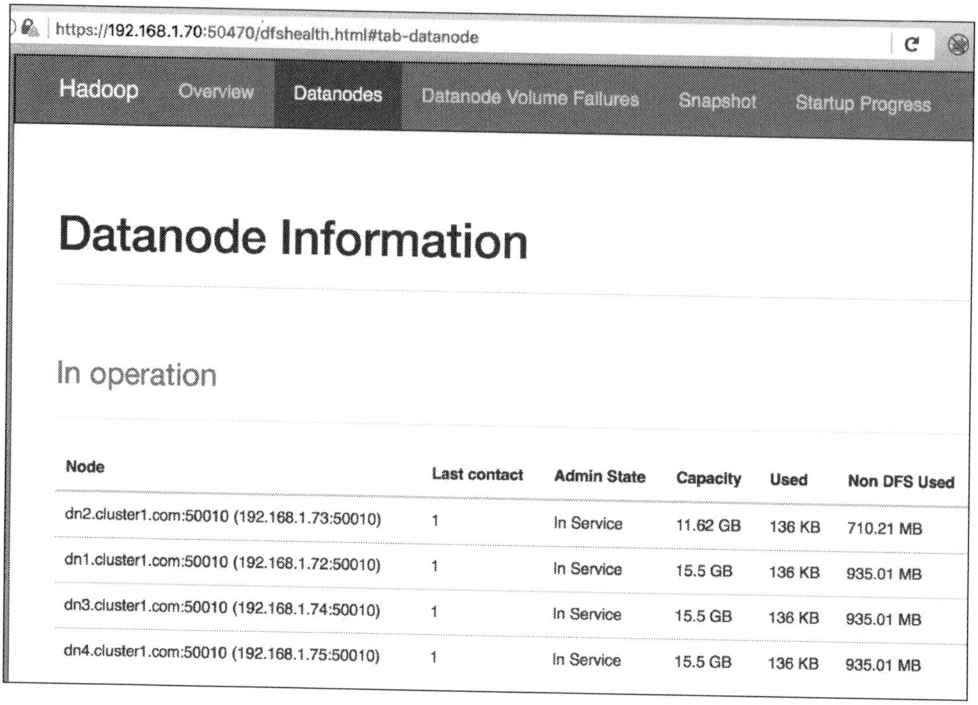

24. Similarly, verify the Resourcemanager Web UI at port `8089`, as shown in the following screenshot:

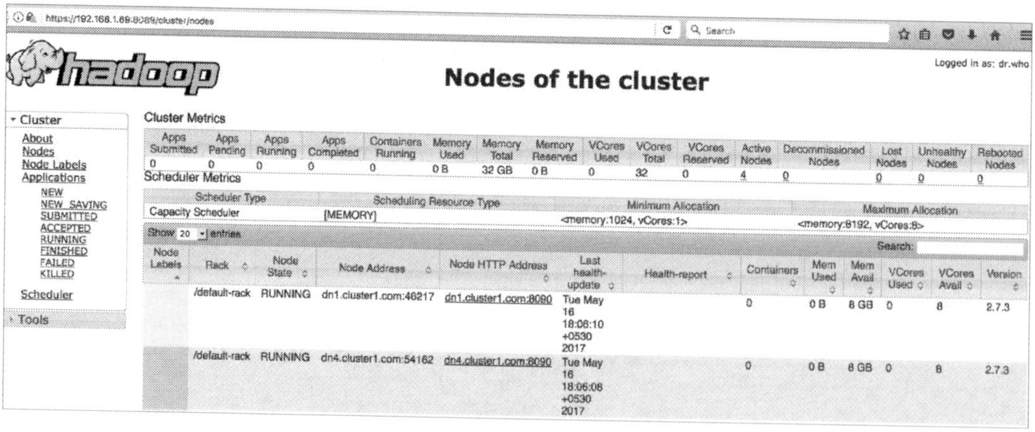

As we have also enabled web HDFS, we can perform operations such as list, create, and delete files using REST API calls, as shown in the following screenshot. We can perform HDFS operations using the CURL command-line tool as well:

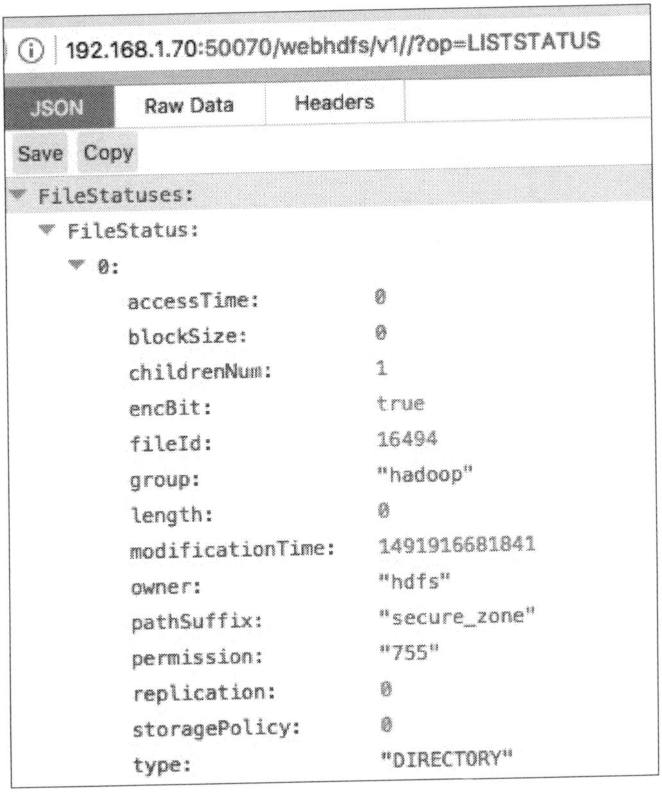

How it works...

The server and client talk to each other using SSL encryption and the store keys. In this recipe, we have configured SSL over HTTP, and in the next recipe, we will secure the in-transit data during the shuffle phase.

See also

- The *In-transit encryption* recipe

In-transit encryption

In this recipe, we will configure in-transit encryption for securing the transfer of data between nodes during the shuffle phase. The mapper output is consumed by reducers, which can run on different nodes, so to secure the transfer channel, we secure the communication between Mappers and Reducers. We will be securing the RPC communication channel as well, although it induces a slight overhead and must be setup only if it is absolutely necessary.

Getting ready

To complete the recipe, the user must have completed the previous *Configure SSL in Hadoop* recipe. We will be extending the configuration already set up in that section by adding a few more options.

> It is recommended that the users explore SSL and learn more about ciphers to understand its security and performance implications.

How to do it...

1. Connect to the `nn1.cluster1.com` master node and switch to user `hadoop`.
2. To enable RPC privacy, edit `core-site.xml` to add the following lines on each node in the cluster:

   ```
   <property>
       <name>hadoop.rpc.protection</name>
       <value>privacy</value>
   </property>
   ```

3. To enable SSL for shuffle, edit the `mapred-site.xml` file and add the following lines:

   ```
   <property>
       <name>hadoop.ssl.enabled</name>
       <value>true</value>
   </property>
   ```

4. Now edit the `mapred-site.xml` file and add all the following steps in the file, unless stated otherwise.

5. Enable SSL for shuffle by adding the following lines:

```
<property>
    <name>mapreduce.shuffle.ssl.enabled</name>
    <value>true</value>
</property>
```

6. Enable hostname verification by adding the following lines to the file:

```
<property>
    <name>hadoop.ssl.require.client.cert</name>
    <value>false</value>
</property>

<property>
    <name>hadoop.ssl.hostname.verifier</name>
    <value>DEFAULT</value>
    <final>true</final>
</property>
```

7. Add configuration for `keystore factory` class and reference to files, which load the ssl configurations:

```
<property>
    <name>hadoop.ssl.keystores.factory.class</name>
    <value>org.apache.hadoop.security.ssl.
FileBasedKeyStoresFactory</value>
    <final>true</final>
</property>

<property>
    <name>hadoop.ssl.server.conf</name>
    <value>ssl-server.xml</value>
    <final>true</final>
</property>

<property>
    <name>hadoop.ssl.client.conf</name>
    <value>ssl-client.xml</value>
    <final>true</final>
</property>
```

8. Add setting for `jobhistory` server to the file as follows:

```
<property>
    <name>mapreduce.jobhistory.http.policy</name>
    <value>HTTPS_ONLY</value>
</property>

<property>
    <name>mapreduce.jobhistory.webapp.https.address</name>
    <value>jt1.cluster1.com:19889</value>
</property>
```

9. Now edit the `hdfs-site.xml` file and add the following lines to enable transit encryption:

```
<property>
    <name>dfs.encrypt.data.transfer</name>
    <value>true</value>
</property>
```

10. Copy the file to all the nodes in the cluster and restart services.
11. Test by running a simple MapReduce example to test the encryption of shuffle phase.

There's more...

In addition to what we have discussed in the previous two recipes, we can add configurations for securing the job history server by adding the following code to `yarn-site.xml`:

```
<property>
    <name>yarn.log.server.url</name>
    <value>https://nn1.cluster1.com:19889/jobhistory/logs</value>
</property>
```

See also

- The *Enabling service level authorization* recipe

Enabling service level authorization

In this recipe, we will look at service level authorization, which is a mechanism to ensure that the clients connecting to Hadoop services have the right permissions and authorization to access them. This is more of a global control in comparison to the control at the job queue level. Which users can submit jobs to the cluster or which Datanodes can connect to the Namenode based on the Datanode service user.

Service level authorization checks are performed much before any other checks, such as file permissions or permissions on sub queues.

Getting ready

For this recipe, you will need a running cluster with HDFS and YARN configured, and it is good to have a basic understanding of Linux users and permissions.

How to do it...

1. Connect to the `nn1.cluster1.com` master node and switch to user `hadoop`.
2. All the configuration goes into the `hadoop-policy.xml` file on each node in the cluster.
3. Firstly, allow all users to connect as DFSclient using the following configuration - this is the default value:

   ```
   <property>
       <name>security.client.protocol.acl</name>
       <value>*</value>
   </property>
   ```

4. In our cluster, Datanodes are running with user `hdfs`. Allow only the Datanodes running with this user to connect to Namenode by using the following configuration. Users can be specified using a comma-separated list, and a group by using a space:

   ```
   <property>
       <name>security.datanode.protocol.acl</name>
       <value>hdfs</value>
   </property>
   ```

5. Control which users can submit jobs to the `mapreduce` cluster using the following configuration:

   ```
   <property>
       <name>security.job.client.protocol.acl</name>
       <value>user1 mapreduce</value>
   </property>
   ```

6. Control Secondary Namenode using the following configuration and control which group can run a functional Secondary Namenode.

```
<property>
    <name>security.job.client.protocol.acl</name>
    <value>user1 mapreduce</value>
</property>
```

7. Which users can run admin commands in the cluster.

```
<property>
    <name>security.admin.operations.protocol.acl</name>
    <value>hdfs</value>
</property>
```

8. Which users can refresh user Mapping in the cluster using the following settings:

```
<property>
    <name>security.refresh.policy.protocol.acl</name>
    <value>Hadoop,hdfs</value>
</property>
```

9. Copy the `hadoop-policy.xml` file to all the nodes in the cluster and use the following commands to load the changes. There are two authorization controls, one for each master:

```
$ hdfs dfsadmin -refreshServiceAcl
$ yarn rmadmin -refreshServiceAcl
```

How it works...

In this recipe, we configured service level authorization to control which users can perform which operations. These controls are exclusive in nature, as we have to either allow or deny the user. This can be done by simply using a property with a specific user and to deny it to use the same property with the `.deny` extension.

For example, to allow hosts for a service, we use the `security.service.authorization.default.hosts` property, and to deny a particular host we use `security.service.authorization.default.hosts.deny`.

See also

- The *Configuring Kerberos for Hadoop* recipe

Securing ZooKeeper

Another important component to secure is ZooKeeper, as it is a very important component in the Hadoop cluster. The nodes contributing towards quorum should communicate over a secure channel and should be safeguarded against any clear text exchanges.

In this recipe, we will configure ZooKeeper to run in secure mode by enabling SSL. The ZooKeeper to be used for this secure connection must support Netty and we will enable Netty in the existing ZooKeeper setup previously in *Chapter 11, Troubleshooting, Diagnostics, and Best Practices*.

Getting ready

Make sure that the user has completed the *ZooKeeper configuration* recipe in *Chapter 4, High Availability*. We will be using the existing ZooKeeper cluster and adding the configuration for securing it. Also, the user must have completed the *Configuring SSL in Hadoop* recipe, as we will be using the existing `keystore` file and truststore for this recipe.

How to do it...

1. Connect to the `nn1.cluster1.com` Namenode and switch to user `hadoop`.
2. We are using the nodes `nn1.cluster1.com`, `dn1.cluster1.com`, and `jt1.cluster1.com`, but you can choose any node.
3. Edit the `zoo.cfg` file and enable ZooKeeper to run in secure mode, as shown here:

   ```
   zookeeper.client.secure=true
   ```

4. Edit the `zoo.cfg` file and enable Netty by adding the following configuration:

   ```
   zookeeper.serverCnxnFactory="org.apache.zookeeper.server.
   NettyServerCnxnFactory"
   zookeeper.clientCnxnSocket="org.apache.zookeeper.
   ClientCnxnSocketNetty"
   ```

5. Enable the secure port `2281`, which is in addition to the default port `2181`:

   ```
   secureClientPort=2281
   ```

6. Use the existing `keystore` file and trust store from the earlier recipe *In-transit encryption* in this chapter. This is shown in the following screenshot:

```
zookeeper.ssl.keyStore.location="/opt/cluster/security/certs/host-keystore.jks"
zookeeper.ssl.keyStore.password="hadoop@123"
zookeeper.ssl.trustStore.location="/opt/cluster/security/certs/host-truststore.jks"
zookeeper.ssl.trustStore.password="hadoop@123"
```

7. Next is to make a change to the script which starts the ZooKeeper server. Edit the `bin/zkServer.sh` file and add the lines, as shown in the following screenshot:

```
[hadoop@nn1 conf]$ pwd
/opt/cluster/zoo/conf
[hadoop@nn1 conf]$ cat ../bin/zkServer.sh
#!/usr/bin/env bash

export SERVER_JVMFLAGS="
-Dzookeeper.serverCnxnFactory=org.apache.zookeeper.server.NettyServerCnxnFactory
-Dzookeeper.ssl.keyStore.location=/opt/cluster/security/certs/host-keystore.jks
-Dzookeeper.ssl.keyStore.password=hadoop@123
-Dzookeeper.ssl.trustStore.location=/opt/cluster/security/certs/host-truststore.jks
-Dzookeeper.ssl.trustStore.password=hadoop@123"
```

8. Copy the `zoo.cfg` and `zkServer.sh` files to all the ZooKeeper nodes and restart the services.

9. As said initially, we are using the existing ZooKeeper from the recipe *Securing Zookeeper*, so it is configured to form a ZooKeeper cluster. Start the ZooKeeper server using the zkServer.sh start command and verify using the command shown in the following screenshot:

```
[hadoop@nn1 ~]$ jps
15183 QuorumPeerMain
15247 Jps
```

How it works...

In this recipe, we configured ZooKeeper to use SSL to secure the communication between peers and the clients connecting to the ZooKeeper. Clients with Netty-enabled ZooKeeper `zookeeper.clientCnxnSocket="org.apache.zookeeper.ClientCnxnSocketNetty` will connect on port `2281`.

Configuring auditing

In this recipe, we will touch base upon auditing in Hadoop, which is important to keep track of who did what and at what time. All users must hold accountability for their actions, and to make that possible, we need to track the activities of users by enabling audit logs. There are two audit logs, one for users and the other for services, which help to answer important questions such as Who touched my files? Is data accessed from protected IPs?

Getting ready

For this recipe, you will again need a running cluster with HDFS and YARN. Users must have completed the *Configuring multi-node cluster* recipe.

How to do it...

1. Connect to the `nn1.cluster1.com` master node and switch to user `hadoop`.
2. The file where these changes will be made is `log4j.properties`.
3. The categories which control audit logging are `log4j.category.SecurityLogger` for service, and for each of HDFS, Mapred, and YARN, we have audit log handlers categories implementing `log4j.logger.org.apache.hadoop`.
4. To enable audits for service, edit the `log4j.properties` file and make the following changes for location, size, and log level:

```
hadoop.security.logger=INFO,RFAAUDIT
hadoop.security.log.maxfilesize=256MB
log4j.category.SecurityLogger=${hadoop.security.logger}
hadoop.security.log.file=SecurityAuth-${user.name}.audit
log4j.appender.RFAS.File=${hadoop.log.dir}/${hadoop.security.log.
file}
```

5. To enable HDFS audit logging, use the following configuration to add rules:

```
hdfs.audit.logger=INFO,RFAAUDIT
log4j.logger.org.apache.hadoop.hdfs.server.namenode.FSNamesystem.
audit=${hdfs.audit.logger}
log4j.additivity.org.apache.hadoop.hdfs.server.namenode.
FSNamesystem.audit=true
log4j.appender.RFAAUDIT.File=${hadoop.log.dir}/hdfs-audit.log
```

6. To enable MapReduce audit logging, enable it using the following configuration:

```
mapred.audit.logger=INFO,RFAAUDIT
log4j.logger.org.apache.hadoop.mapred.AuditLogger=${mapred.audit.
logger}
log4j.additivity.org.apache.hadoop.mapred.AuditLogger=true
log4j.appender.MRAUDIT.File=${hadoop.log.dir}/mapred-audit.log
```

7. To enable other audit logs, such as for YARN, Hive, and HBase, we need to make the change and use the following appenders:

```
log4j.category.SecurityLogger
org.apache.hadoop.hive.metastore.HiveMetaStore.audit
log4j.logger.org.apache.hadoop.mapreduce.v2.hs.HSAuditLogger
```

8. If using RFAS log appender, then we need to change the configuration specifically for that, as shown here:

```
log4j.appender.RFAS=org.apache.log4j.RollingFileAppender
log4j.appender.RFAS.File=${hadoop.log.dir}/${hadoop.security.log.file}
log4j.appender.RFAS.layout=org.apache.log4j.PatternLayout
log4j.appender.RFAS.layout.ConversionPattern=%d{ISO8601} %p %c: %m%n
log4j.appender.RFAS.MaxFileSize=256MB
log4j.appender.RFAS.MaxBackupIndex=20
```

9. Change the respective logger for RPC, HDFS, YARN, MapReduce, and HBase using the settings shown in the following screenshot:

```
log4j.logger.SecurityLogger=INFO, RFAS
log4j.logger.org.apache.hadoop.hdfs.server.namenode.FSNamesystem.audit = INFO, RFAS
log4j.logger.org.apache.hadoop.mapred.AuditLogger = INFO, RFAS
log4j.logger.oozieaudit = INFO, RFAS
log4j.logger.SecurityLogger.org.apache.hadoop.hbase.security.access.AccessController= INFO, RFAS
```

10. Similarly, we can see audit logs for the KMS service we configured in the previous recipe *HDFS encryption at rest*, as shown in the following screenshot:

```
$ ls -l ../../logs/*audit*
 hdfs    4348 Apr 11 20:23 ../../logs/kms-audit.log
 hadoop     0 Apr 11 05:11 ../../logs/SecurityAuth-hdfs.audit
```

11. The key exchange, authentication, and KMS truststore is logged as shown in the following screenshot:

```
OK[op=DECRYPT_EEK, key=key1, user=hdfs, accessCount=1, interval=0ms]
OK[op=DECRYPT_EEK, key=key2, user=hdfs, accessCount=1, interval=0ms]
OK[op=DECRYPT_EEK, key=key1, user=hdfs, accessCount=1, interval=10247ms]
OK[op=DECRYPT_EEK, key=key2, user=hdfs, accessCount=1, interval=10059ms]
```

How it works...

In this recipe, we saw how audit logs can be enabled to track activity. Generating too many logs can also be an overhead. We can use a job summary appender as shown in the following screenshot:

```
hadoop.mapreduce.jobsummary.logger=${hadoop.root.logger}
hadoop.mapreduce.jobsummary.log.file=hadoop-mapreduce.jobsummary.log
hadoop.mapreduce.jobsummary.log.maxfilesize=256MB
hadoop.mapreduce.jobsummary.log.maxbackupindex=20
log4j.appender.JSA=org.apache.log4j.RollingFileAppender
log4j.appender.JSA.File=${hadoop.log.dir}/${hadoop.mapreduce.jobsummary.log.file}
log4j.appender.JSA.MaxFileSize=${hadoop.mapreduce.jobsummary.log.maxfilesize}
log4j.appender.JSA.MaxBackupIndex=${hadoop.mapreduce.jobsummary.log.maxbackupindex}
log4j.appender.JSA.layout=org.apache.log4j.PatternLayout
log4j.appender.JSA.layout.ConversionPattern=%d{yy/MM/dd HH:mm:ss} %p %c{2}: %m%n
log4j.logger.org.apache.hadoop.mapred.JobInProgress$JobSummary=${hadoop.mapreduce.jobsummary.logger}
log4j.additivity.org.apache.hadoop.mapred.JobInProgress$JobSummary=false
```

We can use Apache Ranger for auditing and can do aggregation of the logs to a single cluster.

Configuring Kerberos server

In this recipe, we will configure Kerberos server and look at some of the fundamental components of Kerberos, which are important to understand its working and lay the foundation for setting up Kerberos for Hadoop. Refer to the following diagram, which explains the working of Kerberos:

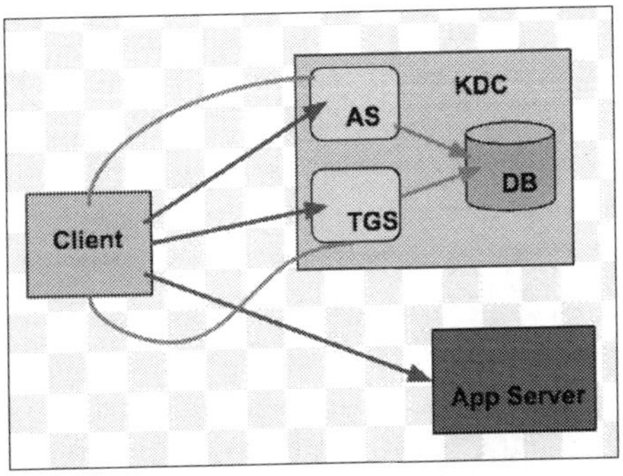

Kerberos consists of two main components, **authentication server** (**AS**) and **Key distribution center** (**KDC, subcomponent KGS**). The clients, which could be users, hosts, or services are called principal, authenticate to AS and, on being successful, are granted a **ticket** (**TGT**), which is a token to use other services in the respective realm (domain).

The password is never sent over the wire and the TGT granted to the client by the KDC is encapsulated with the client password. The TGT received will be cached by the client and can be used to connect to any service or host within the realm or across domains, if a trust relationship is configured.

KDC is the middleman between clients and services and facilitates single sign-on by providing tickets.

Getting ready

Make sure that the user has at least one Linux server to install Kerberos or it can be installed on the master node in the cluster. Users can use an existing Windows server if they want, but we will be setting up a Kerberos server on the `repo.cluster1.com node` and using it to authenticate the Hadoop cluster.

One of the important prerequisites for running Kerberos is that all the clients participating in the ticket exchange must have the time synced and there should not be more than 5 minutes of time skew between any node, else Kerberos authentication will fail. For this, you can use NTP server and sync time with that server. The following screenshot shows that all the nodes in the cluster are within 1 second of time difference:

```
[root@repo ~]# clush -g all -b "date"
---------------
dn[1-4].cluster1.com,jt1.cluster1.com,nn1.cluster1.com (6)
---------------
Mon Apr 17 04:40:33 IST 2017
```

The other way to make sure that the DNS resolution is working fine is by making sure that both forward and reverse lookups are working fine. The assumption is that users are well versed in the Linux package installation and can navigate the filesystem easily.

Also make sure that SELinux is disabled on all the nodes.

How to do it...

1. Connect to the `repo.cluster1.com` node, which is a CentOS 7 server, but this can be set up on any node in the cluster for this recipe. But, in production, Kerberos will always be running on a dedicated host outside the Hadoop cluster.
2. Change to user `root` or you must have `sudo` privileges.
3. Install the Kerberos server, client, and libraries using the following command:

   ```
   # yum install -y krb5-server krb5-libs krb5-workstation
   ```

4. Enable `krb5kdc` to start at system boot and disable the firewall for the initial configuration:

   ```
   # chkconfig krb5kdc on
   # chkconfig kadmin on
   # chkconfig iptables off
   ```

5. Now edit the `/etc/krb5.conf` file and add the following lines with changes according to your domain. The domain/realm we are using is `cluster1.com`, which in Kerberos is represented as `CLUSTER1.COM`. This is more of a client-side configuration and it is used to connect the KDC server running on that node itself:

```
[realms]
 CLUSTER1.COM = {
 kdc = repo.cluster1.com
 admin_server = repo.cluster1.com
 }

[domain_realm]
 .cluster1.com = CLUSTER1.COM
  cluster1.com = CLUSTER1.COM
```

6. Now edit the `/var/kerberos/krb5kdc/kdc.conf` file and make the changes shown in the following screenshot:

```
[root@repo ~]# cat /var/kerberos/krb5kdc/kdc.conf
[kdcdefaults]
 kdc_ports = 88
 kdc_tcp_ports = 88

[realms]
 CLUSTER1.COM = {
  #master_key_type = aes256-cts
  acl_file = /var/kerberos/krb5kdc/kadm5.acl
  dict_file = /usr/share/dict/words
  admin_keytab = /var/kerberos/krb5kdc/kadm5.keytab
  supported_enctypes = aes256-cts:normal aes128-cts:normal des3-hmac-sha1:normal arcfour-hmac:normal
 camellia256-cts:normal camellia128-cts:normal des-hmac-sha1:normal des-cbc-md5:normal des-cbc-crc:n
ormal
 }
```

7. Now start the `krb5kdc` daemons using the following command, depending upon the Linux version you are using:

```
# service kdb5kdc start
```

8. The next step is to create the KDC database using the following command. Remember the password; if you forget this, you will have to recreate KDC, losing all principals:

```
# kdb5_util create -s
```

9. Now configure the kadmin acl to control which users can manage the principals in KDC by editing the `/var/kerberos/krb5kdc/kadm5.acl` file and adding the following configuration:

```
[root@repo ~]# cat /var/kerberos/krb5kdc/kadm5.
kadm5.acl     kadm5.keytab
[root@repo ~]# cat /var/kerberos/krb5kdc/kadm5.acl
*/admin@CLUSTER1.COM    *
```

10. Now start the Kadmin service using the following command:

    # service kadmin start

11. Now, if we logged on the KDC server with `root` privileges, then to create the first admin principal, use the following command. It will prompt you for the password; remember this in order to be able to connect from other nodes in the cluster:

    # kadmin.local -q "addprinc root/admin"

12. We can connect to the kadmin in interactive mode using the `kadmin.local` command and add users as shown in the following screenshot:

```
kadmin.local:  addprinc hadoop
WARNING: no policy specified for hadoop@CLUSTER1.COM;
Enter password for principal "hadoop@CLUSTER1.COM":
Re-enter password for principal "hadoop@CLUSTER1.COM":
Principal "hadoop@CLUSTER1.COM" created.
```

13. Add a few other users such as `hdfs`, `yarn`, and `mapred`. This can be seen in the following screenshot:

```
kadmin.local:  listprincs
K/M@CLUSTER1.COM
hadoop@CLUSTER1.COM
hdfs@CLUSTER1.COM
kadmin/admin@CLUSTER1.COM
kadmin/changepw@CLUSTER1.COM
kadmin/repo.cluster1.com@CLUSTER1.COM
krbtgt/CLUSTER1.COM@CLUSTER1.COM
root/admin@CLUSTER1.COM
yarn@CLUSTER1.COM
```

14. To add a principal for host we can use the command shown in the following screenshot:

```
kadmin.local:  addprinc -randkey host/repo.cluster1.com
WARNING: no policy specified for host/repo.cluster1.com@CLUSTER1.COM
Principal "host/repo.cluster1.com@CLUSTER1.COM" created.
```

15. This host principal needs to be added to the keytab file /etc/krb5.keytab so that, when prompted for a password, it can be supplied by the application from the file directly:

```
kadmin.local:  ktadd host/repo.cluster1.com
Entry for principal host/repo.cluster1.com with kvno 2,
FILE:/etc/krb5.keytab.
Entry for principal host/repo.cluster1.com with kvno 2,
FILE:/etc/krb5.keytab.
Entry for principal host/repo.cluster1.com with kvno 2,
krb5.keytab.
```

16. We can check the principals loaded in a keytab file using the command shown in the following screenshot – there is a host key for each supported cipher:

```
[root@repo ~]# ktutil
ktutil:  rkt /etc/krb5.keytab
ktutil:  l
slot KVNO Principal
---- ---- ---------------------------------------------
   1    2      host/repo.cluster1.com@CLUSTER1.COM
   2    2      host/repo.cluster1.com@CLUSTER1.COM
   3    2      host/repo.cluster1.com@CLUSTER1.COM
```

17. Now we need to configure Kerberos client to talk to the server and authenticate using tickets. We have already installed the krb5-workstation package; this is needed on all clients that want to talk to KDC.
18. An easy way to configure the client is to use the authconfig-tui command and select the authentication method, as shown in the following screenshot:

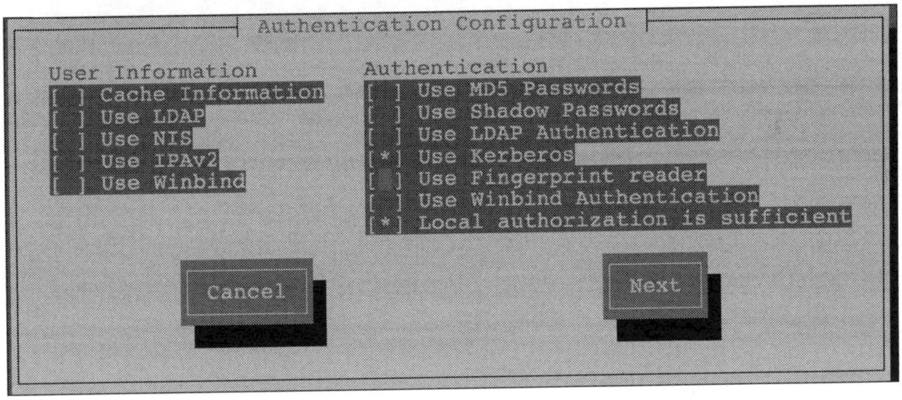

19. Then, specify the configuration shown in the following screenshot to connect to the server:

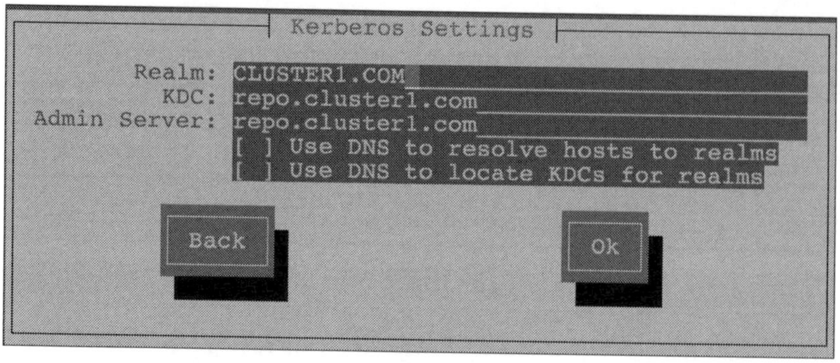

20. The preceding configuration actually generates the `/etc/krb5.conf` file, which can be added manually as well, and there is no need to use any tool.
21. Now the setup is complete and we should test the Kerberos server by connecting to it and then later configuring SSH for single sign on. Create a user `hadoop` on the `repo.cluster1.com` node and test whether it can get the TGT from the server or not, as shown in the following screenshot:

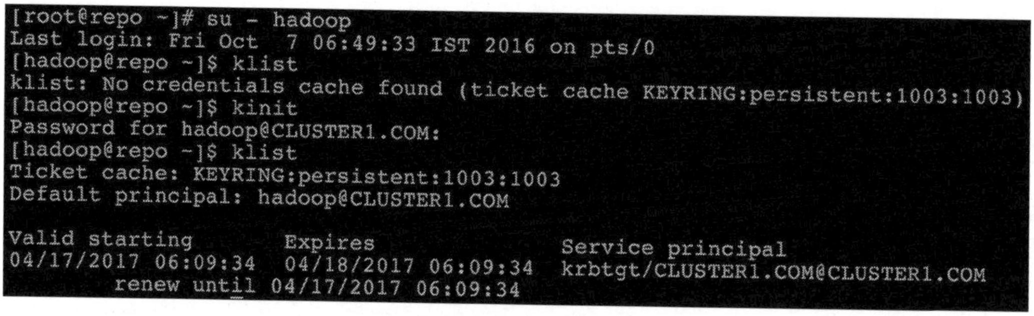
[root@repo ~]# su - hadoop
Last login: Fri Oct 7 06:49:33 IST 2016 on pts/0
[hadoop@repo ~]$ klist
klist: No credentials cache found (ticket cache KEYRING:persistent:1003:1003)
[hadoop@repo ~]$ kinit
Password for hadoop@CLUSTER1.COM:
[hadoop@repo ~]$ klist
Ticket cache: KEYRING:persistent:1003:1003
Default principal: hadoop@CLUSTER1.COM
Valid starting Expires Service principal
04/17/2017 06:09:34 04/18/2017 06:09:34 krbtgt/CLUSTER1.COM@CLUSTER1.COM
renew until 04/17/2017 06:09:34

22. We can see in the preceding screenshot that, to get a ticket, we executed the `kinit` command and now we can connect to any node in the same domain without being prompted for the password. For this to work, we need to add the other hosts to the Kerberos realm and create host keys.
23. For single sign-on to work for SSH across the cluster, we need to perform the following steps. This is not mandatory for Hadoop, but it is a good way to test Kerberos.
24. The first thing is to edit the `/etc/ssh/sshd_config` file and enable token forwarding, as shown here:

```
GSSAPIAuthentication yes
GSSAPIDelegateCredentials yes
```

25. Save the file and restart the SSH server using the following command:

```
# service restart sshd
```

26. Now add all the nodes in the Kerberos realm by adding and installing the following packages. This must be done on all the nodes in the cluster:

```
# yum install -y krb5-libs krb5-workstation
```

27. Edit the `/etc/krb5.conf` file to point to the KDC server using the following settings. The best would be to copy the file from the `repo.cluster1.com` server on all the nodes in the cluster:

```
[realms]
 CLUSTER1.COM = {
 kdc = repo.cluster1.com
 admin_server = repo.cluster1.com
 }

[domain_realm]
 .cluster1.com = CLUSTER1.COM
 cluster1.com = CLUSTER1.COM
```

28. Now add the host principal for all the nodes in the cluster, which could be done using either `kadmin.local` on the Kerberos server or kadmin tool from remote nodes, as shown in the following screenshot. Notice that we have added the principal to the `keytab` file:

CLUSTER1.COM:
.cluster1.com
/nn1.cluster1.com with kvno 5, encryption type aes256-cts-hmac-sha1-96 added
/nn1.cluster1.com with kvno 5, encryption type aes128-cts-hmac-sha1-96 added
/nn1.cluster1.com with kvno 5, encryption type des3-cbc-sha1 added to keytab
/nn1.cluster1.com with kvno 5, encryption type arcfour-hmac added to keytab

29. Now, on the `repo.cluster1.com` node, switch to user `hadoop` and make sure you have the token by using the kinit command. Then, `ssh` to the `nn1.cluster1.com` node without being prompted for the password, as shown in the following screenshot. Notice that there is no `ssh` private/public key set up:

[hadoop@repo ~]$ ls -l .ssh/
total 4
-rw-r--r-- 1 hadoop hadoop 1341 Oct 7 2016 known_hosts
[hadoop@repo ~]$ ssh nn1.cluster1.com
Last login: Mon Apr 17 06:29:35 2017 from repo.cluster1.com

30. What if we try to now jump to the `dn1.cluster1.com` node? It will prompt us for a password, as the SSH on `nn1.cluster1.com` is not forwarding the tokens.
31. Make the change, shown here, to the `/etc/ssh/sshd_config` file, on all the nodes in the cluster:

    ```
    GSSAPIAuthentication yes
    GSSAPIKeyExchange yes
    ```

32. As stated initially, this is not mandatory for Hadoop to run, but helps in making sure we have set up everything correctly.

How it works...

In this recipe, we configured Kerberos across the nodes and tested single sign-on across the nodes to make sure the ticket/token forwarding works.

It is recommended that users play around with Kerberos and understand its workings before moving to the *Configuring and enabling Kerberos for Hadoop* recipe.

Configuring and enabling Kerberos for Hadoop

In this recipe, we will be configuring Kerberos for a Hadoop cluster and enabling the authentication of services using tokens. Each service and user must have its principal created and imported to the `keytab` files. These `keytab` files should be available to the Hadoop daemons to read the passwords and perform operations.

It is assumed that the user has completed the previous recipe "Kerberos Server Setup" and is comfortable using Kerberos.

Getting ready

Make sure that the user has a running cluster with HDFS or YARN fully functional in a multinode cluster and a Kerberos server set up.

How to do it...

1. The first thing is to make sure all the nodes are in sync with time and DNS is fully set up.
2. On each node in the cluster, install the Kerberos workstation packages using the following commands:

    ```
    # yum install -y krb5-libs krb5-workstation
    ```

3. Connect to the KDC server `rep.cluster1.com` and create a host key for each host in the cluster, as shown in the following screenshot:

```
kadmin.local:  listprincs
K/M@CLUSTER1.COM
hadoop@CLUSTER1.COM
hdfs@CLUSTER1.COM
host/dn1.cluster.com@CLUSTER1.COM
host/dn2.cluster.com@CLUSTER1.COM
host/dn3.cluster.com@CLUSTER1.COM
host/dn4.cluster.com@CLUSTER1.COM
host/jt1.cluster.com@CLUSTER1.COM
host/nn1.cluster1.com@CLUSTER1.COM
host/repo.cluster1.com@CLUSTER1.COM
```

4. Now add the principals for each of the Hadoop service roles, such as Namenode, Datanode, Resourcemanager, and HTTP, as shown in the following screenshot:

```
kadmin.local:  addprinc -randkey yarn/nn1.cluster1.com
WARNING: no policy specified for yarn/nn1.cluster1.com@C
Principal "yarn/nn1.cluster1.com@CLUSTER1.COM" created.
kadmin.local:  addprinc -randkey mapred/nn1.cluster1.com
WARNING: no policy specified for mapred/nn1.cluster1.com
Principal "mapred/nn1.cluster1.com@CLUSTER1.COM" created
kadmin.local:  addprinc -randkey HTTP/nn1.cluster1.com
WARNING: no policy specified for HTTP/nn1.cluster1.com@C
Principal "HTTP/nn1.cluster1.com@CLUSTER1.COM" created.
kadmin.local:  addprinc -randkey hdfs/nn1.cluster1.com
WARNING: no policy specified for hdfs/nn1.cluster1.com@C
Principal "hdfs/nn1.cluster1.com@CLUSTER1.COM" created.
```

5. This needs to be done to all the hosts in the cluster. To make things easy, it is good to script this out.
6. Import each of these principals into the `keytab` file on each node, as shown in the following command:

```
kadmin: xst -norandkey -k /opt/cluster/security/nn.hdfs.key hdfs/
nn1.cluster1.com
kadmin: xst -norandkey -k /opt/cluster/security/ nn.hdfs.key yarn/
nn1.cluster1.com
kadmin: xst -norandkey -k /opt/cluster/security/ nn.hdfs.key
mapred/nn1.cluster1.com
kadmin: xst -norandkey -k /opt/cluster/security/ nn.hdfs.key HTTP/
nn1.cluster1.com
```

7. Now edit the Hadoop configuration files and make the changes, as shown in the following step. Ensure that the `keytab` files have just read permissions.

8. The first thing is to edit the `core-site.xml` file and add the following lines:

```
<property>
    <name>hadoop.security.authentication</name>
    <value>kerberos</value>
</property>

<property>
    <name>hadoop.security.authorization</name>
    <value>true</value>
</property>
```

9. Now edit the `hdfs-site.xml` file on Namenode, as shown in the following screenshot:

```
<property>
    <name>dfs.block.access.token.enable</name>
    <value>true</value>
</property>

<property>
    <name>dfs.namenode.keytab.file</name>
    <value>/opt/cluster/security/nn.hdfs.keytab</value>
</property>

<property>
    <name>dfs.namenode.kerberos.principal</name>
    <value>nn/_HOST@CLUSTER1.COM</value>
</property>

<property>
    <name>dfs.namenode.kerberos.http.principal</name>
    <value>host/_HOST@CLUSTER1.COM</value>
</property>

<property>
    <name>dfs.namenode.kerberos.internal.spnego.principal</name>
    <value>HTTP/_HOST@CLUSTER1.COM</value>
</property>
```

10. Now edit the `hdfs-site.xml` file on Datanodes, as shown here:

```
<property>
    <name>dfs.datanode.keytab.file</name>
    <value>/opt/cluster/security/dn.hdfs.keytab</value>
</property>
```

```
<property>
    <name>dfs.datanode.kerberos.principal</name>
    <value>dn/_HOST@CLUSTER1.COM</value>
</property>

<property>
    <name>dfs.datanode.kerberos.https.principal</name>
    <value>host/_HOST@CLUSTER1.COM</value>
</property>

<property>
    <name>dfs.namenode.kerberos.principal</name>
    <value>nn/_HOST@CLUSTER1.COM</value>
</property>
```

11. Now edit the `yarn-site.xml` file, as shown in the following screenshot:

```
<property>
    <name>yarn.resourcemanager.principal</name>
    <value>yarn/_HOST@HADOOP.COM</value>
</property>
<property>
    <name>yarn.resourcemanager.keytab</name>
    <value>/opt/cluster/security/yarn.keytab</value>
</property>
<property>
    <name>yarn.nodemanager.principal</name>
    <value>yarn/_HOST@HADOOP.COM</value>
</property>

<The below is only for the respective nodemanagers>
<property>
    <name>yarn.nodemanager.keytab</name>
    <value>/opt/cluster/security/yarn.keytab</value>
</property>
```

12. Make the changes on all the nodes in the cluster and make sure you use the correct `keytab` files per host.
13. Restart the services and, if everything is fine, you should be all set to go.
14. Execute the `$ hadoop fs -ls /` command; we will see the error if you have directly connected to the Namenode and do not have the token, as shown in the following screenshot:

```
[hdfs@nn1 ~]$ hadoop fs -ls /
Apr 17 07:40:04 WARN ipc.Client: Exception encountered while connecting to the server :
javax.security.sasl.SaslException: GSS initiate failed [Caused by GSSException: No valid credentials
provided (Mechanism level: Failed to find any Kerberos tgt)]
```

15. Now get the ticket by using the `kinit` command and try executing the command again. This time, it will succeed, as shown in the following screenshot:

```
[hdfs@nn1 ~]$ klist
Ticket cache: FILE:/tmp/krb5cc_1011
Default principal: hdfs@CLUSTER1.COM

Valid starting       Expires              Service principal
04/17/2017 07:45:29  04/18/2017 07:43:43  krbtgt/CLUSTER1.COM@CLUSTER1.COM
        renew until 04/17/2017 07:45:29
[hdfs@nn1 ~]$ hadoop fs -ls /
Found 4 items
drwxr-xr-x   - hdfs hadoop          0 2017-04-11 18:48 /secure_zone
drwxr-xr-x   - hdfs hadoop          0 2017-04-11 19:22 /secure_zone2
-rw-r--r--   2 hdfs hadoop         19 2017-04-17 03:34 /test_audit
-rw-r--r--   2 hdfs hadoop         20 2017-04-11 19:22 /tmp
```

16. We can set up Kerberos for Hive and HBase and also integrate the security option we discussed in the *Configuring SSL in Hadoop* recipe. Creating the principals and keytabs can be cumbersome; it is better to create a simple script to generate all these things for you.

17. To create the Namenode principals, we can use the script shown in the following screenshot:

```
#!/bin/bash

# Generate Hosts principals

for i in `cat dn_host_list`
do
    kadmin.local -q "addprinc -randkey host/$i"
    kadmin.local -q "addprinc -randkey http/$i"
    kadmin.local -q "addprinc -randkey dn/$i"
    kadmin.local -q "xst -norandkey -k dn.hdfs.keytab host/$i"
    kadmin.local -q "xst -norandkey -k dn.hdfs.keytab http/$i"
    kadmin.local -q "xst -norandkey -k dn.hdfs.keytab dn/$i"
done
```

18. To create principals for Datanode, we can use the script shown in the following screenshot:

```
#!/bin/bash

for k in `cat nn_host_list`
do
    echo "$k"
        kadmin.local -q "addprinc -randkey host/$k"
        kadmin.local -q "addprinc -randkey http/$k"
        kadmin.local -q "addprinc -randkey nn/$k"

        kadmin.local -q "xst -norandkey -k nn.hdfs.keytab host/$k"
        kadmin.local -q "xst -norandkey -k nn.hdfs.keytab http/$k"
        kadmin.local -q "xst -norandkey -k nn.hdfs.keytab nn/$k"
        kadmin.local -q "xst -norandkey -k dn.hdfs.keytab host/$k"
        kadmin.local -q "xst -norandkey -k dn.hdfs.keytab http/$k"
        kadmin.local -q "xst -norandkey -k dn.hdfs.keytab nn/$k"
done
```

19. To create user keytabs, we can use the script shown in the following screenshot:

```
#!/bin/bash

for k in `cat user_host_list`
do
        kadmin.local -q "xst -norandkey -k user.hdfs.keytab host/$k"
done

for p in `cat user_list`
do
        kadmin.local -q "xst -norandkey -k user.hdfs.keytab $p"
done
```

20. All these scripts use hostname and users one per line in the files `dn_host_list`, `nn_host_list`, and `user_host_list`, respectively.

How it works...

In this recipe, we configured Kerberos across the nodes and configured the Hadoop configuration files to point to the Kerberos server.

Another important thing to keep in mind is that running Datanode in secure mode requires root privileges. It is mandatory to set up **Java Cryptographic Extension** (**JCE**) to allow the unlimited strength to elevate the privileges and run the daemons in secure mode.

To do this, copy the `local_policy.jar` and `US_export_policy.jar` files from the package at `http://www.oracle.com/technetwork/java/javase/downloads/jce-7-download-432124.html`, according to the Java version. The location is as shown in the following screenshot:

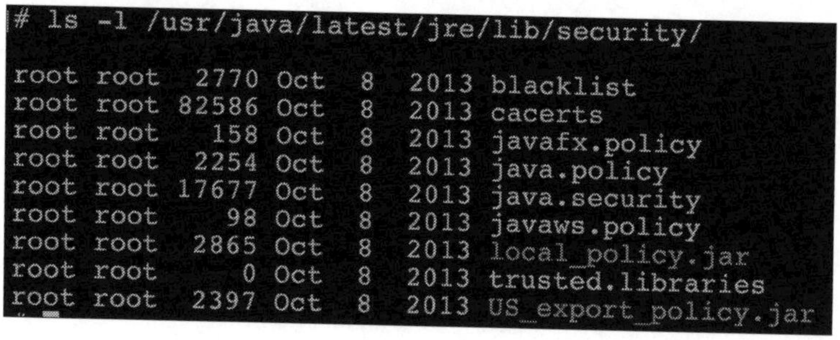

ls -l /usr/java/latest/jre/lib/security/
root root 2770 Oct 8 2013 blacklist
root root 82586 Oct 8 2013 cacerts
root root 158 Oct 8 2013 javafx.policy
root root 2254 Oct 8 2013 java.policy
root root 17677 Oct 8 2013 java.security
root root 98 Oct 8 2013 javaws.policy
root root 2865 Oct 8 2013 local_policy.jar
root root 0 Oct 8 2013 trusted.libraries
root root 2397 Oct 8 2013 US_export_policy.jar

Another very important thing to keep in mind is the Kerberos ticket default expiration time, which is 14 hours. What will happen to a job that takes more than 14 hours to finish? Once the Kerberos ticket expires, any other containers fired after that time will fail. There are two ways of solving this; one is to increase the default ticket expiration time, which is not the right way, as it will increase the time for all tokens. The recommended way is to call `k5renew`, for long-running jobs. This can be done by configuring the Nodemanager to refresh it before the expiration period. Hadoop implements an automatic re-login mechanism directly inside the RPC client layer.

Index

A

B

C

D

E

F

I

J

K

L

M

N

67629351R00194

Made in the USA
Middletown, DE
24 March 2018